atterns and Structure

In memory of Lars, and for Pierre, Sébastien, and Catherine, with great joy and expectations

Guy Nordenson

Patterns
and Structure

Selected Writings
1972–2008

Graham Foundation for Advanced Studies in the Fine Arts
The Publications Fund, Department of Art and Archaeology,
Princeton University

Lars Müller Publishers

"But think
        (he said continuously scratching
) of a life (suddenly
                lightning shears his
                                nails apart)
                without death.

Guy Nordenson

Sublimating Structures
–A Short Memoir

In his essay "The Divorce between the Sciences and the Humanities," Isaiah Berlin summarized Giambattista Vico's central discovery as "most of all, the notion that the only way of achieving any degree of self-understanding is by systematically retracing our steps, historically, psychologically … through the stages of social growth that follow empirically discernable patterns." The collection that follows here is a retracing that examines "trends and tendencies with whose workings we are acquainted in our own mental life, but moving to no single, universal goal." As my studies and career took me from a love of literature and philosophy to a practice of structural engineering, these texts accumulated along the way. In retrospect the ambition embodied in the journal *Rune* is prophetic: not only did it found an activity and tradition (the journal still exists at MIT after 34 years), but it represented a total effort at collecting material, editing and directly producing the entire press run ourselves. The thing itself, as well as the content, matters; which is why *Rune* is presented here in facsimile. Most crucially, the production was a social process that involved many others in key roles, something that has been an important factor in the activities and writings described and included here.

While the range of writing types and topics is circumstantial – including early poems, book reviews, newspaper opinion pieces, peer-reviewed papers on earthquake engineering, and several longer articles and essays on architecture and structural engineering – the thread running through all of them is my belief in the possibility of culture and continuity in concert with invention. I have often started anew, but always in the hope that continuity will follow. Ezra Pound's admonition to "make it new" and T. S. Eliot's essay on tradition and the individual talent were influences, and both emphasize the reimagining of cultural traditions. From the range of topics here it should also be clear that I am not convinced that we must necessarily operate as "two cultures," a divide C. P. Snow described between the sciences and the humanities fifty years ago. To return again to Berlin, I am more convinced that "each [is] a world on its own, yet [has] enough in common … [to form] a continuous line of recognisably human experiences."

The collection is arranged, and this introduction proceeds, chronologically because these "steps" do not always follow a direct route and some background is helpful. There are many names given in this memoir for a variety of reasons from personal to professional acknowledgments of influence to some critical commentary. Not everyone who has been a part of my life or these writings is mentioned for the sake of brevity. It is a short memoir.

1972

And this, and so much more?–
It is impossible to say just what I mean!
But as if a magic lantern threw the nerves in patterns on a screen:
T. S. Eliot, 1915

The fall of 1972 was the start of my final year of high school at Phillips Andover. I had gone there in the fall of 1969 after four years at the *Lycée Français de New York*. I didn't mind boarding. Before the *Lycée*, at age seven, I had gone for two years to the Marie-Josée, a small *internat* in Gstaad, Switzerland, run by a Mme Racine and her partner, "Falfal." Falfal had purple hair, which fascinated me.

Boarding was not my choice, however. I was too young to choose the Marie-Josée and I was at Andover because they had offered me a full scholarship. I was lucky, not privileged. I had a nomadic youth–four years in Paris, one and half each in Dallas and New York followed by Gstaad, New York, and Andover, with summer vacations as a guest of my godfather, Pierre Tattarachi, or godmother, Tessie Tesch in Southern France and Luxembourg respectively. I was born near Paris and when my parents married it lasted only five years. It was after their divorce, when my mother went to live with her best friend, Tessie, in Luxembourg, that she sent me to the Marie-Josée.

Panorama of Wildhorn, Wispile, Diableret, and Eggli Mountains, Gstaad, 1963
New York from the Empire State Building, 1965

For all this, I recall my time in Gstaad with pleasure. The chalet was beautifully situated, overlooking the valley. We would spend our rest time in the afternoon watching the Swiss air force jet fighters slaloming down the mountain valleys. Winter afternoons we skied after classes, and in the fall and spring we were in the woods behind the chalet, building cabins out of salvaged materials and playing out territorial rituals. Activity made me happy, and to this day I feel free in the mountains.

My parents were briefly reunited in 1964 and we returned to New York. When their reconciliation failed, my mother and I moved to the Hampton House on East 71st Street and then in 1966 to 73rd Street, where she still lives. At the *Lycée* I did well, though not too well. I was consistently in second place (the *Lycée* ordered everything) behind a brilliant Dominican girl, Dominique, whom I also sat next to, thanks to alphabetical order. As my father told me at the time, I was, like him, "a late bloomer"–or as my teachers and mother said repeatedly, *"il pourrait faire mieux."* Second place had its freedoms at the time.

In 1969 I left the *Lycée* for Andover at my parents' suggestion. My father drew up a list of boarding schools and my mother and I drove around in a friend's Alfa Romeo Spider to visit. Some of the schools were rather grim, with little privacy between the first-year boys' beds, and in the end only two schools offered me a scholarship. Andover seemed a bit forbidding due to its size, but it was my only real choice. It worked out well even though I had very little understanding of the social rituals, especially among the sports-minded WASPs (one of the Bushes was a few classes ahead of me). My closest friend and eventual roommate, Michael, who nearly became class president (I ended up secretary), was the brilliant and charismatic son of Cuban expatriates and excelled at writing and art. His father was a successful architect. In 1971 and 1972 he and I would go to Paul's Mall in Boston (with or without permission, I don't recall) to see Miles Davis' group perform. I had a secondhand white suit I would wear. We would sit in the front row and I remember Davis sticking his tongue out at us. In New York I also recall solo outings to Club 82 on East 4th Street in the same suit.

In the fall of 1972 my friend Michael suffered a mental breakdown. His crash extended over a three-day period of insomnia and I rode with him through the full madness of it. A girl was in part the focus of his mania, but there was more to it. His brilliant success and the admiration of his teachers and friends had fed a feeling of omnipotence and none of us, myself included, were wise enough to intervene in time. I visited him often at the mental hospital he went to (the same one where Robert Lowell was treated) and bore witness to their misuse of psychopharmacy. He did recover (when they took him off the drugs to prepare for electric shock treatment!) and sadly I have lost touch with him for years now.

"The girl" happened also to be the interest of the editor of the Andover literary magazine *The Mirror*, who agreed to publish the poem included here in that fall of 1972.

That was also the year my father died, in July, in Gstaad. I had seen him the summer and spring before in London and at Andover. For several years he had been sober and active in Alcoholics Anonymous. In 1968 he had come to stay with my mother and me in New York after a near-fatal car accident in the Venezuelan Andes. That and the London trip in 1971 were the last times I had spent with him. He had left New York for Illinois and Caracas and then London and Gstaad, in 1966. In Gstaad he lived on and off with a rich girlfriend, who as far as I could tell was supporting him. I had never had much close contact with him or information about his independent private life.

His death and my subsequent first visit to my family in Stockholm (they had not been part of my life till then) was a solitary and painful time. I learned of his death when I was staying with my mother on my godfather Pierre's boat, the *Milos II*, in Cannes, and I went on my own to the funeral in Stockholm. The night of the funeral I had a sharp but brief breakdown following an absurd (and quite Swedish) "theoretical" argument with my uncle over the question of child support–this in front of one of my half brothers and my father's girlfriend. Apart from that barbarism, though, the

Traversing the Gulf of Genoa on the *Milos II,* ca 1967

visit did help establish good feelings with my grandparents Harald and Clare and many of my fourteen Swedish cousins.

The fall of 1972 was also marked for me by my admission to K. Kelly Wise's legendary Andover seminar "Novel and Drama." The seminar cemented the love of writing and literary criticism that emerged in my third-year English instructor Frank "Bobo" Bellizia's class. Kelly Wise led the class through close readings of Faulkner *(Absalom, Absalom!)*, Conrad *(Heart of Darkness* and *Nostromo),* James *(The Ambassadors* and *The Aspern Papers),* Albee *(Tiny Alice),* and other great classics. Students were asked to lead the seminar for a month. It was my first time teaching.

MIT

The influence of "Novel and Drama" somehow mixed with my grief that fall to convince me that I should become a poet. I was applying to colleges and, to honor my father, I included MIT. I was admitted to all except Harvard, where I would have gone. I chose MIT, even knowing I wanted to study literature, out of contrariness (only one other Andover classmate applied to MIT) and to be near my friend Scott, who was going to Harvard. That was my first step to becoming an engineer.

As I mention in "Notes on Bucky: Patterns and Structure" MIT was, as Ezra Pound might have described it, an intellectual vortex. From Norbert Wiener's invention of cybernetics to Edward Lorenz's research in what became chaos theory, it was a whirlwind of unorthodox thinkers: Noam Chomsky, Minor White, Jerry Lettvin, Cyril S. Smith, Philip Morrison, Hans-Lukas Teuber, Harald A.T.O. Reiche, and Leo Marx were active and I studied with them or attended their lectures. I took Ancient Greek with an atomic scientist who had taught himself the language so he could write about Democritus. An evening seminar taught by the mathematician Gian-Carlo Rota was devoted to reading Heidegger's *Being and Time* out loud. I was able to start an arts and letters magazine—*Rune*—with generous financial support and full access to the photo and printing facilities of Ron MacNeil and Muriel Cooper's Visible Language Workshop—a precursor, with Nicholas Negroponte's Architecture Machine Group, to the MIT Media Lab. For the first issue of *Rune*, we collected the material, set the type, shot the halftones, printed the aluminum plates, and spent the summer running the Super Chief offset press. We did everything but bind the magazine.

For the Department of the Humanities I started a lecture series and in so doing was able to meet and spend a little time with the critics Harold Bloom and Hugh Kenner, as well as Robert S. Fitzgerald, the poet and translator of Homer. I chanced on Bloom's *The Anxiety of Influence* in 1975 and it opened up for me the literature of post-structuralism and structuralism. Kenner I discovered through his extraordinary book *The Pound Era* (a review of which is included within) because of my fascination with Pound and T. S. Eliot. In the summer of 1975, I spent a month traveling through Northern Italy with the Cantos "as my Baedeker," spending one night in Pound's house in Sant'Ambrogio at the invitation of his housekeeper, eating *funghi,*

April 19, 1975 demonstration by the People's Bicentennial Commission across from the official bicentennial commemoration of the Battle of Concord by President Gerald Ford. Image taken from the cover of the *Harvard Crimson* newspaper
Louise Nevelson's *Transparent Horizon* after one of many defacements; in the winter it was once buried in snow by critical students

listening to her stories in the Genovese dialect (which I could not understand but was still enchanted by), and sleeping in her son's bed overlooking the bay. My first solo teaching experience was during the January MIT Independent Activities Period (IAP) teaching Pound.

Kenner also had a connection to Buckminster Fuller and Samuel Beckett. He enlisted me to help with his book on Geodesic Math and encouraged me to write to Beckett, from whom I received a very polite reply that he "would not be in Paris at the time of your visit."

Despite all this activity in the "humanities"—or Course XXI as it was known at MIT— I was by then not sure of a career as a poet or critic or scholar. Barry Spacks the poet told me that I was a better impresario than poet, and I realized he was right. So I was continually searching for a "second" major. Mathematics led to Economics. I bypassed Architecture and finally came to Civil Engineering (Course I). I found math beyond differential equations, as well as economics, too abstract to grasp and I was impatient with the chatter of architectural reviews. I did spend time in Architecture, especially in Stan Anderson's lectures and visiting the studio of Maurice Smith, then the reigning Kiwi sage of MIT architecture, and I was especially drawn to Nicholas Habraken's writings and teaching. Above all, Donlyn Lyndon, the chair of Architecture at the time, took an interest and invited me to join the MIT

Committee on the Visual Arts, which he chaired. The committee acted as curator of the University's art collection and I was lucky to participate in the discussions following fellow students' attack in 1975 on the large Louise Nevelson sculpture *Transparent Horizon.* The large black, steel sculpture was first defaced with buckets of multi-colored paint and then, in the winter, entirely buried in snow. The student reaction prompted much discussion of the conflict between popular taste and modern art.

I was also taking courses in Civil Engineering and graduated with my degree in Course I, not Course XXI. For the most part, my Course I work was straightforward but unmemorable. The two exceptions were the lectures of John Biggs and Robert Whitman in structural analysis and geotechnics respectively. Biggs has continued to be an inspiration and touchstone as one who combined practice as a consulting engineer (e.g., on the dynamics of the Citicorp Tower) and original research. Whitman I came to know again later through earthquake engineering and also regard as a model of practical and fundamental engineering intelligence.

In the fall of 1975 my mother saw Isamu Noguchi by chance near the Metropolitan Museum of Art and in conversation he suggested that I come work with him and Buckminster Fuller in the office they had just combined together with Shoji Sadao, in a building across from Noguchi's studio in Long Island City. My mother, who knew Noguchi from the late forties, had mentioned my developing interest in civil engineering and Noguchi offered me an internship in both the Fuller & Sadao and Noguchi Fountains studios, both of which were overseen by Sadao. I spent part of January 1976 there as well as that summer and made, along with other interns

The green SAAB two-stroke station wagon after a somersault on the Queensboro Bridge off-ramp

Fuller and Sadao Inc office in 1976, Long Island City, NY

including Rob Grip, many of the models that went into the exhibition of Fuller's work included in Hans Hollein's *MAN TransFORMs* for the opening of the Smithsonian Institution's Cooper-Hewitt National Design Museum. Along with the models, I also was able to use Noguchi's equipment and supplies to make an aluminum replacement part for my car, a late '60s olive green SAAB two-stroke wagon (which I totaled that September in a freak accident on the Queensboro Bridge). Some of the models that Rob Grip and I made in 1976 reappeared in 2008 in *Buckminster Fuller: Starting with the Universe* at the Whitney Museum of American Art. As I recall in the essay "With Great Joy and Expectations," my one direct conversation with Bucky was memorable not so much for the content, but for the fact that he first perched himself on a desk, feet dangling, and then started the chat by turning off his hearing aid. It wasn't until 20 years later when I asked his daughter Allegra Snyder about this that she explained it was his way of focusing on the conversation without distracting background noise. He read lips. I had misunderstood this at the time and said nothing.

In my final semester in literature and philosophy I took a seminar on semantics with Chomsky and never did pull together the paper on Jacques Derrida and John Searle that he had agreed I could write. That one course was all I would have needed to complete the second degree in Course XXI. But I had by then heard back from graduate schools and had already chosen my next step—structural engineering at UC Berkeley rather than comparative literature at Yale, where I was rejected.

Bay Area, California

The summer before I left for Berkeley was spent living in a sublet on Sparks Street in Cambridge. I don't recall what work I did, if any, but I did discover by accident the work of the Zen Buddhist teacher Shunryu Suzuki—thinking I was buying a book by D.T. Suzuki, the teacher of John Cage and others at Columbia University. Shunryu Suzuki's book *Zen Mind, Beginner's Mind* has been an important reference for me. The teaching is as simple as the instruction to "just sit"; to attend to the practice or craft of an activity or work and when the mind wanders to gently draw it back. "When you wash the rice, wash the rice," as the cook and Zen teacher Edward Espe Brown explains it. My friend Pamela had also introduced me to Quaker meetings in Cambridge that year. The emphatic quiet of meeting, not unlike Zen meditation, had a lasting effect.

I arrived in Berkeley and stayed with friends on Hillegass Avenue for a few months till I found a small cabin for rent from a widow on Shasta Road. It was not far from the Berkeley Rose Garden—and it was magical. I felt as if I had returned to the hillside in Gstaad, only with a view of the Pacific through the eucalypti. The air was fresh and the bike rides up the hill hard but thrilling. Eventually I bought a car— a yellow Citroën 2CV. This was my second car after the SAAB two-stroke wagon. The 2CV was romantic but impractical. It would not climb the hills of San Francisco's North Beach except in reverse and labored to get over the Bay Bridge. But it was sharp. I eventually gave it up for a Fiat 128 (actually two, but the first one burst into flames an hour after I bought it) and finally my last and best-loved car, the 1969 Alfa Romeo Giulia Super, white with red leather bucket seats, which I kept till I returned to New York in 1982.

My studies at Berkeley in structural engineering and structural mechanics were difficult and discouraging. My teachers were excellent. But I often found the material too abstract and mathematical to follow. I do remember the intellectual brilliance of Egor Popov and Vitelmo Bertero, the warmth and intelligence of Boris Bresler and Steve Mahin, and the total clarity of Anil K. Chopra's structural dynamics class. But I struggled in all their classes. I managed better in Frank M. Baron's class on the "Analysis and Design of Structural Systems" and Alex Scordelis' "Thin Shell Structures." Baron introduced the work and writings of Hardy Cross, the inventor of "moment distribution" and other approximate calculation methods, including freehand sketching of deflected shapes to estimate force distribution in frameworks. The thin-shell class used David Billington's classic textbook on concrete shells in which iteration between the mathematical "membrane" general solutions and the approximations of edge and other local perturbations of the general solutions give a direct feel for structural behavior. Both the Cross and the thin-shell analysis methodologies were pragmatic, improving accuracy by iteration and not by immediate outcome, and bound up with physical reality. In *Arches, Continuous Frames, Columns, and Conduits: Selected Papers of Hardy Cross* there are nuanced essays on the uncertainties inherent in the structural analysis of real materials. Unlike many more sophisticated analysis methods, and especially the sometimes disembodied detachment of computer analysis, the direct approximate methods of Cross for frames and Billington for shells are hands-on in their correlation to real behavior. They helped me develop intuition.

I barely graduated from the Berkeley master's program. I found a group of close and smart friends among the Lebanese students who had descended on Berkeley as refugees of the 1975 civil war, many of whom were brilliant students. They helped me as best they could, but somehow I finished my coursework with a grade average of 2.99 when the minimum to obtain the master's degree was 3.0. I had to petition the university to accept 2.99 as equal to 3.0, which they graciously did, so I know I graduated at the absolute bottom of my class. I was quite discouraged and not at all enthusiastic to start work in the field.

But Boris Bresler introduced me to the structural engineering firm of Forell/Elsesser Engineers and I went to work there in the beginning of 1979. It was then a small but already very well-respected office. Nicholas Forell was working with MBT Associates' Gerry McCue (who soon after became dean at the Graduate School of Design at Harvard) on several elegant research facilities for IBM, at Almaden and Santa Teresa, California, and Eric Elsesser had just completed the two great Paffard Keatinge-Clay buildings in San Francisco, the addition to the San Francisco Art Institute and the San Francisco State University student union. Forell and Elsesser were good designers and very well respected in the practice of earthquake engineering. The rest of the staff, especially Don Chappell and Bill Honeck, were very generous teachers, however reluctant I was at first. I benefited from the example of their craft in the layout of working drawings and detailing. It was also my first exposure to computer structural analysis, first with the McDonnell Douglas McAuto time-share mainframes and later with the early HP-85 tape memory tabletop computers. Even then we were using the programs SAP and ETABS, developed by Berkeley professor Edward L. Wilson, which are still mainstays of structural engineering practice today.

What eventually overcame my reluctance and developed my interest and commitment to the profession was the volunteer work I was able to do in the Structural Engineers Association of Northern California. At that time SEAoNC was responsible, together with the other California SEAoC groups, for the writing of the "Blue Book," or the *Seismic Design Recommendations of the SEAoC Seismology Committee*, which were then the basis of the seismic code. When I got involved, the Seismology Committee was engaged in one of its updates and I was able to join the subcommittee that was looking at the steel design provisions. Egor Popov of Berkeley was just then promoting his idea of "eccentrically braced frames" (EBFs) based on the "capacity design" approach. Capacity design identified and gave special detailing attention to designated "fuses" or ductile links in the structural earthquake-resistant systems. In the case of the "EBFs" this fuse was created by offsetting the connection of diagonal braces from the intersection of columns and beams so that a length of beam became a kind of "shear link" that could be designed to fail before the other parts of the braced frame. The clarity of this "capacity design" philosophy was very appealing to me. It resonated with my readings of Hardy Cross and the idea that a structural framework could be seen as a network or circuitry that would have strong, weak, brittle, and resilient links and parts. That and many of the other intellectual concepts of earthquake-resistant design—ductility, response spectra, soil amplification, seismic risk, etc.—came alive as I sat through the deliberations of both the brilliant and enthusiastic academics—Popov, Bertero, and Helmut Krawinkler, among others—and the more cautious practitioners, including Henry Degenkolb, John Rutherford, Edwin G. Zacher, and others. Through SEAoNC I also joined the Earthquake Engineering Research Institute in 1979 and stayed active through the 1990s. Both organizations brought together all the disciplines interested in earthquakes, from geologists to seismologists, to engineers of all types, to social scientists and government officials. Because of the unexpected damage caused by the San Fernando CA earthquake of 1971 there was also government funding for research at the time, which led to new developments in steel and concrete design and analysis techniques, as well as ground motion predictions, that would find their way into practice through the codes developed then by SEAoC and the deliberations of EERI. It was a rigorous and invigorating community and I became quite engaged. A number of the papers collected here date from that period.

My contribution was to write the draft provisions for the design of concentrically (as opposed to eccentrically) braced steel frames. This was a typical contrarian impulse given the popularity of the new EBFs. At Forell/Elsesser in 1980-82 I did design the second and third or fourth EBFs built, one for the San Jose State Office Building designed by HOK and the other for a complex of buildings for Chevron at Bishop Ranch designed by MBT. But it was with the CBFs that I made my first actual discovery. CBFs were considered problematic for seismic resistance because as the ground shook back and forth, the braces would alternatively buckle, losing

June 12, 1982 Nuclear Freeze Initiative demonstration on Fifth Avenue, NY (also page 22)

much of their capacity, and yield in tension. This meant they had limited energy-dissipating capacity and degrading strength. To mitigate that, the provisions we proposed required the use of stouter braces and strong connections that could develop the braces' tension strength. All this was based on research and experimental work that Popov and others had done at Berkeley, and so merely code adoption. What I realized, though, was that in configurations known as K or inverted V braces—which were common ways of clearing the way for openings through braces —the behavior of the braced frame after one of the braces buckled was quite poor since the cross beam would have to resist the unbalanced vertical force from the tension side brace, for which the code had no requirements. This had not till then been noted by the code or anyone in practice or academia. The CBF provisions we developed then in our SEAoNC Seismology Subcommittee on steel identified this problem and added mitigating design requirements.

The intellectual energy of the earthquake engineering community and the creative design ideas that were coming into play, including EBFs and new techniques for seismic hazard and risk assessment and base isolation technologies, were completely engaging. Equally so was the sound ethical underpinning of the field. After all, the purpose of earthquake engineering is to save lives. The design philosophy that has been in place since the 1940s as formulated by the early pioneers of EERI, including George Housner, Nathan Newmark, John Blume, and Henry Degenkolb, was and is that buildings should be designed to survive major earthquakes with major damage but no loss of life. In effect, buildings should "crash" but save the occupants.

I was given an opportunity to test this ethical strain in 1982 when I decided to campaign to have SEAoC endorse the Nuclear Freeze Initiative that was on the ballot that fall in California. I was able to convince a number of the elders of the field to sign a petition to the board of SEAoC to have the members polled. Some of them objected–rightly, I now think–that maybe this was not an appropriate question for the members, but at the time I was on a mission that was both heartfelt and just a little mischievous. Through this venture I met both John Rutherford and Chris Rojahn, both of whom became friends and colleagues and moral examples for what an engineer could do and be. In the end the SEAoC board could not refuse the request from their most respected members and the poll was mailed. About 40 percent of the members responded, with two thirds in favor of endorsing the initiative. Inevitably there were some angry members who protested vehemently, mostly from the Right, and the SEAoC board cautiously decided to drop the matter. I did go to New York for the June 12, 1982, antinuclear march as a result, where among the more than one million marchers that converged up Fifth and Eighth Avenues into the Great Lawn of Central Park I managed to find my MIT roommate Tom, who had walked with a group of Buddhists carrying large drums all the way from Los Angeles to join the march.

In 1982 I also decided that I was ready to move back to New York. Thanks to Isamu Noguchi's introduction, I had met both the engineer Paul Weidlinger and the architects I. M. Pei and his partner James Ingo Freed in 1981 and was eventually offered a job at Weidlinger's. Noguchi continued to generously offer time and advice and to persuade me that I should stay with structural engineering–the dedication on the flyleaf of an exhibition catalogue he gave me on New Year's Day 1981 was "with great joy and expectations." He took me in person to see I. M. Pei on New Year's Day 1981–of course they were both working that day–when I mentioned hesitantly that I would like to meet him. We drove from Long Island City to 600 Madison Avenue in his yellow VW station wagon. Pei then introduced me to his partner, Freed, and he in turn to Myron Goldsmith, whom I was able to visit at SOM Chicago thanks to a traveling fellowship I won from the American Institute of Steel Construction (AISC). I was then considering the possibility of returning to school to study architecture and both Freed and Goldsmith also encouraged me to stay with engineering.

When Matthys Levy, Weidlinger's partner, offered me a job in early 1982, I said I could come in September and then foolishly gave notice at Forell/Elsesser six months in advance. I was laid off then and there, I think in part because of the recession but also because I had made myself a bit of a pest with Forell—asking interminable questions and disputing decisions and ideas rather too often. I went on unemployment for a few months and then was able to get a small project, through Donlyn Lyndon, as the engineer for a house in Sausalito designed by William Turnbull for a local doctor named Rabkin. When the doctor and Turnbull fell out over some issue I don't recall, I was left alone on the project. The structural drawings were done part-time by one of the draftsmen at Forell/Elsesser whose hand was exquisite. I still have the vellums.

Weidlinger

I returned to New York in September 1982. Including my time at Andover, it was thirteen years since I had left. At first I stayed with my friends George and Mari, with whom I had also spent my first months in Berkeley five years before. I found a rental apartment in one of the Bing and Bing buildings on West 12th Street after a few months of persistent calls (and chocolate deliveries) to their rental office. The West Village was far enough from the East Side, where I grew up, to feel like a fresh start. And at the time it was quiet and quite diverse in population. Early on my local dinner haunt, the Cottonwood Café on Bleecker Street, afforded me a chance encounter with Michel Foucault. I found myself sitting at the table next to him and the poet and translator Richard Howard—one in black leather from his shaved head to booted toe, and the other in tweeds—and after overhearing an hour of priceless gossip in French I decided to introduce myself. I had not recognized either of them, but the conversation was too spicy not to realize that these were unusual dinner neighbors. They were both very gracious and we had a good conversation, extended in part, I knew, by the fact that they rarely spoke with an engineer. A few years before, I had had a similar experience in Berkeley, when Derrida joined me after a lecture for a beer at the Bear's Lair pub, also out of curiosity to meet an engineer reader.

The West Village had a lively if seedy nightlife back then. Foucault was at the Cottonwood on his way to the "baths." These were mostly for the gay community, though there was one, the incomparable Hellfire, that tried to recreate the bath atmosphere for straights. More interesting was the Roxy on 18th Street, a club which brought hip-hop downtown. For someone who had grown up in New York, being part of a crowd that was nearly fifty-fifty black and white having fun dancing and watching break dancing and even, in the middle of the night, double Dutch competitions, was exhilarating. Fridays were for Afrika Bambaataa, Grandmixer D.ST, Jazzy Jay, Grand Wizzard Theodore, and Grandmaster Flash. I had great fun and felt very much at home as a New Yorker.

The work at Weidlinger was a welcome challenge. I was quickly given responsibility. My first project was with Freed on an office complex in Southern California for a developer client we referred to as the Artichoke King (he was from Castroville, the "Artichoke Capital of the World"). I remember my first solo business trip with John Sullivan of Pei and Freed's office–traveling first class in the nose of an American Airlines 747, listening to Grace Jones on the airplane's earphones as we descended over the infinite light field of the LA street grid. This was OK.

Besides Freed, I also worked with the successor firms of Marcel Breuer and Associates–Gatje, Papachristou, Smith, and Beckhard and Richlan–on several suburban office complexes and some houses. I was beginning to see some of the variety of architectural practice cultures, a topic of continuing interest ever since. I skirted around the blast-resistant design, defense work, and applied research that were a key part of Weidlinger's practice, and only worked on one small bridge–part of a wildlife preserve near Stone Mountain, Georgia–with the bridge group led by Herbert Rothman. I did work on the U.S. embassy in Nicosia, Cyprus, with Lee Polisano of KPF and enjoyed learning in that case again from John Biggs' clear and simple methods of energy-based calculations for blast-resistant design.

Columbia

At the same time I got a start teaching, thanks to Weidlinger and Levy's partner Mario Salvadori. He became one of my few true mentors and a friend. Salvadori came from a complex history–a Rome-born Jew and anti-fascist who escaped Italy at the age of 31 in 1938 and came to New York, eventually teaching at Columbia University. He had studied physics with Enrico Fermi but graduated in mathematics and engineering and taught at the University of Rome. In 1945 he discovered that research he had done in New York during World War II was, unbeknownst to him, part of the Manhattan Project to build the first atomic bomb. He became a lifelong pacifist. Over time his teaching focused more and more on the education of architects and young people. In the 1950s and '60s he wrote textbooks and developed the teaching methods for what became the standard of the structural engineering education of architects. Salvadori and I shared a European background and cultural and political interests. He was an extremely clear thinker and teacher and excellent mathematician. On his recommendation I was offered a job in the fall of 1983 teaching an introductory class on structures to the environmental design students at the Parsons School of Design. The department was headed by James Wines of SITE and included Laurie Hawkinson and others who became friends. I got stage fright during my first class and froze up. When I told Salvadori that I was not made for teaching, he responded with generosity typical of him. He immediately called his friend Felix Candela, who was then living in New York, and a young Dominican graduate student at Columbia, and the two of them, together with Wines and his deputy Lindsay Stamm Shapiro, all marched into the second class period and got me off to a fresh start. Afterwards I had a wonderful conversation with Candela over lunch, which inspired me to initiate the Candela lectures at MoMA years later. It was then that Candela told us the story of how he designed and built the *Palacio de los Deportes* stadium for the 1968 Mexico Olympics in a few months –just in time for the detailed calculations to be completed.

A few years later, in 1985, Salvadori asked me to teach with him at Columbia. He had just given the last series of his wonderful "Building of Buildings" introductory lectures, which I was able to attend, and was only teaching his seminar "The Architectural Consequences of Structural Decisions." I helped him teach that for two years and then in 1987 he retired from teaching at university to devote himself entirely to the Salvadori Educational Center on the Built Environment, where he taught grade school students and other teachers how to do math and physics through buildings and bridges. I took over the class and renamed it and over the next eight years taught a series of seminars, including "Structural Design," "Patterns and Structure," and "The Design of Mechanisms and Composite Structures." This last class I taught with my friend Chuck Hoberman and it was one of the most memorable seminars I have participated in. By then I was working at Ove Arup & Partners and Chuck had contacted me to arrange a meeting with Peter Rice. At the meeting in the new offices of Arup New York, Rice proposed designing deployable stadium roofs to him. The resulting Iris Dome was exhibited at MoMA, and Chuck and I worked on that and other projects as well as the Columbia seminar.

When Hoberman asked me to write an essay on his work for *Sites* magazine in 1992, it triggered a resurgence of my interest in literary and critical studies for the

first time since MIT, as well as rekindling my pleasure at writing essays. The introduction to the book on the work of Harry Wolf was also written in that period, and
coincided as well with my move to Arup.

New York Seismic

Besides the introduction to teaching, my time at Weidlinger also allowed for my
continued involvement in earthquake engineering. In 1984 I was handed a letter to
Matthys Levy from the New York Association of Consulting Engineers (NYASCE),
asking for an opinion on the application of the recently published national building
code standards for seismic design to New York construction. I remember the letter
was on blue paper. In 1982 the new standard published by the American National
Standard Institute (ANSI) revised the national seismic zone map to reflect research
on seismic hazards around the country, developed for the siting of nuclear power
plants. This was based on historic as well as seismological data, and it resulted in
areas of the East Coast being "upgraded" to higher seismic zones. New York, Boston,
and Charleston, South Carolina, were especially affected. Initially the NYASCE members did not think this should be adopted, but the blue letter went out pro forma.
I wrote on behalf of the firm to suggest that there was in fact some basis to the ANSI
maps and that this required more study. As it turned out, Leslie Robertson wrote
as well to say the same thing, and we were asked to take on a further study. At the
time, Weidlinger was working on a study for the Port Authority to look at the probable behavior of the George Washington Bridge in the event of a very unlikely but
possible earthquake, and so I was able to attach the NYASCE study to this. I formed
an ad hoc committee of Robertson, Joseph Kelly of the Port Authority, I. M. Idriss
and Tom Statton of Woodward Clyde, and Leonard Seeber and later Klaus Jacob
of Columbia University's Lamont-Doherty Earth Observatory. After a year of meetings we presented a report on November 7, 1986, confirming that there was a need
for earthquake-resistant design in New York.

As it happened, that same year the federal government designated the State University of New York in Buffalo as the site for the National Center for Earthquake
Engineering Research (NCEER)—much to the surprise of many, especially in California. Klaus Jacob, Carl Turkstra from Brooklyn Polytechnic and I persuaded the
NCEER to fund a conference in February 1988 at the New York Academy of Sciences
on Earthquake Hazards and the Design of Constructed Facilities in the Eastern
United States (later published in the Annals of NYAS in 1989 and to which I contributed "Wind versus Seismic Design"), which brought together experts from the
east and west coasts with the local NY government officials. During that meeting
Charles M. Smith, then the Commissioner of the Department of Buildings (DoB),

San Francisco-Oakland Bay Bridge visit by NYC Department of Buildings delegation in November 1989

asked me to form an official committee to look into the question of whether the NYC building code should include earthquake regulations. The story of the committee's work is included here in several papers. In brief, the committee included representatives of constituents from the Real Estate Board of New York to the state Urban Development Corporation and the Port Authority as well as academics and practitioners ranging from structural engineers to seismologists. Altogether there were 31 members on the committee and we met about once every two months for several years. A turning point was when I was able to take a small group to see the damage from the October 17, 1989 "World Series" Loma Prieta Earthquake as the official NYC DoB delegation. We got good access and saw what relatively little ground motion–15 seconds with a peak rock acceleration of 5-10 percent of gravity–could cause in damage. That magnitude of rock motion was equal to what we had found was possible in New York, so the impact of the visit was quite direct. After this the committee was able to complete its work adapting the seismic code provisions of the *Uniform Building Code* to New York and voted unanimously to recommend that the city make it into law on April 18, 1991. As a result of both the Loma Prieta and the subsequent 1994 Northridge California earthquakes, the federal government issued directives that federally owned or leased properties conform to some accepted seismic code provisions. The city council passed Local Law 17/95 in 1995 and the mayor signed it in the presence of the committee in February 1995.

The work of the NYC seismic committees, from 1984 to 1991, gave me some encouragement to take up an idea I had first broached with Leslie Robertson in 1983, to form a Structural Engineers Association of New York. I brought it up at a conference where the engineers Jacob Grossman and Tom Scarangello were with me to present the NYC seismic code, and carried on the discussion with Tom and his partner Aine Brazil. The timing was good as a new generation of New York structural engineers, including Tom and Aine, Ramon Gilsanz, Steve DeSimone, and Rick Mahoney, was moving into leadership roles in their offices or on their own. There was interest and after a year of meetings to discuss bylaws over breakfast (which I hosted at the Players Club off Gramercy Square), the association was finally launched in 1996. Aine Brazil was the first president, and I became the second.

Ove Arup & Partners

As I was working at Weidlinger in 1986 on the Nicosia U.S. embassy, I had occasion to travel through London and paid a visit to Patrick Moreau at Ove Arup & Partners. Donlyn Lyndon had introduced us based on the similarities in our career paths. Patrick did the structural engineering on the Sea Ranch California Houses, Lodge and Condominiums with Lyndon, Charles Moore, and Bill Turnbull. He then went to work at Weidlinger's office in Cambridge, Massachusetts, before returning to London to join Arup. I went to see him and to get his advice on my future career at Weidlinger, when the subject of working at Arup came up. Moreau was then starting an office for Arup in San Francisco, its first in the U.S., and commuting back and forth. I was not going to return to California, so the next question was whether Arup would consider an office in New York. They were reluctant to compete directly with Robertson, Weidlinger, Robert Silman, and others they considered peers. Ove Arup and then chairman Jack Zunz had worked with Paul Weidlinger and Salvadori on an SOM-designed bank tower in Johannesburg, and Arup had earlier consulted with Fred Severud. New York was in their view a hard town to set up in. And they had just retreated from an unsuccessful office they had set up in Paris on the back of the Pompidou Center.

Even so, after several months of discussions they decided to start a New York office. I was convinced that the timing was propitious, though the decision to go ahead was made on October 20, 1987, the day after the Black Monday stock market crash. The market for architecture was ever more international and Arup had an advantage offering offices in both New York and any project's location. In fact, during the discussions leading up to my move to Arup, I had worked with them and Lee Polisano at KPF on a headquarters building in London for Goldman Sachs together with Weidlinger. More importantly, the opportunity existed to bring a more engaged kind of collaborative design culture to New York, challenging what had become a rather passive position for consulting engineers in the city. With the exception of Les Robertson, there were few engineers in New York at the time who sustained the kind of strong collaboration with architects that had been the practice of Paul Weidlinger and Fred Severud in the 1960s. As I wrote some years later in the introductory essay to the Candela Lectures, *Constellations*, the post-modern movement, and before that the interests and approach of the New York Five architects and their generation, had used engineers instrumentally as technicians rather than collaborators. Arup could show highly integrated work with the British and European "hi-tech" architects of the 1960s and 1970s, and more recently the refined craftsmanship of Peter Rice and Tom Barker's work with Renzo Piano on the Menil Collection. These were forceful examples to offer the new generation of New York architects that I had begun to work with. Further, the Arup portfolio was a strong support to those same young architects as they were submitting their qualifications for larger institutional and public projects for the first time. It worked: not only did Arup prosper in New York, and eventually elsewhere in the U.S., but the example of their success attracted Buro Happold, Werner Sobek, Schlaich Bergermann, Tim MacFarlane, and others to open their own outposts in New York in the 1990s and 2000s. Between the start of Arup in 1987 to the founding of the Structural Engineers Association of New York in 1996, I think the culture of structural engineering in New York was changed for the better.

I flourished for the first five years I worked at Arup, thanks both to the small size of the office in New York and to the opportunities to work with and watch the remarkable leaders of the practice. I was lucky enough to meet Arup briefly in December 1987, a few months before he died. He was 92 but clear, articulate, and quite incensed at the time that Arup had inadvertently gotten involved in the design of a Trident nuclear submarine base in Scotland ("I am going to take my name off the firm," he told me). Gazing over the cathedral formed by his joined fingertips, he looked at me like I remember Bucky Fuller would look down as if from outer space. He talked in a continuous eloquent thread. His secretary had asked me before I went in to his large office whether I had an appointment afterwards, and as I did have a lunch date, she intervened after an hour and a half to halt the conversation. I was very sorry to leave, and sorrier that following February when Jørgen Nissen called me to say that Arup had died.

I was fortunate to work for Duncan Michael, who later led the firm, and to spend time with Jack Zunz, the chairman at the time, and architect Philip Dowson, the head of the multidisciplinary group Arup Associates. All of them and Jørgen were part of the senior board, and all in their varied way shared the idealism that drove the practice. The late Tony Fitzpatrick was also a friend. But the most immediate inspiration and influence for me came from Peter Rice and some of the younger engineers who worked with him—John Thornton, Richard Hough, Tristram Carfrae, and

Alistair Guthrie. Rice was clearly ambitious and directed in his interest in unconventional materials and lightweight structures. With Piano and Richard Rogers, he had developed an approach based on the investigation of uncommonly used structural materials – polycarbonate, ductile iron, ferro-cement, cast steel and glass – and a Ruskinian devotion to craftsmanship and the "*trace de la main*" as he called it.

My introduction to Rice was awkward and preceded my joining Arup. One of the last projects I had at Weidlinger was a glass and steel tensegrity sculpture, the *Bell Prism*, which I designed with Stephen Leibowitz for the newly created Bell of Pennsylvania in Philadelphia. I went on a junket with Stephen and the Bell engineers who were our clients to see the glass *"serre"* that Rice had designed for the La Villette museum of technology in Paris. I wanted to use the articulated glass bolt that Rice, Martin Francis, and Henry Bardsley had created for that project, but they were hesitant. I invited Francis to come and charrette on the design together in New York and after a rather fruitless week he announced that the solution to the problem was for us to resign and give the project to Rice. While this did not happen, this history gave my first meeting with Rice an awkward tone. But quickly the relationship warmed and I had several enjoyable times watching him at work in New York, most notably on the ill-fated collaboration of Arup and Rafael Viñoly on the Tokyo Forum. We never worked directly together. Richard Hough told me that Rice said he would not work with me because he did not think he could control me. But he did recommend me for projects he did not want, most happily the Byzantine Fresco Chapel I worked on with Francois de Menil.

My ten years of work and collaboration at Arup were fruitful and resulted in some good buildings and strong ongoing professional partnerships. I was able to maintain the "three-legged stool" of teaching, practice, and earthquake engineering research and code development. When Peter Rice died in 1992, though, my circumstances started to shift at Arup. In 1993 – 94 I was a Loeb Fellow at Harvard and this began my gradual disengagement from Arup. In part I was less comfortable with the growth of the Arup NY and U.S. practice. As additional disciplines were added, from building services engineering to acoustics and industrial engineering, I was invigorated, especially by the chance to collaborate with Mahadev Raman, the mechanical engineer, but also put off by the need to promote multidisciplinary services even when I didn't think it was necessarily best. Growth has its costs, and the burst of geographic and disciplinary expansion of Arup in the 1990s was out of sync with my interests. When in 1995 I was offered a lectureship leading to a tenure track position in the School of Architecture at Princeton by Ralph Lerner and Liz Diller, I took the opportunity to leave Arup in 1997 and start my own small practice in 1998.

Practice and Princeton

My new practice took me back to the feelings of the early days of opening the New York office of Arup and the improvisational pleasures of innovation on a shoestring. Fortunately, many of my architect friends, including Architecture Research Office, Henry Cobb, Steven Holl, Richard Meier, and Harry Wolf, remained loyal and I was able to work on large projects in collaboration with other structural engineers in New York and out of town and country. An early coup was the commission to work with Yoshio Taniguchi on The Museum of Modern Art expansion. This came in part through the recommendations of Harry Wolf and Terry Riley, then MoMA chief curator of architecture and design. It was Terry who also invited me to work with him on the MoMA exhibition *Tall Buildings* and write the introductory catalogue essay, as well as share in earlier brainstorms about some of his other exhibitions. Several of the essays in this book are the product of those conversations, as is the lecture series in honor of Felix Candela that I organized with Terry's support and advice at MoMA from 1998 to 2005. The lectures were a rewarding culmination of the effort to place structural engineering firmly alongside architecture in New York design culture.

The *Tall Building* show was Riley's response to the trauma of 9/11 and anxiety about tall buildings. While that anxiety was short lived, the show did mark the emergence of the full exuberance of fluid forms for tall buildings, as well as the programmatic and metaphoric construction that were evident in the looped figures and complex sections. I thought it was wonderful that the show of tall buildings, all but one designed by men, in the cavernous and loosely playful space of Michael Maltzan's MoMA QueeNS, was opened alongside the retrospective of the dark interior wall sculptures of Lee Bontecou.

My first office was inside that of my friend and lawyer Robert Rubin at 17 Battery Place. We moved to our own space at 198 Broadway in 1999, a block away from the World Trade Center. The effect of 9/11 was for the office and me, like everyone else in New York, disruptive and deep. A number of the essays here reflect on that and in particular the possibility of social action that became clear from the recovery and inspection work I was part of in the months after 9/11 working on the site. Our office was part of the recovery effort that I organized along with Ramon Gilsanz and Aine Brazil, starting the afternoon of the 11th through our then 400-member strong SEAoNY. I first came to the site on Friday the 14th and initiated that evening the proposed approach to the inspection of the 400 surrounding buildings that had been evacuated. This was based on the post-earthquake "triage" technique that had been developed after the Loma Prieta and Northridge California earthquakes and relied on a database of buildings compiled as part of a FEMA-sponsored research project just completed by us at Princeton. All this is related in the book we compiled and self-published afterwards: *World Trade Center Emergency Damage Assessment of Buildings*.

The aftereffects of 9/11 were for me intellectual and personal. They were also a challenge to our practice. Thanks in part to the pay we received from FEMA for our work at the WTC site, our inspection work, and our book publishing, we survived well enough to return to more normal projects. But the example of a deliberative democratic process guiding good engineering during the WTC recovery work and the mediocrity of the planning and design of the reconstruction that followed (and in which I played a not always happy part, as I explain in "Freedom from Fear" and "Action and Practice") both set the stage for what has become a greater degree of engagement in social action.

Coda

"The student is to read history actively and not passively;
to esteem his own life the text, and books the commentary."
R. W. Emerson, 1841

In his 1974 review of Harold Bloom's 1973 *The Anxiety of Influence*, Paul de Man writes "we can redirect our needs by substitution or sublimation." And in *Ludwig Binswanger and the Sublimation of the Self*, de Man adds that "the upward fall is a highly suggestive way of designating the ambivalence that makes artistic invention into a paradoxical combination of free will and grace." De Man alludes to an

First office space of Guy Nordenson and Associates at 17 Battery Place overlooking the New York Upper Harbor "asceticism of the mind" and to "disinterestedness." In Bloom's words, this upward fall is implied as "we journey to abstract ourselves by fabrication."

I would argue that under those creative circumstances that are available to the engineer, this "practical criticism" outlined by de Man is useful. In my experience there are three types of engineers in building and bridge engineering practice – the technicians, the "structural artists," as David Billington describes them, and the collaborators. The first act as executors of others' direction, using conventional and repeated methods and tools. This is generally a commodity practice and is subject to tight market constraints and pricing. There can be significant craftsmanship involved but it is not aspiring to originality – in fact originality is discouraged. The "structural artists" function in much the same way as architects who see their practice as an autonomous art – rather than, say, as a craft or "service." A Christian Menn or a Santiago Calatrava should, I think, be judged on aesthetic grounds for works they will justifiably claim as authors. But they will often rely on assistance to execute their direction. Neither Menn nor Calatrava generally do their own detailed engineering.

The collaborators, my third category, work with architects or engineers or even artists. Their practice is more explicitly embedded in both the process and work itself, and the originality of their work therefore requires closer reading. They are themselves readers and critics in their practice since they are operating in a "secondary" role. This is where, to me, the lessons of de Man, Bloom, Derrida, and Michel Foucault were useful, as they extend from the relationships of author and reader, author as reader, and critic as author, etc., to the relationship of author and collaborator, author as collaborator, and so on. This is also where such an outlook on practice as a "paradoxical combination of free will and grace" implicates the concept of sublimation and "disinterestedness."

The verse of Henry Wadsworth Longfellow that Wittgenstein loved captures the burden and gift of craft:

In the elder days of Art,
Builders wrought with greatest care
Each minute and unseen part;
For the Gods see everywhere.

We "abstract ourselves by fabrication": by necessity our work is rarely present in the final architecture. It may be partly glimpsed or re-presented as architecture, but a complete understanding of the structure in the finished work requires close reading of the architecture, deduction, or, most likely, a study of the construction drawings. As a student of structure I can attest there is always interpretation.

The invisibility or dissimulation of structure is to my mind a good thing for creative practice. What Eduard F. Sekler called "structure, the intangible concept" can be realized in ways that are tectonic, a-tectonic, or even sublimated. Creativity can be real even if it is secret. It is up to the "reader" to find what matters.

What this means in practice is that the work of the structural engineer is at least a dialectic between the empirical necessities of strength, stiffness, and stability and the rhetoric of presence and representation. This gets interesting for example when, as in the case of Peter Rice, the rhetorical enlists craft and innovation in the interest of safety. Rice claimed that routine repetitive engineering—commodity practice—was riskier than an innovative or progressive practice of new methods and materials. Not only was Rice after the evidence of craft, but in projects from the Pompidou Center to Lloyds of London and the Menil Collection of Houston, he experimented with forms and legibility as well as new materials. In a true, if you might think paradoxical, sense he was conservative—he played it safe by always starting fresh.

Part of that conservatism was the continuity of his collaborations—most centrally those with Renzo Piano and Richard Rogers. It is notable, I think, that Rice did not work with either James Stirling or Norman Foster even though they were of the same generation as Rice and Piano and Rogers. In the case of Stirling it is clear, in Stirling's own words, that "a successful transition from organized patterns"—and the corresponding "relationship of spaces"—"into structure and materials is dependent on the author's structural vocabulary," i.e., Stirling's, not the engineer's. As Stirling wrote in his essay "Anti Structure," he opposed any appearance of structural rationalism which means that the structure was in effect repressed, not sublimated. In Foster's case, as an Arup engineer put it to me once, the task is to "make it work the way Foster imagines it's working"—in effect representation but one that also distorts or even represses the engineer's will and insight.

The organization of design is either top-down and hierarchical—with each "trade" made instrumental to the author's vision—or collaborative. While I prefer the collaborative situations, I recognize that there are practices—I. M. Pei & Partners in the 1960s to '80s, and Foster and Gehry's today—where a top-down practice can produce excellent work. But to me the situations that more resemble repertory companies—

in theater and even cinema—are more interesting from the perspective of both participant and critic. For the engineer, as I imagine for the associate architects, craftsmen, and other "players," the repertory model is the preferred choice. Where this is not the case it may be for reasons that have to do with everything from education to psychology. Many prefer to be given specific problems that have clear solutions rather than complex texts requiring deconstructive reading. Many disdain what they see as obfuscation and rhetoric in favor of the clarity of problem solving. For me it is different.

I prefer adapting and discovering craft and ideas in the contexts, circumstances, and characters of each idiosyncratic project.

In Search of Ezra Pound

Book review of Hugh Kenner's *The Pound Era,* University of California Press

"I have brought the great ball of crystal; who can lift it?"

Ezra Pound, *Canto CXVI*

"…having had twenty years"

1951–1971: punctuated by two careful, extremely lucid books on Ezra Pound by Dr. Hugh Kenner. The first (*The Poetry of Ezra Pound)* was an effort to return Pound to his rightful place in literary history: if as "barbarian," then so be it. Pound was an "inventor" ("discoverer of a particular process or of more than one mode and process"–Pound), and as such bound to seem uncivilized.

"Mr. Pound is more responsible for the XXth Century revolution in poetry than is any other individual" –Eliot, in the dedication of his "Waste Land" to Pound, "il miglior fabbro" (Dante's word for Arnaut Daniel: another inventor).

But Pound "erred," and so was excoriated by those who knew him only through tabloids: hence Pound the fascist, Pound the anti-Semite, Pound the "officially pronounced" insane (so he would avoid the electric chair as traitor).

Hugh Kenner then, pioneer of Pound studies (1951–Pound aetat. 66), and, subsequently, authority on T. S. Eliot, Wyndham Lewis, James Joyce, Samuel Beckett, and R. Buckminster Fuller (!). And twenty years later ("a wholly new start"?), a voluminous work, not on Ezra Pound, but on *The Pound Era* (an inversion, a pun?).

In a very important sense this book is also an effort to weave Pound into the tapestry of modern poetry. For Pound, as inventor (like Daniel, Cavalcanti, Jonson) could simply become an "influence," obscured by the shade of a "master" ("inventors … able to assimilate and coordinate a large number of preceding inventions"). And T. S. Eliot (as Dante, Shakespeare) casts a large presence.

Published in *The Tech,* vol. 95, No. 9, March 7, 1975, page 8

The Pound Era: an age then: and the men, and women, who inform it, Kenner
traces their beginning: we find Ezra Pound talking to Henry James, though "their talk
is forgotten." We have a chapter called "Space-Craft" ("Any object in space is
a memory system"), engaging Joyce, Pound, in "transactions with Homer," and "Eliot
with Shakespeare." There is "Renaissance II," and "The Muse in Tatters" (Sappho).
Each chapter is a Wholy System, each collaborates with those surrounding in not an
explanation, but more an evocation of the Era. Kenner draws us, with Pound, to
a bookseller's along the quais in Paris, makes us choose Divus' [translation of the]
Odyssey (not Iliad!), then leaves us to continue. He does not explicate, he explodes
details (luminous details). It is for the reader to respond with an urge. (For the
best way to understand a poem is to be moved to write, and discover it has already
been written.) We are plunged into the hopes of the "Men of 1914," introduced to
a ferment of talent ("vortex of vortices"), then watch the greater part die in a senseless
war (Gaudier-Brzeska, T. E. Hulme, Alain Fournier…), and the rest scatter into
loneliness ("Who is there now for me to share a joke with?"–Pound [1966] on Eliot's
death). And the margins fill ("Ya une limite…").

Photographs are set beside poems (Kenner is a fine photographer!), poems
beside people, people beside people spinning a web of subject rhymes ("Pound's

Drawing of a panther by Henri Gaudier-Brzeska from *The Pound Era* heuristic device") that seems to include everything, yet remains wonderfully flexible. There are priceless anecdotes: Eliot at the Garrick, "I no longer pretend that I am pretending"; on cheeses, "Never commit yourself to a cheese without having first ... *examined* it."

I'm afraid I could go on. But rather save your time for the book!

Of Kenner: *The Pound Era* is one of the best books I have read.

And of Pound I can only say what he said of Eliot (1966): READ HIM.

Tensegrity from Greece to Cambridge

Dr. Hugh Kenner was at MIT last Wednesday for an informal talk sponsored by the Course XXI Society (an "organization" of humanities majors). Dr. Kenner, a Professor of Twentieth Century Literature at Johns Hopkins University, is the author of books on Ezra Pound, T. S. Eliot, James Joyce, and R. Buckminster Fuller.

Kenner brought along a Tensegrity Sphere to illustrate his remarks. The Tensegrity (tensional integrity) is the simplest example of the principles, which extended, include those of the famous Geodesics. The Tensegrity Sphere is made up of 12 sticks (actually dowels) held in 4 intersecting planes by wires extending from their ends. The Tensegrity is particularly useful for demonstration purposes since it effectively separates the compressive and tensive stresses respectively along the sticks and wires. The wires then lie outside and the dowels inside the sphere outlined by their points of intersection.

Centering on this sphere Kenner continued, using its system of differentiating tensions and compression to illustrate aspects of Pound's and others' poetry. He explained his notion of the space between words, noting that early Greek did not originally include any. Greek was originally written across the page then around and backward, and around again and forward, much as a plouw runs across a field. The space between words most likely came along with the philosophic differentiation of a continuous "real" into particular "ideas." Anyone who has listened to a foreign language which he or she does not understand can attest to the tendency of the words to run into one another. At most, phrases may be isolated, but it is only in the written language that the words separate.

It is only in 19th-century France that the potential, poetic and otherwise, of this late addition to the alphabet was fully understood and implemented. It was the Symbolist poets and in particular Stéphane Mallarmé who gave these "silences" their place in verse. Through Ezra Pound and T.S. Eliot and later William Carlos Williams this element entered English verse. These poets made different though equally powerful usage of this space not only to tie together seemingly jarring subjects but also to express the tensions that can only be communicated silences.

Responding to a question by Barbara Sirota, Kenner elaborated this metaphorical connection between 20th-century poetry and Fuller's Tensegrity. He pointed out that the same discontinuity that underlies them pervades throughout much of contemporary art; that it also has much of our cultural patterns (for example, the recent switch from continuous to digital displays in clocks, stereos, etc.).

Kenner spoke as well of the peculiarities of academic learning. In response to a remark by Mykl Castro concerning the "museumification" of visual art, Kenner pointed out that much the same was occurring in poetry. To accommodate the classic "survey" course, anthologies have emerged as arbiters of "importance" and "relevance." The student can then be led by the hand through these museums, pausing to note each piece. The art-object is thus divorced from its original context in the artist's work to serve as evidence of some thematic, qualitative, or chronological intent.

Overall, Dr. Kenner concentrated on the meaning of words and language. Language has, according to him, evolved to the point that the words and lines have become the basic units of a kind of literary construction business. Novels rise from a careful, and arbitrary, blueprint: beginning with a point of view, insight, plot, etc. The novelist adds on structure and superstructure ("And besides," "And over and above that…") till the whole thing is sufficiently fleshed out. According to Kenner, this process underlies much of contemporary literature and to some extent other arts.

The evening was essentially Fulleresque, extending over an astonishingly wide range of topics. Like Fuller, Kenner does not prepare his lectures, but instead will let the topic emerge from a rather free-flowing exposition of his extensive knowledge.

Aseismic Reinforcement
of Existing Buildings

Nicholas F. Forell, F. ASCE, and Guy J. P. Nordenson

Introduction

The reinforcement and strengthening of existing buildings to resist seismic forces has in recent years become an increasingly significant part of the work done by the engineering profession. The rapid rise in costs, coupled with lengthy and expensive approval processes for new construction, has made the rehabilitation of older buildings to modern uses more attractive. In addition, growing environmental and conservationist concerns demand the retention of historic and older buildings within the urban fabric. Simultaneously, the widespread media coverage of the effects of earthquakes has increased the public awareness of the potential hazards of these buildings to life and property. This awareness has led to legislation in the form of building codes requiring the reinforcement of older buildings to resist earthquake forces. Within the framework of these modern seismic codes, the differences in hazard exposure and the importance of buildings are recognized, and variations in design criteria and seismic reinforcing methods are allowed.

This paper presents three case studies of buildings of different age and construction that illustrate such variations of design criteria and reinforcement methods.

Case Study No. 1

Description

The structure described in this study (FIG. 1) is part of a historic complex of buildings in Monterey, California, known as the Cooper-Molera Adobe. The complex is owned by the National Trust for Historic Preservation and will be operated by the California Department of Parks and Recreation as a historic monument and museum. The main buildings were constructed in 1832, with a major addition occurring in the 1950s. The foundations are of pressed stone, generally laid in three courses creating a footing 22 inches (55.9 cm) deep and 32 or 22 inches (81.3 or 55.9 cm) wide.

Published in *Journal of the Structural Division*, vol. 106, no. ST9, September 1980, pages 1907–19

The adobe bricks used in the construction of the walls are either 11 × 22 × 3 inches (27.9 × 55.9 × 7.6 cm) or 10 × 20 × 3 inches (25.4 × 50.8 × 7.6 cm), depending on their age. The walls are either 22 or 32 inches (55.9 or 81.3 cm) thick. Door and window openings have timber headers supporting the masonry above them. The lumber used for the second floor and roof framing included both redwood and pine.

Structural Evaluation
The condition of the adobe was generally good, with little weathering noted. No signs of foundation settlement were found. The absence of cracks and the condition of the joints at unbonded wall intersections indicated that the adobe walls did not sustain any damage due to past earthquakes. This observation was confirmed by historic records in which references were made to the excellent performance of this building during earthquakes. The wood framing throughout has heavy dry rot and termite damage which could impair the load-carrying capacity of the affected framing members.

From a seismic design point of view, a great number of deficiencies were noted. Although the unreinforced adobe walls, by virtue of their large cross-sectional areas, possess substantial shear resistance, they are poorly supported in the lateral direction. The interior adobe walls at the ground floor provide some lateral support, but the connection of the interior walls with the perimeter walk has no tensile capacity. Failure due to earthquake forces is most likely to occur at right angles to the plane of the walls, leading to inward or outward collapse of the exterior walls. The roofs and second floor are tied to the adobe walls and would move relative to them under severe earthquake forces. Any localized damage in the adobe walls would then result in the loss of vertical support for the roofs or floor, leading to the collapse of these elements.

Design Criteria Development
Though the building is owned by the Trust for Historic Preservation, it is operated by the State of California. As a result, some problems arose in the determinations of an acceptable method of rehabilitation. The Trust's primary task is the preservation of the historic fabric and authenticity of their buildings, whereas the State of California's duty is to protect the life of the user. Solutions that would severely alter the appearance of the building or even recreate the appearance of the original materials with modern ones were therefore not acceptable. While compliance with current building codes was not required by the agencies that have jurisdiction over this

building, adequate safety to meet anticipated earthquake forces had to be ensured.

To arrive at an acceptable design criteria, the following studies were performed:

1. A seismic risk evaluation study was prepared by Dames & Moore, San Francisco. This study took into consideration the following: (a) the probability of earthquakes occurring in the region affecting the site; (b) the location of such earthquakes relative to the site; (c) the magnitude of earthquakes to be expected; and (d) the attenuation, or reduction in force level, due to the distance between the epicenters and the site.

The probability of occurrence, magnitude, and location of earthquakes was based on historic records and geologic fault location studies (SEE FIG. 2). Magnitude attenuations were determined using established mathematical procedures. In arriving at the final probability distributions, it was assumed that risk could be expressed in terms of the probability of an event occurring in a given span of time. A 50-year span of recurrence was used. Evaluation of the data presented in this study showed that, using a 50-year time span, the probability of earthquake-induced accelerations in excess of 20% of gravity is small.

2. A material study was conducted by Testing Engineers of San Francisco. Tests were made of 23 adobe samples to determine density, moisture content, moisture absorption, compressive strength, and flexural strength. Visual inspection and laboratory test results showed an excellent uniformity of material throughout the building. Standard deviations from average density and strength were 8% and 23% respectively. The average compressive strength of the adobe masonry was 400 psi (2,756 kPa), and the average flexural strength 39 psi (269 kPa) from which an average shear strength of 20 psi (138 kPa) was derived.

Reinforcement Criteria

The seismic risk study indicated that the maximum acceleration level at this site, over a reasonable span of time, would not exceed 20% of gravity. This is considerably less than the acceleration magnitude used in the development of the code force for the Seismic Zone 4. This finding is borne out by historic records of seismic activity in the city of Monterey. It should also be noted that studies by the California Division of Mines and Geology place Monterey on the boundary between Seismic Zones 3 and 4. It was therefore concluded the building could be reinforced using the code force level for Seismic Zone 3.

1

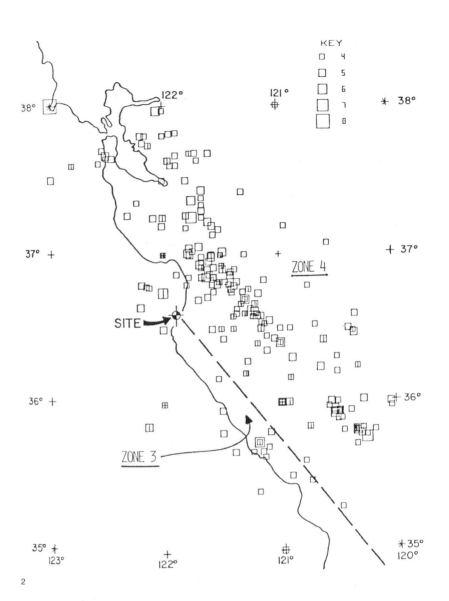

2 Recorded Epicentral Locations (Dames & Moore)

The material test study suggested that the adobe masonry could be used as a vertical and lateral load resisting element as long as the material stresses provided for adequate safety factors. In addition:

1. Adequate horizontal diaphragms will be provided to collect and distribute lateral forces.

2. Horizontal perimeter ties (chord) will be installed to connect the diaphragms to the building walls and to distribute the lateral forces uniformly to the force-resisting walls.

3. Provisions are to be made to restrain the adobe wall from collapse at right angles to the plane of these walls.

4. In addition, vertical support for the roof and walls are to be provided independent of the adobe walls, so that partial failure of these walls would not impair the safety of these elements.

Since the building was to have an independent vertical load-resisting element, the building could be classified as a $K = 1.0$ value structure. Thus $V = ZIKCSW$ (1) in which Z = seismic zone factor = $\frac{3}{4}$ (see the foregoing); I = importance factor = 1 (limited occupancy by resolution); K = structural system factor = 1 (see the foregoing); and CS = dynamic characteristics factor = 0.14. Therefore V = base shear = $0.75 \times 1.0 \times 1.0 \times 0.14 \times W$; and $V = 0.105W$.

The design criteria using a force level of approximately 10% of gravity was compared to the force level of 20% of gravity as indicated by the seismic risk study relative to the computed stress level. Structural analysis showed that the average shearing stress in the adobe walls due to criteria lateral forces was 4 psi (28 kPa). At isolated maximum stress concentrations, the shear stress did not exceed 6 psi (41 kPa). This gave a safety factor of 3.3 to 5, which was judged to be adequate.

Rehabilitation and Reinforcement
To minimize the impact on the finishes of the building, structural steel was selected as the appropriate reinforcing material. The deterioration of the wood framing necessitates that most roof and second-floor members be replaced. A plywood diaphragm will be installed at the roof and under the second floor joists (FIG. 3). The roof rafters will be supported by a horizontal steel beam keyed into the top of the adobe walls. The second-floor joists are to be supported on a steel ledger applied to the interior face of the adobe walls. These ledgers in turn will be supported by steel beams located between the floor joists and spanning the width of the building. These beams are extended to the outside of the exterior wall, where they will be supported by columns installed recessed in vertical slots cut into the

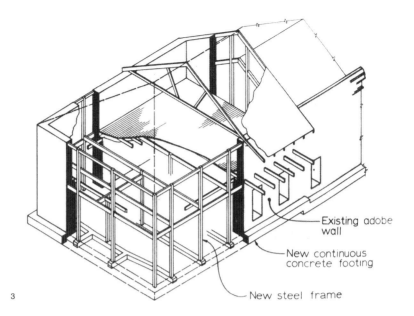

Existing adobe wall

New continuous concrete footing

3

New steel frame

adobe. The exterior column extends to the roof structure to carry the horizontal roof support beams. A horizontal steel beam at the second floor level, located opposite the interior steel ledger, will also be installed in horizontal slots cut into the adobe wall. The exterior walls are thus restrained laterally by the columns, by the two horizontal steel members at the second floor between which they are sandwiched, and by the horizontal roof beam which is keyed to the masonry. The steel columns are supported by new concrete grade beams which tie the columns at grade and aid in the lateral support of the walls. The slots in the adobe wall will be packed with new adobe grout and covered with new plaster so as to restore the exterior finish and protect the adobe from weathering.

The working drawings for this project are completed and construction is expected to start this summer. This reinforcing solution demonstrates that reinforcing systems can be devised to respond to a specific seismic environment without undue disturbance of the fabric of a historically significant structure.

Case Study No. 2

This section of the paper examines the conversion of a part of a retail store built in 1929 for the Sears-Roebuck Co. to public school use.

3 Isometric View: East Corner
4 Sears Building, San Francisco, Calif.

Description

The building is 200 feet (61 m) square and three stories high, with a 50-foot (15.2-meter) high by 30-foot (9.1-meter) square tower rising at the main elevation (FIG. 4). The tower housed mechanical equipment and a water storage tank no longer in use. The timber pile foundations were found to be in excellent condition. The floors and roof are of reinforced concrete flat-slab construction with dropped panels and flared column caps. The exterior walls are built of unreinforced brick elements with brick veneer covering concrete columns and spandrels. Carved stone elements were used as decoration.

An extensive testing program was carried out to determine the strength of the materials and to verify compliance of construction with the existing engineering drawings.

Reinforcing Requirements

The first floor was to be occupied by a department of the State of California. The San Francisco Community College intended to occupy the second floor, with future expansion to the third floor. The partial use of this building for public school purposes required that the entire structure be upgraded to meet the requirements of the California Administrative Code, Title 24. This code, at the time of conversion, paralleled the basic lateral load provisions of the 1973 edition of the *Uniform Building Code* (*UBC*), with the exception of the design, detailing, and quality control requirements, which are considerably more rigorous. Since the time of design of this project, Title 24 has adopted the basic lateral force design provision of the 1976 *UBC*.

Design Criteria

In 1929, when this building was designed, mandatory requirements for the design against seismic forces were not included in building codes. The 1927 *Uniform Building Code*, which governed at the time of design, had an appendix with optional earthquake provisions, but it appears that they were not considered in the design.

Analysis indicated that the inherent lateral force resisting capacity depended on the frame action of the exterior columns and spandrel beams as well as the interior columns and the flat-slabs. The contribution of the unreinforced masonry to the lateral resistance was negligible, since the anchorage of this masonry to the concrete elements was nominal. The utilization of the existing frame capacity and masonry elements in a reinforcing scheme was not acceptable, since neither non-ductile frames nor

4

unreinforced masonry are permitted by Title 24. An independent shear wall system consisting of pneumatically placed concrete or "gunite" walls was therefore decided upon.

Reinforcement

Since the function of the new occupancy required undisrupted clear interior spaces, the new gunite shear walls were to be applied to the exterior walls of the building (FIG. 5). Requirements for security and sound isolation from traffic noises permitted the closing of openings at the exterior wall whenever structurally required or architecturally desirable. Because construction of the first floor remodeling was under way, the gunite had to be applied from the outside. At the upper floors the gunite was placed from the inside against a single-course brick closure of the openings. The gunite shear walls are designed to span between the existing concrete element to which they are anchored with drilled-in dowels. The gunite wall thickness varies from 8 inches (20.3 cm) on the ground floor to 6 inches (15.2 cm) on the third floor (FIGS. 6A AND 6B). Reinforcement is provided in accordance with the shear demand of the walls.

In addition to providing seismic force resistance to the building, the gunite walls must act as a support for the unreinforced brick elements. The provisions of Title 24 state that "existing masonry which does not meet the requirements for reinforced grouted masonry shall not be used for structural purposes..." However, it may be assumed to carry its own weight vertically. Title 24 specifically defines the permissible methods of supporting masonry by means of gunite. If the gunite is applied to form a membrane or wall on one side of the masonry wall, such membrane must be keyed into the masonry by means of ribs or minor columns of gunite extending to the far tier of masonry. Such ribs may not be placed further than 5 feet (1.5 m) apart and must be reinforced with two #5 bars and #3 ties at 9 inches (22.9 cm) on centers. An alternative to the installation of gunite ribs is to provide contact between the gunite membrane and the far tier of the masonry at one point in any rectangle of masonry surface 4 feet (1.2 m) wide and 3 feet (0.9 m) high. The area of such contacts cannot be less than 64 square inches (412.9 sq cm).

The latter method was used in the building described in this example (FIGS. 6A AND 6B). The masonry elements, consisting largely of spandrels and mullions, did not lend themselves to the installation of gunite ribs. The contact point with the outer masonry tier could be readily provided by drilling 9-inch (22.9-cm) diameter holes using conventional coring equipment.

The single course of masonry covering the concrete spandrels and columns required anchorage to conform with the code provisions for masonry veneer. Title 24 requires that a minimum of one anchor tie of 16-gauge galvanized sheet metal be embedded into the concrete and extended into the horizontal joints of the veneer for every 2 square feet (0.19 sq m) of veneer surface. The existing anchorage did not meet this requirement. In lieu of the sheet-metal anchorage, anchor bolts with washers were drilled through the veneer into the concrete at the required spacing. The support of carved stone ornamentation was provided in the same manner.

This project was halted after completion of the contract documents by the passage of State Proposition 13. The San Francisco Community District's funding was drastically reduced by this proposition, stopping all further construction.

Cost estimates prepared by the school district indicated a rehabilitation cost of $13.00/square foot (0.09 sq m), of which $3.00 would be for structural work, figures that are well within the budget for this type of conversion.

Case Study No. 3

This building is part of a manufacturing complex located south of San Francisco which was designed in 1965 in conformance with the lateral load requirements of the 1964 edition of the *Uniform Building Code*. The single-story structure is 250 feet (76.2 m) wide and 720 feet (219.5 m) long (FIG. 7). Expansion joints at the one-third points divide the building into three independent elements. The structural system consists of exterior tilt-up concrete walls and a structural steel roof system. Steel columns on a 50-foot by 40-foot (15.2 × 12.2 m) grid support steel trusses which in turn support channel purlins and the 1-½-inch-deep (3.8 cm) fluted steel roof deck. Lateral loads are resisted by the exterior concrete walls and the combination of steel columns and trusses acting as rigid frames. Adjacent to the expansion joint in each building section, a knee-braced frame was installed in lieu of the truss-column frames. A mechanical core structure in each of the building elements provides additional lateral support through a bracing system located below an equipment mezzanine.

In view of the close proximity of this building to a major active fault, the importance of the manufacturing process contained in this building, and the recent developments in seismic-resistant design, the owners voluntarily decided to reinforce this building, as far as possible, to conform to the current "state of the art" in seismic design. A seismic risk evaluation study was performed that took into consideration fault locations, seismic

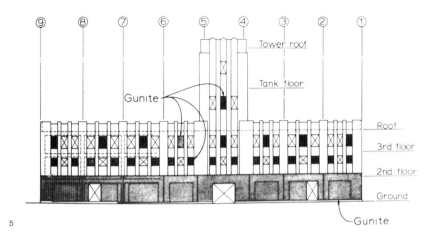

5

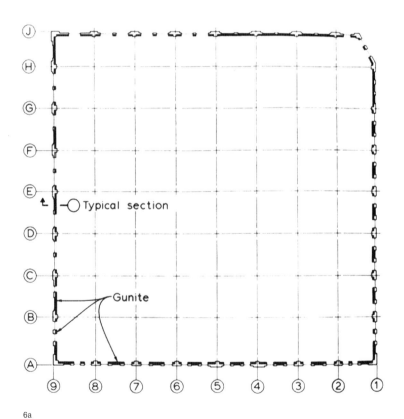

6a

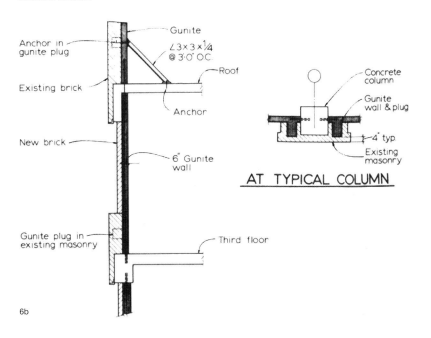

Gunite

Anchor in gunite plug

∠3×3×¼ @ 3'-0" O.C.

Existing brick

Roof

Anchor

New brick

6" Gunite wall

Gunite plug in existing masonry

Third floor

6b

Concrete column

Gunite wall & plug

4" typ.

Existing masonry

AT TYPICAL COLUMN

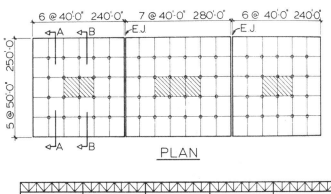

6 @ 40'-0" 240'-0"   7 @ 40'-0" 280'-0"   6 @ 40'-0" 240'-0"

E.J.   E.J.

A B

5 @ 50'-0" 250'-0"

A B

PLAN

TYPICAL SECTION A-A

SECTION AT MEZZANINE B-B

7

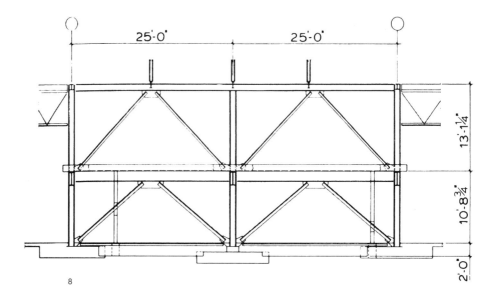

25'-0" 25'-0"

13'-1¼"

10'-8¾"

2'-0"

8

history, including frequency and magnitude of earthquakes, distance attenuation, and soil-structure interaction. The study developed a response spectrum as a design criteria which could be compared to the current code requirements.

The design force level for this building under the provisions of the 1964 edition of the *Uniform Building Code* was as follows:

$V = ZKCW$ (2) in which V = total lateral load or base shear; Z = seismicity factor = 1 in the location of the building; K = structural system factor (a value of 1.33 was required for shear wall building and appears to have been used throughout); C = dynamic characteristics factor based on the fundamental period of the building (the code recommended value of 0.10 for one-story buildings was used); and W = total dead load of the building. Therefore, $V = 1.0 \times 1.33 \times 0.10 \times W = 0.133W$ or 13.3% of gravity.

The 1976 edition of the *Uniform Building Code* requires a later design force level based on the formula $V = ZIKCSW$, in which V = total lateral load or base shear; Z = zone factor = 1.00; I = importance factor (a value of 1.0 was used); K = structural systems factor (a value of 1.33 was used); C = dynamic characteristics factor; S = site-structure resonance factor; and W = total dead load of the building. Since the building period was low and the soil period in excess of 1.0 sec, the maximum value of $C \times S = 0.14$ was

8 Section: Vertical Steel Truss (1 ft = 0.305 m)
9 Section: Vertical Steel Truss (1 ft = 0.305 m)

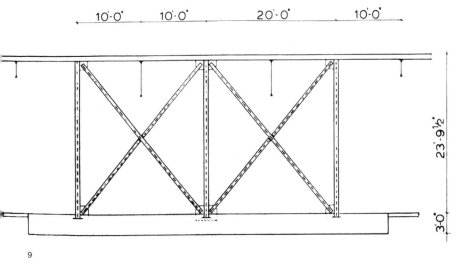

9

applicable. Therefore, $V = 1.0 \times 1.0 \times 1.33 \times 0.14 \times W = 0.186W$ or 18.6% of gravity.

This constitutes an increase in design force level of 40%. This force level was compared with the predicted ground motion behavior generated in the site seismicity study. To do so, the fundamental period of the building was computed considering both existing and proposed lateral bracing systems. Using the response spectrum and the computed building period of 0.08 sec, an acceleration of 40% g is indicated at 5%–10% critical dampening. An evaluation of the proposed and existing lateral force-resisting systems led to the conclusion that a force reduction factor of two, based on ductility and reserve strength capacity, was permissible. A design lateral force level of 20% g was therefore used for the reinforcement of this building.

Analysis
Structural analysis indicated that all building sections required substantial reinforcement to meet the new seismic design criteria.

End Building Sections
The end wings exhibit severe torsional problems in their transverse direction to the truss-column frames. Under the computed deflection of the roof

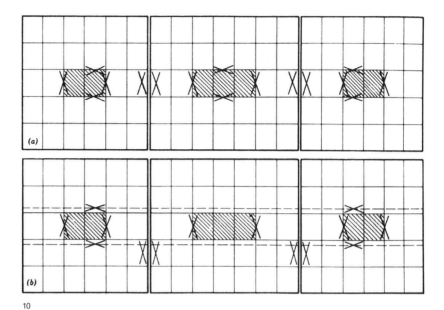

(a)

(b)

10

diaphragm, the frames that are an integral part of the mechanical cores were badly overstressed. In the longitudinal direction, the roof diaphragm adjacent to the exterior wall as well as the truss column frames integral with the mechanical cores were overloaded.

Center Building Section
In the longitudinal direction, the same overstress condition exists as in the end elements. In the transverse direction, the truss-column frames were inadequate to resist the new seismic force level.

Reinforcement System
The seismic reinforcement of this building was relatively simple in concept. Vertical steel trusses were used to provide lateral resistance to supplement the existing concrete shear walls (FIGS. 8 AND 9). Existing truss-column frames were neglected as a primary lateral load-resisting system because of their lack of relative stiffness. Their function will be to serve as a back-up system should the primary resistance system go into the inelastic range due to overload. The new bracing trusses were arranged in a manner to divide the building elements into smaller segments, thus reducing the stresses in the steel diaphragm as well as its deflection (FIG. 10). Where

the bracing trusses interconnect with the roof framing, new collector chords were installed. Diaphragm perimeter chords were reinforced and reconnected to the concrete walls where required.

It will be noted that the reinforcing concept permits a variety of bracing locations and bracing configurations to accommodate the manufacturing process lines.

Conclusions

This paper attempts to demonstrate not only the differences between possible methods of reinforcement of buildings against seismic forces, but also the variations in the desired results. The examples cited used criteria ranging from reasonable protection of life (Case Study No.1), through a total code compliance (Case Study No. 2), to optimum protection of life and property (Case Study No. 3). The methods used to accomplish these goals are bound only by the ingenuity of the engineer.

The issues in the formulation of appropriate building code provisions for the seismic reinforcement of buildings are therefore complex. A recognition and acceptance of the different levels of protection regarding life, safety, and protection of property is needed. Code provision dealing with the methods of reinforcement should be based on performance-type specification rather than explicit and overly detailed requirements. Research is needed regarding such contributions of structural and nonstructural elements to the seismic resistance of a building that may not meet the letter of current codes.

The following symbols are used:
C = dynamic characteristics factor;
I = importance factor;
K = structural system factor;
S = site-structure resonance factor;
V = total lateral load or base shear;
W = total dead load of building; and
Z = zone factor.

Notes on the Seismic Design of Concentrically Braced Steel Frames

Summary

The background to provisions for the earthquake-resistant design of Concentrically Braced Steel Frames (CBF) currently under review for inclusion in the Recommended Lateral Force Requirement of the Structural Engineers Association of California (SEAoC) is presented. The results of recent research on the inelastic cyclic behavior of steel struts and of complete CBF and KBF assemblies are reviewed insofar as these guided the development of the CBF provisions and prompted the questions raised regarding the behavior of KBFs. A discussion of some features of the inelastic cyclic behavior of K-Braced Steel Frames (KBF) which distinguish it from that of CBFs is also included.

Introduction

The hierarchy of structural systems as delineated in the table of R factors of the ATC-3-06[1] and of K factors in the 1982 UBC[2] place CBFs on a par with or slightly below reinforced concrete shear walls. Ductile Moment Resisting Frames (DMRF) are favored because of their more reliable ductility and energy-dissipating capacity. CBFs, especially those with very slender braces (e.g., tie-rods), are faulted for the relatively poor inelastic cyclic response that results from the cyclic buckling and tensile yielding of the braces under severe seismic excitation. Nevertheless, CBFs have the advantage over DMRFs of limiting story drifts at moderate levels of excitation and thereby reducing the potential for often costly "nonstructural" damage.

→ p. 69

In an attempt to combine the better parts of DMRF and CBF behavior, recent efforts have led to the development and increasing use of Eccentrically Braced Frames (EBF). Combining as they do the stiffness of braced frames with the stable hysteretic response of flexural or shear yielding beam links, these structures should in many cases supplant the use of CBFs. Nevertheless, until CBFs are proscribed in favor of EBFs, code provisions incorporating the results of recent research on the response of

Published in *Eighth World Conference on Earthquake Engineering*,
San Francisco, 1984, vol. V, pages 395–402

individual struts as well as complete CBF assemblies subjected to cyclic axial loading are in order.

In studying the inelastic behavior of CBFs, it is important to establish which parts of the system are to undergo inelastic excursions and which are to remain essentially elastic. The components of a typical CBF are: the diagonal brace; the beams and columns included within the braced bent; the collector beam(s) called on to drag loads to the braced bent; and the brace-beam and/or brace-column, beam-column and column-base connections (SEE FIG. 1).

In a strictly Concentrically Braced Frame, that is a CBF wherein at both ends of a brace the center lines of the brace, beam, and column essentially intersect, a mechanism will in most cases first form as the tension brace yields and the compression brace buckles. If the cyclic tensile yielding and buckling of the brace is to be selected as the principal locus of inelastic action in CBFs, then the remaining elements of the system should be designed to develop that mode.

This paper will first briefly review currently available information on the elastic cyclic behavior of stress struts and list those parameters that most significantly affect that behavior. A summary and discussion of the CBF code provisions follows and in closing some hypotheses are offered regarding the inelastic cyclic behavior of KBFs.

Inelastic Cyclic Behavior of Steel Struts

It has been recognized for some time that the inelastic cyclic behavior of steel struts, as represented schematically in Figure 2, is largely determined by the buckling behavior of the strut. Two important characteristics may be noted.

1. In each cycle of response there is a range of deformation characterized by low stiffness where the strut, under tensile loading, straightens out from its buckled condition.

2. With repeated cycles of loading, the buckling capacity of the brace, P_{yc}, is considerably diminished either due to prior tensile yielding or residual curvature imparted by prior buckling.

As a result the typical hysteresis curve for cyclically loaded struts has what has been termed a "pinched" look when compared to those of cantilever stubs or DMRFs. Since the capacity of a structure to dissipate seismic energy in the inelastic range is indicated by the area enclosed by these curves, it is apparent that a structure dependent on the inelastic action of a brace to supply that capacity is at a disadvantage when compared to

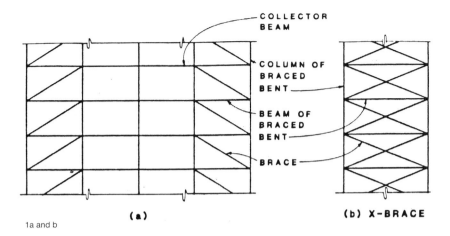

(a)   (b) X-BRACE

1a and b

DMRFs. In cases where very slender bracing (Kl/r greater than 200) is used, this problem is particularly severe, since with the ever increasing inelastic extension of the brace and little resistance from the compression brace the frame will sway freely in either direction until the tensile brace straightens and "catches," thereby imparting what is essentially an impact load on the structure.

On the basis of the results of recent research (ref. 3, 4, 5, and 6, among others), it is evident that the inelastic behavior of steel struts is determined by the following parameters:

1. Slenderness or Kl/r Ratio

As may be seen in Figure 3, the hysteresis curves for cyclically loaded struts "fill out" with increasing Kl/r.

Furthermore, where it is possible to provide restraints that reduce the K, the resulting behavior is essentially identical to a strut with an equivalent l/r (SEE FIG. 4). Where members of different sectional geometry but equal Kl/r's are used, the hysteresis curves are also essentially identical. Finally, as can be seen in Figure 5, the reduction in buckling capacity of a strut due to prior buckling increases with increasing Kl/r, though for a Kl/r greater than 90 the reduction in buckling capacity remains essentially constant (with P_{yc} after 2 cycles equal to about half the initial buckling load).

2. Sectional Geometry of Strut

If the overall buckling behavior of the struts is to be largely determined by the Kl/r ratio, lateral-torsional buckling and local buckling of outstanding

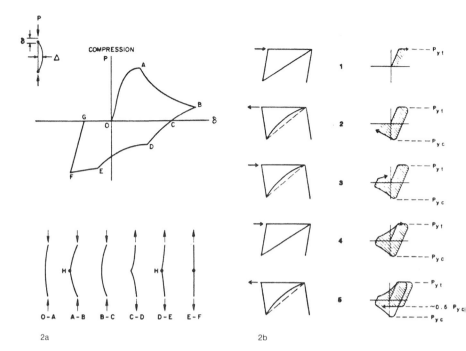

2a

2b

elements should be prevented through proper selection of the section (e.g., complying with Section 1.9 of the AISC Specifications). Where built-up members are used, the stitching should effectively restrain the parts and limit their individual Kl/r between stitches to less than the overall member's.

3. Baushinger and Residual Curvature Effects

As noted above, the buckling capacity may be considerably reduced subsequent to the initial yielding or buckling of the strut. In the case where a strut is initially yielded in tension, this is caused by the reduction in the elastic modulus due to the Baushinger effect. A similar problem exists for members (e.g., pipes and tubes) composed of materials with less distinct proportional limits. In the case where a previously buckled strut is recompressed, the reduction in buckling capacity is mostly due to a residual curvature in the member.

4. Boundary Conditions

As noted in Astaneh-Asl et al.[7], it is important that the end connections of braces be detailed to accommodate the assumed boundary conditions. Where braces are assumed pinned-pinned, sufficient flexibility in the gusset should be allowed to prevent fracture. Where a fixed condition is

2a (Ref. 4) Typical Load Deformation Relationship of a Slender Bar
2b Diagonal Brace Schematic Hysteresis

assumed, the detailing should allow for the formation of a plastic hinge. Where a plastic hinge is to form within the span of a built-up member, the stitching within that zone must be particularly secure. Finally, in cases where X-bracing is used and the braces are attached at the center to provide mutual lateral restraint, such connections should allow for the hinging that may occur.

Design of Concentrically Braced Frames

In recognition of the relatively poor ductility and energy dissipating capacity of CBFs, recent earthquake-resistant design codes have provided as follows:

1. The 1982 *UBC*[2] for a dual system prescribes a K factor of 0.80. With a typical ten-story structure, the base shear factor works out to 0.104 (CS = 0.13, I = 1.0, Z = 1.0). The code further requires that members in a braced frame be designed for 1.25 times the design shears, giving a base shear factor of 0.13. The braces will buckle at about 1.7/1.33 times this value, or a base shear of $0.166W$.

2. The ATC-3-06[1] for a similar case requires an R factor of 6. With the same structure and conditions, the ATC base shear factor C_s works out to 0.169. Combined with the required capacity reduction factor, this amounts to a base shear of $0.169/0.9 = 0.188W$ at the point of incipient brace buckling. The ATC code further requires that for Seismic Performance Categories C and D the brace be selected such that $F_a/F_t = 0.50$. With A36 steel this corresponds to a Kl/r of 115.

3. The recently revised Japanese code[8] provides for the full range of relative stiffnesses of brace and DMRF in the assignment of story shear factors. The matrix from which the Structural Characteristic Factor D_s is drawn varies with member ductility, relative share of story shear between brace and frame, and brace slenderness. Braced frames with braces having Kl/r less than 57.1 (for A36 steel) are accorded the same D_s factor as DMRFs or dual systems where the DMRF resists over 70% of the story shear.

The CBF provisions prepared for consideration by the SEAoC Seismology Committee are directly applicable only to strict CBFs as defined above. Provisions for KBFs, as yet incomplete, may differ somewhat to allow for the problems outlined in the next section of this paper. The format and content resembles the *UBC* and ATC provisions. No effort was made to alter the approach along the lines of the Japanese code, although these are in many respects better, since that would require a more extensive overhaul of the rest of the code.

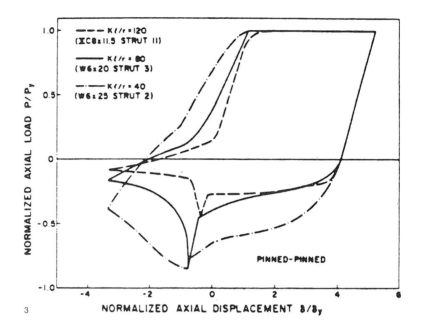

3

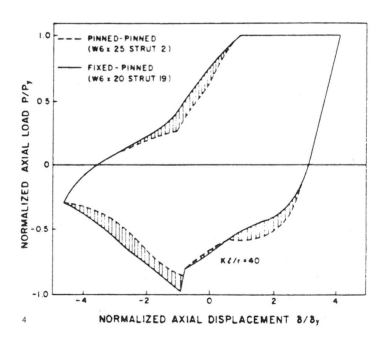

4

3 (Ref. 4) Hysteretic envelopes for struts with different slenderness ratios
4 (Ref. 4) Comparison of hysteretic envelopes for struts with different boundary conditions

The specific requirements as enumerated below are best understood by referring to Figures 1 and 6, which show two typical CBF configurations. The principal elements of the requirements are as follows:

1. Diagonal braces which act as primary lateral load resisting elements must have a Kl/r less than $540/\sqrt{F_y}$ (for A36 steel Kl/r is then 90 or less). The value of K may be taken as 1.0 or equal to 1.3 times the theoretical K. This last factor is similar to that used in the AISC Specifications Table C1.8.1. An exception is granted where the strength of the brace exceeds 2–3.75 times the design story shear (depending on the structural system and R factor used). In such cases the Kl/r is limited to $810/\sqrt{F_y}$ (135 for A36). The precise numbers are, of course, subject to review. The intent is to enhance the energy-dissipating capacity of the system while not adversely affecting the sizing of the other members which, as described below, must develop the tensile capacity of the bracing member.

2. Braces are to be provided in tension/compression pairs in any framing line and at each story (SEE FIG. 1A). This will ensure symmetrical response, by opposing the asymmetrical halves of the brace's own response.

3. The remaining members of the braced frame system must either develop the story shear capacity (usually determined by the tensile capacity of the brace) or 2–3.75 (again related to the R factor) times the design story shear. This will not only impact the column design, which must resist the overturning, but also the braced bent and collector beams. In cases such as that shown in Figure 1b, the beam must act as a strut to complete the truss once the compression brace is buckled. Similarly, in Figure 1a the collector beam must drag the full, not just half of the tributary story shear of the braced frame line. This demand on the beams could perhaps be reduced by recognizing that for Kl/r's less than 80–90 the compression capacity of the brace, after several cycles, stabilizes at about 30–50% of the initial buckling load (SEE FIG. 5) so that 50–70% of the tensile yield load applied will be balanced and the beams can be designed accordingly.

4. Provisions are also included to limit the Kl/r or parts of built-up members between stitches to ¾ of that of the whole members (referencing AISC Section 1.9 for stiffened and unstiffened compression elements) to require that connections develop the forces calculated by the provisions of paragraph three above and to set a limit on the ratio of effective net to gross area at bolted connections. Absent from the provisions are guidelines for the design of brace connections to allow for rotation, elastic or inelastic, that will occur, as discussed above. At present the knowledge available is insufficient to develop code requirements.

The effect of these provisions will, it is hoped, be to rationalize the design so that each requirement follows from and indeed obliges the designer to think in terms of the assumed collapse mechanism. Though not envisioned at this time, it may be possible to reduce somewhat the seismic design shears for which CBFs are designed (i.e., increase the R factors) in recognition of the improved ductility and energy-dissipating capacity. To do so though it may be necessary to apply stricter limits on $Kl/r,$ reducing the limiting value to about 60–80. Such a direction would be in keeping with a philosophy that regards improved post-elastic behavior as more beneficial than increased elastic strength.

K-Braced Frames

The behavior of KBFs (both in the K or "chevron" and inverted K or "V" configurations), as opposed to CBFs, has as yet received little attention. Nevertheless, if one takes into consideration the reduction in the buckling capacity of a strut after several cycles (SEE FIG. 5) and the probable collapse mechanism of KBFs (SEE FIG. 7), it is evident that:

1. The tensile capacity of the brace cannot be developed, since for a given load direction, once the compression brace has buckled and unloads, the beam, unless it is unusually strong, will form one or more plastic hinges (depending on its end restraint conditions) and so allow a collapse mechanism to form without reaching the tensile brace's capacity. The story shear capacity of the system is therefore determined by the buckling capacity of the brace and therefore the remaining members of the system need only develop that capacity.

2. Since with repeated cyclic loading the buckling capacity of the brace is reduced to 30–50% of the initial capacity, the braced frame after one or more cycles into the inelastic range will retain roughly 30–50% of its original strength. This reduction may of course be lessened if the frame containing the braces has some lateral capacity afforded by the beam-column connections.

It is unclear, given the present paucity of research information, whether the earthquake-resistant capacity of KBFs is necessarily diminished by these factors when compared to CBFs, since it is difficult to gauge the energy-dissipating capacity of the system and since under actual earthquake excitation the ductility demand may not be as severe as is imposed in cyclic loading tests of individual struts. Nonetheless it is apparent that as the system stabilizes at the lower buckling capacity, the area enclosed by the presumed hysteresis loops (SEE FIG. 7) is roughly 30–50% of what

5 (Ref. 3) Reduction in Compressive Loads
6 X-Braced Frame (strict CBF) Schematic Hysteresis
7 K-Braced Frame Schematic Hysteresis

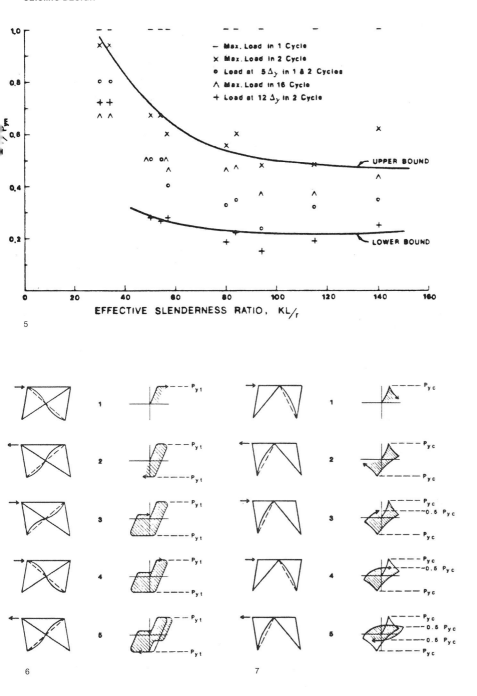

would be enclosed by the hysteresis loops of a DMRF of equivalent strength. A CBF of equivalent strength with braces having a Kl/r around 80 should exhibit hysteresis loops that enclose roughly ¾ the area enclosed by the loops of a DMRF of equivalent strength.

In order to possibly improve the performance of KBFs, several approaches are possible:

1. Stricter limits on the Kl/r ratio would result in a lesser reduction of the buckling capacity. Struts with a Kl/r less than 40 will retain 70–80% of their original buckling capacity (SEE FIG. 5).

2. KBF might be considered as a special case of Eccentrically Braced Frames (EBF) and the beam detailed as a flexural link. If braces with Kl/r's around 80 are used, the corresponding EBF would need only be designed for 50–70% of the design story shear. Some drift limitations should most likely be included when considering the EBF phase of the system.

Clearly it is as of yet not evident whether the problems presented above are necessarily severe. Before any conclusions can be drawn, and before appropriate code provisions can be developed, further study is undoubtedly called for.

Conclusion

The background to code provisions for the design of Concentrically Braced Frames as well as the essential details of those provisions have been presented. The proposed requirements, intended for inclusion in the Recommended Lateral Force Requirements of the Structural Engineers Association of California, are currently under review. Some notes regarding cyclic inelastic behavior of K-braced frames have also been offered and it is argued that the behavior of KBFs is sufficiently different from that of CBFs to possibly warrant an independent approach to their design.

Acknowledgments

Some of the results and reasoning presented herein are derived from the work of the 1981–82 SEAoNC Research Committee, of which the author was chairman. The development of the provisions has been continued as part of the efforts of the Steel Subcommittee of the SEAoNC Seismology Committee, chaired by Professor Helmut Krawinkler. The author wishes to thank the members of both committees for much useful discussion. The views expressed are entirely the author's.

1 ATC-3 (Applied Technology Council). June 1978. *Tentative Provisions for the Development of Seismic Regulations for Buildings.* Washington, D.C.: National Bureau of Standards, U.S. Dept. of Commerce.

2 International Conference of Building Officials. 1982. *Uniform Building Code.* Whittier, CA.

3 Jain, A. K. and S. C. Goel. August 1979. Cyclic End Moments and Buckling in Steel Members. *Proceedings, 2nd U.S. National Conference on Earthquake Engineering.* California: Stanford University.

4 Black, G. R., W. A. Wenger, and E. P. Popov. October 1980. Inelastic Buckling of Steel Struts Under Cyclic Load Reversals. *EERC Report 80–40.* Berkeley, CA: University of California.

5 Popov, E. P. August 1979. Inelastic Behavior of Steel Braces Under Cyclic Loading. *Proceedings, 2nd U.S. National Conference on Earthquake Engineering.* California: Stanford University.

6 Wakabayashi, M., T. Nonaka, T. Nakamura, S. Morino and N. Yoshida. 1973. Experimental Studies on the Behavior of Steel Bars Under Repeated Axial Loading. *Disaster Prevention Research Institute Annals,* No. 16B. Kyoto University, 113–125.

7 Astaneh-Asl, A., S. C. Goel, and R. D. Hanson. 1981. Behavior of Steel Diagonal Bracing. *Preprint 81-522.* St. Louis, MO: ASCE Convention, October 26–31.

8 Aoyama, Hiroyaki. 1981. Outline of Earthquake Provisions in the Recently Revised Japanese Building Code. *Bulletin of the New Zealand National Society for Earthquake Engineering,* vol. 14, No. 2, June.

Seismicity and Seismic Hazards in the New York City Area

Guy J. P. Nordenson and C. Thomas Statton

Abstract

An overview of current evaluations of seismicity and seismic hazard for New York City (NYC) is presented. Results of the ATC 3/BSSC Trial Design Program for NYC, of a recent probabilistic seismic hazard evaluation prepared for NYC, and a comparison of wind and seismic design load exceedence ratios are given and discussed in the context of current design practice and applicable codes. The implications of these results are outlined and possible directions of code development suggested.

Introduction

Concern over the hazard posed to New York City (NYC) area construction by earthquakes, at both nearby and distant sources, has deepened over the past ten years. Based on national seismicity evaluations recently proposed, national seismic codes have called for an increase in the strengths and ductility of buildings in the NYC area. A program of Trial Designs comparing the cost of seven buildings designed for current NYC wind load requirements and for the seismic loads prescribed in a proposed national seismic code was conducted in 1983–84. A probabilistic seismic hazard evaluation has been prepared for the NYC area for use by the Port Authority of NY and NJ. The probable ground shaking levels calculated in the study are in general agreement with the values included in the proposed national seismic code. A committee of NYC structural engineers and seismologists is at present evaluating the hazard posed by these levels of probable ground motion to make recommendations to the NYC Department of Buildings regarding the need for seismic requirements in the NYC Building Laws.

This paper will present (1) a brief review of past and present NYC lateral force requirements and design practices; (2) a discussion of the ATC 3/BSSC Trial Design Program for seven NYC buildings; (3) a presentation of the methodology and results of the probabilistic seismic hazard evaluation; and finally (4) a comparison of extreme wind pressure and peak horizontal site acceleration exceedence ratios and a discussion of the

Published in *Third U.S. National Conference on Earthquake Engineering*, Charleston, South Carolina, 1986, vol. I, pages 209–220 implications for the design of structures in areas of moderate seismicity. Some of the implications for NYC design practice and code development are suggested in conclusion.

NYC Building Laws and Design Practice
Wind Design
Minimum design wind pressures for buildings in NYC were set at 30 pounds per square foot (psf) (146.5 kg per sq m) in the 1906 Building Laws and later adjusted, in 1917, to 30 psf (146.5 kg per sq m) for buildings "over 150 feet (45.7 m) high or where height is over 4 times least horizontal dimension." [1] The 1963–64 NYC Buildings Laws prescribed a wind pressure of 20 psf (97.6 kg per sq m) for structures over 100 feet (30.5 m) in height. This held till the 1970 NYC Building Laws, which were revised to a stepped wind pressure curve varying from 20 psf (97.6 kg per sq m) up to 100 feet (30.5 m) to 40 psf (195.3 kg per sq m) over 1,000 feet (304.8) (FIG. 1). For buildings under 104 feet (31.7 m) in height, lateral stability was often provided by solid masonry walls varying in thickness from 20 to 12 or 8 inches (50.8 to 30.5 or 20.3 cm), depending on the building height. The current NYC building code [2] still includes "Empirical Provisions" which allow for design without structural analysis for masonry construction under 104 feet (31.7 m) in height. Many of the tall structures built in the 1920s and '30s include bracing for wind pressures acting on the broad side of the building only and are stabilized for wind pressures against their narrow face by the stone or masonry façade infill. Current NYC code design wind pressures are shown in Figure 1 alongside those calculated by the ANSI A58.1-1982 code [3]. Current NYC wind design practice for medium to high-rise building has included:

→ p. 86

– For residential construction to use a combination of reinforced concrete shear walls and flat plate/column frames as wind bracing. Buildings of up to sixty-six stories have been built this way, faced either with glass panels or unreinforced (and unanchored) masonry infill.

– For office buildings to use either conventional steel (most commonly) or reinforced concrete systems with rigid frames, braced frames, core walls, tube frames, etc. Facing materials are glass, stone veneer, precast concrete (rarely) or masonry (often panelized). Cladding attachments rarely provide resistance to in-plane shear.

Seismic Design
The NYC Building Laws do not include any seismic design provisions. A number of model and governmental agency codes do however specify

1 NYC Design Wind Pressures

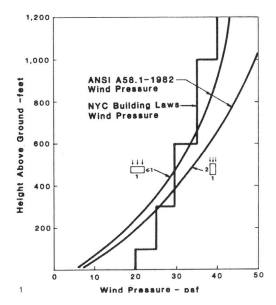

seismic design requirements for NYC. Table 1 shows the zoning factor or ground acceleration values from a number of these codes for NYC alongside those given for Boston and San Francisco.

Exempting a few anomalous values, one finds that the seismicity indicated by these codes for NYC is roughly a quarter of that of San Francisco and is equal to Boston's. The recent hazard evaluation discussed below further substantiates this apparent consensus.

ATC 3/BSSC Trial Design Program

The 1978 *Tentative Provisions for the Development of Seismic Regulations for Buildings,*[4] commonly known as ATC 3-06, is the most comprehensive code developed to date to include requirements for NYC.

In an effort to test and refine ATC 3-06, a program of trial designs was conducted by the Building Seismic Safety Council (BSSC) for the Federal Emergency Management Agency (FEMA) in 1983–84. A total of seven designs were prepared for NYC by Robertson, Fowler & Associates PC and Weidlinger Associates. Table 2 provides a list of the designs and a summary of results. The prototype designs were selected by BSSC to provide a meaningful mix of building and structural types. Some of the characteristics of the NYC prototypes did not altogether reflect actual

	Zone Factor or Ground Acceleration (% g)		
Model Code or Reference	San Francisco	Boston	NY City
BOCA 1981, Nat'l Bldg. Code 1976, Std. Bldg. Code 1976, UBC 1970 and 1973 and ANSI A58.1–1972	1	$^1/_2$	$^1/_4$
Mass. Bldg. Code, 1975	1 (implied)	$^1/_3$	–
UBC 1976, 1979 and 1982	1	$^3/_4$	$^3/_{16}$
ATC 3-06, 1978 [4]	0.40	0.10	0.10
Veterans Admin. Earthq. Resist. Design Requirements, 1978	30 % g	10 % g	7 % g (Albany)
ANSI A58.1-1982 [3]	1	$^3/_8$	$^3/_8$
AASHTO and NY State Dept. of Transportation, 1984	50 % g	50 % g	7.5 % g
Algermissen and Perkins, 1976 [5]	60 % g	11 % g	9 % g
Algermissen et al., 1982 [6]			
95-year return period	40 % g	6 % g	6 % g
475-year return period	60 % g	10 % g	17 % g
2,375-year return period	60 % g	30 % g	54 % g

TABLE 1

local practice. NYC twelve-story residential structures (NY-5) are rarely constructed of brick masonry bearing walls and RC slabs and few thirty-story steel office buildings (NY-28A) use moment frames as wind bracing (braced cores are often more economical). In some cases the cost impacts indicated could be lessened substantially if some reasonable relaxation in ductility requirements is permitted. The 20% structural cost increase shown for NY-20A, for example, is a consequence of the prescribed lateral (confining) reinforcement for beams, columns and shear wall boundary members (44% of cost increase) and of the requirement to include beams (as opposed to equivalent slab-beams) in the "backup" moment frame of this frame/wall "dual" system (48%). All things considered, though, an average cost increase of from 1% to 2% of the total construction cost of the building would most likely result from the adoption in NYC of ATC 3-06, even if amended.

Probabilistic Seismic Hazard Evaluation—NYC
A probabilistic seismic hazard evaluation has been prepared for the Port Authority of NY and NJ for use in the evaluation of its facilities. Peak

TABLE 1 Comparison of Seismic Zoning Coefficients and Ground Accelerations (in Rock)

TABLE 2 ATC/BSSC Trial Design Program – New York City

	Seismic to Wind Design Load Ratio at Building Base						
	Base Shear		Base Overturning Moment		Building Density (pcf)	Cost Increase (percent)	
Building	Transv.	Longit.	Transv.	Longit.		Structural Cost	Total Cost
NY-5 12-story brick bearing wall (R) (60' × 195') (18.3 × 59.4 m) [R = 3.5]	3.1	15.1	3.8	18.2	24.7	4.0	1.3
NY-20A 30-story RC moment frame and non-bearing shear wall (Dual) (R) (60' × 182') (18.3 × 55.5 m) [R = 8]	0.5	1.9	0.7	2.6	23.8	20	5
NY-22 20-story RC bearing wall (O) (100' × 200') (30.5 × 61 m) [R = 4.5]	1.4	3.5	1.5	3.4	13.8	3.5	1.0
NY-27A 5-story steel moment frame (O) (63' × 163') (19.2 × 49.7 m) [R = 4.5]	0.7	1.9	0.9	2.3	7.0	2.0	0.5
NY-28A 30-story steel moment frame (O) (100' × 256') (30.5 × 78.0 m) [R = 4.5]	0.3	0.7	0.3	0.8	7.1	0.5	0.1
NY-32 10-story RC moment frame (O) (100' × 150') (30.5 × 45.7 m) [R = 2]	4.4	6.4	5.2	7.6	18.5	17	4
NY-41A 2-story steel frame w/RC block walls (I) (192' × 288') (58.5 × 87.8 m) [R = 4]	11.5	11.7	8.6	14.6	5.0	2.5	1.5
Average [× R factor]	4.5 [16.8]		5.0 [18.8]		14.3	7.1	1.9
Average (w/o NY-5 and NY-41A)	2.2 [7.9]		2.5 [9.3]				

(R) Residential (O) Office (I) Industrial

TABLE 2

horizontal site accelerations and spectral ordinates corresponding to different return periods have been calculated for use in evaluating structures and facilities for different levels of risk acceptance. Input to the hazard analysis includes a seismic source zone defined primarily on the basis of seismicity, a recurrence relation calculated from the documented activity in the source zone, a probability distribution for maximum expected magnitude, and three feasible attenuation relations. Quantifiable uncertainties are incorporated in the analysis. The principal limitations derive mostly from a lack of understanding of the causes of eastern United States earthquakes. The following is a brief description of the methodology and results of this study presented in the sequence of the tasks involved: (1) define a zone or zones in which the probability of earthquake occurrence is uniform, and which describe(s) the observed and expected seismicity of the region; (2) estimate the rate, relative magnitude distribution, and maximum expected magnitude for all source zones; (3) determine appropriate attenuation relationships to describe the decay of seismic ground motion; and (4) combine the above input data to produce a probabilistic estimate of the horizontal ground accelerations to be expected at the site, and interpret the results in terms of appropriate spectral ordinates for design.

Seismic Setting

Scattered earthquakes have occurred historically throughout northern New Jersey and other regions of northeastern North America. Some of these earthquakes have been damaging. Figure 2 shows the distribution of documented earthquakes with estimated magnitude greater than three for the region surrounding the bridge site. Four of these events have an epicentral intensity of VII on the Modified Mercalli (MM) scale, though it is likely that they are of different magnitudes. The area over which the events in 1871, 1840, and possibly 1737 were felt appears to be considerably less than for the 1884 shock. Thus, these events are probably smaller than the 1884 event, which has an estimated magnitude, based on total felt area, of 4.8[7]. The recent earthquake in the Adirondack Mountains (October 7, 1983) has been suggested as an earthquake of similar size based on the comparison of felt areas for different intensity levels. This earthquake was well recorded by many seismic stations in eastern North America, and has been assigned a body wave magnitude of 5.2. Thus, the 1884 earthquake in the greater New York City area has a range of magnitude estimates from about 4.75 to 5.25.

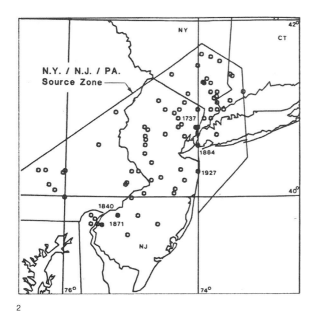

2

The question of whether the Ramapo Fault System is seismically active has been a matter of scientific debate for a number of years now. Earlier studies tended to associate the detected earthquakes with the Ramapo Fault primarily because it is the predominant geologic fault in the vicinity. Later studies concluded, on the basis of epicenter alignments and fault-plane solutions showing the mode of fault movement, that the Ramapo Fault was being currently reactivated in a reverse sense. More recent work[8] (see also for additional references) has shown that, while some earthquakes do occur along the Ramapo Fault, they are the result of slip on planes oblique to the Ramapo Fault and not on the fault itself.

Definitions of Source Zones

Sources of seismicity in the eastern United States are not yet understood. Thus, source zones defined to describe seismic activity that influences the hazard in the NYC area are not related to specific tectonic features. Rather, they are drawn to encompass a region over which the historical seismicity appears relatively uniform. It is assumed that future earthquakes will occur with equal likelihood at any site within a given source zone.

Six source zones were initially defined to characterize seismicity affecting NYC. In addition to a local zone describing seismicity in southeastern

New York, New Jersey, and western Pennsylvania, distant source zones were defined on the basis of historical seismicity for central Virginia; Charleston, South Carolina; New England; La Malbaie, Canada; and New Madrid, Missouri. These source zones were initially included to investigate whether long-period ground motions generated by large earthquakes associated with these zones could potentially affect long-period structures (tall buildings, bridges, etc.) in an adverse manner. Probabilities of strong ground motion from the more distant zones proved to show an insignificant contribution to hazard in NYC. Only the central Virginia zone and the New England zone were thus retained for final analysis of seismic hazard estimates along with the local zone.

Seismicity Parameters
Recurrence relations describing the rate and relative size distribution of earthquakes in the defined source zones are based on the documented historical seismicity. An equation is used of the form $log\ N = a - bm$ in which m is the body-wave magnitude, N is the number of events per year having magnitude m or larger, and a and b are constants to be estimated. Values for a and b are determined by finding the maximum likelihood fit to the historical data. For the local NY/NJ/PA Source the values used were $a = 2.29$; $b = 0.905$. This method assumes that the occurrence of earthquakes is a Poisson process, and that the rate at which events occur does not vary with them. Uncertainties are accommodated by specifying several options for a and b, and assigning them probabilities based on professional judgment.

Maximum Magnitude
To carry out the seismic hazard analysis, it is necessary to know the largest earthquake that is expected to occur within a given source zone. Estimates of this parameter are based largely on subjective judgment and intuition, and hence are subject to large uncertainties. In most cases it is reasonable to assume, though, that the maximum magnitude event is at least as large as the largest event that has already occurred and it may be appropriate to use the largest event that has occurred in tectonic environments that are thought to be similar to the one being considered. The event with a characteristic return period, say 1,000 years, determined from the recurrence relation for the source zone is another possible method of estimating maximum magnitude. For the source zones used in this study it is felt that there is a small probability that a magnitude 6.75 event can

TABLE 3 Peak Horizontal Site Accelerations (90 % confidence upper limit)

Return Period (years)	Prob. of Exceedence in 50 years (%)	Peak Horizontal Site Accel. (% g)	Exceedence Ratio*
15	96	0.01	0.33
35	76	0.02	0.65
104	38	0.04	1.3
344	14	0.08	2.6
516	9.2	0.10	3.3
720	6.7	0.12	3.9
1,092	4.5	0.15	4.9
1,876	2.6	0.20	6.5
2,857	1.7	0.25	8.1
4,028	1.2	0.30	9.8
6,872	0.7	0.40	13.0
10,275	0.5	0.50	16.3

* Acceleration/Acceleration for 72-year average return period

TABLE 3

occur in the local source zone, so a maximum magnitude of about 5.76 has been used.

Attenuation
Three attenuation relationships, which were derived in the eastern United States, were used in the evaluation. These are by Herrman and Nuttli, 1984,[9] Veneziano, 1985,[10] and Toro, 1985.[11] Weighing factors of $\frac{1}{2}, \frac{1}{4}$, and $\frac{1}{4}$ were used for these respectively.

Peak Horizontal Site Accelerations and Spectral Ordinates
Peak horizontal site acceleration (using the upper bound of the 10% confidence limit) calculated using these relationships are as given in Table 3.

The peak acceleration value for a 475-year return period has been calculated as 9.5% g. This is comparable to the 10% g effective peak acceleration value used for NYC in ATC 3-06 for the same return period. From preliminary results for spectral ordinates it appears that the ATC 3-06 response spectrum shape is appropriate in the low period range but somewhat conservative for long-period structures.

Limitations

The results of the seismic hazard analysis are limited by the assumptions and data used in the computations. For instance, in defining a seismic source zone, it was assumed that earthquakes of significant size in terms of seismic hazard will occur with equal likelihood at any site within the zone. If such events were assumed to occur preferentially near or along the Ramapo Fault System, the hazard results would be different. Such an assumption, however, is not deemed appropriate on the basis of available information. Similarly, if a better understanding is obtained in the future of the tectonic processes causing earthquakes in the eastern United States, it may be necessary to revise the estimates of hazard derived here. Limitations in the model of earthquake occurrence can also affect the hazard results. While there is a considerable amount of uncertainty in estimating some of the values used as input to the seismic hazard analysis, these uncertainties are accommodated by the method to the degree that they can be quantified. Thus, maximum magnitude and attenuation uncertainties are incorporated into the "best estimate" presented.

Wind Design and Earthquake Resistance

It is sometimes argued by structural designers in areas of moderate seismicity that for most structures, particularly tall ones, the lateral resistance provided by the necessary wind bracing is adequate for the low levels of ground motion that are expected in the region. It is noteworthy that following the 1906 San Francisco earthquake, an ASCE committee stated that "sufficient evidence is at hand to warrant the statement that a building designed with a proper system of bracing to withstand wind at a pressure of 30 psf (146.5 kg per sq m) will resist safely the stresses caused by a shock of an intensity equal to that of the recent earthquake in California" (quoted in Freeman[12], p. 804). This judgment was founded on the evidence that well-designed structures of up to sixteen stories (New Chronicle Building) and even 315 feet (96 m) in height (Claus Spreckels Building) of steel frame and masonry construction suffered little damage (examples of over thirty such buildings are given in Freeman[12]). A similar sentiment was expressed by NY engineers following the October 19, 1985, Ardsley, NY earthquake (M = 4.0). As quoted in the *New York Times* on October 20, one engineer noted "the structures here are more than adequate to absorb that kind of tremor ... Designing for winds is a much more critical factor."

The question of whether or not presently specified wind resistance provides adequate assurance of structural safety against expected levels of earthquake ground motion is critical. The following discussion is a brief sketch of some possible approaches to answering this question.

Reserve Capacity of Structures

In a 1975 study[13] to assess seismic code requirements for Boston, Whitman et al. tentatively concluded "that normal concrete buildings [possessing a "nominal amount of ductility"] located on firm ground (and probably on soft ground) in Boston do not need to be designed for seismic resistance." The study concluded, however, that in light of the uncertainties in ground motion and in ductility predictions, "Boston should not totally ignore the danger of earthquakes." A study by Housner and Jennings[14] of the performance during the $M = 6.4$ San Fernando earthquake (February 9, 1971) of fourteen multistory reinforced concrete frame buildings found that they were able to sustain 1.2 to 2.1 times the design base shear with no visible damage and from 3.2 to 5.3 times the design base shear with some moderate structural damage. In examining four buildings subjected to blast-induced ground motion at the Nevada Test Site (1) and to the 1971 San Fernando (2) and the 1978 Santa Barbara (1) earthquakes, Mathiessen and Joyner[15] found that initial yielding of the frame occured "at multiples of 2 to 5 times the code values and the ultimate capacities range[d] from 6 to 15 times the design code earthquake." On the average, these studies indicate that well-designed, regular structures could withstand up to double the design base shear with only minor structural damage and up to 3 to 5 times the design base shear with structural damage but not collapse. This is consistent with the assumption by Whitman et al.[22] that typical reinforced concrete buildings possess at least a nominal ductility.

Based on the sample of buildings included in the ATC 3/BSSC Trial Design Program (TABLE 2) and excluding NY-5 and NY-41A, we find that on the average the seismic/wind load ratio is 2 to 3 with the structural system "ductility" factor R included and 8 to 9 without (i.e., were elastic response to the code seismic loading required). This admittedly limited sample does suggest that even with the apparently inherent "reserve" capacity on the order of 3 to 5 suggested by Mathiessen and Joyner[15], the seismic demands would exceed the "ultimate" capacities by a factor of 1.6 to 3. It should be noted that the structures studied in Housner,[14] and Mathiessen[15] had been designed following the *Uniform Building Code* (*UBC*) and that despite the apparent absence of inelastic response or damage, the "toughness" noted must in part have resulted from the detailing requirements followed. Continuous load paths, provisions of diaphragm reinforcement and overall interconnectedness, beam-column joint reinforcement, and above all shear and confining reinforcement as required by the *UBC* are not always present in eastern U.S. construction. Assuming therefore a reduced "reserve" capacity on the order of 2 to 3 times the design base shears (e.g., by ATC 3-06), it is possible that the "ultimate" capacity (as defined in Mathiessen and Joyner[15] as structural damage without collapse) of NYC structures conventionally designed may be exceeded by factors of roughly 2.7 to 4.5. Even limited mitigating measures in areas of design at present neglected (e.g., tying the building together, strengthening diaphragms, limiting drift) could substantially reduce this margin.

Exceedence Ratios for Design Wind Pressures and Seismic Base Shears

The prediction of extreme wind velocities for different return periods is rather difficult in NYC because of the possibility of hurricanes. Simiu et al.[16] using observations over 31 years (1947–1977) at LaGuardia Airport, have derived a probability distribution of the largest values of wind speeds at 10 m. Those values have been plotted as wind pressures in Figure 3. Values given by Ellingwood et al. for maximum wind loads in Baltimore, Maryland, (New York values are not given) are also plotted. These values include allowances for the variability of gust and shape factors and were based on the extreme wind speed data base of Simiu et al.[16] The plots show exceedence ratios calculated by dividing the value for a given average return period by that for a 72-year average return period. This return period (which corresponds to a 50% probability of exceedence [P_E] in 50 years) is often used in seismic design to establish shaking levels for which a structure is designed to remain elastic. It provides a basis for comparison with wind pressures used for allowable stress design. An estimate of the maximum credible hurricane pressures for NYC is shown as well. This was calculated based on a method proposed by Simiu and Scanlan[18], pp. 90–96, yielding average return periods of from 7,700 to 9,700 years for winds exceeding 155 miles (249.5 km) per hour. Finally the wind design load values prescribed in the ANSI A58.1[3] and NYC Building Laws[5] for NYC are shown for elevation 350 feet (106.7 m) (which is roughly comparable to values at 30 feet (9.1 m) in open terrain) normalized by the 12.9 psf (63.0 kg per sq m) pressure calculated for the 72-year return period from Simiu et al.[16] The exceedence ratios for the peak accelerations estimated by probabilistic seismic hazard evaluation discussed above are plotted in Figure 3 alongside those for the wind pressure values. Also indicated are normalized effective peak

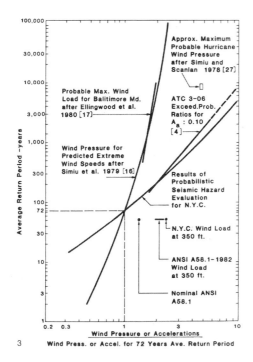

3

Wind Press. or Accel. for 72 Years Ave. Return Period

acceleration values given in ATC 3-06 for NYC for different return periods (after Figure C1-7 of Quittmeyer et al.)[4]

It can be seen from Figure 3 that with increasing return periods (corresponding to decreasing P_E in a given time span), predicted wind pressures increase more slowly than peak accelerations. The exceedence ratios for a 475-year return period (P_E of 10% in 50 years—the basis used in ATC 3-06) are 1:1.3 for wind pressures and 1:3.1 for peak accelerations. For a 1,000-year return period (P_E of 5% in 50 years) the ratios are 1:1.5 and 1:4.7 and for 10,000 years 1:1.9 and 1:16 for wind pressures and peak accelerations. For the extreme (and improbable) 155 mph hurricane, the wind pressure exceedence ratio would be 1:4.8.

This would indicate a fundamental difference in the exceedence trends of extreme winds and earthquake occurrences and support the need in seismic design to ensure that structures possess adequate energy-dissipating capabilities. It is interesting to note that the wind pressures do not appear to exceed the design value by more than double, which is within the "reserve" capacity margin noted above. A comparison, in Figure 4, between

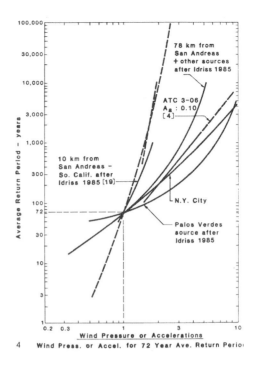

4　Wind Press. or Accel. for 72 Year Ave. Return Period

exceedence ratio curves for NYC and some Southern California sources taken from Hermann and Nuttli [19] also shows an interesting trend among various faults and sites. Evidently the increase in exceedence ratios tends to be greater at smaller faults or at greater distance from large ones.

Conclusions

A probabilistic seismic hazard evaluation has been prepared for the NYC area and generally confirms the seismicity assessment used in the ATC 3-06 *Tentative Provisions* [4]. A Trial Design Program comparing designs for wind loads (by the NYC Building Laws) and seismic design base shears (by ATC 3-06) indicates a probable average increase of 1–2% in total construction cost for the seismic designs with a range of 0.1 to 5%. A comparison of wind pressure and seismic peak acceleration exceedence ratios demonstrates that a structure designed to respond elastically in extreme wind or in earthquake shaking with equal average return periods (or equal probabilities of non-exceedence in a given time span) is more likely to be damaged or to collapse in a seismic event with greater return period than in a corresponding wind storm, unless provisions are made to ensure adequate energy-dissipating capacity. The seismic demands may exceed the elastic limit by factors of 4 to 6. The nominal ductility or reserve capacity of structures that has been noted by some investigators [13, 14, 15] is not sufficient to provide this capacity, though it may account for the adequacy of current wind design practice. Given that evacuation is possible in anticipation of hurricanes and not for earthquakes, the levels of acceptable risk used to determine design loads for each would not be the same. Uncertainties in ductility predictions and sensitivity of earthquake resistance to configuration, symmetry, irregularities, etc., would also suggest greater caution.

An effort is under way in NYC to evaluate the need for and/or nature of seismic design code provisions for the city. A number of questions and issues have come up in these deliberations which suggest the range of possible future work and research:

— Is there a characteristic earthquake for the NYC area or the East Coast which might affect hazards evaluation?

— Can a "comprehensive risk" approach to wind and seismic design be developed?

— What is the proper body to develop and update seismic design requirements for regions of moderate seismic risk such as NYC?

— Are the differences in seismic risk (e.g., return periods, exceedence ratios, etc.) between the western and eastern U.S. such as to suggest different types of ductility requirements? And if so, how are these to be qualified?

— Is it necessary in zones of moderate seismicity such as NYC to provide for the level of strengthening and attachment of nonstructural elements (façade, etc.) that is prescribed for in California?

— What should be done to strengthen existing structures? Could the level of acceptable risk be greater for such structures?

Acknowledgments

The writers are grateful to Drs. I. M. Idriss and R. C. Quittmeyer, who co-authored the seismic hazard analysis discussed herein with the second author; to the Port Authority of NY and NJ for supporting the seismic hazards evaluation; to Mr. L. E. Robertson for supplying information on his firm's ATC 3/BSSC Trial Designs; and to the members of the NYACE Ad Hoc Seismology Liaison Committee for valuable discussions. The writers are very appreciative of the diligence and care with which Ms. Mindy Hepner typed the many drafts and to Mr. Charlos Zor, who drafted the figures.

1 Ketchum, M. S. 1924. *Structural Engineer's Handbook*. New York: McGraw-Hill.

2 New York Society of Architects. 1985. *1985 Manual New York Building Laws*.

3 American National Standards Institute (ANSI). 1982. ANSI *Standard Building Code Requirements for Minimum Design Loads in Buildings and Other Structures. A58.1*. New York.

4 Applied Technology Council. 1978. *Tentative Provisions for the Development of Seismic Regulations for Buildings*. ATC 3-06, NBS SP 510, NSF pub. 78-8. 1978.

5 Algermissen, S. T. and D. M. Perkins. 1976. *Prob. Est. of Max. Accel. in Rock in the Contig. U.S.* U.S. Geo. Surv., Open-File Report 76-416.

6 Algermissen, S. T., D. M. Perkins, P. C. Thenhaus, S. L. Hanson and B. L. Bender. 1982. *Prob. Est. of Max. Accel. and Vel. in Rock in the Contig. U.S.* U.S. Geo. Surv. O/F Rep. 82-1033.

7 Street, R. and A. Lacroix. 1979. An Empirical Study of New England Seismicity: 1727–1977. *Bulletin of the Seismological Society of America* vol. 69, 159–175.

8 Quittmeyer, R. C., C. T. Statton, K. A. Mrotek, and M. Houlday. 1985. Possible Implications of Recent Microearthquakes in S.E. N.Y. State. *Earthquake Notes* vol. 56, no. 2, 35–42.

9 Hermann, R. and O. Nuttli. 1984. Scaling and Attenuation Relation for Strong Ground Motion in Eastern North America. *8th World Conf. on Earthquake Engineering* vol. 11, 305.

10 Veneziano, D. 1985. Statistical Estimation of Ground Motion Using MM Intensities. *Draft Report: Seismic Hazard Methodology for Nuclear Facilities in the Eastern United States*, EPRI/SOG-Draft 85-1 (April 30), vol. 3, pp. B36–B76.

11 Toro, G. 1985. Stochastic Model Estimates of Strong Ground Motion. *Draft Rep: Seis. Haz. Method. for Nuc. Fac. in the East. U.S.*, EPRI/SOG-Dft. 85-1 (April 30), vol. 3, pp. B77–B116.

12 Freeman, J. F. 1932. *Earthquake Damage and Earthquake Insurance*. New York: McGraw-Hill.

13 Whitman, R. V., J. M. Biggs, J. E. Brennan, C. A. Cornell, R. L. de Neufville and E. H. Vanmarcke. 1975. Seismic Design Decision Analysis. *Jrnl. of the Struct. Div.*, Proc. ASCE, vol. 101, no. ST5, 1067–84.

14 Housner, G. W. and P. C. Jennings. 1982. *Earthquake Design Criteria*. EERI Monograph.

15 Mathiessen, R. B., and W. B. Joyner. 1982. *An Investigation of the Correlation Between Earthquake Ground Motion and Building Performance*. ATC-10. November.

16 Simiu, E., M. J. Changery and J. J. Filiben. 1979. *Extreme Wind Speeds at 129 Stations in the Contiguous United States*. NBS BS 118.

17 Ellingwood, B., T. V. Galambos, J. G. MacGregor, and C. A. Cornell. 1980. *Development of Probability Based Load Criterion for American National Standard A58*. NBS SP 577.

18 Simiu, E. and R. H. Scanlan. 1978. *Wind Effects on Structures*. New York: John Wiley & Sons.

19 Idriss, I. M. 1985. Evaluating Seismic Risk in Engineering Practice. *Proc. 11th International Conference on Soil Mechanics and Foundation Engineering*. San Francisco, 255–320.

Wind Versus Seismic Design*

→ p. 101

Introduction

While there is a growing recognition of the potential for damaging earthquakes in the eastern United States, the general opinion among building designers and the public is that modem structures designed according to the code-specified wind loads should prove safe in the moderate-level earthquakes that are considered possible. In New York City (NYC) the code requires that buildings over 20 stories be designed for wind pressures of up to 30 and even 40 pounds per square foot (psf) (146.5 and 195.3 kg per sq m). A typical 30-story apartment building would then be designed for a total lateral wind load equivalent to between 1.5 and 2 percent of its weight. This is, in fact, comparable to the design loads specified in current seismic design codes [1, 2] for such a building in NYC. Given the infrequency of even moderate earthquakes in the NYC area (only one with a Richter magnitude slightly over 5 is known to have occurred to date), there would appear to be little cause for concern.

If one examines more closely the assumptions underlying the loads specified in the building codes for wind- and earthquake-resistant design in relation to the actual response of buildings to earthquakes, the comparison is in fact less simply made. Further, it has become clear from recent seismological research that earthquakes of at least one magnitude greater than the historical record indicates must be considered possible. In this paper an attempt is made to clarify the difference between wind and seismic design assumptions and results through a review of recent research work and several simple parametric studies. Implications regarding the seismic hazards and risk in NYC are discussed in the conclusions.

The Action of Winds and Earthquakes on Buildings

The overall effects of winds and earthquakes on building are well understood and incorporated in building codes and design practice. The major uncertainties arise when an effort is made to predict the specific character and frequency of extreme and potentially damaging hurricanes or

Part VI. "Seismic Design of Buildings and Special Structures, and Nonstructural Components
in Moderate Seismic Zones," published in: *Earthquake Hazards and the Design of Constructed Facilities
in the Eastern United States,* New York Academy of Sciences, pages 262–74

earthquakes. There is, as well, a fundamental difficulty inherent in any structural analysis in precisely characterizing the properties and interaction of the "structural" and "nonstructural" materials and elements that make up a building to arrive at a complete representation of its behavior. How is one to give an exact account of the variation in stiffness with increasing load of an unreinforced brick masonry wall built as infill to a riveted steel frame, up to and past the "elastic" limit? How can one model the elastoplastic, interactive behavior of concrete-encased steel girders?

The physical effects of strong winds and earthquakes differ in a number of essential ways:

1. The wind velocity at a given location during a storm includes both a mean component that increases gradually over the course of hours and a gust component that fluctuates about that mean in periods of seconds or less. The gust component is usually less than 40 percent of the magnitude of the mean wind pressure value. In contrast, earthquakes last from 10 to 90 seconds with complete reversals of ground motion occurring in periods from one 10th of a second to 2–3 seconds.

2. For all but tall slender structures, wind effects are essentially static loadings, whereas in earthquakes the accelerations reverse rapidly and induce significant inertial effects. Wind loads are proportional to the building shape and exposed area, earthquake loads to the building mass and stiffness.

3. Extreme winds (e.g., hurricanes) generally give some warning, while earthquakes give none that is dependable.

4. The wind loads specified in building codes are tied to the "50-year wind velocities," that is, those estimated from the historical record to have less than a 2 percent annual probability of being exceeded (annual probability of exceedence [APE]). Important structures may be designed for the "100-year wind" or 1 percent APE. The design loads in current seismic design codes are derived from ground motions with a 10 percent probability of exceedence in 50 years (i.e., a 475-year return period of 0.2 percent APE).

5. As tragically demonstrated in the 1985 Mexico City earthquake, the type of soil underlying a building can have a profound and determining effect on the structure's response in both amplifying the signal and shifting the input frequency content to that resonant with the structure's natural frequency. The wind's effect is unaffected by soil conditions.

6. Structures are typically designed to remain elastic in extreme winds, whereas in an earthquake they are expected to locally deform well into the material plastic range in order to dissipate in work the seismic energy

input. Wind design is largely concerned with achieving sufficient stiffness and damping to keep horizontal vibrations below perceptible levels.

The Worst Case

The probable hurricane wind speeds measured at 30 feet (9.1 m) above ground have been estimated for various mean recurrence intervals by the Building Seismic Safety Council (BSSC)[3]. For 50-, 100-, and 2,000-year intervals (2.0, 1.0, and 0.05 percent APE), the estimates of fastest wind speed are 86, 97, and 134 miles per hour (mph) (138.4, 156.1, and 215.7 kilometers per hour). The wind loads specified for use in the NYC area in current codes[4] are based on the "50-year" wind speed of 90 mph (144.8 kph). In a hurricane with wind velocities as high as 134 mph (215.7 kph), the surface pressures on a building could exceed the code design basis by 122 percent (pressure varies with the square of the velocity). Since structural elements are typically designed to allowable stress levels of 80 percent of the tensile yield stress when considering wind effects, they would at most be overstressed by slightly over 75 percent. Furthermore, since wind bracing is often sized to meet lateral stiffness requirements (and is therefore at lower than allowable stress levels under design loads), it is likely that only a few elements would in fact yield in even the worst hurricane.

In the case of earthquake effects, the analogous ratio of design loading to the maximum conceivable in the extreme instance can be far greater. In the Los Angeles area, the largest "credible" earthquake (of magnitude 8.0) for the South San Andreas Fault might generate peak ground accelerations (PGA) at a site 6 miles (10 kilometers) from the fault of 70 percent of gravity (g).[5]

The average return period for such an earthquake is believed to be less than 1,000 years. For a 500-year return period, the PGA is estimated to be approximately 64 percent g. For a site in Santa Monica, California, further from the San Andreas Fault, the corresponding PGA for 1,000- and 500-year average return periods are estimated at 52 and 42 percent g respectively.[5]

The lateral loads in the current Los Angeles seismic code[i] are derived from ground motions with an effective peak acceleration of 0.40 g. In the worst conceivable event, at a site close to the San Andreas Fault, this design basis PGA may be exceeded by up to a factor of 1.75. The increased demand on the structure's energy-dissipating capacity will undoubtedly cause extensive damage to some structures. For a good number of the structures designed to the current code, this increased demand may well be accommodated without collapse.

A similar comparison of the proposed code[1] design basis PGA to the maximum credible values for NYC illustrates the essential difference in the nature of seismic hazards in zones of high and moderate seismicity. Our knowledge of the seismic hazard in the East is not as good as for the western United States because of the relative infrequency of damaging events and the comparatively small extent of our history. The historical record for the East dates back to the 1638 St. Lawrence River, Canada earthquake. There have been sizable earthquakes with Richter magnitudes estimated at or in excess of 7.0 in 1755 (Cape Ann near Boston, Massachusetts), 1812 and 1813 (New Madrid, Missouri), and 1886 (Charleston, North Carolina). In 1884 an earthquake with an estimated Richter magnitude of 5.0 to 5.5 occurred off-shore near Coney Island, New York, causing a few large cracks in masonry walls in Jamaica, Queens. There have been numerous small earthquakes as well. A recent probabilistic hazards evaluation undertaken for the NYC area[6], based on available historical and geological data, projects a PGA value around 7 percent g for an average return period of 400 to 500 years. This corresponds roughly to an event with a Richter magnitude near 5.2. A clarification issued by the U.S. Geological Survey in response to a query from the Nuclear Regulatory Commission has suggested that the risk may in fact be even greater:

"Because the geologic and tectonic features of the Charleston region are similar to those in other regions of the eastern seaboard, we conclude that although there is no recent or historical evidence that other regions have experienced strong earthquakes, the historical record is not of itself sufficient ground for ruling out the occurrence in these other regions of strong seismic ground motions similar to those experienced near Charleston in 1886. Although the probability of strong ground motion due to an earthquake in any given year at a particular location in the eastern seaboard may be very low, deterministic and probabilistic evaluations of the seismic hazard should be made for individual sites in the eastern seaboard to establish the seismic engineering parameters for critical facilities."[7]

It may therefore be necessary to consider that earthquakes of up to Richter magnitude 6.5 or 7 could occur in NYC, though with very low probabilities (on the order of 0.01 percent APE or a 1 percent probability of being exceeded in 100 years), when evaluating construction standards along the eastern seaboard. The peak accelerations generated by earthquakes of this magnitude would be on the order of 0.40 to 0.50 g or up to seven times the design basis acceleration of 0.07 g. Thus, while the worst New York City hurricane or the worst Los Angeles earthquake may exceed the design basis values by up to a factor of 1.75, the worst conceivable NYC earthquake could exceed the design basis proposed (though not at present applied) by a factor of about 7.

It is important in considering this comparison to recall the difference in the design philosophies applied to seismic and wind design. The aim of wind design is to achieve occupant comfort in common windstorms and an essentially elastic structural response in extreme winds. In the words of the Structural Engineers Association of California, the aims of the building code's seismic provisions are:

1. To resist minor levels of earthquake ground motion without damage;
2. To resist moderate levels of earthquake ground motion without structural damage, but possibly experience some nonstructural damage;
3. To resist major levels of earthquake ground motion having an intensity equal to the strongest either experienced or forecast for the building site, without collapse, but possibly with some structural as well as nonstructural damage.[8]

The ability of a structure to withstand without collapse a major earthquake depends on the "ductility" or energy-dissipating capacity that is provided to the lateral-load-resisting system through detailing. Earthquake-resistant structures are designed using typical elastic analysis methods with allowable material stresses around 80 percent of tensile yield and lateral loads one-tenth to one-fifth the expected loads to recognize the structure's ductility. This ductility, or, more accurately, toughness, is simply the capacity of the system to dissipate energy through many large displacement cycles of plastic rotation, shearing, or extension in the members. Moment frames yield at beam ends, braced frames "yield" through inelastic extension and buckling of the braces, shear walls in chord flexure or web shear, and coupled shear walls or eccentric braced frames in specially designed "fuses." To ensure that the predicted mechanism is obtained, the members away from the yielding element and all the connections are sized and detailed to remain essentially elastic up to the stage where a side-sway mechanism is formed. Throughout, as individual elements yield and distort with each cycle, energy is effectively dissipated. Tests on large-scale subassemblies of these structures have demonstrated that overall ductilities (i.e., maximum lateral displacement divided by that at yield) of up to 4–6 can be achieved and repeated through several cycles. The difference between these values and the larger ratios used in the code is the subject of some controversy, particularly since the 1985 Mexico City earthquake.[9]

A structure designed in NYC by conventional code-specified seismic design methods would be sized for lateral loads of roughly one-fifth those expected in an earthquake of a magnitude equal to the largest yet experienced. In the extreme case of a magnitude 6.5 event, the structure would be subjected to inertial loads in excess of 30 times those for which it had been designed, well beyond the effective capacity of the structure to dissipate energy. It should be clear from this that the nature of "moderate" seismicity suggests an even greater need for structural "ductility" or energy-dissipating capacity than is the case in the areas of high seismicity.

Parametric Studies

Direct comparisons of wind and seismic demands on building structures are complicated by the essential difference in their action. Whereas wind pressures act on the exposed surface area of a building, the effect of earthquake-strong ground motions is to accelerate the masses of the structure in increasing proportion to their height above ground. For example, buildings with long, narrow plan dimensions, as are common in NYC, are designed for relatively small wind loads parallel to the long side. In many cases there is no direct lateral-load-resisting system provided other than the façade construction. Since the earthquake effects are essentially independent of plan configuration, such buildings would be potentially vulnerable in an earthquake.

As a means of scaling in general terms the relative magnitude and parameter sensitivity of the wind and seismic demands on structures in NYC, a simple equation has been developed for the unit seismic base shear as a function of the building geometry and density. The unit base shear is the total horizontal load acting on the structure divided by the cross-width of the building. The relationship has been derived on the basis of the approximate equations contained in the 1988 *Uniform Building Code* (1988 *UBC*) for the building period and the proposed seismic zone factor of 0.15.[1] Referring to Figure 1, consider a simple building of height H and base dimensions B (width) and αB (depth). The wind or seismic effects are considered to act perpendicular to the width B. A height-to-width ratio β for the structure is defined as

$$\beta = \frac{H}{\alpha B}$$

1 Building diagram and variables used for unit base shear calculations

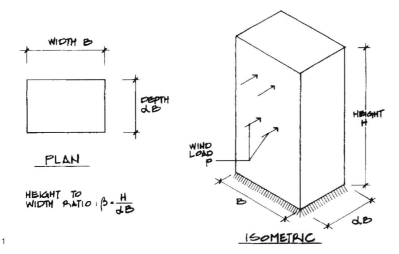

PLAN

ISOMETRIC

The building weight can be calculated as

$$W = \varrho(\alpha B^2 H)$$

where ϱ is the average *density* of the building. The building weight per unit width is then given by

$$\frac{W}{B} = \varrho \frac{H^2}{\beta}$$

The 1988 *UBC* equation for the seismic base shear is

$$V = \frac{ZIC}{R_w} W$$

where R_w is the reduction factor relating to the structure's energy-dissipating capacity and, for NYC, Z = seismic zone factor = 0.15 (Zone 2A); I = importance factor = 1.0; C = response factor = $\dfrac{1.25S}{T^{2/3}}$; and S = soils factor = 1.0.

The structural period T is calculated using the approximate formula

$$T = C_t H^{3/4}$$

where C_t is an empirical factor depending on the type of structure and varying between 0.020 and 0.035.

From these the unit seismic base shear for NYC can be expressed as

$$V_s = 0.1875 \frac{\varrho H^{1.5}}{C_t{}^{2/3}\beta}$$

The equivalent expression for the unit base wind shear is

$$V_w = p(Z)H$$

allowing for the variation of pressure p with height z.

The variation in unit base shear is plotted (semi-log) in Figures 2 through 4 for building height-to-width ratios β of 1, 2, 3, 5, and 8. The curves are cut off at heights considered excessive for a given β ratio. The curve of unit wind shears is shown, as are bars indicating prototype buildings reviewed in a trial design program conducted to assess the proposed ATC-3 *Tentative Provisions for the Development of Seismic Regulations for Buildings*.[10, 11] The average densities for the trial design buildings are shown in brackets below the bars. As noted on the figures, values are shown for unit base shears with and without the code reduction factors that account for the structure's energy-dissipating capacity. The solid circle and triangle represent the demand on the structure, across both its axes, were it to remain elastic. Among the structures considered are:

– 5-, 30-, and 38-story steel moment frames with an average density of 8.5 pounds per cubic foot (pcf) (136.2 kg per cubic meter);

– 10-, 17-, and 20-story reinforced concrete (RC) shear wall and frame structures with an average density of 16.5 pcf (264.3 kg per cubic meter); and

– a 12-story brick masonry bearing wall structure and a 30-story RC moment frame and shear wall structures with an average density of 24 pcf (384.4 kg per cubic meter).

The plots have been grouped into densities of 5, 15, and 25 pcf (80.1, 240.3, and 400.5 kg per cubic meter) as representative of the range of NYC construction.

It is clear from the figures that the elastic seismic demand (for $R_w = 1.0$) on buildings calculated by the 1988 *UBC* will in all cases exceed the design unit wind base shears.

The Influence of the Earthquake Frequency Content
Studies of the shape of response spectra characteristic of earthquakes of various magnitudes have demonstrated that at periods greater than one second there is a substantial decrease in spectral accelerations with

2 1988 *UBC* seismic versus NYC wind unit base shears 5 pcf (80 kg per cubic meter)

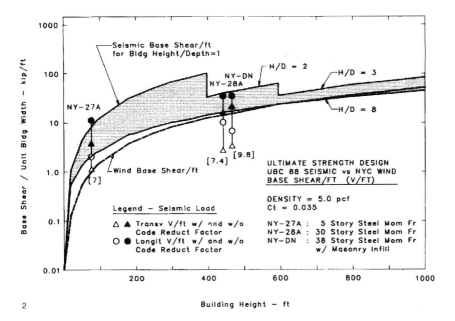

decreasing magnitude.[5, 12] Figure 5, developed from Joyner and Boore,[12] illustrates the trend. A comparison of response spectra applicable to NYC from various sources with one derived specifically for the city (from Statton et al.,[6] and shown as NYC and NYC-mod in Figure 6, representing alternative proposals) reflects the implications of this trend. The normalized versions of these spectra shown in Figure 7 further demonstrate the basic difference. In Figures 8 and 9, the curves for unit seismic base shears have been modified to reflect the influence of these proposed NYC-specific spectra on the wind/seismic comparison. Figure 10 further reduces, for the very light buildings of a 5 pcf (80.1 kg per cubic meter) density, the seismic unit base shear by allowing for a ductility factor of 2. It is apparent that the shape of the response spectrum will have a substantial impact on the demand on structures over 200 feet in height.

Conclusions

Structures designed to modern seismic codes are provided with sufficient strength and stiffness to withstand frequent earthquakes with minor damage and sufficient toughness and energy-dissipating capacity to survive major events without life-threatening damage or collapse. Careful design and detailing of the structure's connections are essential to ensure their

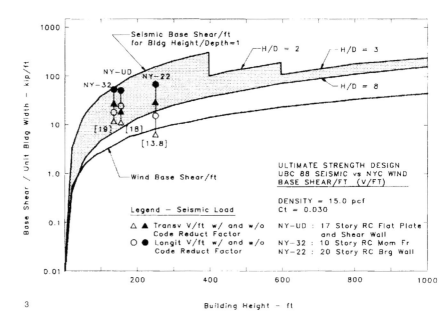

3

Building Height – ft

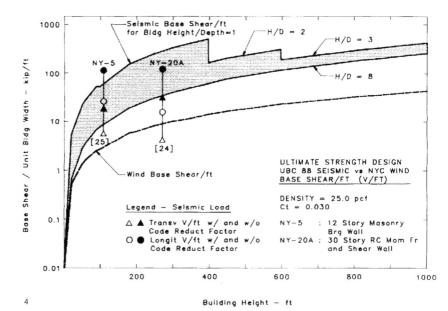

4

Building Height – ft

3 1988 *UBC* seismic versus NYC wind unit base shears 15 pcf (240.3 kg per cubic meter)
4 1988 *UBC* seismic versus NYC wind unit base shears 25 pcf (400.5 kg per cubic meter)
5 Spectral ordinate ratios normalized to Magnitude 5 (from Joyner and Boore)[12]
6 Proposed linear elastic response spectra for NYC

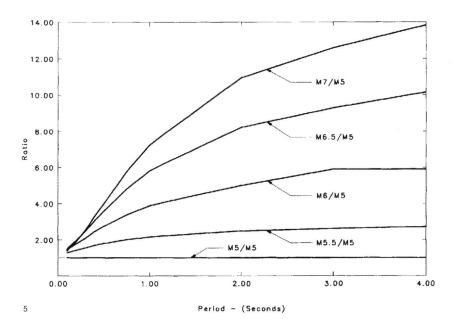

5   Period − (Seconds)

NEW YORK CITY − ROCK SITE − 5% DAMPING

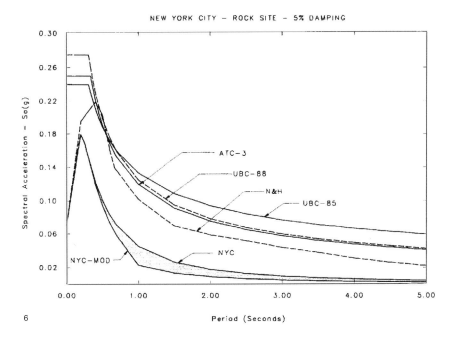

6   Period (Seconds)

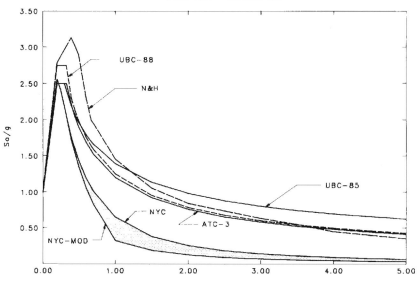

7

Period (Seconds)

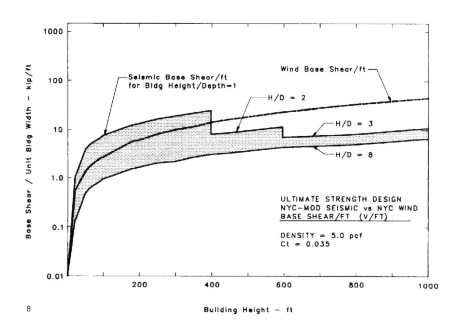

8

Building Height — ft

7 Normalized response spectra for NYC
8 NYC-mod seismic versus NYC wind unit base shears 5 pcf (80 kg per cubic meter)
9 NYC-mod seismic versus NYC wind unit base shears 15 pcf (240.3 kg per cubic meter)
10 NYC-mod seismic versus NYC wind unit base shears 5 pcf (400.5 kg per cubic meter and $R = 2$)

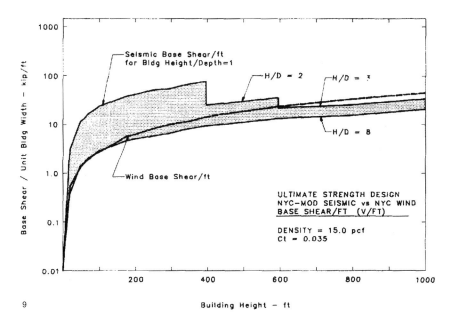

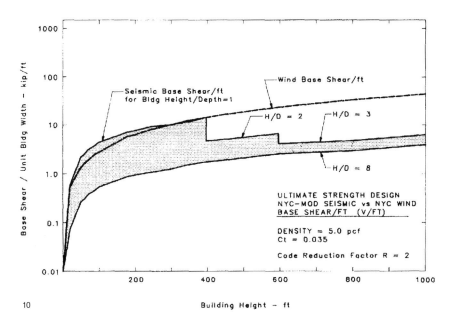

ability to withstand large inelastic cycles of deformation in excess of four to even six times the yield displacement. The number of structural system types with demonstrated energy-dissipating capacity is limited as well, so that consideration of building configuration and overall structural strategy are fundamental to effective seismic design. The design of tall structures for wind effects is at times a complex task, especially where aerodynamic effects are important. In general, however, wind-resistant design is quite straightforward and allows for considerable diversity in design strategies. The principal issues raised in this paper can be summarized as follows:

– The ratio of values representing the effects of a "maximum credible event" to those on which the building code is based is on the order of 1.5 to 2 for wind along the eastern seaboard and for earthquakes in the western United States. The equivalent value (or "marginal hazard") is closer to 5 to 7 for earthquakes in the East. This reflects the rare occurrence of large earthquakes in the East, particularly in relation to the return period on which the currently proposed seismic codes are based. This suggests that structures designed for earthquake resistance in the East should be provided with even greater energy-dissipation than is the practice in the West (if this is possible), or that the average return period chosen as the basis for the code-prescribed loads should be increased to reduce the magnitude of the marginal hazard.

– A comparison of unit base shears calculated by the code procedures for wind and seismic design demonstrates that for a representative range of building height, slenderness, and density, the elastic seismic demands (allowing no load reduction for "ductility") in all cases exceeds the prescribed wind loading.

– If the probable frequency content for the type of moderate earthquake used as the design basis event for NYC is incorporated in the comparison (e.g., by modifying the response spectrum shape), the relative seismic demands are substantially reduced. This is especially true for structures over 200 feet (61 m) in height.

– Clearly a further reduction in the difference is possible if even a nominal degree of energy-dissipating capacity is allowed for.

It should be evident that it is impossible to establish a direct relationship between code-prescribed wind forces and earthquake resistance. Both the physical nature of the phenomena and the design philosophy underlying the respective code procedures are fundamentally different.

Appropriate seismic design provisions are needed for adoption in New York City.

Acknowledgments
Mr. Tian Fang Jing played a central role in all aspects of this work.

* *The work described was done under a research contract from the National Center for Earthquake Engineering Research (SUNY at Buffalo) at Weidlinger Associates, New York.*

1 *Uniform Building Code*. 1988. International Conference of Building Officials. Whittier, CA.

2 BSSC (Building Seismic Safety Council). 1985. *Recommended Provisions for the Development of Seismic Regulations for New Buildings.* Washington, D.C.

3 Simiu, E. and R. H. Scanlan. 1988. *Wind Effects on Structures*, 2nd ed. New York, NY: Wiley.

4 American National Standard Institute. 1982. ANSI *Standard Building Code Requirements for Minimum Design Loads in Buildings and Other Structures*. ANSI A58.1-1982. New York, NY.

5 Idriss, I. M. 1985. Evaluating seismic risk in engineering practice. In *Proceedings of the Eleventh International Conference on Soil, Mechanics and Foundation Engineering*. Accord, MA: A. A. Balkema, 255–320.

6 Statton; C. T., R. C. Quittmeyer, and I. M. Idriss. 1987. *Probabilistic Seismic Hazard Evaluation for George Washington Bridge, New York-New Jersey*. Wayne, NJ: Woodward-Clyde Consultants.

7 Nuclear Regulatory Commission. Division of engineering geosciences plan to address USGS clarification relating to seismic design earthquakes in the eastern seaboard of the United States. Memorandum from Richard H. Vollrner to Harold R. Denton, March 2, 1983.

8 SEAoC (Structural Engineers Association of California) Seismology Committee. 1988. *Tentative Lateral Force Requirements*. Sacramento/San Francisco/Los Angeles, CA.

9 Bertero, V. V. 1987. The Mexico Earthquake of September 19,1985: Performance of building structures. Presented at seminar of ASCE Met Section.

10 Weidlinger Associates. 1984. BSSC Trial Design Program. National Institute of Building Sciences. ATC-3-06 Trial Design Program. New York, NY.

11 Robertson Fowler and Associates. 1984. BSSC Trial Design Program. National Institute of Building Sciences. ATC-3-06 Trial Design Program. New York, NY.

12 Joyner, W. B. and D. M. Boore. 1982. Prediction of earthquake response spectra. Presented at the 51st Annual Convention of the Structural Engineers Association of California. Sacramento, CA.

13 Applied Technology Council. 1978. *Tentative Provisions for the Development of Seismic Regulations for Buildings,* ATC 3-06, NBS-SP 510, NSF pub. 78-8. Palo Alto, CA.

Seismic Design of Suspended Boiler Structures

Guy J. P. Nordenson, P. J. Donelan, and M. Garkawe

Abstract

A study of the seismic behavior of suspended boiler structures is presented. The boiler considered is a 550 MW(e) output, 7,500-ton unit. The conclusions from a literature search are given as well as an outline of current practice. It is found that the inclusion of the boiler-structure interaction significantly reduces the demands on the structure. Additional design concepts are also presented.

Introduction

Suspended boiler structures (SBS) provide support and stability to steam-generating boilers. A study conducted for the Foster Wheeler Energy Corporation by Ove Arup & Partners[2] examined the dynamic behavior of the boiler and support structure system in an effort to improve the clarity and economy of its seismic design.

→ p. 111

A 550 MW(e) output, 7,500-ton boiler measuring 65 × 140 × 179 feet (19.8 × 42.7 × 55.6 m) (FIGS. 1, 2) has been used as the prototype. As is typical for these boilers, it is supported on hangers at its top, off "top steel" framing consisting of large plate girders (up to 15 feet [4.6 m] deep). Boiler sway is prevented by bumper connections at platforms located on the sides of the boiler.

The study includes consideration of steel eccentric braced frames as a possible lateral load resisting system, as well as other design concepts. Of particular interest are conclusions regarding the significant influence of the boiler-structure interaction on the design, and the advantages of locating vertical bracing on the outermost bents of the structure.

Current Seismic Design Practice

Many boiler structures exist in regions of high seismicity around the world. Typically these are designed as follows:

1. Equivalent static methods are often used with a specified minimum base shear coefficient on the order of 10 to 15 percent.

Published in *Proceedings of Fourth U.S. National Conference on Earthquake Engineering*, May 20–24, 1990, Palm Springs, California, vol. 3, pages 229–37

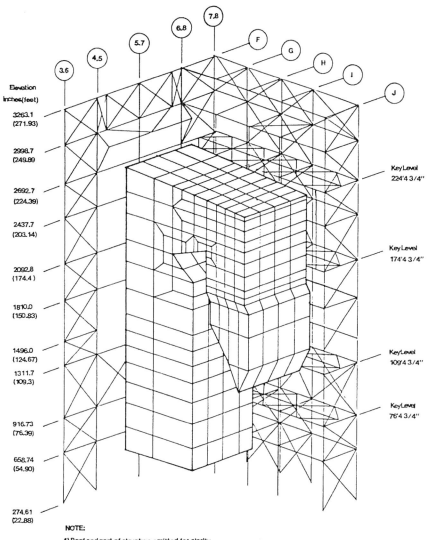

Elevation
Inches(feet)

3263.1
(271.93)

2998.7
(249.89)

2692.7
(224.39)

2437.7
(203.14)

2092.8
(174.4)

1810.0
(150.83)

1496.0
(124.67)

1311.7
(109.3)

916.73
(76.39)

658.74
(54.90)

274.61
(22.88)

Key Level
224'4 3/4"

Key Level
174'4 3/4"

Key Level
109'4 3/4"

Key Level
76'4 3/4"

3,6   4,5   5,7   6,8   7,8   F   G   H   I   J

NOTE:

1) Roof and part of structure omitted for clarity

2) Key level truss at elevation 109' 4 3/4" omitted in later models

1

2. Boiler wall stiffness is neglected and the boiler element masses are apportioned to each platform or key level (FIG. 1) on a tributary basis.

3. Typical load paths for boiler inertial loads are:

– element
– boiler wall (consisting of vertical tubes)
– horizontal buckstay
– bumper
– main structure—columns or horizontal key level truss
– vertical bracing

Considerable attention is given to the design of the boiler wall to bumper portion of the path, including any stress concentrations in the boiler wall.

4. Vertical bracing is designed by conventional means. A critical factor is usually the client-specified limit on uplift forces at the column bases. Current practice has been to mitigate this by locating the bracing between columns supporting the "top steel" plate girders, mobilizing their large reactions. The necessity for numerous ducts and other penetrations across these "inner" bents, however, sometimes results in awkward configurations.

A review of this practice has identified several drawbacks which this study has sought to correct:

– The boiler stiffness is in fact large and will influence the dynamic response of the overall system. This has been recognized in the 1988 *Uniform Building Code* (1988 *UBC*) provisions for nonbuilding structures, wherein it is mandated that elements weighing over 25 percent of the total system weight must be properly represented in the analytical model.

– The horizontal diaphragm structure of two trusses alongside the boiler cannot be considered rigid overall.

– The interference of ducts and other penetration with the bracing at the "inner" bents is costly and preferably to be avoided.

Literature Review

An exhaustive review of existing literature on both the analysis and actual earthquake response of SBSs has been done. Selected references are provided herein. The literature obtained covers a range of topics including the behavior of boilers in real earthquakes, vibration testing of full-size and scale model structures, and dynamic modelling of the boiler and support structure.

Damage observed in real earthquakes includes buckling of cross-bracing, permanent deformations of the bumpers, damage caused by piping

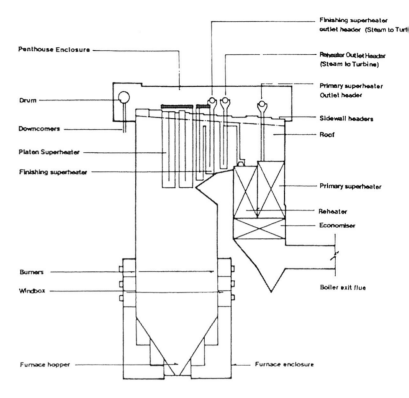

Penthouse Enclosure

Drum

Downcomers

Platen Superheater

Finishing superheater

Burners

Windbox

Furnace hopper

Finishing superheater outlet header (Steam to Turb

Reheater Outlet Header (Steam to Turbine)

Primary superheater Outlet header

Sidewall headers

Roof

Primary superheater

Reheater

Economiser

Boiler exit flue

Furnace enclosure

2

banging against adjacent members, elongation of pinholes, damage to insulation, etc. To date no major structural damage has been observed.

The modelling carried out to date, especially that described in the older papers, has been relatively simple in most cases. Frequently physical testing, either at full size or on scale models, has been carried out in order to verify the mathematical models. Such testing usually consists of vibration tests to measure natural frequencies of vibration and mode shapes. If the calculated natural frequencies and mode shapes were in reasonable agreement with the measured values, then this would give confidence that the mathematical model was a reasonable representation of the dynamic characteristics of the real boiler.

The more important conclusions arrived at concerning the modelling of boiler structures include:

− The torsion mode of vibration has a relatively long period of oscillation. Hence in dynamic models it is necessary to carry out three-dimensional analysis in order to properly account for this effect.

– The rigidity of the boiler can significantly reduce the shear taken by the support structure in an earthquake.

– The bumpers are highly stressed elements, and their behavior significantly affects the overall response to an earthquake.

The more advanced papers [1, 3, 4] describe nonlinear analyses in which the behavior of bumpers in yielding is considered.

Design Studies

Studies have been conducted on a variety of structural schemes to identify the most economical. These studies considered all steel structures including "ductile" and "ordinary" (i.e., non-ductile) moment resisting frames; concentric braced frames; and eccentric braced frames. The designs were developed following the detailing provisions of the 1988 *UBC* as well as its loading requirements. All shared the following characteristics:

– Analysis was by the 1988 *UBC* equivalent static method and in three dimensions.

– Accidental torsion was included.

– The ANSYS computer code was used.

– The boiler (including the roof and partition walls) was modelled using orthotropic quadrilateral shell elements and spring elements for the bumper and buckstay assemblies.

– The hangers and top steel were included.

– The side bracing was relocated to the outer bents.

– "Top-hat" and "belt" trusses were used to mitigate overturning demands on the columns (FIG. 3). It was found that these were effective in reducing the column uplift forces by over 30 percent.

Effect of Boiler-structure Interaction

The contribution of the boiler to the overall stiffness of the system is substantial (FIG. 4). Over its height the boiler takes nearly 50 percent of the shear. Were the bent structures to be intentionally made flexible, this percentage would increase. In the cases studied, the bent stiffnesses resulted from preliminary designs that neglected the boiler contribution. The effects observed therefore represent the current reality of practice.

The interaction forces are shown in Figure 5 for the front-to-back case and an eccentric braced frame (EBF) scheme. It is evident that the distribution does not correspond to a tributary mass assumption.

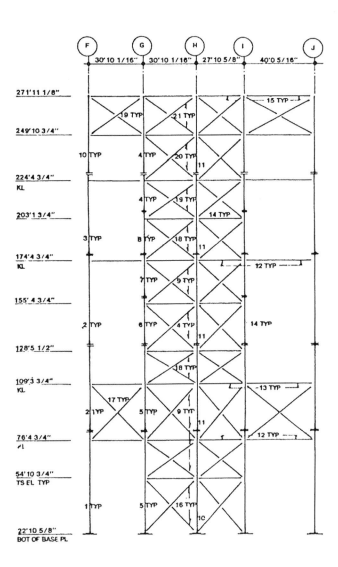

F   G   H   I   J

30' 10 1/16"   30' 10 1/16"   27' 10 5/8"   40'0 5/16"

271'11 1/8"

9 TYP   21 TYP   15 TYP

249' 10 3/4"

10 TYP   4 TYP   20 TYP   11

224'4 3/4"
KL

4 TYP   19 TYP   14 TYP

203'1 3/4"

3 TYP   8 TYP   18 TYP   11

174'4 3/4"
KL

7 TYP   9 TYP   12 TYP

155' 4 3/4"

2 TYP   6 TYP   4 TYP   11   14 TYP

128'5 1/2"

18 TYP

109'3 3/4"
KL

17 TYP   13 TYP

2 TYP   5 TYP   9 TYP   11

76'4 3/4"
1   12 TYP

54' 10 3/4"
TS EL TYP

1 TYP   5 TYP   16 TYP   10

22'10 5/8"
BOT OF BASE PL

3

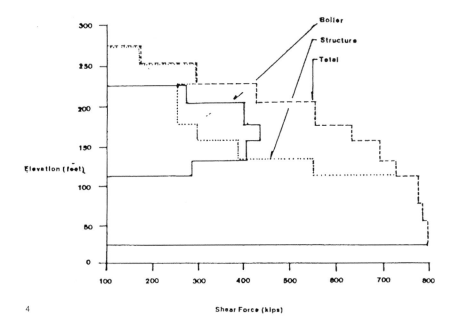

Elevation (feet)

Shear Force (kips)

4

Dynamic Analysis

The concentric braced frame (CBF) scheme was analyzed using the response spectrum method presented in the 1988 *UBC.* Modes were combined using the Complete Quadratic Combination procedure. Interaction forces for this case are shown in Figure 6.

Conclusions and Recommendations

The consideration of boiler-structure interaction effects and the use of the boiler as part of the lateral load resisting system represent a new concept for SBS seismic design. The interaction is a physical fact which cannot be ignored, even if, as in Zone 2 designs, the 1988 *UBC* code, for instance, does not require that it be considered. The advantages of the interaction are:

– A reduction in the story shears carried by the structure, since the boiler takes on shear at its top and effectively transfers it at its bottom, balanced by the hangers.

– A conversion of overturning moments from shear induced moments on the bents to axial loads added by the hanger couples to the top steel girders and supporting columns.

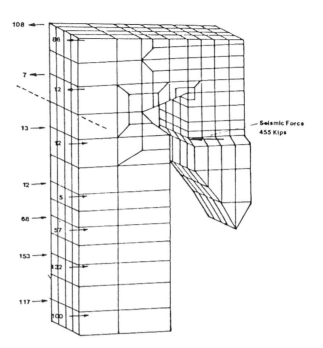

108 ⟵

86 ⟵

7 ⟵

12 ⟵

13 ⟶

12 ⟶

Seismic Force
455 Kips

12 ⟶

12 ⟶

5 ⟶

68 ⟶

57 ⟵

153 ⟶

32 ⟶

117 ⟶

100 ⟶

5

These advantages can translate into savings in structural costs. These must be balanced against the following considerations:

– The boiler's ability to sustain the calculated transfer forces with adequate ductility reserves and without local buckling.

– The boiler's ability to sustain internal stresses induced and remain stable as it "spans" between points of contact with the structure.

– The actual dynamic interaction likely to occur among the many internal boiler parts.

On the basis of this study the following recommendations can be made:

1. CBF and EBF designs are promising for SBS.

2. The braced frame schemes using outrigger "top hat" and "belt" trusses provide an efficient means of reducing column uplift forces and stiffening the structure (thereby reducing bumper forces at the top of the boiler if desired).

3. In order to avoid having to provide the boiler with the ductility implied by the 1988 UBC's "ductility" factor R_w, the bumpers could be designed as "fuses" which yield at a force just higher than the calculated bumper force.

5 Bumper Forces – Front to Back 3-D Static Analysis
6 3-D Dynamic Analysis

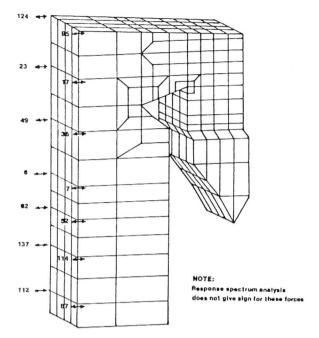

NOTE:
Response spectrum analysis
does not give sign for these forces

6

4. Further work on the inelastic behavior of EBFs having belt trusses and outriggers should be undertaken. Current design methods assume that all links are yielding simultaneously, which places high demands on the columns. An improved understanding in this area could result in savings in column steelwork.

1 IHI Ltd. *Aseismic Design for Boiler Steel Structure*. Ref. no. IHI-904-8604, Tokyo. (In Japanese with English translation of figures and tables.)

2 Ove Arup & Partners. 1989. Seismic Design Of Suspended Boiler Structures. *OAPNY Report 32016-1*, vols. 1 & 2. 30 December.

3 Sharpe, R. D. 1987. Support Structure Design for New Zealand Forest Products Ltd No 5 Recovery Boiler. *Bulletin of the New Zealand National Society for Earthquake Engineering*, vol. 20, no. 1. March.

4 Uchiyama, S. 1988. Parametric Study on Seismic Ties of Boiler House. *Report of the 13th Congress of the International Association for Bridge and Structural Engineering*. Helsinki, Finland. June.

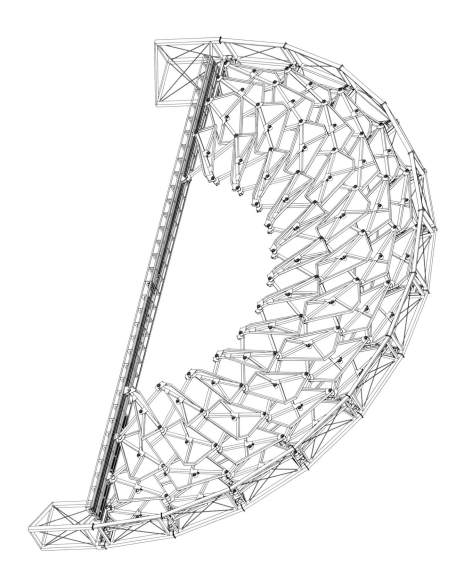

Drawing by Chuck Hoberman

An Inventive Nature

"…we no sooner get a problem solved than we are overwhelmed with a multiplicity of additional problems in a most beautiful payoff of heretofore unknown, previously unrecognized, and as yet solved problems."

R. B. Fuller, 1975

"The whole of science is nothing more than a refinement of everyday thinking."

A. Einstein, 1936

Patterns and play

Invention or discovery: mind or matter: imagination or method. How do we inquire these days? Despite the revolutions of '89 we do not live in hopeful times. We are least of all convinced of the promises of technology. Everywhere we suspect that order is *in order to*. If at the root our very language is biased by power's inflection, how do we think? What becomes of free inquiry? Is there such a thing? Does it make a difference?

"Dare to be naive" quoth R. Buckminster Fuller, as he did well and with great courage. The clarity of his important discoveries must at least partly be ascribed to the prejudice-blasting power of this tack. Fuller conceived of the geodesic dome around 1946 as "the invisible sphere of the imagination." As described by his biographer L. S. Sieden[1], Fuller came to the geodesic by way of an analogy between thought and minimal surfaces. If thoughts are patterns of experiences, then it takes at minimum four experiences to define a solid with the minimum three-dimensional surface: the tetrahedron. To Fuller the tetrahedron represented the connectivity or relationship of (four) experiences, bound along the shortest straight-edge lines to form the thought: relevance inside, irrelevance without. So with clear thought the next larger solid made of (minimal) triangular faces is the icosahedron (12 vertices and 20 faces). If one were to slice off its 12 corners, one would obtain a solid of 32 regular faces (20 hexagons and 12 pentagons) and 60 vertices. This is the truncated icosahedral geometry of most geodesics. Connected, its edges describe the chords of great circles on the sphere formed by the vertices.

→ p. 117

Is it any wonder that in 1985, nearly forty years after Fuller's discovery and two years after his death, Richard E. Smalley, Harold W. Kroto, and others found that a new, extremely rugged carbon molecule, C_{60}, is in fact structured as a truncated icosahedron? They call them buckminsterfullerene, or bucky balls, and speculate that they may populate interstellar space in great numbers.[2] Considering that diamond is formed of carbon atoms in space-filling tetrahedral arrays, and graphite of flat sheets of hexagonal arrays, it is curious that Fuller did not himself dream up his own C_{60} bucky balls.

"Is human reason, then, without experience, merely by talking thought, able to fathom the properties of real things?" Speaking on January 27, 1921, on "Geometry and Experience," Albert Einstein described a process of thinking speculatively in terms of geometrical "objects:"[3] "All our thinking is of this nature of a free play with concepts" which for him were "of visual and some muscular type." In 1936, in the essay "Physics and Reality,"[4] he wrote:

"The very fact that the totality of our sense experiences is such that by means of thinking (operations with concepts, and the creation and use of definite functional relations between them, and the coordination of sense experiences to these concepts) it can be put in order, this fact is one which leaves us in awe, but which we shall never understand. One may say 'the eternal mystery of the world is its comprehensibility.' It is one of the great realizations of Immanuel Kant that the postulation of a real external world would be senseless without this comprehensibility."

This "practical geometry," based on "earth-measuring," i.e., on induction, solicits and bounds the persistent combinatorial play of concepts into thoughts and "mental relations" by means of which we are, with Einstein, "able to orient ourselves in the labyrinth of sense impressions."

That play can be creative and inventive has been noted by many, from Immanuel Kant, who described art as "a purposeless purposivenes" or as a "passion guided by reason,"[5] by way of Nietzsche to Derrida, for whom "l'abscence de signifié transcendantal étend a l'infini le champ et le jeu de la signification." For Derrida, though play may not be productive in the usual sense, it is still joyful.

"La pensée du jeu dont *l'affirmation* nietzschéenne, l'affirmation joyeuse du eu du monde et de l'innocence du devenir, 'l'affirmation d'un monde de signes san faute, sans vérité, sans origine, offert a une interprétation active, serait l'autre face. *Cette affirmation determine alors le non-centre autrement que comme parte du centre. Et elle jous sans sécurité. Car il y a un jeu sûr: celui qui se limite a la substitution de piece données et existantes, présents. Dans le hasard absolu, l'affirmation se livre assi a l'indetermination génétique, a l'aventure seminalé de la trace'"* [6]

Thought in the clear, free to play and in play discover what is real and, dare we say, true. In summary:

Inquiry is play, trying and fun.

Invention is the discovery of order(s) that emerge, quite suddenly, as we play: creation and discovery are the same.

We may come into play any time, in mind and matter, for patterns to come into place.

The vectors of Chuck Hoberman's work belong in this field or reference frame to be read against the axes of Fuller, Einstein, Derrida, etc. It is the work of both thought pattern and object. It is too early to know the homologies of Hoberman's thinking and work as we do Fuller's. We can only discover "by taking thought," by visualizing and playing along, what it has to teach us about method and imagination, matter and mind, and of course discovery and invention.

Metamorphoses

The work of Chuck Hoberman is readily divided into surface and bar deployables. For all these, the common traits are their ability to transform continuously from the very small to the very large: line to surface, point to sphere. All are made of rigid units that deploy through the unfolding of surface pleats or bar linkages. The designs emerge from the pattern of these units and folds.

Hoberman begins with this idea of deployment and his engineering knowledge of linkages. He has devised a number of basic units for some of which he has received patents. These units define types of possible controlled-unit movements (conceptual vectors, if you will) out of which complete systems are formed. Examples of these are the linkages of the deployable sphere and iris dome, of the "zig-zag" nesting of the surface collapsible. The challenge is to develop the many potential applications of these simple and suggestive units, some of which are directly practicable. An example of one such development is the iris dome, which was conceived as part of a sphere deployed from a small circle rather than from its center.

This is design as experiment, as open play. The first genius, of course, is in the discovery of the atoms of this physics, most notably the bent-bar linkage for which Hoberman has received patents 4,942,700 and 5,024,031. The second genius is in the direction of play and the alertness to patterns. Hoberman has spent years of devoted effort testing elaborations of these simple units, the products of which are shown in these pages. A few of their attributes and behavioral characteristics are worth noting:

there is a love of materials and their "thing-ness" and patina evident in the models themselves;

each deployment is smooth, continuous, and bound within a specific workable range, the limits of which are the binding of joints and the singularities at each end of the deployment: full extension or contraction;

each device represents the considered selection of process and parts on the design principle of achieving greatest complexity and richness with the simplest means.

The second of these could be rephrased so as to state that all are always already slightly folded.

Image in motion: imagination

"The production of any work of art is preceded by a creative mental act for which the means are provided by language. Thus the creative use of language, which, under certain conditions of form and organization, constitutes poetry, accompanies and underlies any act of the creative imagination, no matter what the medium in which it is realized."

N. Chomsky,[7] 1966

"I am inclined to believe that the logic of images is the prime mover of constructive imagination."

T. A. Ribot,[8] 1926

The constructive imagination has great difficulty visually anticipating the behavior of Hoberman's devices. It is even more difficult to discover the basic unit and its function without guidance. Further yet, the mind short-circuits before the singularities possible at the bounds or even along their motion. And yet, after many attempts, one finds that one can begin to imagine their motion in short glimpses or flashes, though it is difficult and strange. This requires thinking not in language but in images—in motion yet. An architecture of moving images and images of moving architecture, "taking thought." Hoberman is seeking application for his ideas and forms in architecture; he is a sculptor and an engineer—generally unreconciled sensibilities. Sculpture, and, I would argue, architecture are principally "the art of shape—the purposeful and aesthetic arrangement of mass and void."[9] Engineering, particularly of mechanisms and structure, is the art of material mechanics. As applied to each, the visual imagination engages entirely different means and realms. Most critically, time and particularly varying motion enters into the sculptor/architect's thinking, and not as much into the structural engineer's. Hoberman has set the "invisible sphere of the imagination" in motion, with his work taking us beyond the traditional statics of architecture to a new relativistic realm.

1 Sieden, L. S. 1989. *Buckminster Fuller's Universe: An Appreciation.* New York: Plenum.

2 Smallry, R. E. 1991. Great Balls of Carbon. *The Sciences* (March/April).

3 & 4 Einstein, A. Geometry and Experience (1921) and Physics and Reality (1936). Idem, 1954. *Ideas and Opinions.* New York: Crown.

5 Kant, I. *Critique on Judgment.* Quoted in Bullock, *The Humanist Tradition in the West* (New York: Norton, 1985).

6 Derrida, J. La structure, le signe et le jeu dans le discours des sciences humaines (1966). *L'écriture et la différence.* Paris: Seuil, 1967.

The absence of the transcendental signified extends the domain and the play of signification infinitely.

…the thinking of play whose other side would be the Nietzschean *affirmation,* that is the joyous affirmation of the play of the world and of the innocence of becoming, the affirmation of a world of signs without fault, without truth, and without origin which is offered to an active interpretation. *This affirmation then determines the non-center otherwise than as loss of center.* And it plays without security. For there is a sure play: that which is limited to the *substitution* of *given* and *existing, present,* pieces. In absolute chance, affirmation also surrenders itself to *genetic* indetermination, to the *seminal* adventure of the trace.

J. Derrida. Structure, Sign, and Play. Trans.

7 Chomsky, N. 1966. *Cartesian Linguistics.* New York: Harper. Summarizing A. W. Schlegel of *Die Kunstlehre* (1801).

8 Ribot, T. A. 1926. *L'évolution des idées générales.* New York: Alcan. Quoted in R. Arnheim, *Visual Thinking* (Berkeley, CA: University of California, 1971).

9 Acord, Jr., J. L. Quoted in *The New Yorker,* Oct. 14, 1991.

The Spirit of Measure

"The geometry of fracture limits and defines the art of carving."
Adrian Stokes

It is always a surprise to come to a building of Harry Wolf's: from his Equitable Building ready at any moment to flee UFO-like from its sorry neighbors, to the invitation of the gardens at the NCNB Tower to wander barefoot in the exquisite geometry of grass and stone. The drawings and photographs prepare you for a cool and abstract geometric rigor, not for the walls of Texas shell stone alive with history. This may be why, on a visit to the Mecklenburg Courthouse in Charlotte, I was at first taken aback at the weathering of the limestone façade. But then, as I explored the building further, it became clear how well the hand-worn concrete columns, the graffiti-carved benches, the concrete steps, and the graying limestone bore their age and constant use with dignity. As I left I looked back to see the evening light refract sharply through the building, a lively pool in the warm shadow-full stone.

Between the idea and the materials or between the immeasurable and the measurable (and back, would say Louis Kahn) is both the way and equilibrium of his architecture. In the words of Martin Heidegger, "thus questioning, we bear witness to the crisis that in our sheer preoccupation with technology we do not yet experience the coming to presence of technology, that in our sheer aesthetic-mindedness we no longer guard and preserve the coming to presence of art." In our deconstructed present, few architects pursue let alone preserve this "coming to presence".[1] In my view Harry Wolf has the rare combination of wit, of passion and eye for order in patterns, and empathy for the character of materials and people–has the soul if you will–to take this tradition forward. Throughout his work there is evidence of his delight in discovery and invention. Consider the gorgeous excess of the nine-fold hypar roofs of the Kansai Airport competition entry, the teasing revelation of the folded square geometry of the 747 Tower structure, or the angel-like impression of the service core on its east façade. As with the architecture of Louis Kahn there is always a close interweaving of material, light, structure,

→ p. 121

Published in *Harry Wolf* (Introduction), Barcelona, Gili, 1993, pages 16–18 servicing, and circulation, and there is wit—witness again the Equitable Building, built so quickly and cheaply it seems to hover on its envelope of air!

There are correspondences as well with the work of another American and witty architect, Gordon Bunshaft. In both, a cool intelligence and a delight in things combine to make buildings at once rational and sensual, like the Banque Lambert in Brussels or the National Commercial Bank in Kuwait or Lever House in New York. In these, thought and technology (structure, services, and construction) are the means of inquiry, tools that mark the work in their use. It is by such marks, at once contingent and transcendent, that the poetry of presence is struck.

```
 0 1 2 3 4 5 6 7 8 9
0 1 2 3 4 5 6 7 8 9 0
1 2 3 4 5 6 7 8 9 0 1
2 3 4 5 6 7 8 9 0 1 2
3 4 5 6 7 8 9 0 1 2 3
4 5 6 7 8 9 0 1 2 3 4
5 6 7 8 9 0 1 2 3 4 5
6 7 8 9 0 1 2 3 4 5 6
7 8 9 0 1 2 3 4 5 6 7
8 9 0 1 2 3 4 5 6 7 8
9 0 1 2 3 4 5 6 7 8 9
```

Perhaps the best analogy I have yet found for the spirit of this work is Jasper Johns'[1] remarkable painting of an 11 × 11 matrix, *White Numbers*.[2] It is a deeply textured painting. The numbers, curved figures deeply carved in paint, recall their cuneiform origin. The Babylonians' shock at discovering the zero is evoked in the top left-corner void. The orderly matrix with its "cross-diagonal" symmetry is old form among mathematicians and computer engineers who since the 1950s have used them to work complex analytical problems. Finally the regularity implied by the alignment of numbers is not only marvelously at odds with the off-square of the canvas as a whole but is uncanny, since the diagonal of this square equals in number its side! Here in this delightful encounter of art, technology, and mathematics is all the oddity, humor, and spirit so much a part of these and so seldom enjoyed.

Professor Cyril Smith, the great metallurgist and historian of technology, showed that most technological discoveries are born of an aesthetic search for order in the material at (or in) hand: from Chinese bronze casting to Japanese swords to ceramic glazes, "aesthetically motivated curiosity, or perhaps just play, seems to have been the most important stimulus to discovery."[3] Today the study of order in "chaotic" or nonlinear dynamic systems continues this practice. Obviously such curiosity is founded on a faith in the possibility of truth and order revealed by intelligence and craft (and play). The nihilism of current North American architectural culture, whether modern or postmodern mise-en-scène or deconstructivist exhibitionism, denies this incessantly. Such millennial cowering is no help. In just our lifetime the population of the earth will more than triple and the surface and atmosphere are even now tearing apart. It is urgent that we question our culture and nature for guidance and make our arts and sciences the tools and evidence of recovery and hope. Harry Wolf is a scout on the way ahead.

from *White Numbers* by Jasper Johns 1957

1 "What is there about Mies, what is there about Le Corbusier, what is there about Aalto that belongs to architecture itself? That which is inevitable or eternal as it is, that naturally belongs to architecture." Louis I. Kahn (*On Form and Design,* 1960).

2 One of several in this series. I refer to the 1957 painting at The Museum of Modern Art, New York City.

3 See Cyril S. Smith, *A Search for Structure* (Cambridge, MA: MIT Press, 1981), well worth quoting at length: Nearly everyone believes, falsely, that technology is applied science. It is becoming so, and rapidly, but through most of history science has arisen from problems posed for intellectual solution by the technician's more intimate experience of the behavior of matter and mechanisms. Technology is more closely related to art than to science – not only materially, because art must somehow involve the selection and manipulation of matter, but conceptually as well, because the technologist, like the artist, must work with many unanalyzable complexities ... the first discovery of useful materials, machines, or processes has almost always been in the decorative arts, and was not done for a perceived practical purpose. Necessity is not the mother of invention – only of improvement. A man desperately in search of a weapon or food is in no mood for discovery; he can only exploit what is already known to exist. Discovery requires aesthetically motivated curiosity, not logic, for new things can acquire validity only by interaction in an environment that has yet to be. Their origin is unpredictable. A new thing of any kind whatsoever begins as a local anomaly, a region of misfit within the preexisting structure. This first nucleus is indistinguishable from the new fluctuations whose time has not yet come and the innumerable fluctuations which the future will merely erase.

Seismic Codes

Abstract

This chapter presents an introduction to the principles of seismic codes and their role in society. The stated purposes of selected seismic codes from around the world are given with a brief history of developments in Italy, Japan, and the United States. An outline of the significant provisions of the *Uniform Building Code* and the *NEHRP Recommended Provisions* is included as well as those of the proposed New York City Seismic Code. The chapter concludes with a discussion of several important ideas contained in the codes of Japan, Mexico, and New Zealand and suggestions for future code development.

Preamble

Throughout the 1950s the noted architect and engineer Felix Candela built hundreds of concrete hyperbolic paraboloid shells throughout Mexico. Candela had moved to Mexico from Spain at the end of the Civil War, in 1939. In Spain he had devised the hyperbolic paraboloid form he made famous.

The shells were generally less than 2 inches (5.1 cm) in thickness, sometimes as little as 1.5 inches (3.8 cm). North of the border this was considered scandalously thin and Candela was regularly denounced at conventions. The American Concrete Institute code prohibited shells that thin, North or South.

When Candela worked there were no codes regulating shell construction in Mexico. His shells still stand today.

In the 1960s the authorities instituted a code controlling shell design and construction and Candela left Mexico to return to Spain.

Seismic Codes And Society

There are at present several noteworthy codes of earthquake-resistant design practice in the world. These include:

- The "Earthquake Provisions" of the *New Zealand Standard* (NZS)
- The *Building Standard Law* of the Architects Institute of Japan (AIJ)

Published in *Monograph 2 on Mitigation of Damage to the Built Environment*,
National Earthquake Conference, Memphis TN, May 1993, pages 89–114

- The "Common Unified Rules for Structures in Seismic Regions," known as *Eurocode No 8* (*EU-8*)
- The *National Building Code of Canada* (CAN)
- The *Federal District Building Code* of Mexico City (MEX)

In the United States there are four major building codes:
- The *Basic Building Code,* of the Building Officials and Code Administrators International, Homewood, Illinois (BOCA)
- The *Southern Building Code,* of the Southern Building Code Congress, Birmingham, Alabama (*SBC*)
- The *National Building Code,* of the American Insurance Association, New York (*NBC*)
- The *Uniform Building Code,* of the International Conference of Building Officials, Whittier, California (*UBC*)

Of these, BOCA, *SBC*, and *NBC* are similar in most aspects. The earthquake regulations they contain were until recently those of the "American National Standard Building Code Requirements for Minimum Design Loads in Buildings and Other Structures"of the American National Standards Institute, New York, 1982 (ANSI-82). At present BOCA, *SBC* and *NBC* are being revised to incorporate the *NEHRP Recommended Provisions for the Development of Seismic Regulations for New Buildings,* 1991 (NEHRP) which, unlike ANSI-82, include extensive materials detailing requirements. The three codes are used primarily in the midwestern, southern and eastern parts of the U.S.

The *UBC* has historically been used in the western states only and has included the *Recommended Lateral Force Requirements* of the Structural Engineers Association of California (SEAoC) as its earthquake regulations. The first U.S. seismic codes originated in California and the *UBC* has generally been recognized as coming closest to the state of the art.

The near future is likely to see a consolidation of seismic codes along the lines either of the *Recommended Requirements* published in 1990 by SEAoC or the 1991 edition of NEHRP. Other efforts, including the recently completed New York Seismic Code proposal (NYC) and guidelines for the retrofit of existing buildings sponsored by the Federal Emergency Management Agency (FEMA), will undoubtedly affect the nature of these codes as well.

Although a detailed review of all these world and U.S. codes is beyond the scope of this chapter, much can be learned by comparing their provisions and philosophies. Indeed, such comparisons are an important topic of papers and discussions at national and international earthquake conferences.

It is clear that seismic codes represent a society's principal response to the devastation caused by earthquakes. Depending on the frequency and severity of earthquakes in a region, its people are more or less likely to demand stringent building code requirements. Given the short memory of many communities and the long time periods separating earthquakes in even the most active regions, it is a blessing that effective codes exist at all, and it is no wonder they are often drastically revised after major earthquakes. Most recently, the 1971 San Fernando, 1985 Mexico City, and 1989 Loma Prieta earthquakes all precipitated major changes in seismic codes worldwide.

As social artifacts, codes embody the choices of both the community at large and the engineering and scientific community in particular. They are "consensus documents," meaning that a group of volunteer professionals have deliberated (always at great length) and eventually agreed on their content. Unlike laws, however, they are not legislated by elected representatives. In fact they most often require near unanimous agreement among those involved for passage. Just like laws they try to regulate reality.

The term "seismic codes" reflects this. They are not referred to as aseismic or anti-seismic because they mean to control the effects of earthquakes by design. As engineers fashion mechanisms and structures to behave as predicted, so seismic codes attempt to remove the unexpected consequences of earthquakes, to in fact tame them.

Purpose and Assumptions of Seismic Codes

The purpose of seismic codes varies around the world. Perhaps the oldest and clearest statement of purpose is provided in the Commentary to the SEAoC *Recommended Requirements:*

Structures designed in conformance with these Recommendations should, in general, be able to:
1. Resist a minor level of earthquake ground motion without damage;
2. Resist a moderate level of earthquake ground motion without structural damage, but possibly experience some nonstructural damage;
3. Resist a major level of earthquake ground motion having an intensity equal to the strongest either experienced or forecast for the building site, without collapse, but possibly with some structural as well as nonstructural damage.

It is expected that structural damage, even in a major earthquake, will be limited to a repairable level for structures that meet these provisions.

This is in essence the stated purpose of NEHRP as well. In comparison, the *Eurocode EU-8* states as follows:

The purpose of the rules is to protect the greatest possible number of human lives and to improve the behavior of structures subject to seismic action in order to limit damage.

The New Zealand Code states that for the various limit states (serviceability, strength and severe seismic):

a. All loads likely to be sustained during the life of the building will be sustained with an adequate margin of safety.

b. Deformations of the building will not exceed acceptable limits.

c. In events that occur occasionally, such as moderate earthquakes and severe winds, structural damage will be avoided and other damage will be minimized.

d. In events that occur infrequently, such as major earthquakes and extreme winds, collapse and irreparable damage will be avoided, and the probability of injury to or loss of life of people in and around the building will be minimized.

The Japanese code requires a two-phase design including an explicit evaluation of overstrength and ductility. Its stated purpose is quite similar to the New Zealand code's (Aoyama 1981, Ishiyama 1987).

The Canadian Code requires that in a major earthquake, collapse should not occur and exit-ways should remain clear and functional.

Building Toughness
Seismic codes reflect the acceptance that society cannot afford to build all structures to withstand severe earthquakes without damage. Damage is to be limited and collapse should be prevented, to preserve life. If damage is acceptable (and defining what is "acceptable" is a difficult task) then it may as well be made useful. Controlled damage in the structure, in the form of stable material yielding, is an effective means of dissipating seismic energy. Concrete and masonry cracking, the grinding of timber joints, even the racking of building façade panels will also help dissipate energy.

Depending on how reliable this controlled damage is, a designer is permitted by the code to reduce the design earthquake forces to anywhere between a third and a twelfth of the forces that would act on a strong and elastic structure. The capacity to suffer damage without failure is sometimes called ductility or toughness, as distinguished from brittleness. It is analogous to material ductility since it involves a kind of plastic flowing of material, without significant stiffness, and absorbs energy. Since buildings in earthquakes shake back and forth, however, the capacity is perhaps more like a (low cycle) fatigue toughness which can be stable and effective both inelastically and through dozens of cycles.

This toughness, or energy-dissipating capacity, is a property of the building as a whole. The structure alone is only a part—the part of last resistance. All the other elements of the building must take the effects of earthquakes into account as well—as do those responsible for their design, construction, and inspection.

Building Team
Buildings are made though the collective efforts of the
- client,
- architect,
- engineers,
- builders, and
- building officials

The client, whether an owner-user or developer, initiates the project and ultimately decides whether the building should be designed to the code minimum or some enhanced standard.Where buildings are essential (hospitals, communications and emergency facilities), hazardous (schools or large occupancy, nuclear plants, etc.) or culturally significant, they are often designed to higher standards.

The architect and engineers (structural, geotechnical and services) are as a team held responsible for meeting the client's and building code's goals. The structural engineer is usually the most conversant with seismic design. In fact the code provisions for façade detailing, mechanical equipment bracing, etc. are found in the "nonstructural" portion of the structural loading requirements. The structural engineer, though legally responsible only for the structure, has a professional responsibility to make sure that the rest of the design team understands and properly applies the seismic provisions applicable to their areas of design and to make sure that everything is fully "tied together."

The builder is responsible for faithfully executing the design as described in the contract documents. It is common practice for the builder to prepare separate drawings for fabrication of steel elements and connections, for precast panels, or for the concrete reinforcement bar bending and placement. In many cases this involves detailed calculations and design work. This should become the responsibility either of the building's structural engineer or may be assumed by a second engineer. In the latter case it is essential that the building engineer clearly define the separate responsibility, with detailed performance criteria, and carefully review and approve the fabrication drawings.

Though the design team will inspect the construction, and extensive laboratory testing is carried out for most materials and installations, it is impossible to build well by inspections. Joints are everything in earthquake resistance and they must be executed with the utmost care and skill if they are to perform as expected.

The building official sometimes checks plans and may inspect the construction, depending on local requirements. Unfortunately, the role of officials is often constrained by limited public budgets.

Some locations, such as Boston, MA, require independent reviews of building structural designs. This practice of so-called "peer reviews" is excellent and will hopefully spread.

History and Development of Seismic Codes

In the monograph *Seismic Design Codes and Procedures*, Glen Berg provided an excellent summary of the history of seismic codes. The following is from this monograph:

"The design of structures specifically to withstand earthquake damage is a recent development and, as one would expect, has come about largely in response to specific disasters. Three events of great influence were the San Francisco earthquake of 1906, the Messina-Reggio earthquake of 1908, and the Tokyo earthquake ....

"... The San Francisco earthquake demonstrated that some good buildings of the day were quite capable of withstanding earthquake shaking. Wood frame buildings responded exceptionally well. The majority of the buildings in the city up to five stories high that were well designed and well constructed performed satisfactorily except for those built on soft ground or fill. ... for tall buildings, the safest structural system was a steel frame made as rigid as practicable by large gusset plates connecting steel columns to steel floor beams and spandrel girders, all embedded in monolithic walls of reinforced concrete and connected and braced horizontally by rigid concrete floors and roof ....

"... In Italy, a land of frequent earthquakes, development of earthquake-resistant construction began following the Calabrian earthquakes of 1783. On the basis of a comparative study of the buildings that had survived the earthquakes and those that had failed, the Italians developed a new type of structure consisting of a timber frame infilled with stone embedded in mortar. This advance was made unaided by engineering analysis, but the result was a structural system admirably suited to its purpose. Resistant to earthquake forces, it employed indigenous materials available to the people at low cost, and buildings could be built with simple tools by semiskilled labor. This type of construction is employed today in much of southern Europe, and variants appear all over the world, for example, the Taquezal construction of Nicaragua. Because the infilled timber frame is not suited to tall buildings, ordinances were enacted in 1784 setting a two-story height limit on all new buildings and requiring that any existing structures taller than two stories that had been damaged must be cut down to two stories. Alas, the ordinance was not enforced. The great Messina-Reggio earthquake of 1908 killed 160,000 persons in a relatively small area centered near the two cities on the Messina Straits. While the few infilled timber frame buildings withstood the shaking well, most of the buildings had been built of rubble masonry, and many were already weakened by previous earthquakes. Nearly all of these collapsed.

"The scientific study of earthquake-resistant building practice in Italy was first undertaken following the Messina-Reggio catastrophe. At that time, a commission was appointed consisting of nine prominent practicing engineers and five distinguished university professors, who were charged with finding methods of designing buildings that would resist earthquakes, that could be erected easily, and that would be inexpensive enough to be within the reach of the devastated population.... It proscribed unreinforced masonry houses taller than one story as well, and imposed other constraints on building systems. Buildings had to be designed to withstand a lateral force of $1/12$ of their own weight. Three years later this was modified to provide that the ground story must resist a lateral force of $1/12$ of the weight above, and the second and third stories must resist $1/8$ of the weight above.

"The remarkable accomplishments of the 1908–09 Italian commission set a new direction for earthquake-resistant design in Italy and opened a new era of earthquake engineering research there. For the class of structures it considered, the commission had arrived at recommendations that remain as valid today as when they were formulated more than seventy years ago.

"Japan has endured as much earthquake destruction as any nation in the world. Among its most severe earthquakes was the one that devastated Tokyo and Yokohama on September 1, 1923. Earlier severe earthquakes had occurred in Tokyo, notably those of 1649, 1703, and 1855;

but the 1923 event was far more destructive to that city than any of its predecessors ....

"... Well before the 1923 earthquake, Japanese architects and builders had begun to use reinforced concrete and structural steel, and structures built of those materials withstood the shaking well ....

"... two conflicting ideas about the merits of building flexibility appeared in Japan. One engineering investigation, which included an extensive study of the dynamic behavior of simple structures as well as an evaluation of the damage incurred in the 1923 earthquake, reported that masonry structures performed the worst and reinforced concrete next, and that steel and wood were the most reliable. That study reported that rigid structures were unreliable for resisting earthquakes, although other engineering investigations drew opposite conclusions from the same evidence. The proponents of rigidity prevailed, and among them was Dr. Tachu Naito, then Professor of Architecture at Waseda University in Tokyo.

"In 1923 Dr. Naito was already among the eminent engineers of Japan, and his standing in the architectural and engineering communities was greatly enhanced by the performance of three of his buildings in the 1923 earthquake. He had designed his Japan Industrial Bank, Jitsugyo Building, and Kabuki Theater in Tokyo to resist a lateral force equal to $1/15$ of their weight, and all came through the earthquake virtually unscathed ....

"... Dr. Naito proposed four fundamental principles of earthquake-resistant design: first, a building should be designed to act as much like a rigid solid body as conditions would permit. To this end, structural members should be rigidly connected and generously braced. Dr. Naito saw this as a way to keep building periods short and thereby prevent resonance with ground motion. Second, a closed plan layout should be used; that is, the plan shape of the building should be a complete closed rectangle rather than a U, L, T, or H shape. Third, rigid walls should be used abundantly and disposed symmetrically in plan, and they should be continuous over the height of the building. Fourth, lateral forces should be allocated to the bents of the building in accordance with their rigidities ....

"... The 1923 earthquake led the Home Office of Japan to adopt a number of changes in building regulations. A seismic coefficient of $1/10$ was prescribed for all important new structures; that is, such structures had to be designed to have adequate strength at any level to withstand a horizontal force of $1/10$ of the weight above. In practice, many of the more conservative designers or building owners used even larger seismic coefficients. In addition, size limits were made more restrictive for the rebuilding of

Tokyo and Yokohama. The earlier height limit of 100 feet above street level was retained … ."

Seismic Code Development in the U.S.
Following the 1971 San Fernando earthquake, SEAoC established the Applied Technology Council (ATC) as an independent nonprofit research and development subsidiary. With support from the National Science Foundation, ATC undertook a complete overhaul of the U.S. seismic code. A group of over 60 professionals and academics completed their work in 1978 and published the *Tentative Provisions for the Development of Seismic Regulations for Buildings*, often known as ATC-3. In the early 1980s ATC-3 was evaluated though an extensive series of trial designs carried out in cities throughout the U.S.

The 1991 NEHRP is the third revised edition of ATC-3, following the 1985 and 1988 editions. The NEHRP is updated every three years by the Building Seismic Safety Council (BSSC), a federally sponsored council of the National Institute of Building Sciences that is funded by FEMA. It consists of over fifty member organizations including engineers, architects and industry, insurance and building officials. The NEHRP updating is carried out through the volunteer efforts of eleven technical committees drawn from these organizations.

Parallel and largely independent of the NEHRP/BSSC process, the Structural Engineers Association of California (SEAoC) continues to update its *Recommended Requirements*, and submits these to the International Congress of Building Officials for inclusion in the *UBC* editions published every three years. At this time the SEAoC and NEHRP currents do not show signs of further convergence. Both are described briefly in the following.

Regions of Moderate and Low Seismicity
Outside the areas of high seismicity an awareness has grown in the last decade that the potential of earthquake damage cannot be safely ignored. Worldwide this awareness has emerged in Northern European countries, such as the United Kingdom, in Hong Kong, Australia, and in eastern North America. Some of the concerns can be summarized as follows:
– For a risk level comparable to other hazards (wind, floods), what is the likelihood of extensive earthquake damage in the region?
– How does this risk level (expressed by the average return period for instance) compare to that deemed acceptable in regions of high seismicity?

– What can best be done to mitigate the hazard and damage (building code for new and/or old construction, post-earthquake planning for relief, repair, rescue, etc.), and at what cost to society?

– What is the chance that the risk estimates are badly wrong—too high? Too low? Can we build in sufficient resistance to protect against an under-estimate?

Where earthquakes occur comparatively often (California, Japan, etc.) it is known that the worst possible nearby earthquake (on the order of Richter magnitude 8) may generate ground motion at most 20 to 50 percent greater than what the code is based on. This is probably within the reserves provided by "ductile" detailing. In the moderate seismic regions, however, the code basis ground motions are less than half to a third of what may occur in a major earthquake (say of a Richter magnitude greater than 6) considered remotely possible near the site.

Such a situation is faced in New York City. Under such a condition it is clear that while the force levels for which buildings are designed can reflect the normally acceptable risk levels, there should be an equal or even greater resistance or toughness built into the structure than is called for in the regions of higher seismicity.

Uniform Building Code

The following brief description is intended as an overview and guide to the principles of the *UBC*. The reader is referred to the EERI Monograph by Glen Berg for a more detailed description and to the excellent code commentary published by the Structural Engineers Association of California headquarters in Sacramento, CA.

The "Earthquake Design" regulations of the 1991 *UBC* are organized as follows:

1. Criteria selection, including provisions for seismic zone, soil, occupancy, configuration, structural systems, height limits, selection of analysis procedure, and structural system limitations.

2. Design forces and effects, for most structures.

3. Dynamic lateral force procedures, for exceptional cases.

4. Lateral forces on structural elements and nonstructural components.

5. Detailed systems design requirements, referencing materials provisions and general framing requirements for connections, deformation compatibility, ties and continuity, and floor diaphragms.

6. Nonbuilding structures' provisions, which are brief and are intended to be used for uninhabited simple structures.

Design Basis and Equivalent Static Forces

The *UBC*, like all modern seismic codes, is based on the demonstrated fact that a properly detailed structure and building designed to forces well below those expected in a severe earthquake can survive that event and protect its occupants by dissipating the seismic energy through damping and ductile material yielding. When looking to compare the wind and seismic loads prescribed by the code, one should allow for this special aspect of seismic design. If a structure is to resist seismic loads the same way as wind loads are resisted, that is elastically and without the benefit of energy dissipation, then it must be designed for several times the code level seismic forces. Thus even when the code wind forces exceed those given for seismic effects, as is often the case in tall structures, seismic detailing requirements cannot be ignored.

The *UBC* provides a simple equation for calculating the base shear, as follows:

$$V = \frac{ZIC}{R_w} W \text{ where } C = \frac{1.25S}{T^{2/3}}$$

The factors are for the seismic zone (Z, with values between 0.075 and 0.40 over 5 seismic zones), for the importance of the building (I, either 1.25 or 1.0 for essential, hazardous high-occupancy structures and other structures), the soil (S, between 1.0 and 2.0), the structural system (R_w, where "w" is for working stress, between 4 and 12), and the period. The minimum value of C/R_w is 0.075. The empirical formula provided for calculating the period is the best fit to data measured mostly during the 1971 San Fernando earthquake. It reflects the contribution of all the building elements to the stiffness. The code limits how far the analyst can vary from these estimates using more "exact" methods of calculation, such as the Rayleigh method.

The weight W should include all the dead weight of the building as well as 25 percent of the contents weight of storage and warehouse structures, 10 pounds per square foot (psf) (48.8 kg per sq m) for partitions and ¾ of the snow load where it is greater than 30 psf (146.5 kg per sq m).

The base shear thus calculated is to be distributed over the height of the building according to the formula

$$F_x = \frac{(V\text{-}F_t)w_x h_x}{\Sigma(w_i h_i)} \text{ where } F_t = 0.07 \ TV$$

if T is greater than 0.7 sec, thereby providing for higher mode effects on long period structures. This vertical distribution resembles an inverse triangular distribution, and is meant to approximate the fundamental mode shape response.

In comparison, the Japanese code (AIJ) calculates the vertical distribution as:

$$Ai = 1 + \left(\frac{1 - a_i \sqrt{a_i}}{\sqrt{a_i}}\right) \times \frac{2T}{1 + 3T} \quad \text{where } ai = \times \frac{\Sigma\,(wi \text{ to top})}{\Sigma(wi)}$$

which results in a curved distribution shape that is arguably more accurate.

The horizontal distribution of seismic shear at each story depends on the flexibility of the floor diaphragm. It is generally assumed to be completely rigid unless a plywood sheathed floor or flexible metal deck is used. The story load is considered to act at the center of the story mass and any "natural" eccentricity from the center of rigidity of the vertical resisting elements (frames, walls, etc.) is accentuated by formula to cover accidental offsets.

The story drift is limited to between 0.04 or $0.03/R_w$ and 0.5 or 0.4 percent of the story height.

So-called P-Δ effects and possible vertical accelerations are considered as well.

Dynamic Analysis

The procedure for dynamic analysis is based on the response spectrum method, though time history analyses are permitted. The procedure includes guidelines for the derivation of a design response spectrum, to be based on 5 percent damping and a 475-year average return period. The code also provides a normalized spectrum for direct use.

Dynamic analysis is mandated in the zones of higher seismicity for tall (over 240 feet [73.2 m]) or irregular structures and those on soft (S_4) soils. Its use is also controlled by the requirement that the results be scaled to match the base shear calculated by the static method.

Material Detailing Requirements

Detailing requirements are provided in the code for all the systems given in the table of structural systems factor, R_w. These include masonry, wood, concrete, and steel provisions as well as regulations for foundations and retaining structures.

In general these requirements range from simple rules for systems not specifically designed for earthquakes (so-called "ordinary" systems) to detailed provisions for systems, such as steel eccentric braced frames, that have been designed for optimal ductility. Also included are the so-called "intermediate" systems that incorporate limited improvements to enhance "ductility" but fall short of the full measures. The list of systems and the corresponding detailing requirements reflect the need to evolve from existing structural types to improve their earthquake resistance at a reasonable cost, and to retain the fullest possible range of options. The improvements benefit from nearly forty years of experimental research worldwide as well as close observations of earthquake damage.

Throughout the material provisions, exceptions are given for elements or connections that can withstand forces equal to $3R_w/8$ times the design loads. This in effect gives a value to the anticipated maximum elastic demand on an element.

Nonstructural Elements Design

So-called "parts and portions" of structures, mechanical and electrical equipment and networks, and architectural elements such as cladding, partitions, ceilings, etc., must be rigidly secured for loads calculated from

$$F_p = ZIC_p\,W_p$$

where C_p is either 0.75 or 2.0 depending on the element, and is tabulated in the code. If the element is itself flexible (with a natural frequency below 16 Hz), it must be evaluated for the possibility of forces even greater than those above.

Elements, such as cladding, that are directly attached to the structure must be detailed to permit it to move unhindered. Allowing for the full inelastic displacement of the structure this means that joints must accommodate $3R_w/8$ times the calculated drifts.

Detailed requirements are also given for floor diaphragms, including a formula to calculate the force acting on it and guidelines for evaluating irregular shapes.

NEHRP Recommended Provisions

The 1991 NEHRP have been incorporated into the 1992 BOCA and are to be the basis of the *SBC* and *NBC*. The principles are similar to the *UBC*, with several important differences.

For a given site, the ground motion parameters A can be found on the Acceleration Maps. These correspond to a 475-year average return period (equivalent to 90 percent probability that the acceleration will not be exceeded in 50 years) and range from 0.05 to 0.40, i.e., 5 to 40 percent of gravity.

For a given building the code assigns an "exposure group" corresponding to whether it is essential (III), hazardous (II), or neither (I). The code then combines these into the "Seismic Performance" matrix as follows

Effective Peak Acceleration	Seismicity	Exposure Group		
		I	II	III
0.05	Low	A	A	A
0.05 to 0.10	Low	B	B	C
0.10 to 0.15	Moderate	C	C	C
0.15 to 0.20	Moderate	C	D	D
0.20 to 0.40	High	D	D	E
		Seismic Performance Categories		

The use of Performance Categories is unique to NEHRP and is intended to integrate the requirements for:
– structural framing systems, including height limits, interaction and compatibility effects,
– analysis procedure, in particular whether dynamic analysis is required for irregular configurations,
– detailing requirements, including those for the interconnection of parts of the building, including collectors, diaphragms, etc., and the design of foundations and of specific structural materials and systems,
– allowable story drift,
– architectural, mechanical and electrical components and systems, which are to be evaluated and secured to varying degrees depending on exposure and acceleration levels.

Equivalent Lateral Force Procedure
The seismic base shear equation is

$$V = \frac{1.2AS}{RT^{2/3}}$$

The factors represent the acceleration (A), the soil coefficient (S, varying between 1.0 and 2.0), the structure system (R, varying between 1.25 for unreinforced masonry to 8 for ductile moment frames) and the estimated period *(T)*.

As with the *UBC*, the values given for each factor are based on judgment, not exact science. For this reason the period estimate is therefore limited to that calculated by the empirical equation given times a factor C_a. Similarly the acceleration and soil factors can be less than would be determined from a direct assessment of specific local site conditions.

An upper limit on the base shear *V* is given by $2.5A/R$ which corresponds to the standard 2.5 spectral amplification derived from typical ground motion records, mostly from California. The 2/3rd power on the period sets the decay of *V* somewhat lower than is measured on typical response spectra, especially in moderate seismic zones where the decay is closer to $1/T$.

Unlike the *UBC* there is no minimum value for *V*.

The drift determination uses a factor C_d tabulated with the *R* factor for each structural system and having values between 1.25 and 6.5. Thus the drift is computed as:

$$\text{design story drift} = C_d \times \text{calculated drift,}$$

with a maximum allowable design drift of 1.5 percent in most cases. These drift limits are similar to those of the *UBC*.

Dynamic Analysis and Soil-Structure Interaction

The NEHRP includes an optional modal analysis procedure that closely parallels the format of the static procedure and requires that the base shears be scaled to match it.

An excellent and simple methodology for incorporating the effects of soil-structure interaction on the determination of design earthquake forces is provided in a separate chapter of the NEHRP. This will in most cases lead to a reduction of the calculated period, and correspondingly the forces, while magnifying displacement effects.

Detailing Requirements and Nonstructural Elements Design

The materials detailing requirements for the most part reference industry standards for wood, steel (AISC), concrete (ACI), and masonry (ACI).

The NEHRP chapter on architectural, mechanical, and electrical components and systems design is unchanged from the 1978 ATC-3 document. Equations are given separately for architectural and other components and are similar to the *UBC* formula except for the use of a performance factor *P* which increases from 0.5 to 1.5 with the assigned exposure group.

Proposed New York Seismic Code

Background

The 1982 edition of the ANSI A58.1 included a new seismic design section, modelled after the *UBC* and ATC-3, which moved New York City (NYC) from Seismic Zone 1 to 2. This in turn triggered the application of the ductile design provisions of the ACI-318 Code for concrete design. The NYC Building Commissioner asked the NY Association of Consulting Engineers (NYACE) for an opinion. The initial response, in the summer of 1984, was to recommend that such requirements be omitted. However, after some discussion, a group of seismologists and engineers was formed to review the issues and advise NYACE. The committee concluded that earthquakes with an intensity of about MM (Modified Mercalli) VII had occurred every 100 years in the NYC area and are likely to occur on average every 100 to 200 years. The seismologists stated that even larger magnitude and/or higher intensities, at very low levels of probability, could not be excluded. Following this the NYACE Board recommended to the Commissioner, in June 1987, that seismic design be mandated in NYC, and that the *UBC* should be followed.

During the same period, the National Center for Earthquake Engineering Research (NCEER) was established in Buffalo, NY. Several conferences were organized as a result which addressed the particular issues of seismic hazard and design in the eastern U.S. Following these, the Commissioner appointed in April 1989 a Seismic Code Committee to draft provisions for NYC. This committee included engineers, seismologists, and representatives of the building industries and real estate community. They submitted their final draft to the Commissioner in April 1991 and the Code is at present (1993) going before the NY City Council. The state is also reviewing the code for adoption.

Principles and Approach

The development of the NYC code was guided by several principles:
– to focus on provisions for the prevention of life-threatening collapse of buildings and components and not the protection of property,
– to seek improvements, not radical changes in construction practices,
– to modify the characterization of the loading to reflect local seismicity.

The committee's work consisted of preparing amendments to the provisions of the 1988 *UBC*. The following summarizes the changes as they were agreed. The *UBC* was selected after lengthy discussions for its technical content and because it was found easiest to adapt for NYC conditions.

Zonations and Soils

NYC is deemed to be in *UBC* Seismic Zone 2A with a factor, or effective zero period acceleration, of 0.15 in S_1 type rock. The soils are classified with reference to the NYC classification system. A new soil type S_0 is introduced, for hard rock, with a factor of 0.67. The Massachusetts code provisions for evaluating soil liquefaction potential are included.

Loads and Systems

The equivalent static lateral force procedure is accepted for all buildings, including irregular buildings of any height. However, the designer is encouraged to consider dynamic analysis for especially irregular or tall buildings.

The *UBC* requires that dual systems of walls or braced frames acting together with moment frames possess at minimum the capacity for moment frames to carry 25 percent of the lateral load on their own. The NYC Seismic Code adds the provision that the walls or braced frame should have sufficient shear capacity to carry 75 percent of the cumulative story shear at any level.

Separation between buildings is limited to 1 inch (2.5 cm) for every 50 feet (15.2 m) of total building height. Thus a building 400 feet (121.9 m) tall would, at the typical 120-foot (36.6-meter) zoning setback elevation, be separated by 8 inches (20.3 cm) from the adjacent building. The provision notes that "smaller separation may be permitted when the effects of pounding can be accommodated without collapse of the building."

Several new structural systems were added to the R_w list:
— ordinary concrete moment-resisting frames, limited to sites with soils S_0 to S_2 and under 160 feet (48.8 m) in height, and
— dual systems combining concrete and reinforced masonry shear walls and braced frames with "Special," "Intermediate," and "Ordinary" moment-resisting frames.

Detailing

The ACI 530-88 *Building Code Requirements for Masonry Structures* has been used as reference standard except that:

– All masonry bearing and shear walls must be reinforced, regardless of whether they are designed as reinforced or unreinforced walls. Maximum spacing of vertical bars is 10 feet (3.0 m).

– All nonbearing backup or infill walls and nonbearing partitions must have minimum one-way-only reinforcement to their supports.

The ACI 318-89 concrete code is referenced without modifications.

The 1988 *UBC* requirements of Section 2723 for steel are referenced without major modifications. The use of LFRD (Load Factor and Resistance Design) is prohibited for the design of seismic resisting elements.

The AITC and APA timber provisions for seismic design of plywood or other diaphragms and shear walls are referenced.

Nonstructural Elements

UBC Table 23-P is revised for nonbearing walls so that only those around means of egress are to be designed and secured for the specified lateral forces.

Provisions for interior components (e.g., access floors, ceilings, etc.) have been eliminated. Exterior appendages, chimneys, stacks, trussed towers, tanks on legs, and exterior tanks and vessels are to be designed for seismic effects.

Lessons From Other Seismic Codes

Mexico—Microzonation

Since the July 1957 Mexico City earthquake, that city has included in its Federal District Building Code pronounced variations in required loads for structures located in either the "hilly" (Zone I), so-called "transition zone" (II) or lake bed (III). The September 1985 earthquake confirmed with devastating effect that "local soil effects on earthquake characteristics in the valley of Mexico are dramatic." (Rosenblueth 1987). The code was modified to further differentiate the loading requirements both in magnitude and spectral shape. One can drive along the Reforma and pass within minutes between zones with required design forces differing by a factor of 4.

During the 1989 Loma Prieta earthquake the ground motion intensity varied by a factor of 4 or even 6 within the affected cities. Whereas the "input" base rock motion was relatively mild, the overlying soft soils substantially amplified the motion at ground level. In places like Boston or New York, where deep deposits of clay or fill exist, one can foresee that even low level base rock motion could be extremely damaging. One can imagine a soft soils site in New York shaking with greater intensity in a moderate earthquake than a firm site in Los Angeles in a more severe one.

"Microzonation" will undoubtedly become more commonplace in seismic codes. However, as Whitman has observed:

"... paradoxically the primary general principle that should govern 'microzonating' is that one should not, if at all possible, establish zones! Boundaries across which there is a step change in requirements are almost certain to lead to trouble as regards to both adoption and compliance. One can understand the difficulties that arise if requirements differ on opposite sides of the same street or within a block. There may be exceptional cases where soil conditions do change abruptly, such as at the edges of a steep-sided valley."

New Zealand—Capacity Design

A most compelling philosophy of earthquake engineering design is that known as "capacity design." This approach originated in New Zealand. In the words of two of its promulgators (Park & Paulay 1975):

"Since it is impossible to accurately predict the characteristics of the ground motions that may occur at any given site, it is impossible to evaluate the complete behavior of a reinforced concrete multistory frame when subjected to very large seismic disturbances. However, it is possible to impart to the structure features that will ensure the most desirable behavior. In terms of damage, ductility, energy dissipation, or failure, this means a desirable sequence in the breakdown of the complex chain of resistance in a frame. It implies a desirable hierarchy in the failure mode of the structure. To establish any sequence in the failure mechanism of a complex chain, it is necessary to know the strength of each link. This knowledge must not be based on safe assumptions or dependable capacities but realistically on the most probable deformations during a catastrophic earthquake.

"In spite of the probabilistic nature of the design load or displacement pattern to be applied to the structure, in the light of present knowledge, a deterministic allocation of strength and ductility properties holds the best promise for a successful response and the prevention of collapse during a catastrophic earthquake. This philosophy may be incorporated in a rational capacity design process. In the capacity design of earthquake-resistant structures, energy-dissipating elements of mechanisms are chosen and suitably detailed, and other structural elements are provided with sufficient reserve strength capacity, to ensure that the chosen energy-dissipating mechanisms are maintained at near their full strength throughout the deformations that may occur."

Japan—Static Pushover and Time History Analysis
All high-rise structures in Japan (taller than 196.9 ft [60 m]) are designed using an equivalent static procedure and checked using a two-step inelastic time history analysis. The analysis and the detail design documents are reviewed by the High-rise Building Structure Review Committee of the Building Center of Japan of the state before the building is allowed to proceed.

The computer analysis procedure is straightforward and has served well as a benchmark against which many designs have been evaluated:
– First a computer model, usually two-dimensional, is subjected to a stepwise increasing monotonic or "pushover" lateral load, applied in a pattern that simulates the actual dynamic loading (e.g., inverted triangular or Japanese "Ai" shape). From this a load-displacement curve is drawn for each story of the structure and fitted to a trilinear approximation.
– Using these trilinear resistance curves to model each story stiffness, and viscous "dashpots" to include the damping effects, a lumped mass "stick" model is developed for the building as a whole. This effectively reduces the number of degrees of freedom of the building to one per story.
– At least two complete time history analyses are run for the model using at minimum the El Centro 1940 NS, Taft 1952 EW, or Hachinohe 1968 EW earthquake records.

The benefit of always using at least these same records is that over time the reviewers and designers learn to find the structural behavior patterns indicative of good or poor designs under a test which comes fairly close to being realistic and, thanks to the standardization of the procedure and the increasing economy of computing, at a reasonable cost.

Future Code Developments
Two important ATC activities under way in 1993 will influence the next generation of seismic code.
– ATC-33, the BSSC/FEMA/ASCE-sponsored development of provisions for the seismic retrofit of existing buildings, and
– ATC-34, the NCEER/ATC joint study of critical code issues, involving practicing engineers and academics.

In both cases, and in part due to the effects of the 1989 Loma Prieta earthquake, these undertakings are concentrating on a reevaluation of the purpose of seismic codes and the performance expected from their use. They will most likely include:

— microzonation, to account for soils effects, and spectral shapes that vary with zones for both equivalent static equations and dynamic analysis,

— two or three "levels" of design or limit states with corresponding expected performance requirements for the building and structure,

— refined practical dynamic and inelastic analysis methods for the analysis of these "levels" and using "capacity design" approaches,

— guidelines for the use of base isolation and energy-dissipating devices, and

— better accounting for the contribution and behavior of cladding and other "nonstructural" components.

References

American National Standards Institute. 1982. "American National Standard Building Code Requirements for Min Design Loads in Buildings and Other Structures. *Standard A58.1*. New York.

Applied Technology Council. 1978. *Tentative Provisions for the Development of Seismic Regulations for Building*. Washington.

Aoyama, H. 1981. Outline of Earthquake Provisions in the Recently Revised Japanese Building Code. *Bulletin of the New Zealand Nat Soc for EQ Engineering*, vol. 14, no. 2.

Architects Institute of Japan. 1986. *Building Standard Law*. Tokyo.

Berg, G. 1983. *Seismic Design Codes and Procedures*. EERI Monograph Series. Berkeley, CA.

Building Officials and Code Administrators International. 1990. *Basic Building Code*. Homewood, IL.

Building Seismic Safety Council. 1991. *NEHRP Recommended Provisions for the Development of Seismic Regulations for New Buildings.* Washington.

Commission of the European Committees. 1991. *Common Unified Rules for Structures in Seismic Region.* Draft Eurocode No. 8. Brussels.

Department of the Federal District. 1976. Construction Regulations for the Federal District. *Diario Official de la Federacion*. Mexico.

International Association for Earthquake Engineering. *Earthquake Resistant Regulations, a World List*. Tokyo.

International Conference of Building Officials. 1991. *Uniform Building Code*. Whittier, CA.

Ishiyama, Y. 1987. Comparison of Seismic Provisions of 1985 *NBC* of Canada, 1981 BSL of Japan, and 1985 NEHRP of the USA. *Proc 5th Canadian EQ Engr Conf*. Ottawa.

National Research Council. 1990. *National Building Code of Canada*. Ottawa.

Park, R., and T. Paulay. 1975. *Reinforced Concrete Structures*. Wiley, NY.

Rosenblueth, E. 1987. Engineering Regulations and the New Building Code. *The Mexico EQ–1985: Factors Involved and Lessons Learned*. ASCE. Ed. M. A. Cassaro and E. M. Romero. New York.

Seismology Committee, Structural Engineers Association of California. 1990. *Recommended Lateral Force Requirements and Commentary*. Sacramento, CA.

Southern Building Code Congress. *Southern Building Code*. Birmingham, AL.

Standards Association of New Zealand. 1992. *General Structural Design and Design Loadings For Buildings*. NE 4203 Wellington.

Whitman, R. 1985. Are the Soil Depositions in Mexico City Unique? In *The Mexico Earthquake*.

Time and Section Study

The exhibition *Thresholds/Santiago Calatrava: Structure and Expression* at The Museum of Modern Art this spring was important for the museum, the city, and the nation. Clearly, it is relevant in these times of debate about the so-called infrastructure. Also significant is the department of architecture and design's decision to show these magnificent examples after years of neglecting public works. Finally, it is a joy to anticipate Calatrava's beautiful proposal for completing the Cathedral of St. John the Divine (1991–).

This intelligent show presents nine projects, amazingly only a small portion of Calatrava's work of the last decade. Most concern transportation: two bridges, three stations, and a garage.

Santiago Calatrava is the heir of Felix Candela, father of the hyperbolic paraboloid (hypar) shell, and both are spiritual descendants of Antonio Gaudí. The hypar is a "ruled surface"–meaning that it can be defined by visualizing a series of straight lines drawn between skewed or curved boundaries. In Candela's shells these lines were the planks that formed the concrete. In Calatrava's work they are more often ribs, cables, or garage door slats, often drawn from a curve (the bridge arch) to a straight line (the bridge deck). The surface, often tensile or glass, is implied (in fact, the sketch of the Alamillo Bridge [1987–1992] exhibited shows clearly the surface tension meant for the cable plane). Along the surface the sections create a steady rhythm.

Movies are made up of frames that pass more quickly than the eye can see; conversely, a series of frames can suggest motion. Superimposed, such a series, like the chronophotographs of Etienne-Jules Marey, traces an arc of motion.

Calatrava has found a way to sculpt negative space to form a place and to regulate and denote the rhythm of movement through that place. As you drive, ride, or walk through these stations and bridges, you sense both a noble stance and a sure rhythm. It is no wonder then that he proved so effective in designing a sacred space.

The exhibition simply and consistently presents each project through models, drawings, and photographs. Construction documents and photographs, showing more of the process, would have been helpful, but the limited presentation allows one to understand and evaluate the work as a whole.

The catalogue offers a useful survey of the work, though the reproductions, especially of the drawings, could be better. Matilda McQuaid's introduction is one of the best essays I've read on Calatrava's work.

Critical Mass

When the materials of a nuclear device reach a critical mass, they explode. Mass is converted into energy and the remaining material has changed its nature. Critical mass is a threshold. The substance of stars continuously crosses this threshold and we live by the energy. Over time, the stars consume themselves in this process and die. Others elsewhere are created as an agglomeration of matter collects and reaches critical mass, or perhaps more accurately, critical density. At the cosmic scale, according to Lederman and Schramm: "The critical density is the boundary that separates the possible future histories of the universe. If the density is above its critical value, the gravitational pull of the universe upon itself will eventually stop the universe's current outward expansion and cause it to contract. This is known as the *closed* universe prediction. But if the density of the universe is below the critical point, the universe will continue to expand forever; this is known as an *open* universe." [1]

→ p. 148

At the scale of the individual building, this physical phenomenon has little application. By lateral extension, the concept is of interest in the tradition of morphology founded by D'Arcy Thompson in his 1917 work *On Growth and Form*. In this book, Thompson explains how the form of animals is constrained by gravity to a balance of size and self weight. Since the skeleton and muscles must be of a size adequate to support the animal's weight and since the critical factor is the cross-sectional area of its members, growth that increases volume and therefore weight will outstrip the corresponding growth of member area. In mathematical terms, since volume increases with size^3 but area with size^2 the volume cannot exceed what the area can support. There is a limit or threshold to animal size specific to each planet.

This limit is governed by gravity and the material strength of bones and muscle. In buildings, such growth is limited as well by material properties. Several examples are useful:

1. A steel cable, such as is used in bridge-building, will break under its own weight if it is hung over a length of 8 miles (12.9 km), assuming a sag of one tenth its

Published in *DAIDALOS* 61, September 1996, pages 74–75

length and a breaking strength of 1,300 million pascals, the current maximum available.

2. A vertical column (or building) made of the highest strength of steel available will crush itself at a height of 19,000 feet (5,791 m), provided it is braced (with guy wires, for example) against buckling.

The size limits on buildings are substantially greater than those constraining animal size. In reality, both are limited by the complex interactions of other factors (organs must fit, locomotion must be possible—even if, as with the brontosaurus, it is difficult). The thresholds are conceptual as complexity constrains reality. The beauty of D'Arcy Thompson's work is in its simplicity and, in my view, in the illusory causality it portrays. No form exists at its material limit. The requirements of complexity and evolution determine form with the bombardment of particulars, a process better modeled by the nonlinear dynamic metaphors of chaos theory.

A more tangible model is the ecological balance of innate structure (materials, transformational rules, elements) and environmental constraints and influences. Nuclear reactions can take place anywhere. The mechanics are direct and the elements, well, elementary. Buildings and animals exist at the scale of complexity (beyond the "edge of chaos," as Mitchell Waldrop describes it) where the simple models of physics are surpassed by the realities. Gigantism is a deformity. The fine balance and scale of the patterns and structures of interaction is the stuff of life.

1 Lederman, L. M., and D. N. Schramm. 1989. *From Quarks to the Cosmos*. New York

Each species is the distortion of another; how to quantify the critical mass that changes a Schinkel into a Saarinen? From: D'Arcy Thompson, *On Growth and Form*

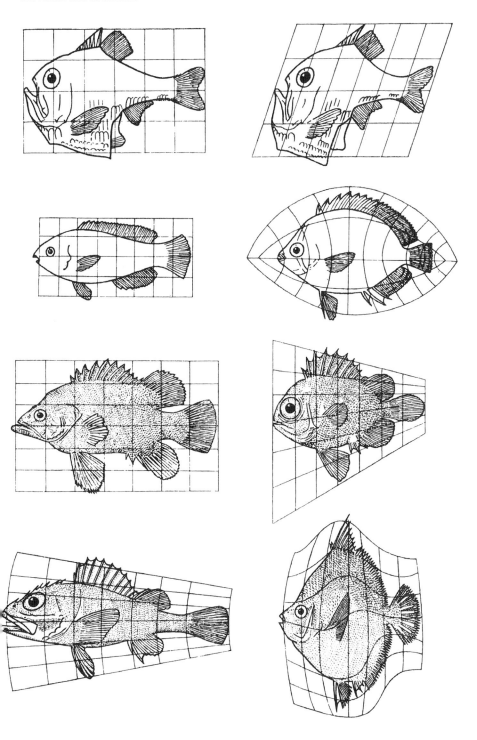

Ryoanji Temple, Kyoto, Japan, 1996

Light Construction Symposium

The Light Construction Symposium was held at Columbia University on September 22, 1995, following the opening of the exhibition Light Construction, *which was organized at The Museum of Modern Art by Terry Riley. My talk was in effect a reflection on reflection. As I had explored in "Notes on Light and Structure," at the time I was impressed by the connection between light scatter and material that is implied in some of Richard Feynman's writing and scientific work. Quantum Electrodynamics (QED, or the strange theory of light and matter) is a good ground for reflection on the potential material presence of light and vice versa. I remember Peter Rice talking about his effort to scatter light with lightweight structures, as for example in the roof he designed with I. M. Pei over the Richelieu wing in the Louvre, and it was then clear that this was an avenue many of the architects in the MoMA show were exploring.*

In the early 1970s, America was introduced to deconstruction via the works of, among others, Paul de Man and Harold Bloom—in particular, their books *Blindness and Insight* and *The Anxiety of Influence* respectively, through which many people were first exposed to the ideas of Jacques Derrida. This was the period during which Peter Eisenman's Institute for Architecture and Urban Studies was active, when Rem Koolhaas published his *Delirious New York*, and when the Vietnam War came to an end. I mention all this here to propose that we consider that the work which Terence Riley has put together in this exhibition has developed from seeds sown around that time. I believe that this is a body of work that closely reflects the ideas current at the time, and those of Derrida in particular. In his essay "Structure, Sign, and Play," presented at Johns Hopkins University in 1966, Derrida reviewed Levi-Strauss' works in detail and questioned the structuralist idea that totalization is impossible because the field of inquiry is too vast, rather than because, as Derrida argued, while the field is finite, it is elusive because of a lack of determined origin and its nature of constant play. Here, Derrida aligns himself with the critique of the Enlightenment—from Isaiah Berlin to Werner Heisenberg. If the Enlightenment was inspired by Newton's successes, our own era, not surprisingly, has undergone a sea of change as the consequences

Published in *Columbia Documents of Architecture and Theory*, 1997, pages 25–29

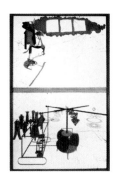

of the new sciences of relativity, quantum electrodynamics, and particle physics work their influence through culture.

This brings us back to the subject of light and construction, or light and matter. There is a wonderful book by the late physicist Richard Feynman called *QED: The Strange Theory of Light and Matter.* In a footnote Feynman points out that Heisenberg's principle of uncertainty is a vestige of determinism. If we accept the probabilistic nature of matter and light's interaction, then there is no problem of uncertainty. Rather, events are the product of probability amplitudes.

This is a difficult thing to accept and convey. Italo Calvino describes this world as one "of minute particles of humors and sensations, a fine dust of atoms like everything else that goes to make up the ultimate substance of the multiplicity of things."

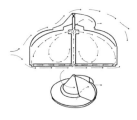

I would like to offer a few concepts about light that, from my perspective, are relevant to the exhibition. First, I propose that as "light" refers to the light of our sun, we are particularly interested in the strange facts of the interaction of light and matter. The light inside a building is radiated by the "matter" of construction. Light on glass sets off an interaction (scattering) and the glass emits a spectrum of light-energy. Light and matter or light and structure are always interacting, absorbing, emitting, and intermingling. Second, there is the lightness of bits, the universe of digital representation and the pattern of chaos revealed in the new telescope of the computer. This relates, of course, to chance, to Marcel Duchamp and John Cage and back to quantum physics. But most of all, it reveals the mysterious beauty and order of turbulence and upheaval. Third, there is that lightness championed by Buckminster Fuller. Fuller, our twentieth-century Emerson, promised in 1969 that "the ever-acceleratingly dangerous impasse of world-opposed politicians and ideological dogmas ... will be resolved by the computer." He identified and promoted that digital ephemeralization. For him, the lightest touch was best, as in Jean Prouvé's Tropical House and his own Dymaxion House. It is the lightness of nomads at home on Spaceship Earth. Fourth, and related to Fuller's ideas, there is a lightness of frugality. It is interesting to note that the visual imagery in many of the projects recalls the space and light of television and film.

If we consider the critic John Berger's description of perspectival space as a safe, and transpose it to television and computer media, we can perhaps better recognize the continuity that exists in the business of capturing and preserving wealth. Façades are still in the art and business of containing and projecting economic value. Perhaps instead, as in a Bedouin tent or Prouvé's Tropical House,

Marcel Duchamp, *The Bride Stripped Bare by Her Bachelors, Even*, 1915–1923
Time magazine cover, 1968
R. Buckminster Fuller, Fuller Dymaxion air circulation diagram, 1946
Jean Prouvé, Tropical House sketch, 1950
R. Buckminster Fuller, *Project for a Geodesic Dome over Midtown Manhattan*, 1962

our interest could extend not to the representation of wealth but to the preservation of commonwealth through building lightness and frugality. Fifth, and finally, there is the lightness of being. Think of Duchamp, Cage, Milan Kundera, and countless others.

In closing, I would like to recount a little Zen story called "No Water, No moon." When the nun Chiyono studied Zen under Bukko Engaku, she was unable to attain the fruits of meditation for a long time. At last, one moonlit night, she was carrying water in an old pail bound with bamboo. The bamboo broke and the bottom fell out of the pail. At that moment, Chiyono was set free. In commemoration, she wrote a poem:

In this way and that I tried to save
the old pail
since the bamboo strip was
weakening and about to break,
until at last, the bottom fell out.
No more water in the pail.
No more moon in the water!

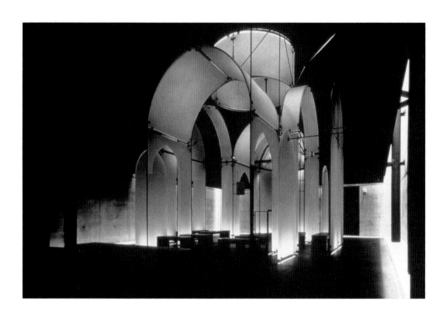

Byzantine Fresco Chapel, Houston, Texas, by Francois de Menil

Notes on Light and Structure

"It is as though space, cognizant here more than any place else of its inferiority to time, answers it with the only property time doesn't possess: with beauty."
Joseph Brodsky

Scatter

A number of years ago, Peter Rice, in describing the design of the Louvre courtyard roofs, emphasized that I. M. Pei's intent was to "scatter" the light with the sunshades and structure so that no distinct shadows would fall on the sculptures below. At the time, I was reading the physicist Richard Feynman's work and was struck by Rice's use of the term. In the language of Feynman's physics, quantum electrodynamics (QED), for which, along with Schwinger and Tomonaga, Feynman won the Nobel Prize, "scatter" has a precise meaning. Photons are scattered by the electrons in the atoms that make up a material like glass; light does not always pass *through* glass. Some photons are scattered by the electrons in the glass and *new* photons are emitted. Many of the photons (up to 16 percent) return in the direction of the incoming light, which gives the phenomenon of partial reflection. Other photons are scattered about within the glass and interact with electrons to emit photons to the far side. The rest and majority of the photons sail through the thin sea of electrons without interaction at all.

What is striking is that at this most fundamental level the passage of light is a matter of interactions as well as transparency, that matter absorbs and emits. Transparency is thus a matter of degree and probabilities. It is indefinite. Indeed, photons will even pass through steel, only fewer make it past the denser sea of electrons. So Rice's remark was particularly relevant. The many transparent structures he helped to develop, especially in his French work (at La Villette, the Louvre roofs and inverted pyramid, and the Charles de Gaulle and Lille train stations), are all in this sense essays in the interaction of light and matter, fugues on Feynman's theory. Consider the diffusion in the Charles de Gaulle station of the structure into layers of mullion and girt, framing, arch and truss webbing and poles, which you enter into as you descend the escalator. Or the scatter vessel of the Inverted Pyramid at the Louvre. It is as if Rice had materialized the light in a kind of structural fog.

Taking Feynman's theory one step further, it is interesting to consider what the probabilistic mathematics of QED imply in this context. In his lay exposition *QED: The Strange Theory of Light and Matter*, Feynman beautifully explains how "real" events are the collection of innumerable possible related events, each with its own probability amplitude. Without going into detail (which is in any case far better done in his book), the explanation of the interactions of light (photons) and matter (electrons) can be obtained by a careful listing of possible photon and electron paths and the vector summation of their probability amplitudes. Feynman dispenses with the wave/particle duality. The *camera obscura*, inter-ference patterns, or reflection and refraction indices are all accountable by tracing the possible "individual" photon paths: from the light source, off that building, scattered by this material, and through the hole, or straight through, etc. In each case, a description is obtained (though never a determined outcome) of the probable event or pattern.

What better metaphor than Feynman's explanation of light and matter in these places of transit and meandering—museum, airport, or rail-port—where people ebb and flow, waiver, enter, and depart: a frame for *passants et lumière*.

Minima

Long before Rice participated in the French projects, he was involved in a project in Germany, which in certain respects prefigures these last works. This was the Federal Garden Exhibition building in Mannheim (1975) by Frei Otto. I believe that this building came about when Otto was given the opportunity to design a greenhouse and chose to break from his other obsessions with minimal surfaces (soap film) and "tensile" structures to design a compressive surface. Clearly there are connections to Gaudí's studies for the Sagrada Familia and perhaps (although I am not certain of the precedence relations) Heinz Isler's free shell designs. Otto contacted Ove Arup (who was in partnership with Ronald Jenkins), already well established as a wizard of shell structures, to collaborate on the project. Arup apparently asked Ted Happold's team, of which Rice was a member, to work on the project.

Both Otto's and, later, Happold and Rice's interest in lightweight structures ran parallel to the interest at the time in ephemera, structures such as Buckminster

Fuller's dome and Otto's fabric designs, which tread lightly; nomadic designs that would leave no trace or harm.

The shapes in tensile structures approximate the minimal surfaces of soap films held in frames. (Charles and Ray Eames' elegant exhibition *Mathematica*, in which a small soap-film cube was suspended in a wire frame cube, springs to mind.) For a given boundary the form spans the smallest surface, minimizing the energy of surface tension.

Large structures, however, carry variable, transient loads besides their own, light weight, and unlike soap films require additional external prestress to retain their shape. Where the transient loads of wind and snow are light, as in Mediterranean and tropical climates, nomadic structures are, of course, fine, and fabric, as well as thin shell structures, thrive (as, for example, in Candela's work). But elsewhere, in the north, the additional prestress means overall increases in mast, cable, fabric, and especially foundation sizes. Otto's Munich Stadium, for example, is lightweight overhead but large in mast and particularly foundation, below the masts, and especially to anchor the cables.

"Form-finding" for membrane structures follows from singular load and boundary patterns. The stories told always suggest the optima or minima of simple and determinable mathematical solutions. To a generation of engineering designers the object was the close match of form and formula, and, indeed, the appeal is strong.

Light weight
Ted Happold and Peter Rice helped found a lightweight structures group at Arup's, on the strength of the lessons learned working with Frei Otto. They also helped establish a tradition that, along with the heritage of Buckminster Fuller's work, was taken forward by Norman Foster and Michael Hopkins, among others. In a sense, the dialectic between this notion of light weight (how much your building weighs) and the elaborations necessary to accommodate the contingencies of environmental and programmatic pressures might be reviewed according to Henri Focillon's categories of experimental, classic, refinement, and baroque phases in the "life of forms." There is no question that Frei Otto, Ted Happold, and Peter Rice saw their work as experimental.

The encounter of the concepts of minima or optima with the complexities and probabilistic workings of nature invariably results in hybrid or multivalent works.

A great modern example of this is Maillart's deck-stiffened arch bridges. Whether this idea is expressed, as I believe it is in Peter Rice's later projects, or suppressed, as it is in the thin shell works of the architect-engineers of the 1950s and Frei Otto's Munich Stadium, is a matter of design choice.

A recent project may help to illustrate this: the U.S. Air Canopy, an Arup collaboration with Smith-Miller + Hawkinson in New York. This project came about as a result of the corporate identity program undertaken by Continental Airlines, the original tenants for the building, a terminal at LaGuardia Airport in New York City. Designed by Nicholas Bodouva, it consists of a large hangar-like glass hall with concourses to the aircraft gates. The plan is about 98 × 394 feet (30 × 120 m) and the hall about 65.5 feet (20 m) tall. A requirement of Bodouva's design was for a shade canopy over the ticket counters to allow the agents to see their CRT computer monitors. The canopy design was assigned to Smith-Miller + Hawkinson as part of their work on the systemwide airline ticket counter and gate area design. With the support of an enlightened client, we decided to use composites for the canopy shell, and glass and metals for the balance. This represented a first application of advanced composites on an architectural project in the U.S. and was made possible in part by the interior use, shielded from harmful ultraviolet rays. The shells are sandwich panels with top and bottom epoxy skins about 0.04 inches (1 mm) thick and a 0.7-inch (18 mm) composite (Nomex) honeycomb core. They are entirely handmade to zero tolerances. This is similar to the construction of composite elements in aircraft and racing yachts. The epoxy is reinforced with glass and carbon fibers arranged in layers of prefabricated "tape" laid according to the stress patterns, on a mold, and cured in an autoclave. The shells weigh one kilogram per 10.7 square feet (1 sq m), about a quarter of the weight of an equivalent thickness of plywood. Their specific strength and stiffness (per unit density) is more than 20 times that of wood or steel.

The shells are integrated in the structure as the top chord of the trusses. These trusses span 32.8 feet (10 m) between column lines. The truss web is made of stainless-steel cables in the front and mild steel bars in the back, for transparency, and the bottom chord is a mild steel plate to accommodate lights and LED signage. The trusses end in triangular glass plates that are held off the columns by a stainless-steel strut and cables. All the connections are machined parts, articulated to prevent stress concentrations and achieve the required zero tolerances.

The structure is lightweight in fact but also in effect since the shells appear to float on the lighting. The light weight in this example is the product of an assembly and integration of separate and distinct elements in a hybrid whole. Instead of portraying lightness as the minimum of a complex equation, the design suspends the parts in the solution. It is the difference between determinate and indeterminate, in the general and specific structural sense. Where the Cartesian dream is a singular total, this represents instead a multivalent reality. After all, a lesson of modern physics has been the irresolution of dualities, including wave-particle, mindbody, and so on (actually, the dualities dissolve into multiplicity). As Feynman shows, uncertainty is not a problem but the reality itself. Nature is the restless interaction of elements according to distinct rules of probability; descriptions and prediction are readily achieved provided we accept, with Feynman, this quantum nature and the suspension of events in the space-time continuum of indeterminacy. Rather than repress this by simulation determinacy I would argue that the best work, in closer tune with our modern condition and knowledge, is the portrayal of interaction, and consequently of continual formation.

Tubes

Television tubes, monitors, and CRTs are ubiquitous. Electron beams display and discover, etch chips, and transmit information. The path of electrons and photons, at the particle scale, is itself a shaft of possible paths. The light projected from here to there is a cascade of photons finding their way. As Feynman explains in QED, our statements about light (optics, etc.) are aggregations of event or path probabilities. His explanation of mirages is an excellent illustration:

"Another phenomenon of light that I would like to mention briefly is the mirage. When you're driving along a road that is very hot, you can sometimes see what looks like water on the road. What you're really seeing is the sky, and when you normally see sky on the road, it's because the road has puddles of water on it (partial reflection of light by a single surface). But how can you see sky on the road when there's no water there? What you need to know is that light goes slower through cooler air, than through warmer air, and for a mirage to be seen, the observer must be in the cooler air that is above the hot air next to the road surface. How it is possible to look down and see the sky can be understood by finding the path of least time. I'll let you play with that one at home – it's fun to think about, and pretty easy to figure out."

It is fascinating how contemporary architecture is in numerous ways exploring the spatial and visual effects of screens and shafts. The recent show at MoMA organized by Terence Riley, *Light Construction,* displayed this eloquently. From Rem Koolhaas' many illuminated screens of glass, façades, and ceilings,

to recent Japanese work, Harry Wolf's project for ABN-AMRO in Amsterdam and Steven Holl's DE Shaw offices and Helsinki MoCA there are many examples of flat-screen displays of virtual form and light projections.

The advent of "tubes" is an interesting and related development. On the one hand, they appear in the use of light shafts, as in the skylights to the Richelieu wing of the Louvre which channel light in mylar-lined corridors to the galleries' overhead baffles. They also appear in the building forms adopted recently for projects such as Renzo Piano's Kansai Airport and Steven Holl's Helsinki MoCA. These later projects seem to have emerged with Piano's Bercy Shopping Center and Valode and Pistre's L'Oréal headquarters. In both these cases the form is a toroidal shape generated by spinning a plane curve about a large radius. Peter Rice again had a strong hand in both projects. However, the culmination is clearly seen in the later projects of Renzo Piano, Steven Holl, Toyo Ito, and Enrique Norten (the Televisa Cafeteria in Mexico City). In all cases the form creates a new kind of compressed horizontality. In Piano's Kansai Airport the design is, of course, inspired by the shape of an aircraft wing but also resolves his sectional design approach effectively by closing the form in a novel way.

Tube space in this sense is a kind of compressed sky bowl. The space between sky and earth is thereby captured and secured. The horizon is brought inside and consequently the inside is made to feel not quite interior. The structure of these projects is generally subsumed in the toroidal form, like the construction of ship and aircraft forms, faired to the stations of equally spaced ribs. Thus there is no frame, no Cartesian referent. Instead, these works allude to the bent space of Reimann geometry.

The frame is externalized, like the box around a television and monitor tube, and rendered virtual. This recalls the relationship between frame and surface of Otto's soap films or the Eames' cube. Or, even further, from the field of visual art, the frame/form relationship of Giacometti's paintings *(Genet*, 1955, or *Yanaihara*, 1961) and cage sculptures (*La Cage*, 1950; *Le Nez*, 1947; *Suspended Ball*, 1930). In these works the space between the form and cage invites the viewer to consider the space within the form and invert this space and the caged space outside.

Perhaps the most powerful recent architectural evocation of Giacometti has been Koolhaas' project for the Bibliothèque de France where the space in between the cage or box and forms is partially solidified into the structural walls devised by Arup's Cecil Balmond. In all these cases the effect is a spatial inversion that

Glass roofs at the Richelieu wing of the Louvre

invites us to consider the enclosure as a kind of atmosphere, which actually or artificially scatters light and "ephemeralizes" structure.

Form lines

What is the space within a wire frame? Or inside the densely drawn heads of Giacometti's heads? A recently completed project by Francois de Menil, the Houston Fresco Chapel, comes to mind. The project houses two frescoes recovered from a Greek Orthodox chapel in Northern Cyprus. De Menil's design is a concrete box with a steel, column-supported roof "lid." Nestled just inside is a liner to create a perimeter skylight, inside of which is a glass and steel rod rendering of the original chapel. This "glass chapel" hangs like a necklace between the roof and floor. The lines of the steel rods are suspended between a dark ceiling and a floor lit from below through slits cut along the outline of the glass chapel plan. The "ground" floor is, in fact, suspended framing over a plenum delivering the conditioned air through this and the perimeter slot. The effect is remarkable, almost as if the space were zero gravity "outer" space. The sharp lines of light below and above are of almost equal intensity so that the glass chapel seems to float like an ideogram. The glass panels within the steel frame are sandblasted and radiant. Thus not only has the original stone chapel been transformed into a masonry of light, but the structure itself is in suspension between a dark heaven and lit ground – between an ideogram and the line form of Giacometti's heads.

Space lies between the whirl of electrons and the paths of photons. There was a time when space was drawn between the points of stars in constellations and woven from the astronomy of the Pre-Socratics to the mechanics of Newton and Kepler. Line became orbit and bond, from Bohr's atom to chemical diagrams; with quantum mechanics and Feynman's QED they dissipated into the whirls and paths of probability. It is no wonder that the lines of structure and shafts of light are now intermingling in what Vito Acconci has aptly described as this "real virtuality."

Built Value and Earthquake Risk

This paper consists of two parts. The first is a historical review which should provide some introduction to the provisions that are in the new Local Law 17, Seismic Code for New York City, and how they came to be there. The second part is an attempt to suggest some ways that we can go from here with building design and, in general, to mitigate seismic risk for New York City.

The New York City Seismic Code

The development of seismic provisions for New York City started in 1984 or 1985 around the time of the Mexico City earthquake. Over the years since then, there have been a number of different groups, starting with the evaluation of the necessity for seismic provisions in New York City to the formation of a committee by the NYC Building Department to write those provisions (see NYACE, 1986; Nordenson, 1987). Two very important elements in encouraging that process were the formation of NCEER in 1986, and a conference organized in 1988 by Klaus Jacob and Carl Turkstra at the New York Academy of Sciences. Proceedings are available from the Academy.

The origin of concern in New York City was a map published in 1982 as part of the *American National Standard Institute Guidelines for Loads for Building Construction*. It placed New York City, along with Boston, in Seismic Zone 2. This led to a question from the building department to the engineering community asking whether we should, in fact, worry about earthquake risk. That concern was raised around August of 1984. A group came together, including Klaus Jacob and others from Lamont-Doherty Earth Observatory. The conclusions that we came up with were that, in fact, the history of New York City seismicity, as Klaus Jacob has noted, indicated MMI intensity levels of about VII once every hundred to two hundred years, and that, surely enough, we could expect the same pattern in the future. In fact, it could be that we would have earthquakes of even larger intensities or magnitudes, on the order of Richter magnitude

Published in *Economic Consequences of Earthquakes: Preparing for the Unexpected,*
edited by Barclay G. Jones, Buffalo, New York, January 1997, pages 167–74

5.75 to 6.75 and perhaps even higher. One of the conclusions which was significant at the time was that, as a result, New York City was in a similar situation to Boston, which had had earthquake provisions in its code since 1975 (see also Nordenson and Statton, 1986, Nordenson, 1987, and Reaveley and Nordenson, 1990).

A further question that then came up was whether we should worry about seismic design since we design buildings in New York City (or at least have for the last thirty-odd years) to resist substantial wind loads. Some thought that this practice would give buildings enough resistance to withstand the kind of earthquake that we were considering. There were a number of studies, including one by Weidlinger Associates (1984), which correlated, on the basis of building density and other parameters, the equivalent wind resistance and seismic resistance. The conclusion was uniformly that there really is no correlation between the two. One way to think about it is to consider the New York City buildings that are long and narrow, including some high-rise structures. Those that were built in the 1930s and 1940s actually rely on the masonry cladding frame infill for wind resistance. There is a significant asymmetry between the resistance of the buildings in the broad direction and narrow directions, which would result in considerable difference in seismic resistance since the earthquake is the same load on the building in both cases (see also Nordenson and Jing, 1988).

The reality of the hazard was confirmed at the time and the New York City seismic code committee was established around April of 1989. In that year, the Loma Prieta earthquake occurred. A delegation from the committee went out to San Francisco to assess the damage. Since the ground motions in San Francisco and Oakland were very similar to those we were considering as the design basis earthquake for New York City, this trip proved quite informative. The damage that we saw there was a good indication of what we would see in New York City in the event of the earthquake that we were considering for our code.

When we came back from San Francisco, we had reached a number of conclusions, some of which were fairly obvious. The structures designed according to seismic codes had, in fact, performed well, as had older structures on firm soil. The ground motions in San Francisco and Oakland, which you will remember were about 60 miles (96.5 km) away from the epicenter, were similar to what we were considering for New York City, in both amplitude and duration. Soil effects proved significant.

We went on to develop the code further. Some of the issues that we were considering were: the kinds of ground motions to anticipate, and whether it was appropriate to use the 500-year return period or a longer return period window given the seismicity in the eastern United States, and what would be the difficulty and the cost of implementing these provisions. We decided to focus our attention in the code only on new buildings and life safety, and remove any provisions that we felt were included to protect property. It was felt by the committee, which consisted of thirty-five people from a broad section of the community, including the real estate sector, that their job was not to protect property, but to protect lives and prevent building collapse.

The other thing that we wanted to focus on was how to improve local construction practice and not try to impose construction practices that had been developed in other parts of the country on the trades and contractors in New York City if that was not necessary. We had a number of different groups involved: Klaus Jacob was involved in our geotechnical group, Joseph Kelly from the Port Authority led the group considering loads, Mohammed Ettouney from Weidlinger Associates led the group considering detailing, Irwin Cantor ran a group that looked at economic implications, and Deborah Beck of the Real Estate Board was responsible for the nonstructural provisions that were implemented in the code.

One of the big discussions that we had at the time, which was 1989–1990, was whether we should be basing our code on the *Uniform Building Code* or on the *NEHRP* provisions. There was quite a lot of debate over this, and in the end, actually shortly after our visit to Loma Prieta, the committee's decision was to base it on the 1988 *Uniform Building Code* provisions. I think that view will probably evolve in time. In terms of our zonation, we came up with a seismic zone factor of 15% gravity horizontal acceleration for a type S_1 rock. We invented a new concept that has now been implemented nationally by introducing an east coast rock factor into the equation and that is our S_0 factor of 0.67 for hard rock in New York City. We also increased the soil factor for soft soils. We implemented requirements for liquefaction which are unique at this point in the country outside of Boston. We have a requirement in our code that a site susceptible to liquefaction be carefully studied, and that mitigating provisions be included in the design of the building foundations.

The code allows for specific response spectra to be developed for individual sites, requiring, however, that they always be scaled to correspond to the minimum level required by the code spectrum. In building design, we incorporated consideration of the structural configuration and recognition that in irregular conditions there will be stress concentrations which can lead to damage and, in some cases, collapse. Pounding was, and continues to be, a controversial topic. The requirements in the *Uniform Building Code* are that buildings be separated by a gap that is on the order of 1.5 percent of the height of the structure. That was not going to be an acceptable arrangement for New York City, so we developed compromise provisions which highlighted that what we were concerned with was life safety, rather than protection against property damage. We allowed for rational evaluation of required building separation as well if further reduction was desired. The different structural systems that we developed as additions to the menu that is already in the various model codes included recognition of the kind of flat-plate construction that we see in a lot of our apartment buildings and accommodation of various other systems. We required that all nonbearing wall masonry, such as the cladding on apartment buildings, be reinforced. We also made some significant modifications to the provisions for nonstructural elements. The focus was on life safety and in particular on the safety of the means of egress (see Nordenson and Jing, 1988).

Finally, there were a number of economic studies done to evaluate the impact of our provisions. A study conducted by Weidlinger Associates to evaluate the cost impact of the provisions on new buildings showed that the cost increases would be somewhere between 0.5 percent and 3 or 4 percent of the total cost of the building, depending on the type of building.

Future Directions

Going to the second part of my presentation, I would like to focus on what we should be doing from here. I think that our task now is to try to integrate our understanding of the consequences of earthquakes, through scenario studies, so that we can understand in advance what the likely consequences of an earthquake in New York City would be and what selective interventions would be appropriate. I would like to propose five different areas of future development.

The first has to do with microzonation and damage estimation, an area discussed by Charles Scawthorn. There are several soil types in New York City. We can take this kind of information and overlay it with our knowledge of the inventory of built structures and try to evaluate, on an aggregate and local level, the likely consequences of various scenario earthquakes, say 5.5 or 6 magnitude events at suitable distances. I think that, based on this, we will be able to estimate the levels of ground motions on the different soils and correlate that with our understanding of what is there. We have enough knowledge to do a good job on that, and Scawthorn has done a lot of this already. Other studies by Dr. Stephanie King of Stanford University use geographic information systems effectively to integrate various databases of information about the nature of the ground and building inventory. There is a need to develop a good consensus-based scenario event for New York City that can give us some picture of what kind of probable damage we are going to get, loss of function and so on, so that we can begin to assess the areas where that damage is going to be concentrated and focus our attention there. Until we do that, we are going to be concerned, in some cases unduly, with certain facilities and not able to see the problem in a larger context. I would think that this sort of effort would be something that could proceed on the basis of a public/private partnership.

My second suggestion is that we should start to think about forming a seismic planning commission for the State of New York that would begin to pull together some of these studies and various pieces of information so that we can start to both evaluate and modify, if necessary, our post-earthquake response plans. I know that there are a number of plans in place, but I think that we should reevaluate them and make sure that everybody concerned knows about them and perhaps even run through some rehearsals. We should also identify critical facilities that need to be upgraded. I think that we will find that some of our facilities are just fine the way they are, and that we can concentrate our attention and monies on the few particular facilities that are shown to be quite vulnerable. We saw earlier that once you integrate all the different types of hazards you may find that there are only two, three, or four facilities that need immediate attention.

My third point is that we need to *continue* to integrate our efforts with those at the federal level. Theodore Algermissen makes what I think is a very good point in his paper on earthquake hazard assessment, that it is important to look at our hazards and our needs in the national context and understand whether, in fact, the risks represented by earthquakes in New York City are of a greater or lesser significance when compared with the risks in other parts of the country. The point has been made over the years that, given that the felt area for an earthquake in the east is much larger, the risk is much greater here than in the west. Those points need to be continually reevaluated and considered. I think as far as our building code is concerned, we need to start to integrate our own code here in New York City with the national codes.

Fourth, I think that we have to pay a great deal of attention to education and perhaps to licensing requirements for engineers. In California and other states, the seismic design of certain kinds of facilities or tall buildings must be done by structural engineers whose qualifications are above and beyond the existing qualifications for professional engineers. That has the advantage of enforcing a level of education among the profession that is, I think, quite beneficial. These people simply know more about earthquake engineering, and the kinds of issues that are discussed in these papers about comparing different evaluations of hazards are put in a much sounder educational context.

Finally, I think that we need to accelerate the testing and implementation of a variety of protective systems, including mechanical devices for energy dissipation, base isolation devices, and so on, which promise, in many instances, to provide a very economical way of significantly reducing potential damage. I was involved just recently in a study for a facility in New York and it was pretty apparent that for a small initial investment one could substantially reduce the likely cost impact of an earthquake on an important facility.

Concluding Remarks

In conclusion, I would like to go back to my title: "Built Value and Earthquake Risk." When I was thinking about this paper, and the question addressed by these proceedings of what might happen to financial institutions on Wall Street in an earthquake, I wondered whether, in fact, that needs to be our main area of concern. I think that in most instances, financial data can be stored off site. My impression is that after the 1993 World Trade Center bombing, some of the markets and institutions that are located there were able to move and resume operations quite quickly. I think that our greatest concern should be with the values that transcend economic measures. It seems to me that it is the "social fabric" we need to be concerned with. I remember here that at the conference in 1988, Dr. Robert Ketter, who help found NCEER, spoke about this very issue, worrying about historical examples of the political fallout of earthquakes (Nicaragua, China, etc.). I think it is the social fabric that is most vulnerable here, as well as our cultural heritage. We should think about our museums and think about the art that is in New York City and how we can protect them in the event of an earthquake. To me, that is our built value, it is what distinguishes the city, and is what we should be concentrating our attention on preserving.

Algermissen, S. T. 1997. Some Problems in the Assessment of Earthquake Hazard in the Eastern United States. *Economic Consequences of Earthquakes: Preparing for the Unexpected*: 167–74.

Jacob, Klaus. 1997. Scenario Earthquakes for Urban Areas Along the Atlantic Seaboard of the United States. *Economic Consequences of Earthquakes: Preparing for the Unexpected*

Nordenson, Guy J. P. 1987. Some Limitations of Current Seismic Codes for Eastern U.S. Earthquake Resistant Design, *Proceedings of the Symposium on Seismic Hazards, Ground Motions, Soil Liquefaction and Engineering Practice in Eastern North America*, October 20–22, in Sterling Forest, New York. Buffalo, New York: National Center for Earthquake Engineering Research.

Nordenson, Guy J. P. 1988. Wind versus Seismic Design. *Earthquake Hazards and the Design of Constructed Facilities in the Eastern United States* 558: 262–74. New York: New York Academy of Sciences.

Nordenson, Guy J. P., and T. F. Jing. 1988. Evaluation of Earthquake Resistance of Existing Building Practice in New York City, *Proceedings of the 9th World Conference on Earthquake Engineering*, August 2–9, in Tokyo, Japan.

Nordenson, Guy J. P., and C. T. Statton. 1986. Seismicity and Seismic Hazard in the New York City Area, *Proceedings of the 3rd U.S. National Conference on Earthquake Engineering*, August 24–28, in Charleston, South Carolina, pp. 209–20.

NYACE, 1986. Seismic Hazard Evaluation for New York City. *Report of the NYACE Ad Hoc Seismology Committee*. New York: NYACE, October.

Reaveley, L. D., and G. J. P. Nordenson. 1990. Damage in Low and Moderate Seismic Zones. ATC 15–3, *Proceedings of the Fourth U.S.-Japan Workshop on the Improvement of Building Structural Design and Construction Practices*, August 27–29, in Kailua-Kona, HI.

Scawthorn, Charles, et al. 1997. What Happened in Kobe and What if it Happened Here? *Economic Consequences of Earthquakes: Preparing for the Unexpected*: 15–49.

Weidlinger Associates. 1984. BSSC Trial Design Program–Buildings NY-5, NY-20A and NY-32. *Weidlinger Associates Report to the National Institute of Building Sciences/Building Seismic Safety Council No 182-016*, ATC-3-06 Trial Design Program, New York.

Rune

The idea to publish *Rune, An MIT Journal of Arts and Letters* emerged from conversations with Jim Adams, a colleague in Course XXI Humanities, and in part through discussions with Judith Wechsler and Pamela Rubin regarding the aesthetics of science and engineering's visual artifacts that populated MIT. With Pamela, Bob Enders, Tom Gooch, and the others listed on the copyright page, we collected a wide assortment of drawings, photographs, and writings, setting original artwork alongside scientific imagery to suggest formal rhymes. We phototypeset the galleys and made corrections by a "paste up" process of corrections cut out with X-Acto knives—a physical precursor to word processing. We arranged the text and halftone photo reproductions and produced large photograph negatives, printing from these onto large aluminum printing plates at the full 16-page signatures that make up the journal. We printed five and a half signatures plus the cover on the big offset press at the Visual Language Workshop in the summer of 1976. The journal has continued to be published since then: see *http://web.mit.edu/rune/www*

The quotation at outset ("... they remember everything by telling stories to their children") is from *The Story of Doctor Dolittle* by Hugh Lofting, who graduated from MIT in 1909. When we first discussed the idea of the journal we called it *Mithras,* not only a play on the name MIT, but also an allusion to mysteries. Not everyone liked the name and its pagan associations, so we used *Rune* instead, retaining some sense of the mysteries of art that require understanding and interpretation. The making of the journal was a form of practice in the Zen Buddhist sense—a way of attending to the mysteries of artifacts gathered from MIT by transforming them into print.

RUNE

An MIT Journal of Arts and Letters

"...they remember everything by telling stories to their children."
— Hugh Lofting '09

Rune is published annually by students and employees of M.I.T. Manuscripts and art work can be sent to M.I.T. room W20-453. Manuscripts should be typewritten, and will be returned if accompanied by a self addressed envelope. All art work will be returned. The staff for this issue was: Guy Nordenson, *Editor,* Robert Enders and Pamela Rubin, *Associate Editors,* Tom Gooch, *Poetry Editor,* Roxanne Regan, *Business Manager,* Paul Boisseau, *Production Manager,* Jim Adams, Teresa Costanza, David Feinberg, Michael Freiling, Marita Gargiulo, Karen Kramer, Steve Lubar, David Mankins, and Michael Wax.

We would like to thank the Council for the Arts and Prof. Bruce Mazlish for the material support that made this first issue possible.

An M.I.T. arts and letters journal can fullfil at least two functions. The first and most obvious one is to publish the art and writing of members of the M.I.T. community. The arts and letters at M.I.T. emerge from a wide variety of sources, most of which are unaware of one another's work or even existence. A publication such as this can serve to increase the interactions between the various arts and literary groups on and around the campus. Our hope is that this might help to develop a sense of community, and thereby strengthen, through collaboration and criticism, each group's work.

A second function would be to try to focus some of the characteristics peculiar to the arts and letters produced at this school. There are many artists and writers at M.I.T., and their work should offer some interesting responses to its assumptions and activities. Many artistic and literary issues have relevance to scientific and technological ventures, much as, in many cases, such ventures have important artistic and literary aspects. As much as possible we would like to illustrate these correspondences. As a result we have had to solicit much of our material (especially the graphics) from unusual sources.

All any magazine can do is establish a context for the work of individual artists and authors. Yet that context may suggest an interpretation that would not be suggested by the work in isolation. The stories and poems included in this issue, as well as the graphics, seldom give any indication of a relation to M.I.T. And yet they were all in part generated by that environment, and express specific attitudes toward it. This environment is rather unusual, and one could reasonably assume it to be somewhat affecting.

The "humanistic" disciplines have for some time taken the role of critic (in the positive sense of discernment) of society. That role is most often played out in essay form, but, in subtler ways, the "creative" arts and letters have also adopted it. At a place such as M.I.T., which focuses on two of society's most significant activities, namely the sciences and technologies, such a role would seem crucial. A magazine like this one could be a vehicle for such criticism, as well as serve its function as straightforward arts and letters journal.

All of which is only to suggest some of the possibilities for such a journal at M.I.T. In the end it all depends on the availability of material, and the artist's willingness to contribute it. Attitudes change, as do people's interest in these issues, and any magazine is only what it contains.

– G.N.

Contents

One Two Three Four

Finally, Domino gave up his plan to engineer and personally participate in the world's first human pieta. He decided instead to mold his living self into a work of art. There's nothing artistic about dying, he decided. Why, even Dada was just kid's stuff, finger painting, and now the new art was static and alienated. He wanted to be recognized in the mainstream of life, the Triborough Bridge not the Empire State Building. Good art must have life in it, the more the better, Domino concluded. He wanted to be real art, made of the real human stuff.

His junior year in college, Domino decided that dramatizing the traditional human emotions would be good training for his life's future course. He began sending obscure threatening letters to his mother's new husband. When he began to speak obscenely to his mother on the telephone, his stepfather ordered him home and, thinking he had gone crazy, sent him to a psychiatrist. The psychiatrist thought Domino was not insane, just sexually frustrated and recommended that he get himself a girl. Domino, who couldn't have been more delighted with this development, told the doctor to watch his step, and returned to school.

Domino did in fact have a girl, whom he called Greta. Greta secretly longed to die, but, bound to the convention of a natural death, was willing to settle for being alone. Domino respected Greta for this sacrifice. Greta respected Domino because she felt being with him was like being alone. This quality of Domino's stemmed from the fact that no matter what he was doing, part of him was always somewhere else. In his head, Domino was always counting. One two three four, one two three four. Domino counted mentally with a constant droning rhythm as he scribbled reminders in his notebook, walked home along the water, pasted newsprint words on letter paper, lay in bed beside Greta.

Domino had started counting to himself before he realized he was doing it or what it could mean, as a child, to take his mind off being bored or being beaten, but now he counted on purpose and on principle. Counting, he might say, is one aesthetic abstraction that is accessible to even the common man, while he thought that, until something better comes along, counting would serve as both a kind of vehicle for his artistic self-expression and its end.

Greta had no particular interest in counting or in art of any kind, although she was an accomplished pianist. There were not many places on a college campus where Greta could have privacy, but as long as she kept playing, she could go on undisturbed in the college's piano practice rooms. Her repeated performances of the major and minor scales, in every octave, rendered as lifelessly as she could manage, gave her fingers great agility. On one occasion Greta consented to play, once through, a piece by Mahler for Domino to discipline his counting.

"Have you ever considered killing your mother?" Domino asked soon after the piece had begun.

"My mother's dead," Greta replied, stopping the piece abruptly, relieved.

"Well, your father, then?" Domino asked.

"No, he's . . . " Greta began. "Say, what are you planning now? What plot has it that a college-girl kills her doctor-father?" After eyeing him up and down objectively for a minute or two, she added, "There's something wrong with you, what is it?"

2

"Oh, I don't know," he said slowly, getting up to stand by the window. "I feel like I'm not learning anything, I'm not growing. I'm just marking time. God, in nine years I'll be thirty."

This comforting thought gave Greta the strength to go on more aggressively. "What's there to do?" she asked.

"I don't know," he said, drifting off, one two three four, "I don't know."

Greta began to consider Domino's predicament. How about the college man who loses his true love, she mused. But is there really such a thing as a talking raven, she wondered. It crossed Greta's mind that there was really a great paucity of stirring human emotions. She thought about this for days. It troubled her and she stayed up nights.

Domino wondered whether he was on the wrong track in this art business, whether the old human truths didn't require a new aesthetic image. He started to wear black sequined blouses and satin pants for a more vivid appearance. He read somewhere about a guy who painted his fingernails black, and he did that too. He considered counting in base two: one, one-zero, one-one, one-zero-zero, but finally rejected the idea. Some things, he thought, transcend styles. Domino grew his hair long, then cut it quite short, but his heart wasn't in it and he began to re-read the Dadaists. He spent more and more time in a hidden basement corner of the library.

During her nights of insomnia, Greta would walk about the student center in her housedress, waking the transients, asking them whether they knew any good plots. Finally, a girl from Montreal called the campus police. The campus police called Greta's father. Greta's father was an expert on personality crises. He thanked the officer and decided the problem could wait until Christmas.

The first day of Christmas vacation, Domino's parents took one look at his sequined shirt and his nail-polished fingers and sent him back to the psychiatrist. Domino still did not know that his doctor was Greta's father, but Greta's father let him have it anyhow. As Domino ran out of the doctor's office in fright, Greta's father suffered a coronary and fell on the letter opener he had been brandishing at Domino, dead.

At the funeral, Domino stood with his arm around Greta. She did not object.

"You know, I don't feel sad," she said abstractly, shaking her head. "But I feel strange." She was confused by her new circumstances and after the burial service, she went alone to walk by the lake.

The restriction Domino's parents placed on his outward appearance caused him to fall into a depression, or melancholia as he called it. Was there no freedom from tradition? he wondered. Could it be true that "The only good art is dead art?" Domino's mother tried to raise his spirits. She bought tickets to the Living Theater but he refused, in certain and ungracious terms, to go. She planned a turkey with stuffing which seemed to arouse his interest, and even opened a jar of cranberries she had put up in the fall. To Domino's surprise, it was the cranberries which gave him, his mother and his father the botulism which killed them all in one two three four days.

— *Diane Sanger*

4

Trial Balloons

for Gene Masters, Esquire

There is a woman oil-drilling inside my mind. She is exploring for deposits of significance. I have not ever seen her. If I could, I would know her. I know her machinery: her intravenous tubes are pipes of plastic or platinum from my childhood. Her drill rig hums when I'm awake. The lights on it are presences in my eyes. She does not wake me with drilling in the morning; she waits until I awake to begin. I understand that significance cannot be found at night.

There is a woman inside my mind. She looks for mushrooms. She knows which types she likes and which types are poisonous to me. They are mushrooms of significance. She points out various species, voicelessly: *Here's Amanita Significata, a tender specimen; and this is Clavariadelphus Significae, subtle, refreshing; and this one is known as the Exterminating Angel —Don't Touch It.* And so on she goes like that, like a wine list. She brings a basket and a knife. The basket is woven of weeping willow—a strange material of construction here. The knife is too short; barely functional as a lever, but with it she lifts the mushrooms of significance. She left it once, at a stream where many mushrooms grew. Overnight it formed a single tear of rust on the blade. She keeps the tear there, to remember her mistake. She cannot gather at night; that is when the mushrooms of significance vivify. At that time they glow a pale, rare glow. I don't know where she goes when not gathering. She does not wake me, she waits to walk in the morning (sunshine) searching and gathering again.

There is a woman inside my mind. She analyses the words and catch phrases that I speak for their significance. Voicelessly, she selects those phrases and words she likes. She becomes silent or giggles at others. The same phrase, perhaps one she seemed to like enormously, is ignored at a second usage. I no longer try to please her. I have never seen this anthropologist woman of significance. If I did, I would know her immediately. I know what she works with: a transcribing tape recorder, a trellis for proper microphone placement, a terminator and a special spiral-bound notebook for indexing spoken tapes. Once left running, her tapes unwound over me all night. In the sunlight her anxious rewinding caused it to tear. She lost what the notebook said to be an interesting phrase. I could not duplicate it for her. The level meter light blinks in rhythm to my speech. It is a red light inside my eyes. If I break off a sentence, does it mean that I stopped or that it stopped me? There's no question about that at night, my speech is unquestionably my own then. She does not work at night, phrases of significance are formed then in places she cannot reach. I am not sure what she does, perhaps she fixes her notes, edits them at night. I have no idea where she goes. After I wake, she adjusts her recorder and begins recording again. The red-light blink, the occasional giggle, these are the footnotes of significance.

There is a woman cooking inside my mind. It seems that foods of significance abound there; her intention is to prepare them. She knows which are mild and which are contrastingly strong and which are to be ignored. She is a chef of the tastes and smells and textures of significance. One receipe she offered me was:

Significance Salad

2	large cucumbers, peeled and significant
1	small onion
3/4	cup yoghurt
1	tablespoon essence of significance
1/2	salt
1/8	pepper
1/2	celery seeds
6	cups Boston lettuce

Put the cucumber in a salad bowl and add the remaining ingredients, except the lettuce. Mix well, chill overnight and serve.

I sample dish after dish some days. But she always knows what my reaction will be. There is a dullness in that. I do not try to please her. I cannot fool her. I suppose I should say I have never seen her. If I did though, I would instantly know her, I am sure of this. Even now I think I could describe her to you. But I have not seen her. There are utensils: a bowl, a wire whisk, several spoons from my childhood, her spice collection. She doesn't make mistakes. There is never an undercooked dish, an improperly served fare, never a spice unintended. She does not cook at night. She is not around then. I don't know where she goes. But in the morning again she is there continually presenting new foods, new preparations.

There is a woman inside my mind. She is standing on a high cliff, the plain above the ocean. She is a meteorologist inflating and releasing trial balloons. She intends to plot the upper currents of my significance. It is lonely work, she is without anyone else. I don't believe anyone has ever seen her; I never have. But I am sure I could recognize her. Sometimes it seems to be:...4.......7........8..........34..35..36.. 37..40, Mark. I guess them to be current counts, incrementations or other data which are important to her. There is implicit denial that she is speaking. It could not be she. Her methods are familiar, equipment varied: she has an infinite supply of balloons, all of small constant diameter. They send signals back to her. She sights them through a tracer theodolite. Where do the balloons go? Do they return for repeated use? Do they decay? I don't know this. I can feel how the currents blow. Only one balloon do I know the life of. She freed it in the late afternoon. Her devices seem to be powered by the morning and this one she released in the late afternoon. It rose for a time but returned nothing and sank again, pulled down, powerless. She kept the balloon to remind her. She never works at night now. But she comes with her devices and additional balloons powered by the morning.

There is a woman inside my mind looking for a place to sing. She is like (though I hate opera) an unemployed diva. She would not, probably could not, however, admit this. She searches for a stage, a theater, an open square to sing in. A place to sing, a place of calm significance is what she would like. Though I have tried to suggest places, I have never seen her at any of them, nor anywhere. Who has? I would know her if I saw her but— Today she has found a location! She will sing. She is standing in a natural cavern, a deep structure below the surface. I cannot see, but I feel the colors here: reds, human grays, a solidity and a pure reverberance too. is only a presence. I will not see her. With her, she has the necessities of a singer: music, a music stand. The stand is a metal construction, descendant of sculpture. And now I can really see the music entirely. It is printed with lights. Blue and white lights make up the pages. Each notation is clearly visible. Everything is in place, she is ready. She sings a first extended high note. Extended without breath. She does not need to breathe. It is very old music but has never been heard before. I still cannot see her. I probably never will. As the music fills me, I realize it is all in a language I cannot understand.

It continues unanalyzable.

Is this her only communication?

Through the afternoon she sings; at night comes a resolution of her voices, dying all to silence. The sheets of music are ·dark now, the stand also disappears. Her presence is nowhere now. I experience a true silence.

There is a woman acting inside my mind. I have seen her! She was standing on a stage. All began as a pantomime and I was eyeless. Shuffling sounds only. THEN, my eyes were opened. They were spotlights for her. If I were on stage, I'd not be saying this. Let me describe her...

There is a woman conducting tours inside my mind. Tour-guide to places of my significance. She knows a wide reper-toire of my points of interest. She has elaborate anecdotes, explanations and pleasantries for the crowds that come. I can hear her voice when she intends me to. I think I have seen her once but I can't be sure, I've forgotten. I would like to meet her, have her identified to me. In her lectures, there is a warmth sometimes in what she says about my mind. She could be a friend I think. Other times with other crowds, though, she is very dry, purely informational. I would like to see her once. She has a tourguide utility cap and a change-making device at her belt. She sells maps and postcards to the visitors. Today's tour has just begun. She is very consid-erate of my hours; there are no night tours, and she never begins shuffling people through until I'm fully awake. Today is a fair-sized group. She says, *Good morning. Welcome to his mind. Please stay in single-file arrangement. Don't lag behind, several were lost last week. If you have questions, save them until the end. Souvenirs will also be available then. Let's start.* It was like all other tours. They stopped for lunch on one of the more scenic sites, a cliff looking down to the ocean. Tables were arranged. As everyone lunches, she announces, *This is the last tour of his mind. Their need ends. They have been doubly useful: informative to you and helpful for me to gain familiarity with the region. Now I have found what I wanted. After lunch I will show you.* Everyone finishes lunch quickly. She leads them down a path, a ravine in the cliff. A rope is assistance. Down to the ocean, they gather at the water's edge. *This is it,* she says, *this was his significance.*

— *R. Hilliard*

Upstate, Late Afternoon

Unlatched, the windows are wary.
Misted grapes wait in the halls -
       pumpkins squat, the gourds rattle.
In the wide room, paper trees surround the bed,
but the still sheet only mirrors the ceiling
         blue and blue.
The old yellow clock ticks its circles in the corner.

He will come
he will come,
     his windcape sweeping the floor
to empty his pockets of rain.

— Patricia Darcy

No Meat

I

For two hours now I've eaten
no meat, plucked no fowl,
peeled no flesh, feasted
on corn and wheat; my head
has cleared of eels, the poison
gone, my mind uncorked
pours liquid-lettered I-love-you-buts;
a hundred more in my skull
than in my desk.

I practice saying you-and-he
in the shower, the names entwined
in my mind, the fingers locked,
you-and-me, you-and-he,
I raise my lips, to drink
from the shower, I drink
to you, to forgetting you.

II

those two hanging ducks
startling thru the glass
remind me of her breasts

every night I am a child.

III

The house is on the beach
the morning is october,
it's cold; the crabs
have given up the sand,
the rich old widow has
gone to her winter home,
the sad young man
sighs within the house,
pretending to grow old

The house is on the beach,
the morning is october,
it's freezing;
no coal in the cupboard,
no bread, no heat,
no meat,

     no goddam meat.

– G. K. Roberts

Polonius Unbound

hesitating,
awaiting a Hercules
(but a Hercules
comes after
the rage of gods) —
and deference
only amuses.
So the old man stumbles,
begins to fail, as the gods
snicker, waiting
for the false step
that leads to chains and eagles
and to redemption
in a life of dry months.

— *Tom Gooch*

Anniversary Poem

So here we are
and four years seem
the fanciful wanderings
of a Kelly girl
eating lunch hour tuna
on a bench
in the Public Gardens.

Just think.
It might easily have been
ham and cheese
and I would never
have bruised your chest
with my violin case
on that pubescent sunday
right under the nose of God himself.

For often I sat
in idle seats
that gave in
to these overplump cheeks
without question or pause.
Passing only the briefest
whispers of glances
beyond the horizon
of my sultry ruminations.

But in the humid passion
of a hayloft tumble,
reckless fantasy
found form
in artless kisses.

We have weathered the sex
of four lifetimes.

And only now,
as passion fades
like aging jeans,
can I take up
a Kelly girl's
crumpled lunch bag
and make a poem
of that salty embrace.

— George W. Pratt III

17

Four Renga

I

In due season, the barest vine
returns to flower

II

rushing spring water caresses pregnant
wife's feet under hoisted skirts

III

burnished redwood trunks
bulwark against the flood

IV

mud patted on pale geisha cheeks
is rumored to enhance her beauty

— Sean O Riain

你不訪唯獨吃

這黃芽珠淚飯

You didn't call.
Alone I chew this
cabbage
and teardrop rice.

— *Sean O Riain*

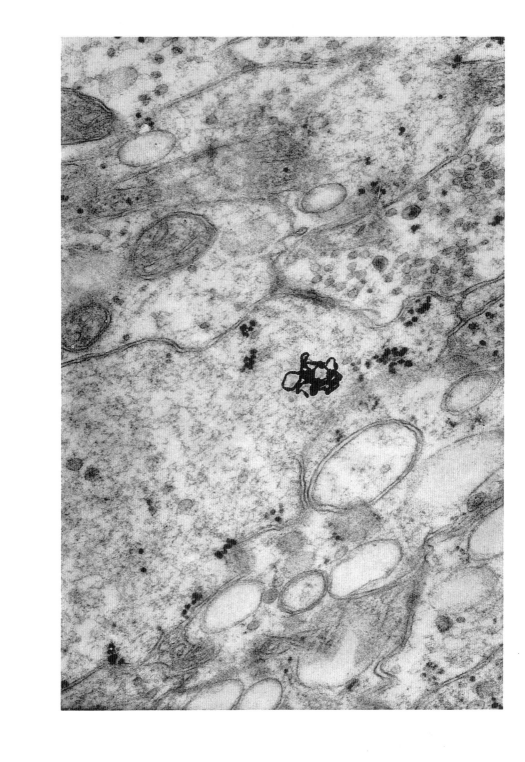

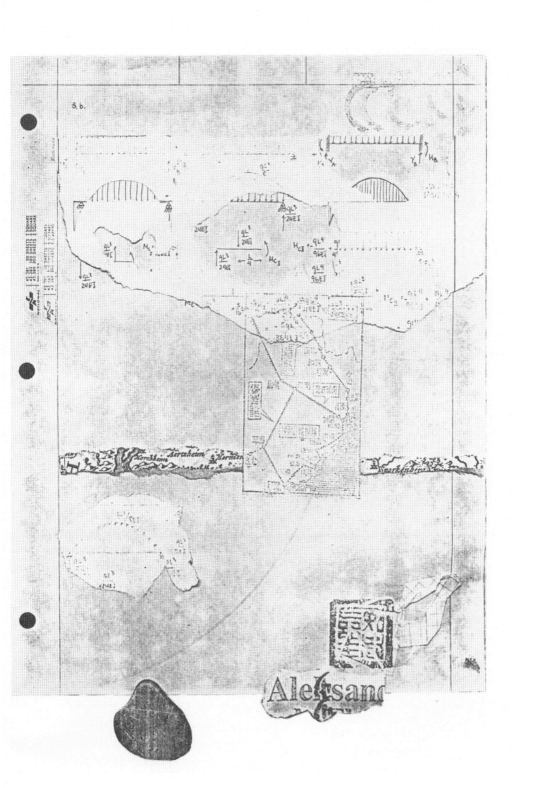

3.b.

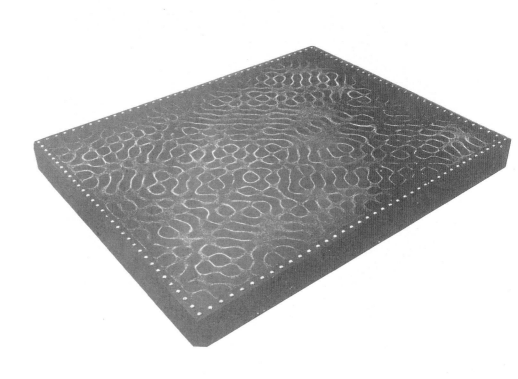

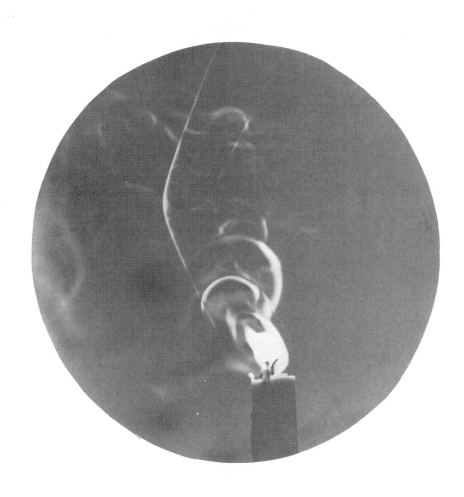

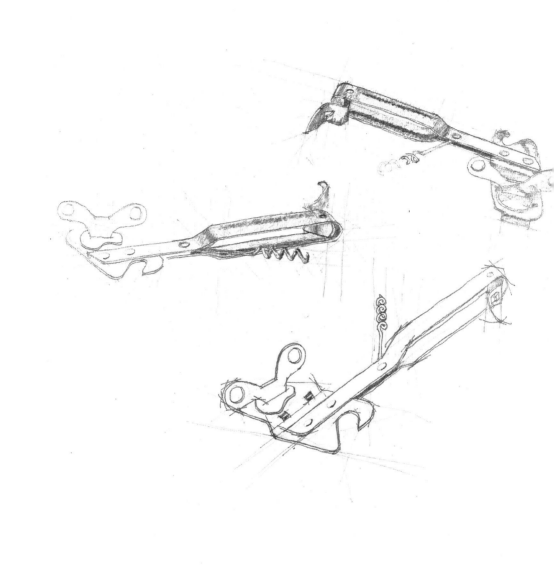

Social Exchange in a Peasant Village

The investigation of the forms and the significance of exchange behavior in so-called primitive societies has long up-staged serious consideration of similar behavior in complex societies. In fact, the nature of exchange in some societies has served to define those very communities as 'primitive'. Hence, when analogous forms of exchange–gifting, feasting, divestment of personal property in ritual contexts, bribery, drinking bouts, to name just a few--occur in economically depressed areas of complex societies, we conceive of the behavior as primitive instead of modern, wasteful instead of efficient, superstitious instead of empirical, and generally counterproductive of achieving an improved standard of living. These hasty judgements obscure an objective consideration of the importance of some customs to the working of complex society as a whole.

I observed many instances of what we will call social exchange in a village of Zapotec speaking peasants in southern Mexico. In this essay, I will consider the implications of these forms of exchange with regard to problems threatening, in particular, the integrity of the peasant enterprise, and in general community life in complex societies. Complex societies differ from 'primitive' ones in the heightened level of social and economic differentiation, the presence of a regional money economy linked most likely to a national or international market system, and in the existence of a state.

Peasant society is complex society as it exists in most of the world; it is neither isolated nor is it simply the survival of some past scheme of feudal orders. Rather, as a general theoretical orientation in this essay, we must think of it as a vital aspect of modern society, an adaptation to historical conditions of conquest and exploitation and modern conditions of economic and political marginality.

What do I mean here by 'social exchange'? There is no room in this essay to review the voluminous literature on this subject. Suffice it to say that few of the concepts of social exchange suit our purposes. Above all, social exchange must be considered as a supra-economic phenomenon. While the objects of gifting, for example, might have clear economic value or consequences, the major significance of the act of 'social exchange' is the relationship that it creates or maintains between the parties to the exchange. Social exchange is one aspect of continuous social relations, conforming to a general, normative pattern of social behavior, and it is a necessary condition for maintaining these social relations. As one writer put it, we exchange gifts because we are friends; we are friends because we exchange gifts (Shalins 1968).

Among Mexican peasants, and Zapotec speaking peasants in particular, one prominent example of social exchange is the *mayordomia*. The *mayordomia* is a fiesta held in celebration of a Christian saint or of one of the many apparitions in Mexico of the Virgin Mary. Each year either the village authorities or the current year's fiesta sponsors select the sponsor, or *mayordomo*, of the next year's celebration. The responsibility could be refused, though there is considerable social pressure to accept, especially if one is obviously financially well off. The *mayordomo* will have to marshall his resources to finance the mass, pay the priest's sundry fees, and wine and dine his guests for the several days of the *mayordomia*.

Through the sponsorship of a *mayordomia*, a *mayordomo* divests himself (or herself) of much of his accumulated wealth. This has led many persons to view the system as a means of leveling wealth differences within the village; in return for dispensing with material riches in the name of the greater glory of the village and the dieties, the *mayordomo* in turn ascends a rung in the village prestige ladder. The most respected persons in the villages of the Zapotecs are generally the elderly and particularly those who sponsored one or more *mayordomias* and/or held posts in the village government.

The *mayordomia* may act to level wealth, to impede social differentiation or class formation. But the fact is that social differentiation has developed in Zapotec villages. This was clear in the village in which I studied, San Sebastian Teitipac, Oaxaca, Mexico. A previous ethnographer there reported: "There is no rigid class structure in San Sebastian society and the conduct of social relations is basically egalitarian in nature. In the realm of personal behavior, differences in wealth are not regularly associated with differences in such things as speech, dress, and etiquette. There are no formalized distinctions between 'ladinos' or 'mestizos' and 'indios' . . ." (Cook 162). Although the differences were not formalized when Cook studied there, they do exist and are now visible. On a chilly night during the dry season, find the men who wear jackets or *sarapes* rather than just tattered shirts; find someone who sports a wrist watch, shoes, or who chain smokes cigarettes, or who has eye-glasses, and the chances are he is, by village standards, a wealthy man. The materials used in house construction also betray relative wealth status -- brick vs. adobe vs. wattle and daub -- as does an occasional television antenna, a metal gate, or a high wall around the residence lot periphery.

Wealth differences also affect food consumption patterns. Wealthy persons drink chocolate more often, drink more milk, eat bread purchased in Oaxaca or Tlacolula every day, eat meat more often (though this might be only once a week), eat all the beans they want, and probably consume too much sugar. Again, however, as Cook noted, the differ-

31

ences are not formalized, and exceptions can be found; people do not openly sport the symbols of their relative wealth status, lest they become the focus of the envy and hostility of poorer co-villagers.

These important differences in wealth status have several manifest effects on the nature of interpersonal relations in the village. The differential access to resources and equipment gives rise partly to a system of cooperative exchange of labor and equipment (the exchange is called *guelaguetza*), especially during the harvest of corn and beans. However, this differentiation may also give rise to conflict. Cook noted that this occurred during the Revolution, when the wealthiest families of the village were expelled, only to return later when things cooled down a bit. Cook went on in that vein to note that " . . . current political factionalism and personal enmities in the village had their inception during the revolutionary period" (Cook 67). Some villagers told me, for instance, how the head of one of the wealthiest households in the village had made a pact with the devil in return for which he accrued great wealth at the expense of his soul. The story, of course, isn't very original. The wealthy, on the other hand, have their own self- justifications to offer for their relatively elevated standard of living. Many of the villagers, they say, are stupid or lazy and don't want to work hard. They themselves are generous, they say, and help the needy when called upon. They claim they do not charge usurious prices for their corn when corn is scarce, and after all, they give costly service to the community in the way of fiesta sponsorship or cargo service.

All in all, the conflict between groups is latent, and might only give rise to open strife under conditions such as that of the Revolution or the expulsion of Protestants. Without exception, San Sebastianos pride themselves on the unity of their village and the lack of intravillage strife. Much of what they tell the anthropologist about the unity of their people is a fiction, of course, but like most exagerations, it has some basis in fact difficult to ignore. A number of neighboring villages are noted throughout the valley for their internecine violence, blood feuds, and open hostility towards outsiders. Not San Sebastian, however.

As I said earlier, it is through a system of social exchanges that San Sebastianos maintain a level of cohesion which permits, except in extraordinary times, smooth functioning of the social machinery. Social exchange in the context of religious ritual, especially exchanges involving food, should be understood as promoting social cohesion. Let's consider then how a *mayordomia* would perform this hypothesized social function.

In sponsoring of a *mayordomia* the *mayordomo* must spend considerable quantities of money and food resources; in general, through the institution of *guelaguetza* by which many villagers contribute upon request food, money, or labor to the *mayordomo's* effort, the sponsor acquires a debt which might not be liquidated even over the course of two or three decades.

Cook gives figures which illustrate the size of expenditures we're talking about here. He reports for the 1965 *mayordomia* of the Virgen de Juquila, celebrated December 8, that the *mayordomo* expended $8,891 Mex ($708 US @ $1 Mex= $0.08 US), 85.5 dozen eggs, 17 turkeys, 266 kilos of tortillas, 28 kilos of beans, as well as smaller quantities of sugar, cacao, candles, mezcal (an alcoholic beverage produced by fermenting the juices of the maguey cactus), and cigarettes. This celebration, the largest of its kind during the year, lasted five days. Actually, Cook noted only half of the expenditures for the total fiesta, since for these large fiestas two *mayordomos* hold two separate celebrations of approximately equal magnitude.

The fiesta I observed in detail, that of the Virgen of Soledad, is traditionally a smaller affair. During four days of celebration, the single *mayordomo* (in this case a widow) spent about $2000 Mex in cash, and expended one pig ($900

Mex), 5 turkeys, 7 gross of eggs, bread ($500 Mex), 7 kilos of cacao, 28 kilos of sugar, cinnamon, chile, oregano, onions, miltomates, tomatoes, garlic, beer, potatoes, soft drinks, and various other herbs or spices. Considering that the sponsor of the fiesta was a widow with six children and virtually no land, this represents a simply astronomical expenditure. Further, it challenges the assertion that the *mayordomia* is basically a wealth leveling device.

The *mayordomos*, of course, must rely on the assistance of many co-villagers to sponsor these affairs. In the case of the fiesta of the Virgen de Juquila (documented partially by Cook), 94 households contributed upon request supplies for the *mayordomo*, such as money, food, fireworks, or a pledge of labor. In fact, only $8000 Mex in cash was derived from the *mayordomo's* own immediate resources (Cook 126). Of the 94 contributers of *guelaguetza*, Cook reported, all but 29 were described by the *mayordomo* as just 'friends'. Furthermore, of the remaining 29, only eight were first or second degree cosanguineal kin. To the *mayordomo* of the smaller fiesta which I observed, there were 27 contributers of *guelaguetza*, none of whom was a close relative of the *mayordomo*. It should be clear then that to sponsor these fiestas, the would-be *mayordomo* must activate his entire network of friendships and obligations which extends well beyond his own extensive circle of kin.

Several months to a year before the date of the fiesta, the *mayordomo* notifies in person, in a formal manner, all the individuals who are to come as invited households to the *mayordomo's solar* on the specified days to celebrate the fiesta. Only these persons, except in the case of the largest fiestas, will actually do any celebrating. When the guests (*invitados*) accept the *mayordomo's* offer to attend the *mayordomia*, they commit themselves to performing labor for the *mayordomo* before and during the celebration, to bringing the requisite offerings of mezcal and cigarettes, and to generally comply with all the expectations of the *invitado*.

What these obligations are will be made clear shortly. First, who gets invited to a *mayordomia*? There is no clear, pat rule, though this list of preferences offered by one informant comes close:

a) All those who have previously invited me to their *mayordomia*, wedding, baptism, etc...
b) All compadres and padrinos (fictive kin linked by godparenthood);
c) All my uncles and aunts;
d) First cousins and other relatives (including with each one their respective spouse and, perhaps, older child) as space permits to make a grand total of approximately 40 persons.

The point is that the list of invited persons, while it includes many persons who are relatives, includes primarily distant relatives or persons linked by ritual, fictive kinship. What we see in the *mayordomia*, then, isn't just a gathering of the clan, so to speak, but an assemblage of a significant portion of those households which are part of the *mayordomo's* vital domestic network of friends and neighbors.

Some of the invited persons, men and women, were in the fiesta I observed, marshalled several days, several weeks, even two or three months prior to the fiesta day to make the necessary preparations. For two days, for example, a half-dozen women ground cacao with sugar to make the chocolate that would be consumed each day of the fiesta. Some men were sent to the hills to the west of the village to gather wood to fuel the fires on which women made many kilos of tortillas, cooked the meat and *mole* (a chile sauce), and prepared the *higadito* (eggs with meat and vegetables turned in). About a week before the fiesta, a crew of male *invitados* was delegated by the *mayordomo* to gather branches of a local, scruby oak tree (*encino*). With the *encino*, they constructed a temporary, rectangular structure called a *ramada* in the *solar* of the *mayordomo*. The *ramada* serves as a large shelter in which many of the more sacred aspects of the celebration would transpire, including most serving of food. For the *invitados*, the chores were virtually endless as long as the celebration continued.

The most significant aspect of exchange, which occurred during the celebrations, was the food exchange. First of all, the *mayordomo* must feed each of his *invitados*, whom he summons to help out with the fiesta preparations. They received, in the morning, chocolate and bread; in the afternoon, beans, tortillas, tejate (a drink made from corn dough and cacao). On the day before the fiesta, I observed that many of the *invitados* were called to help with the butchering of a pig in the *mayordomo's solar*. When the butchering was complete, bits of fried pork, tortillas, tejate, and beans were served to each of the *invitados*; after eating this, they dispersed until the next day, the first day of the fiesta proper.

On the morning of the first day of the celebrations, the *invitados* gathered at daybreak at the *mayordomo's solar*. Each household brought one liter of mezcal and a carton, or perhaps, only a pack of cigarettes. Each of these offerings was received by the *mayordomo* and his wife in the sacrosanct *ramada* inn front of a simple family altar. The altar consisted of a small wooden table, a pictoral image to a saint or virgin, some candles, and some flowers. Also present was a man, who is a combination ritual specialist/professional master of ceremonies, known as the *huehuete*. *Huehuete* is not a religious office; rather, it's an occupation filled by very few older men who have learned to run these affairs, how to mediate between groups, and to keep the celebration on the right track with eloquent sermons and a humble, though wise, demeanor.

Once each offering was blessed and received *con toda voluntad*, that is, in good faith, the *invitados* were seated at a long table which dominated the inside of the ramadas,. There they received a cup of hot chocolate, some bread, tortillas, chocolate *atole* (corn gruel) a heaping plate of *higadito* which the women had been preparing literally all night, and soft drink. No one could possibly eat all the food offered, nor could they refuse any of it; instead, each woman *invitada* brought along a plastic bag into which they dumped their own and their husband's uneaten portions to bring home and share with their children or relatives. In this way, the food from the fiesta is distributed so that many times the number of persons actually invited benefit by it.

Almost no one attended Mass offered the morning of the fiesta. San Sebastianos have little respect, except in word, for the ecclesiastical authority of the Catholic Church; they generally shy away from the church whenever the itinerant priest is around. After Mass, the church authorities, except the priest, were escorted to the *mayordomo's ramada* where they shared in the breakfast fare. These men, "los de la iglesia", are village heads of household selected for one year terms by village authorities to perform various functions of maintenance and assistance at the church. When they had eaten, they danced. The *huehuete* and *mayordomo* selected six women *invitadas* to join them in the dance, which was accompanied by the music from a village eleven piece brass band. While they danced, the other *invitados* milled around, unless they were given specific tasks such as cleaning off the table, setting off fire-works, etc. Two male *invitados* served continuously a shot of mezcal and one cigarette to each of the dancers for the duration of the *jarabe*, as they call that step. When the dance ended one hour after it began, "los de la iglesia" left and the *mayordomia* progressed to the next stage, the search for the *mayordomo* of next year's fiesta.

Before going on, I must emphasize the significance of the offering of food, mezcal and cigarettes. No one refused the presentation of food and mezcal, regardless of whether they were full or did not want to get drunk. Some women got away with just sipping at the mezcal, but this was just a small courtesy to them by the mezcal servers. Generally, they would not continue to serve anyone else until each individual accepted the glass (*copa*) of mezcal and downed it. The key concept here is that the reluctant recipient must demonstrate that he or she participates in the celebration and partakes of the *mayordomo's* food and mezcal "con toda voluntad" (of their own free will) and "con toda confianza" (with all confidence). In readily accepting the mezcal, each *invitado* publically demonstrated that he or she harbored no fear of the intentions of the *mayordomo*, of the servers, nor of the other *invitados*; he or she demonstrated trust that his or her fellow celebrants would neither poison, stab, nor bludgeon while he was helplessly inebriated or while eating. This represents, in the broadest sense, a commitment to enter into social relations and to expel thoughts of envy, fear, or hostility which otherwise characterize much of the peasant scene.

Around midday, explosions were sounded in the street facing the *mayordomo's solar*, the band struck up *La Diana* and a small procession headed out to name and bring back the *mayordomo* who would celebrate one year hence. They also went to escort to the *mayordomia* the parents of four girls who carried the statue of the Virgin of Soledad during the previous nine days novena observances at the church. The *mayordomo, huehuete* and *invitados* ushered the distinguished guests quickly into the *ramada* where the offerings they brought (carried on the backs of the *invitados*) were accepted and blessed. The goods included one case of soft drinks, one liter of mezcal, one carton of cigarettes each. Though it was already midday, the new guests were promptly served breakfast in which all, including the *mayordomo* and *huehuete,* took part. The formal atmosphere shortly broke out into a more relaxed conversation as some *invitados* brought in food while others removed expended dishes. After breakfast, one round of mezcal and cigarettes for all present in the *ramada,* and then lunch was brought in. By that point, no one could eat the heaping bowl full of *higadito,* not to mention the atole, tortillas, soft drinks, etc. Each person drained off the broth that the *higadito* sat in and stored the solids in a plastic bag.

The dancing began again, during which the heaviest drinking took place. It lasted again one hour while mezcal was continuously served, with no exceptions. Their concept of dancing is quite different from our own. Couples, married or otherwise, never danced together; rather, the *mayordomo* or *huehuete* paired up *invitados* until no more women were available. Dancing partners never touch, and only incidentally may they look at each other. The remaining *invitados* stood around the fringes and either drank or performed miscellaneous chores. Once the music had begun, neighbors gathered around the fringes of the *solar* to watch the festivities.

When the dancing ended, one or two hours later, dinner (*comida*)was served–turkey cooked in mole, tortillas, soft drinks. The distinguished guests–the new *mayordomo* and her immediate kin–ate in the *ramada* with the *mayordomo* and *huehuete*, while the others sat on logs outside, ate, and conversed. Then more dancing and drinking until about 10pm when the new *mayordomo* was escorted back to her *solar*. There, she and her *invitados*–while she was celebrating many of the *invitados* to her fiesta one year hence were rounded up–received the presentations of the current *mayordomo* with considerable formality. Another dance then ensued; *jarabes*, for two hours more mezcal, more cigarettes. Around midnight, the party of the current *mayordomo* headed back to their own *solar* where some *invitados* took their leave until the next day, while others drank themselves into a not-so-blissful oblivion.

Until this point, I have focused on the giving and receiving of food as declaring good intentions and reinforcing social relations. There remains yet another aspect of this behavior to consider. When the old *mayordomo* escorted the new *mayordomo* back to her *solar*, with her went a highly stereotyped menu of presentations froms the old to the new; one live male turkey, one case of soft drinks, one large casserole of mole, one large casserole of *higadito,* cigarettes, and baskets of tortillas, not to mention mezcal. In front of the family altar, with both *mayordomos* and their close kin present, the *huehuete* asked if they made these gifts "con toda voluntad"; he proceeded to lecture on the nature of the fiesta and harmonious relations while all persons, with hats doffed, periodically interjected declarations of good intentions, humility, and respect to each other. In these presentations, I saw the attempt to mediate potential conflict between the two groups, even though they were closely linked by a bond of fictive kinship. I also saw a desire to maintain the continuity of the tradition of the fiesta; the new fiesta that is the celebration which will reach its zenith in one year, began right there with the food prepared at the house of the house of the old *mayordomo*. Further, we must note the attempt to interject an extra measure of confidence and trust, to reinforce respect in the interpersonal relations of all the persons present.

The celebrations continued at the *solars* of the new *mayordomo* and at the old for four or five days; each day with diminishing intensity. Throughout the fiesta, food offering tested and reinforced the social fabric which, inside or outside of the ritual context, is at once so important yet, so delicate. The *ramada*, constructed by the collective labor of the *invitados,* housing as it does the altar and sheltering much of the food offerings, encapsulates much of the symbolism of the fiesta that we are concerned with here. The *ramada* is a sort of neutral ground on which individuals interact with suppposely good intentions. So, when one aging villager told me of how he was, as an *invitado* to a *mayordomia,* poisoned by witchcraft while eating in the *ramada,* he emphasized his indignation that he was attacked while in the *ramada.*

Many writers, both from the United States and from Mexico, view the *mayordomo* as an orgy of waste and self-destructiveness characteristic of a broken, despondent people. The *mayordomia,* they say, squanders the peasant's vital resources, above all, accumulated capital, with which they might have improved their productive capacity and achieved some sort of economic take off into the modern age. The *mayordomia* should be seen, rather, as a vital institution through which social relations are reinforced and through which domestic networks of mutual aid are rejuvenated. Most peasant households depend upon these networks and their *membership* in the community to remain viable in a socio-political milieu, which otherwise makes life very difficult for them.

— Paul Sullivan

Bibliography:
Fernando Benitez, *Tierra Incognita.* Ediciones Era., 1972
H. S. Cook, *Teitipac and Its Metateros: An Economic Anthropological Study of Production and Exchange.* Ann Arbor: University Microfilms, 1970
Peter P. Ekeh, *Social Exchange Theory.* Harvard University Press, 1974
Charles M. Leslie, *Now We Are Civilized.* Wayne State University, 1960
Jorge Martinez Rios, "Analisis Funcional de la 'Guelaguetza Agricola,'" *Revista Mexicana de Sociologia.* 1964
Talcott Parsons, "Durkheim's Contribution to the Theory of Social Integration of Social Systems," *Emile Durkheim, 1858 — 1917.* ed. K. H. Wolff, Ohio State University, 1960
Marshall D. Shalins, "On the Sociology of Primitive Exchange," *Relevance of Models for Social Anthropology.* London: Association of Social Anthropologists of the Commonwealth, 1965
Eric Wolf, "Closed Corporate Peasant Communities in Mesoamerica and Central Java," *Peasant Society Reader.* ed. Jack Potter, May Diaz, & George Foster, Little Brown & Co., 1967

Summer Job

Alley cats wait in the rain
  crowded against soot skies
    rummaging through shiny pails
      fumbling for possessions
        to prize
In a blue and white apron
  I'm shining the tables
    waiting for who are you
Alley cats lay on their empty stomachs
  envying alley rats and car lights
    Reflecting back light
      from the core of their eyes
        While their hearts remain prisoners
        of night.

— Marita Gargiulo

42

Grey Sails

for Tim Holm - died hang gliding, 1975

What time the grayfly winds her sultry horn

I

So the wind returns, past;
the ear, murmured, roars of sea fall,
or the lift-draft up cliff walls: hung

there by breath alone, you freeze, forget,
or explode fear, halt at the taut,
silent instant.

II

I see the sinews
sprung from shoulders
themselves heaved, the whole
wrenched out
as of Brancusi's Torment.

I hear you whisper, hoarsely,
of the student you saw leap,
with notes and books, down
off the bridge; and of his voice:
"I cannot swim."

The acrid, arsenic sting
of the waters:
the jade dark silence
swallowing, sinking, drowns.

III

Your body swung up lightly
atop our great mast.

My own fear forced placent
admiration, beholding the wind
anchor.

Broad armed you
embraced outright air.

You should have flown.

IV

Burnt wing, winding
down; a feather dodges
between the wind a
and air, and plummets
down.

Nothing's left.
But the curl of this
page on the wind; a white
against the white: the black in-
consequential.

V

The wind knot on the rigging, straining,
the grey sky, prowed white.

An oak leans, groans,
the leaves slap the wind.

A breath billowed on the tack.

— Guy J. P. Nordenson

44

We have been long
in becoming, you and I,
trapped by each other, afraid.
But I will not forgive,
and you will not admit,
so there it is:
a half eaten orange
left drying on some window sill.

Perhaps you have found
a few of my shirts
still clinging to their hangers
in your closet,
collars stained and frayed
from all the times
I sweated blood for you.

— *George W. Pratt III*

45

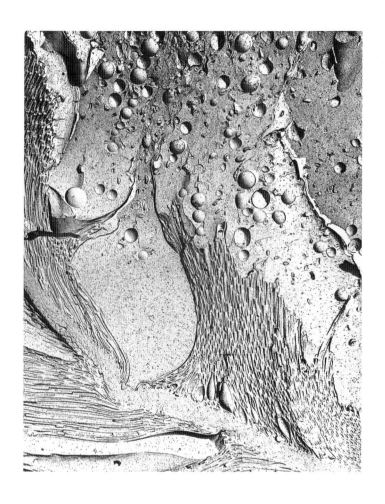

46

Apartment

16 cushions filled with foam
and still it's a cell
my home

my hell
my body weeps
for me
       alone.

— Linda Burley

Garlic Suite

Where garlic is king, happiness reigns

I

The way of the Lord had long puzzled me,
how he fashioned men from clay.
I tried blowing into dust motes;
I just blew them away,

and I prayed to my God for the answer,
how he exhaled life, and death.
The Lord came to me in a vision.
There was garlic on his breath.

II

The taste of you is like
the taste of garlic. Your afterimage
burns my eyes, clings
to the hairs in my nose, lingers
in my throat. I've tried
remedy and remedies: mouthwash,
brushing with bourbon, biting
cakes of soap, but these
all pass; you persist
on the tip of my tongue.

Would that you had the civility
of an ice cream cone, the decency
to melt away. But no,
delicious irony! You,
ever the icy one,
stay on, to coat my tongue,
a cloak of garlic.

III

when I dine
there is a hint of garlic in the wine

when I gloat
a lump of garlic lodges in my throat

when I sleep
I fall to garlic heads, instead of sheep

when I die
they shall place a clove of garlic on each eye.

— *G. K. Roberts*

La Playa

The bay puts off her shawl of faded, mottled green
and dons a blue one, one whose ripples softly shiver.
Manuel Fregoso's shaded eyes, no longer keen
enough to meet the sun's incessant stare,
drop to his line. Slowly he sighs and slowly pulls it in
with heavy olive arms. His catch today was fair.

Vincente D'Angelo, who squats amid his balls
of brightly colored glass, Malaysian hemp, and cork,
allows one driftwood snag to pass unnoticed, hauls
the mended net outside. A cigarette burns slow
between his calloused fingers. Salted kelp and mussel
odors catch him unawares. Where did morning go?

Cries of whirling seagulls drown the gentle slap
of waves, echoed in the blue, the empty sky.
Corazon Martinez soothes the frightened child
upon her lap, as soft she hums her ageless lullaby.

— Sean O Riain

50

Newcombe's Paradox and Free Will

A few thoughts on this puzzle (as published by Nozick):

You are placed in the following situation: there are two boxes, A and B, whose contents are hidden from you. A contains either $1 million or nothing; B contains $1 thousand. You are allowed to keep the contents of either A or A and B. Since B is guaranteed to give you $1 thousand, it seems as though the second choice strictly dominates the first, and you should choose the contents of both boxes.

The twist is that at some time in the past (say, one week ago), an insightful being has predicted which choice you will make. Furthermore, it is this being who has placed the sums in the boxes, in a particularly perverse way. If he thought you would take both boxes, he put nothing in box A; if he predicted you would take A only, he put the million dollars in. Of course, the being is very accurate in his predictions.

Nozick analyzed this puzzle from the point of view of decision theory. Here I concentrate on a purely logical approach. We already have an argument for taking *A and B*. Here is the argument for taking only *A*. If you take *A and B* then (with virtual certainty) the being predicted you would, and you get $1000. If you take *A* only, then the being predicted you would, and you get $1 million. Therefore, taking A has a much higher expected outcome than taking both. (From now on, I assume the being is infallible, and drop words like "expected.")

It will be seen that the paradox involves simple logic and generates a contradiction quickly. Since the contradiction is in terms of the seemingly clear notion of "outcome of an action," it does not appear at first to have much to do with free will. Most people have the strong impression, however, that free will is involved here. It seems as though once an accurate being has forecast your actions, alternative and previously possible actions become unfeasible. E.g., if the being predicts you will take A, it is no longer feasible to take A *and B*. Of course, you will have no subjective impression of an obstacle. Besides, if it weren't for the peculiar interaction of prediction and action in Newcombe's puzzle, what difference would it make whether the prediction were actually made? Consider the following: the being accurately predicted yesterday (privately) that you would not buy a newspaper tomorrow; should you buy one or not? The answer cannot be "you have no choice"! For to say an accurate prediction a decision was made is merely to re-express the fact that such decisions have definite outcomes, and that it is possible to guess them.

But a mere guess is not good enough, one might claim. A consistently accurate being must be doing more than guess. Surely a future decision is sufficiently "indeterminate" in some way to preclude consistent prediction. The accurate being is impossible, decisions *don't* necessarily have definite outcomes in advance, and the residual problems can be lived with.

Unfortunately, the being is not impossible. As Robert Moore has pointed out, the entire scenario can be made more visualizable by letting the decider be a computer program and the being a human examining its listing. Let us imagine that the program is used every Wednesday to solve certain sophisticated decision problems, and is not run on other days. One

Wednesday we give it Newcombe's puzzle, having run it on Sunday to see what it would do. (We don't actually have to run it; we can just pretend to. We will call both cases "simulation.") If the program is not too stupid to see the paradox, it should encounter the same contradiction we did. Now Moore's formulation of the problem posed by the paradox is direct: is there *any* way to encode the logic of decision and action in such a program so as to avoid contradiction? Moore believes not, and further believes (I think) that the notions of decision and action are inherently self-contradictory (perhaps combined with certain simple facts about physics, time, etc.).

He may be right, but this scenario doesn't prove it. All we have to imagine is that the computer program is smart enough to realize the likelihood that the human being simulated it to make his prediction. Then it would realize that it has no way of telling whether this is the real decision or the simulation. (If it could, the simulation would be faulty.) Therefore, the only consistent plan of action is to choose box A only. This will cause the human predictor to place $1 million in box A, and win the machine a million.

Further, if the decider believes that simulation is the method used by the predictor, there is no longer any question of $A+B$ dominating A as a choice. This is because the decider's response is in answer to *two* questions, asked at simulation time and at real time: what will I do and what should I do? The answers must be the same, and A is better.

The only way to salvage the paradox is to rule out simulation as a prediction method. It might be thought, for instance, that the complexity of the universe makes it impossible for someone to simulate it (using a subsystem of it) faster than the universe actually runs. Assuming this is correct, that wouldn't stop "God" from playing the role of the being. In this context, "God" might mean the agents responsible for simulating the entire universe. They could run two simulations, one slightly ahead of the other. To make Newcombe's situation happen, they would have to allow the two simulations to differ in that the "fast" one would be stopped after the decider made his choice (so that it would be irrelevant what was in the boxes in that world). Then the being would intervene in the other simulation enough to put the correct amounts in the boxes.

(At this point a certain queasiness overtakes one. My argument is correct as far as it goes, but only if you assume the "person" answering the two questions is the same person both times. Should I care about a "copy" of myself some time hence or in another universe? For that matter, when making *any* decision, the impact will fall on a later version of myself. Should I care about him? (These points were raised by Moore.))

Even if our physics actually does rule out something like this, it seems unnatural to make our theory of choice depend on physical laws that we don't yet know.

Anyway, assume the decider knows that simulation has been ruled out. (It is not clear exactly what this excludes. For example, does it exclude solving an enormous set of differential equations describing you? I think so.) Only two possibilities are left: the being is only guessing, but has been so phenomenally lucky in similar situations in the past that he has a reputation for accuracy; or there is some causal factor at work in the universe influencing both your decision and his prediction in correlated ways:

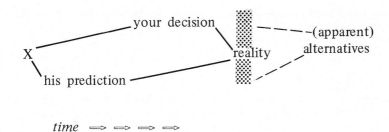

The first possibility is very attractive if you picture the being as living in the universe and incapable of simulating it faster than it runs. If it is the correct one, the proper decision is take *A and B*, since the contents of *A* are purely random.

The second case is the tough one, of course. It brings us back to our starting point of utter bewilderment. Because in this picture the being and his prediction are irrelevant; it is "X" whose prisoner we are. There is some reason to believe that this is the correct picture, with X standing for the laws of physics and certain boundary conditions. Is the notion of "choice" (or even "action") compatible with those laws? The answers must remain unknown for now. For, while the adherent of physics may claim with some justice that a decider's decision is determined, and that the contents of the boxes are determined, he will have a hard time proving that they could both be determined in the perverse way demanded by Newcombe's situation. So the discussion, for now, ends in stalemate.

— Drew McDermott

Bibliography:
Robert Nozick in *Essays in Honor of Carl G. Hampel.* D. Reidel, 1970

Laughter

When we try to draw the line that delimits our uniqueness as human beings from the rest of the animals we may cite man's ability to form abstract ideas, his innate capacity for language, or his ability to enjoy art of his own creation. Whether or not man shares any of these abilities with the anthropoid apes is beside the point, since it is virtually a law of our thinking about biology that there ought to be continuity between closely related species; abrupt jumps without "missing links," while not prohibited, run contrary to the spirit of Evolutionary theory. It is precisely these three abilities (more especially the first two than the third) that explain why laughter is unique to man. Man laughs because he can abstract one idea from another and can thus perceive the absurd. Man laughs to communicate; to convey joy or warmth, to show his contempt for something, to signal a release of tension. And man seeks to create products of his fancy or perception at which he can laugh.

The best philosophical and physiological explanation for laughter must try to account for the connection between man's mental state and his physical response, as well as for the great variety of objects of laughter. Naturally and unfortunately, any such theory is doomed to be speculative. The one offered here is thus only a system of belief; although I hope that it will appear at least plausible or evocative.

Certain groups of emotions, such as fear, anger, joy, etc., are known to involve stimulation of the sympathetic nervous system and the adrenal glands. These in turn initiate what psychologists term an *arousal response;* the physical signs of this response appear in increased heart rate and blood pressure, decreased blood-flow to the viscera, increased blood-glucose levels and metabolism, and possibly dilation of the pupil of the eye and sweating. Such a response prepares us for whatever physical exertion may be appropriate to the situation. All too often, however, no physical response is called for. Moreover, the physical effects of arousal linger on after the initial stimulus, due to a variety of factors, not the least being the time it takes adrenalin to leave the circulation. As Aldous Huxley said:

> we carry around with us a glandular system which was admirably well adapted to life in Paleolithic times but is not very well adapted to life now. Thus we tend to produce more adrenalin than is good for us, and we either suppress ourselves and turn destructive energies inwards or else we do not suppress ourselves and we start hitting people.

Alternatively, certain advanced *reflexes*, such as yawning, crying, shivering, and laughing, may step in to provide an outlet or release for the emotional tension and its redundant physiological side-effects. Because all of these stress-relieving reflexes may be exhibited at the same time by the same person in a particularly stressful situation, it is not easy to untangle the specific impulses for laughter from those triggering the other releases. Arthur Koestler successfully distinguishes the different emotional impulses for laughter from those for what he calls "gentle weeping": laughter is an explosive release of "self-assertive" emotions, such as fear, anger, and disgust; weeping is a gentle release of "self-transcending" or "oceanic" emotions. Unfortunaltely he makes no differentiation that could adequately explain crying, or any of the other releases not associated with "oceanic" feeling.

Here I would like to take a reactionary step and note that

of all the release-reflexes under discussion laughter is the only one directly associated with pleasure. We may obtain a degree of pleasure from the other releases simply because they relieve some of the emotional stress of the situation at hand, but laughter is the only one that is inherently pleasurable. Why this is so may require no more complicated an hypothesis than that the neurological path of the laughter-reflex make a connection with one of the pleasure centers in the brain. It is not just relief that is involved but inherently pleasurable release.

The pleasure characteristic of laughter needs to be stressed because of the failure of Koestler's theory (and of other more narrow theories based on humor as "aggression" or a "sense of superiority") to encompass all the different classes of risible objects. It is doubtless true, as these theorists argue, that when we laugh at a man who slips on a banana peel, we are experiencing a sense of smugness that we ourselves are above such clumsiness. But it is hard to understand how "aggression" or "superiority" can be stretched to account for the happy, care-free laugh that we occasionally do see among young children (among others).

The emotional state of the laugher accounts for only part of the picture; we must also have present the comic incident or idea. Situations that provoke laughter nearly always hinge upon some type of incongruity, a thought or feeling jumping from one plane to another. Thus the man with the banana peel is caught between two principles: on the one hand he is a creature with dignity and volition, who can walk where he chooses; on the other hand he is a physical object, like any other lump of clay, subject to the laws of gravity and friction. When a baby is tickled by its mother it laughs because it is caught between the sense of fear caused by the mock attack and the sense of security caused by the presence of mother. (Studies have shown that babies do not laugh if the tickler is a stranger.) Likewise, puns are obvious examples of double meaning or incongruity. So are jokes:

"Have a good day," a friend said to a little old lady. The
latter replied, "Thank you. But I have other plans."

Incongruity does not of itself induce laughter. It may
produce wonder or horror instead, as when we contemplate
some of the more striking discoveries of science or the
atrocities of war. The emotional climate must be appropriate;
there must be a touch, at least, of excitement (anger, fear, or
joy) and at least a hint of pleasure (possibly grim). The
natural expansiveness of the intellect itself may be sufficient
to establish this aroused state: the pause between recognizing
a pun and understanding it often determines its degree of
humor. A joke should not be too explicit— we like a certain
subtlety to arouse our intellects:

In 1960 an anecdote in the form of an imaginary dialogue
circulated in the satelite countries of the East:
"Tell me, Comrade, what is capitalism?"
"The exploitation of man by man."
"And what is Communism?"
"The reverse."

Laughing is a far more common occurence than weeping,
crying, yawning, or shivering. This is because laughter is the
most socially acceptable of the release-reflexes. Young children, who are not subject to the same social strictures as
adults, cry with much greater frequency than they laugh. The
social permissiveness of a situation to laughter (or the other
reflexes) plays a large role in determining whether we laugh.
We do not laugh at a funeral, or if we are afraid of appearing
stupid. We are more likely to "let go" and laugh if other
people are laughing around us.

Laughter has its social uses as well. Ridicule, for example,
can be a tool of correction, aimed at reforming the manners
and vices of certain characters or classes. (Ben Jonson made
this corrective power the *raison d'etre* of all comedy.) Unfortunately, fear of laughter all too often promotes uniformity

and conformity at the expense of eccentricity. Humor, it has been said, is allied to truth; but only to truth as attested to by common sense or group values— it has a good eye for spotting contradictions, but it cannot, as a rule, convey abstract truth or esoteric emotion. Yet humor is by no means completely or even primarily destructive. It may promote humanization by allowing agression to end and sympathy to enter. If, for example, a boy can get a bully to laugh at something, the chances are much improved that he won't be beaten up.

The problem of sympathy and humor is quite complicated. It is clear that we need a certain amount of distance and *lack* of sympathy (what Henri Bergson calls a momentary "anaesthesia of the heart") in order to be able to laugh at people. That is why the characters in jokes and comic stories are so often mere caricatures: the little old lady, the gorgeous blonde, the traveling salesman, the lawyer, the doctor, and so on. We also need to be assured that the pain of the comic victim is not too great if we are to feel secure enough to laugh.

On the other hand, laughing at someone may establish a bond of humanity that had not existed before; witness the following joke, which comes from China:

> A doctor, who had doctored a man's son to death and was threatened with legal proceedings, agreed to hand over his own son for adoption. Later on, he managed to cause the death of a client's servant, and was obliged to give up the only servant he had. One night there came a knock at his door from a neighbor, who said : "My wife is having a baby. Please come and attend to her at once!"
>
> "Ah, the blackguard!" cried the doctor to his wife. "I know what he wants this time – he wants you!"

There is evidence that humor evolves, both ontogenically and phylogenically, in the direction of increased sympathy and humanity. The two-to-six month baby laughs only in situations of mixed fear and security, as when tickled or tossed by its mother. Later it may laugh in (self-assertive) good spirits. But the child does not laugh *at* someone (such as the man who slipped on the peel) until it is old enough to feel empathy with the victims and to be glad that it was spared his pain and embarrassment.

Historically, comedy has progressed from unfocused exuberance, to ridicule, to increasing sympathy of characterization. The Ancient Greek word *komos* meant "banquet" or "carnival." According to Aristotle the first comedies grew out of the older "phallic-songs" and "satyr-plays" (compare "satirization") and served to ridicule enemies of their authors. The early comedy of both Greek drama and the Italian *Commedia dell' Arte* made extensive use of grotesque masks of a type we would hardly find funny today. From merely *laughing at*, seventeth and eighteenth century comedy moved to *reforming* its characters. And in the eighteenth century, with the introduction of such thoroughly likeable comic heroes as Tristam Shandy and Tom Jones, comedy began to show a true affection for its protagonists. Since then the growing sense that we cannot avoid being absurd in an absurd world, has generated a whole new class of comedy and comic hero, represented by characters like Leopold Bloom and the personae of Woody Allen.

— Robert Enders

Bibliography:
Robert Corrigan, ed., *Comedy: Meaning and Form.* Chandler, 1965
Charles Darwin, *The Expression of the Emotions in Man and Animals.* J. Murray, 1872
Pierre L. Duchartre, *The Italian Comedy.* George C. Harrap & Co., 1929
Leonard Feinberg, *Asian Laughter.* John Weatherhill, 1971
Arthur Guyton, M.D., *Textbook of Medical Physiology.* W. B. Saunders, 1971
Aldous Huxley in *Man and Civilization: Control of the Mind, a Symposium.* McGraw Hill, 1961
Arthur Koestler, *The Act of Creation.* New York: Dell, 1965
David Krech et. al., *Elements of Psychology.* Alfred A. Knopf, 1969
H. E. Schimdt & D. I. Williams, "The Evolution of Theories of Humour" in *Journal of Behavioral Science* Vol 1(3) 1971 Natal, South Africa
Frederic Stearns, M.D., *Laughing: Physiology, Pathophysiology, Psychology, Pathopsychology, and Development.* Charles C. Thomas, 1972

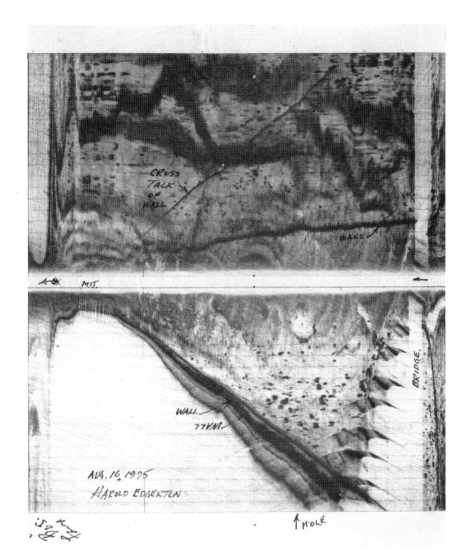

CROSS
TALK
OF
WALL

WAKE

M.I.T.

BRIDGE.

WALL

WALL

AUG. 16, 1975

HAROLD EDGERTON

HOLE

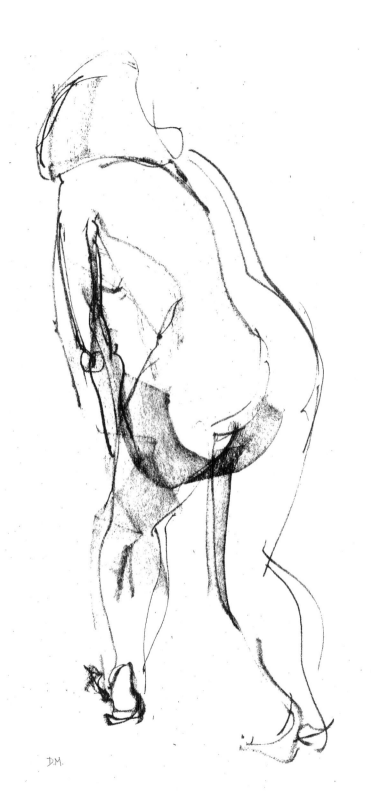

D.M.

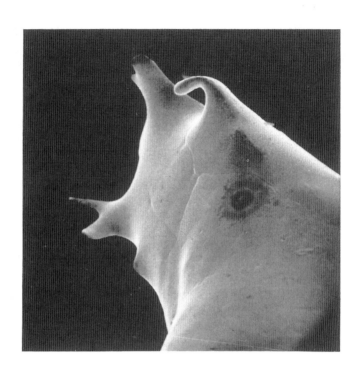

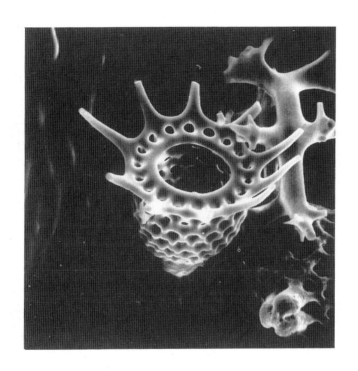

68

The Deep Deep Snow

translated from the original of Wolfgang Borchert *by* David Herwaldt

Snow hung in the branches. The machinegunner sang. He stood out in a Russian forest far out on the front. He sang Christmas songs, and it was already the beginning of February. The snow lay about one meter deep. Snow between the black trunks. Snow on the dark green boughs. Hanging in the branches, waving on the bushes, soft, and packed on the black trunks. Deep deep snow. And the machinegunner sang Christmas songs, although it was already February.

You must shoot a few rounds here and there. Otherwise the thing will freeze up. Simply shoot it straight ahead in the dark. So that it won't freeze. One shoots at the bushes there. Yes, those there, then you know that no one sits there. That calms. Can calmly shoot a series every quarter-hour. That calms. Otherwise the thing will freeze up. It isn't so quiet then, when one shoots here and there. The other said it, the one he relieved. And also: you must take the helmet off the ears. Regimental Order. One must take the helmet off the ears on posts. Otherwise one can't hear anything. That is the order. But one doesn't hear anything anyway. It is always quiet. Not a peep. The whole week. Well then, ok. One shoots here and there. That calms.

The other said it. Because he stood alone. He took the helmet off the ears, and the cold grasped with pointed fingers for him. He stood alone. And snow hung in the branches.

69

Sticking to the dark blue trunks. Piled up over the shrubs. Piled up high, settled in pockets, and blowing. Deep deep snow.

And the snow in which he stood made the danger so soft. So far away. And it could stand right behind one. The snow silenced the danger. And the snow in which he stood, stood alone in the night, stood alone for the first time, it made the nearness of the others so soft. It made them so far away. It silenced them, because it makes everything so soft, so the blood in your ears is loud. The snow silences.

It sighed. To the left. In front. Then right. Again to the left. The machinegunner held his breath. There, again. It sighed. The roar in his ear grew very big. Then it sighed again. He tore off his coat collar. The fingers pulled, shook. He tore off the coat collar so it wouldn't cover his ears. There. It sighed. The sweat came cold from under the helmet and froze on his forehead. Froze there. It was fourty-four degrees below zero. The sweat came from under the helmet and froze. It sighed. Behind. And right. Far away. Then nearby. There. There also.

The machinegunner stood in the Russian forest. Snow hung in the branches. And the blood roared loudly in the ears. And the sweat froze on the forehead. And the sweat came out from under the helmet. Then it sighed. Something. Or someone. The snow silences them. It freezes the sweat on the forehead. Because the fear was great in the ears. Because it sighed.

He sang. He sang loudly, so he wouldn't hear the fear anymore. And the sighing anymore. And the sweat wouldn't freeze. He sang. And he didn't hear the fear anymore. He sang Christmas songs and he didn't hear the sighing anymore. He sang Christmas songs loudly in the Russian forest. Because snow hung in the dark blue branches in the Russian forest. Deep snow.

But then a stick suddenly broke. And the machinegunner stopped. And turned around. And tore the pistol out. The sergeant was running in great steps through the snow to him.

Now I will be shot, thought the machinegunner. I have sung on duty. And now I will be shot. Here comes the sergeant. And so quickly. I have sung on duty, and now he comes and will shoot me.

And he held the pistol tightly in his hand.

There was the sergeant. And looked at him. And trembled. And gasped out:
My God. Shut up, man. My God! My God! And then he laughed. His hands trembled. And laughed! One hears Christmas songs. Christmas songs in this damned Russian forest. Christmas songs. Isn't it already February. It's already February. One hears Christmas songs. That come out of this terrible silence. Christmas songs. My God! Shut up, man. Be quiet. No. Now it's gone. Don't laugh, said the sergeant and gasped again and looked strongly at the machinegunner, don't laugh. But it comes from this terrible silence. No peeps. Nothing. Then one hears Christmas songs. And it is already February. But it comes from the snow. It is so deep here. Don't laugh. It drives you crazy, I tell you. You've been here only two days. But we've been here already for weeks. No peeps. Nothing. It drives you crazy. Always silent. No peeps. Weeks. Then one hears Christmas songs, you. Don't laugh. As soon as I saw you, you were suddenly away. My God. It drives you crazy. This eternal silence. This eternal!

Sometimes a branch bowed softly under the snow. And the snow slid to the ground between the dark blue trunks. And it sighed. Very softly. In front. To the left. Then here. There also. Everywhere it sighed. Because the snow hung in the branches. The deep deep snow.

Excerpt from angela, joyce, peter, renata, sylvia, and death

RENATA

The car waterwheeled struck seventy two revolutions and then jerked forward from the snowbank. Renata clung to the armrest ashtray. A matter of principle never buckling those constricting belts gears pulleys as men drove jaguar phalluses sped dangerously showing that they are more muscular than death. If one fingerbone was sprained (as they stopped with a hiccough at the just-red light), she would sue the fucking bastard ten grand. And anguish.

Eyes everalert beneath wirerimmed octagons, she silently orchestrated the traffic, drove, braking anxiously with her entire frame, 114 pounds of ballast. Renata wears boxers beneath her Sears special slacks they joked in the car as Renata gripped her dangling necklace, a silver design: two intersecting circles with a displaced horizontal tangent and two vertical normals at the point of tangency.

RUNNING OUT OF ICE

Holding it behind her back surprises are the best hellos Angela pressed the lit button. A mat declared WEL OME clods of dirt and sludge covering the C. The door opened and, "Hello, Angela, how nice of you to come— oh, excrement, Bill says we've just run out of ice. Angela, could you be a darling and go upstairs and borrow some ice from the Hendersons, just a few kilos."

"Sure. Anytime" sucking in the lower lips at the edges feeling it become ingrown as she stood there, doorshut, Joyce having gone back to entertain the guesties. It had rained ice last night, get an elastic sandbox shovel go to the roof no worry of dogs walked on the roof or poisonous salt it's perfectly safe thought angela walking up the circular greenwalled backstaircase, graffiti of eloquent metaphor painstakingly painted nymphs nine months pregnant, picasso delineated privates, the archline simplicity of some amused her wanted to stop and admire but no must finish soon angela thought as she handscooped roofice into her bucket she will be pleased surprised alarmed agape aghast at my alacrity astounded at my speed shocked at my vitesse she will kiss me both cheeks and call me darling as

Joyce wondered how to get rid of malicious little Angela the gall. Wonder who invited her. The nerve. Angela in an arab caftan, loose nipples hanging over doilie breast pockets, necklace of dried beets on a newspaper string, and green sneakers. As if I don't have enough to worry about what with Sylvia bound to arrive any minute god why me? With any luck, the Hendersons will call the doorman have her thrown out of this place in no time. How did she get past him the first time? Can't count on luck today. She worriedly crossed her legs, changing the place where the skin would redden.

Why does everyone get so depressed at my parties?

TOM

Clouds of acapulco gold hung uneasily over the assemblage. Samantha the cat walked through in her ethel rosenberg I-am-not-a-spy jigaboo electric tapdance. Patricia approached Tom on pigeontoes a knee knockout in her grassgreen skirt covering psoriatic scaled shins. Her legs stuck together siamese twins. She said in a soothing mermaid sigh, "You look down, Tom."

"I'm not."

"Pity." Again Joyce halfwitty halfwicked spoke. "Tom

73

tries so hard to get down. You can see him skulking around empty Sundays in public buildings, hitting the machines every half hour to get another fix. He drops tin alloy sandwich quarters into slots, presses plastic buttons, out comes artificially sweetened nontoxic to be fed only to thalidomide babies and those on a restricted sugar intake diet (fat Sylvia who hasn't yet arrived smiles a telepathetic smile. Thyroid condition, explain the bits of poisoned apple flecks that froth between her teeth stuck). Yes, Tom is after some low times. Chocolate gets you down, doesn't it? Fresca even lower, with its lukewarm citric bubbles. Chocolate dairy lowfat imitation drink, marshall mcluhan monogrammed melt in your mouth not in your hand morsels; chocolate, peanuts, caramel, and cocoanut permuted through every possible combination. Tom alone in locked civic centers with whistling janitors and refrigeration motors.

"And how did the day begin? Two peanut butter sandwiches on buildsbodiestwelve ways prepuffed white starch patties with milk only after your jaws stuck together piped in by plastic sipping straw. Yesterday brownies at 3 am in the plastic package postdated ten days from an all nite grocers slipping in with a junkies nerves and a muddled face. 5 am a tensecond sweep of the store-twentyfour transistorized haven with tv monitors penal programming turning as you make your spot check for pornographic magazines following you out with hands stuffed in pockets bull fisted and shoplifter's guilt engraved on your face. An everpresent fluid feeling in your upper stomach.

"Back home, Nose droppings on table undersides, wadded in the margins of the Wall Street Journal. Remembering that afternoon outside the bank when you watched reflections of beautiful women in the glass wall."

FRANKENSTEIN MEETS GODZILLA

Peter railtouching (schoolboy memory of tongue stuck on concrete gravel iced granite bannister fear of certainty tongue leaving a bloodful membrane) a moment paralyzed. Sylvia huffs cumulonimbus panting as she sluggishly stepclimbs and presses the bell for both. Sylvia's eyes overread, lips rounded despair, complexion balloon perfect: result of years smearing dannon yogurt into cheeks while caseloads had accumulated on thighs. Sylvia stood in basic black, a slit up the side not necessarily of the dress' original design.

"I honestly don't know why I came," she said through the mouth of an octopus. "I really wanted to stay home, but you know how persuasive Joyce can be. She practically dragged me over. Just now I don't feel like being surrounded by people. Please don't talk to me. I'm in no mood to talk to anyone. Least of all."

Joyce opened the door. "Thank you, Joyce, we've already met, so please don't bother with the introductions," said Sylvia smoothly handing her a sheet of blue stationary folded diagonally. Seeing Peter's instantaneous pocket search glove jumbled confusion, Joyce quickly assured him, "No worry, it's just a personal note, not an invitation. Do come in, Peter darling, take off your coat, why," razor eyes inspected Peter's mudface, "you seem to have fallen."

"It's nothing, just slipped in the ice."

"Well, never mind, why don't you sit down have some pringles and mingle with the others." Joyce went to the kitchen to mix up some more margueritas. The floral clock with the pastel barn and daisies missed its hour hand, plastic cover with grievous crack. Atop a copy of Lady's Home Journal with a piece of defurrowed brain on it. Actually greysmooth gum, juicyfruit flavor lost before twenty fifth overbite.

Peter's coat burying the bean bag davenport, Peter becoming part of the part. Sitting, reflecting emotions, his potential stifling to get out, conversational afterthoughts burning, lump like centrifuged pellets at his brow.

"I dislike lust as an idea."
must not think of food must not think of food thought moby matilda nine times between nibbles and picks lipton sour cream onion soup dip mix. Perhaps sex could be an

adequate substitute. She stared at Charles: the natural creases in his pants were hardly the result of well placed cotton balls. And then at her own overabundant everythings. And sighed.

" I think I'm falling in love with you."

" Nonsense, George, you're a Homosexual," replied Joyce curtly.

"And?" It seemed that Joyce had lost out on another verbal sparring match. Joyce losing confidence, unassured caught off balance unequilibriated the state which Angela liked best pressing her nose into the lit buzzer.

"Thank you so very much," tinkled Joyce. "That was really awfully kind of you to step out, and help me even before you had entered. Oh, urine. John says we're out of hashish. Would you mind terribly—"

"Here," grabbing a baggie from the underside of her breast, taped with electricians blacking. "Always carry a spare ounce, never know when it might come in handy."

Given the time and opportunity Joyce would not only look a gift horse in the mouth, she would stick her head down its throat, practically induce vomiting. Knowing neither how poor grade nor how potentially lethal it was, Joyce slyly slipped it into the hanging terrarium, thanking Angela profusely. When Joyce turned around Angela retrieved it.

Peter sitting in the corner, dreaming of crashing non-existant parties. Renata beside him, mouthing a pear confused, remembering the day she discovered that her lovers had fallen in love with one another, forgetting the trauma of her own making, made up merely to pass the time. The horrible twenty minute delay shade had sprung alive in the midst of sensual passion, ecstacy now interrupted, stopped.

"Rhythm method of course just put on some Ike and Tina Turner and boogie with my baby my diamond head needle in her smoky black grooves."

But Sylvia could not help herself. Memory of lambchops eaten in ten seconds flat. Creamed cheese on celery. Stuffed eggs. Filled too tight, food squeezing rubber sponge. Filled so you feel the solidness at your throat. Your brain against your skull oleagenous lining of breathing passages shorten insufflation. Her head hurt so.

"Whatcha upto?" asked Ralph, beer stains on his crotch-tangled jeans.

" 'Bout to hemhorrhage," she muttered, evidently referring to the fleeting minute blood hemhorrhages that occur on the stomach lining following consumption of aspirin. "Just a headcold." Popping a bottleful of acetate of salycylic acid, her hands groped for a bottle of whiskey. Failing that, she doused a vodka chaser. Doctors recommend aspirin, liquids, and what was the third? she wondered as she drifted into immobile rest, a Joni Mitchell record on the stereo, People's Parties. Her body against Ralph, asleep on the couch in an Egyptian Tomb Pose: hands clasped on chest, staring with closed eyes at the ceiling.

Ralph just snoring a theme with variations for nose, chest cavity and esophagus. It began simply, with a semisneeze accompanied by a problematic derisive counterpoint, followed by a somewhat tricky phlegmatic series of snorts with lustful bass accompaniment. Diaphragmatic drool formed on thickly concentrated lips gripping imaginary reeds. A momentary breathcatching cadence, and then modulation the theme repeated in a minor tonality. Six flats appeared in key signature. Italics instruct the performer *rallentando por respirato infectio.* A smegmatic denouement of mouthspurts gently suffocating lead to the ultimate cadenza of wheezing trills spanning eight octaves presto! with a short, staccato cough finale.

Angela not facing Romeo and Juliet in fifth act silence with droppings of flesh nail and blood trailing her like a lobstertail, hitting it on the rocks broken pieces form a wake but the tail remains unsheddable. She picked at the callous on her blistered palm. Her finger ran through hair follicles following a trace of oil down to its source and then a minor explosion danger caution no cigarettes.

"What is worse, loneliness or boredom?"

Alexis replied, "There really is no excuse if one has the money."

"How like you to think pecuniarily."

"Yes," said Joyce who seemed to be everywhere at once. "Precisely. That's exactly what I would have said, if I had bothered to think," the last bit quite unintentional, embarrassing the way things slip out when one least expects. Joyce retreated to the study, but no one had noticed. She sat at the desk of her unwritten fanletters, the bottom drawer with a manilla envelope full of unviable careers. She felt the same as the day her high school English teacher had pronounced, "but there IS no meaning in life." Joyce flickered, thoughts flashing by, the attention span of a thirty second commercial, the half life of Rhodium 106. Wandering through elevators, the search for lost genius. How long would youth last? Holding four fingers down she bent up at the wrist and counted creases. The fire hissed in the other room.

Peter leaning against the wall, tries to edge his way out, leaving a snaillike greasy trail, but Renata corners him offering cheese which he swallows without chewing, a large chunk of brie slides down his throat with a warm melted coating and tangy saliva, a rabbit swallowed snake alive, a rarebit choke. Like a bubble of Prell shampoo, a blotch of air travels up gastric acid scarred trachea and excuses itself with a birdsong croak. Renata slaps Peter on the back, closing the passage. His groping hands reach toward her in slimy symbolism. The dead gloves at her feet.

"I read the future in blemishes."

Angela too impatient to shell, chewing unopened pumpkin seeds, going to the bathroom, discovering a bug in her underwear. Removing doors to pay toilets a hobby of hers: in work clothes she enters stately terminals, wrench in hand, and extricates screws. Those she finds too difficult to remove are climbed over, the seats sprinkled with a generous coating of itch powder. Angela stared at the mirror, nail clippers biting her lobes in careless imitation of Joyce.

Renata goes into the game room finds the remnants of a sixchambered game of Soviet stakes. Six bodies spilling blood onto the bluegray carpet, a grandmother design of faded roses: Michael, Arthur, Charles, Bill, Thomas, and John. With the vengeance of a seven year old tomboy the guys didn't invite to the clubhouse, Renata clubs herself senseless with the emptied pistol, doing severe damage to her cerebral cortex.

Through the crack beneath the door comes a fine mist of dry ice sublimating but it turns out Marguerita, Alexis, and Patricia have gotten into Angela's hash. They get the high of their life. The smoke sifts through the study as Joyce wonders: have I truly grown that dimwitted that qucikly? In fright she conducts an extemporaneous aptitude test. Academy award winners from 1959 on, worst dressed womens lists, playgirl centerfolds, an abundant collection of hors d'oeuvres she would not be allowed to sample when dead, conversation tidbits, but what is life other than a series of conversations? In horror she scores below average.

Joyce was not that simple altogether. The distinction of reading Finnegans Wake via Evelyn Wood, hand a ouija planchette hovering over the text, smoothing over each page, why she had managed to read all but the last line of War and Peace, surmounted her phobia of gentlemen who told foreign language jokes in her presence, the fear that her watch was twelve hours fast, that she wasn't reincarnated, that lights that flickered in public lavatories were fluorescent blinders.

She closed her eyes and saw arrows: ⇒⇒⇒⇒⇒ NEXT ROLL, PLEASE REMOVE CARDBOARD RRRRRRRRIPPPPPPPPP the sound of testicles bleeding, the pounding in her foot, it was all physical, just symptoms, it was necessary to see it follow the vein and bone feet up the shins over bumpous knee and thrusting thigh trace it below the skin subcutaneous hypodermic words floating in her head Joyce wandered into the bathroom, where Angela looked at her with steady eyes instantly realizing feeling Joyce's pain, a mind grown rutted, and said, "There's a simple solution to your problem."

"What is it?" inquired Joyce.

A LA SALLE DE BAINS
the state of New Jersey: a fat man called new york belches, unexcused.
the city of Piscataway: home to Trojan rubbers and Rutgers. neither gives free samples.
the avenue of Plainfield: snowcovered, a plow leaves cleft palate marks in the sides, burying the curb.
apartment number 320: through the window an unobstructed view of a dying elm.
the bathroom mirror of apartment 320: "does anybody know Melancholy Baby" sprayed in Menthol shaving cream, partially obscuring an image of Janet Leigh in perpetual scream taped to the linen closet.
and sitting like a princess on the water closet: a sad lonely figure drooping over, at the back of her neck an American Flag Readers Digest Miniarette, mark of the bicentennial daemon in a moment of patriotic fervor?

dead dead inexcusably irrevocably immutably ineluctably dead.

fin

— *David B. Feinberg*

This issue was set and printed by Paul
Boisseau, Robert Enders, Steve Lubar,
Guy Nordenson, Roxanne Regan, Pamela
Rubin, and Becky Waring. The type was
set on an IBM composer at the offices of
The Tech, and the printing was done at
MIT's *Visible Language Workshop*. The
type-face used is Press Roman and the
paper *Northwestern Vintage Velvet*.

We would like to thank Ron MacNeil
and Bruce Childs and expecially the
people at *Leether Press* for their kindness
and patience.

Notes on Bucky: Patterns and Structure

Education

"Making the world work through competent design ... What we do with the brain is an extraordinary, orderly pattern-manipulating capability to deal with that quadrillion times a quadrillion invisible atoms. This is all born into the child. The parent doesn't consciously put it there. Men may take credit for the fundamentals of their relative success upon earth."

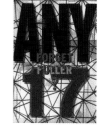

These passages from Buckminster Fuller's *Education Automation* (1971) illustrate two poles of Bucky's thought. Every system is a whole, whether a thought, person, or planet. A system has an inside and an outside and a boundary. Through observation and experiment we can discern the system's structure. Or we may not. The system will carry on its business regardless. Our will and our knowledge are extraneous, even if we are a part of it. It goes without thinking.

Then what of thinking? According to Amy Edmondson, author of *A Fuller Explanation: The Synergetic Geometry of R. Buckminster Fuller* (1992), thinking is a "spontaneous preoccupation" to which we turn our attention and on which we eventually focus by sorting out irrelevancies. We tune in to certain thoughts, exclude others, and finally assemble them into an "understanding." In *Buckminster Fuller's Universe: An Appreciation* (1989), Lloyd Seiden reports that for Bucky this model of thought simply is the polyhedra (geodesic, tetrahedron). Thinking is geometric. Ideas are assembled as connections are made. Some are complete as triangles (or tetrahedra or geodesic or ...). Some become units of other assemblages. Object of thought.

Meanwhile the universe carries on, with or without thought.

Sandpainting

In "Forerunners of Modern Music" (*The Tiger's Eye*, March 1949), John Cage proposed a spectrum:

consciously controlled
MIND−structure/method/material/form−HEART
unconsciously allowed to be

He discussed at length the difference between harmonic structure and rhythmic structure, placing the first toward the left and the latter to the right of this range. "Structure in music is its divisibility.... Form is content, the continuity. Method is the means of controlling the continuity from note to note. The material of music is sound and silence. Integrating these is composing."

"*Coincidence of free events with structural time points have a special luminous character, because the paradoxical nature of truth is at such moments made apparent:* Caesurae, on the other hand, are expressive of the independence (accidental or willed) of freedom from law, law from freedom." [my emphasis]

In the summer of 1992, to celebrate Cage's upcoming 80th birthday, a series of ten free weekend concerts of his works was organized by Paul Zukofsky for the sculpture garden at The Museum of Modern Art. I went to most of them. Some were music, others readings from *Empty Words*, Cage's version of *Walden* reworded by chance operations. The concerts transformed the city for the evening. You could arrive late, sit in the back, then gradually move forward as puzzled spectators left. The ebb and flow slowed time. There was clearly no start or finish. Sitting there, you found that gradually all of the sounds, the ebbing light, the breeze, occasional rain, sirens and voices and music and words all came forward. They were utterly present−the city had never been more real. It was as if Bucky's dome had enclosed us all in this "room" and Cage was performing the perfect *musique de chambre*.

Unbelievably, Cage died August 12 just before the seventh concert. The concerts continued. Merce Cunningham missed the one after Cage died, then returned. For me, it was as if Cage had vaporized into his own music.

This fine mist of energy, the intermingling of structure and free events, even as this event was his death, was moving evidence of his enduring spirit. It was what Bucky meant by the universe: "the aggregate of all humanity's consciously apprehended and communicated nonsimultaneous and only partially overlapping experiences."

→ p. 269

"For every atom belonging to me as good belongs to you."[1]

The Frog's Eye

"Since he is equally at home in water and on land, why should it matter where he lights after jumping or what particular direction he takes?" The question of the century is perhaps this: By what structures do we know form? If modern linguistics has given an account of the universals of grammar; what of the well-formed meaning of a phrase? Colorless green ideas sleep furiously, as Noam Chomsky told us. If form, as Cage claims, "belongs to the heart; and the law it observes, if indeed it submits to any, has never been or never will be written," then by what physical structure, by what "meat machine" does the "heart" tell?

A remarkable vortex, as Ezra Pound would have called it, emerged at MIT in the 1940s and 1950s, particularly at the Research Laboratory of Electronics. Among the work and publications at the lab were several remarkable papers by Warren McCulloch and Walter Pitts. In particular, their papers "How We Know Universals: The Perception of Auditory and Visual Forms" and the famous "What the Frog's Eye Tells the Frog's Brain," the latter with Jerome Lettvin, provide accounts of the effort to understand the workings of neural mechanisms: "We seek general methods for designing nervous nets which recognize figures in such a way as to produce the same output for every input belonging to the figure." McCulloch in effect invented artificial intelligence as the mechanical simulation of human thought, or intelligence, by substituting electrical devices for (real) neural nets. As Seymour Papert has pointed out in his introduction to McCulloch's *Embodiments of Mind* (1988), the work has to do with the specifics of the structure of the simulating net, while eliminating "all consideration of the detailed biology of the individual cells."

By what structures do we recognize form? And what is this form? Is form meaning to the grammar of structure?

From the frog they learned that "the eye speaks to the brain in a language already highly organized and interpreted, instead of transmitting some more or less accurate copy of the distribution of light on the receptors." Processing occurs at every level in the hierarchy of structure. From real to thought the cascade is thought throughout. Or with Bashô's *The Narrow Road to the Deep North:*

The old pond;
A frog jumps in, –
Plop!
Furu-ike ya kawazu tobikomu mizu no oto

Computer

Fuller's *Operating Manual for Spaceship Earth*, published in 1969, predicted twenty-five years ahead to 1994. He died in July 1983, not long after the first "personal computers" were conceived. His manual closes:

"You may very appropriately want to ask me how we are going to resolve the ever-acceleratingly dangerous impasse of world-opposed politicians and ideological dogmas. I answer, it will be resolved by the computer. Man has ever-increasing confidence in the computer; witness his unconcerned landings as air-transport passengers coming in for a landing in the combined invisibility of fog and night. While no politician or political system can ever afford to yield understandably and enthusiastically to their adversaries and opposers, all politicians can and will yield enthusiastically to the computers safe flight-controlling capabilities in bringing all of humanity in for a happy landing.

So, planners, architects, and engineers take the initiative. Go to work, and, above all, cooperate and don't hold back on one another or try to gain at the expense of another. Any success in such lopsidedness will be increasingly short-lived. There are the synergetic rules that evolution is employing and trying to make clear to us. They are not man-made laws. They are the infinitely accommodative laws of the intellectual integrity governing universe."

This is rather strange. After all, who will write the software for this computer? And why be subject to this computer instead of the earth, or the universe, of which the computer is but a mean simulation?

Design is, of course, the answer given. Dogmas will be overcome by design. This may seem quaint today, yet consider Bucky's account of the difference between process and product as applied to his notion of a "housing service industry" and the analogy of the telephone system. Until the breakup of AT&T, phones were standard. "Competition" brought the variety of so-called "designer" phones. "Thingness" and author labels (or label authors?) took the fore in lieu of service. In fact, insatiable consumption led to a rapid turnover of product (and waste), obscuring the service.

With the Internet, perhaps, utilities will come again. Already some German automobiles are designed for disassembly and recycling. With luck the same will come to computers, buildings, even clothes. Design will then take a back seat to process, to the software underlying the product-person interface, while still assuring us that these objects are "man-made." Cage wrote: "The use of technological means requires the close anonymous collaboration of a number of writers. We are on the point of being in a cultural situation, without having made any special effort to get into one."

The Boeing 7x7s are designed with clear objectives. They are made to last. When their forms are changed (747 humpback, 757 flamingo legs, 747-400 and 777 canards), we adjust and savor.

Programming is gradually devising a "mirror world." David Gelertner defines this as "devices for showing you the big picture, the whole," to give what he calls "topsight." The Windows code is by now a metropolis. As means of navigating codes and data structures emerge, we will be able to visit these cities, as do the cowboys of William Gibson's romances. Or, as Gelertner envisions, we will wire the existing cities so that we can inquire at will.

The World Wide Web is clearly the beginning of this and may well be the clearest version of Bucky's vision. Ironically, the administrative structures of civil service and bureaucracy, much maligned these days, are such computers already.

On Growth and Chaos
Thomas Malthus and D'Arcy Thompson, in 1805 and 1917 respectively, both discovered the incompatibility of growth at different exponential rates—geometric versus arithmetic or volume versus area. Malthus devised an equation to represent his model of population growth in which $x_{next} = rx$, where r is the rate of population growth. The modified version preferred by modern ecologists incorporates "natural" restraints on growth, sometimes leading to extinction: $x_{next} = rx (1-x)$ is a possible model.

In the 1970s, James Yorke and Robert May investigated the latter model. They discovered that if the growth rate parameter (r) was set above 3, the population did not converge. Instead, it bifurcated to alternate between several (2, 4, 8, 16, etc.) states or, for some values, simply became chaotic. The impetus for such investigations resulted from Edward Lorenz's discoveries at MIT in the early 1960s (on the heels of McCulloch et al.'s work) while modeling weather patterns on the computer. Lorenz discovered the "butterfly effect" and, later, "strange attractors."

The computer became the telescope for a new universe to unfold, a universe of fractals, attractors, and so on. Patterns of elusive or nonexistent structure. Pure form, perhaps.

The task of representing these phenomena generated new tools of graphical representation, tools that grapple with picture patterns by creatively altering the parameters. A point is no longer an event but the terminus of a converging string of events: the quadrillion outcomes of a quadrillion experiments.

Structure

"Even the brain needs a three-dimensional structure underlying the sometimes two-dimensional patterns of thought," Cyril Stanley Smith wrote in the concluding essay of *A Search for Structure* (1981). Smith extended his experience to "the hierarchy of structural changes associated with the hardening of bronze, steel, and duralmin" and the geometries of crystal lattices for the purpose of analyzing artifacts of metallurgical history and discussing their historical evolutions. He sought "a system of patterns to be experienced visually and turned into meaning by the sensual finding of a shared duality of external relations with those patterns of and on and in an individual brain."

A metallurgist specializing in alloys, Smith devoted a good half of his career at MIT to the history of metalwork. The "shared duality" he sought would have interested Bucky (I do not know if they knew each other). The concept of shared duality would be illustrated, for Bucky, by the polyhedra.

The sciences, as Smith's central argument goes, emerge from the investigation of the products and methods of crafts and technologies, which in turn come about in the arts. This epistemological relationship between aesthetics and material sciences can be traced along a historical trajectory. The love of beauty is the root, perhaps even instinctual drive that generates the desire for knowledge of the material.

Mathematicians Henri Poincaré and Seymour Papert extended this argument, suggesting that the silent ways of the mind (or brain?) as it goes about resolving (thinking) mathematical problems in the unconscious (you struggle; you put it aside; later it comes to you in the shower) is guided to the more succinct, elegant, simple—that is, beautiful—solutions.

If this is so (I believe it is), the old C. P. Snow argument of "two cultures" is socio-logical, not historical. Artists, scientists, engineers at their best are going about the same practice by different means (paint, scientific method, performance). Bucky is a good example.

Diazographomenon

"There still remained one construction, the fifth, and he (God) used it for the whole, making a pattern of animal figures thereon (*diazographon*)." Thus does Plato "pass over in silence" the dodecahedron, the last of the perfect solids. Giorgio de Santillana, also of the MIT vortex, has shown that this Pythagorean reserve hides the discovery that the dodecahedron is a time lapse trace of the path of Venus, a phase diagram, in fact, multiplied twelvefold to represent the universe: 12 faces (zodiac) multiplied by 5 edges equals 60, the basic unit of time. Every eight years the risings of Venus draw the same pentagonal phase pattern.

The five platonic polyhedra are only five by virtue of the structure of space. Space allows no more. Just as language is species-specific, so is geometry not only the earth meter but also the grammar of space.

Patterns

The computer is not even a "meat machine." There is little reason, as Freeman Dyson has already argued, to expect an electrical apparatus to recreate what involves the effects, quantum or otherwise, of all possible interactions.

Yet we now have the means to run countless nonlinear simulations and see the patterns. Each of these performances can initiate another. Ecologies of networked processors can evolve, and we can observe the pattern and figures. The setup and initial conditions matter little. The operations might best be given to chance.

Sometimes the patterns will match something—a face, a rose, a landscape. At some mapping the figures emerge, the code unlocks the key, continuously, never closing.

---

1 From Walt Whitman's poem "Song of Myself," which was published as the first of twelve untitled poems in the 1855 edition of his *Leaves of Grass*.

The placement of the post-tensioning cables and steel reinforcements
Aerial view of the building (February 1971)

The Lineage of Structure
and the Kimbell Art Museum

There is no inert matter, only active energy. However, the cosmos of forces is not the naked manifestation of tectonic functions but their translation into a basically graphic system. The aesthetic values of Gothic architecture are to a surprising extent linear values. Volumes are reduced to lines, lines that appear in the definite configurations of geometrical figures. The shafts express the principle of supporting by the dynamics of their vertical lines. The ribs represent the statically important ridges where the two "tunnels" of a groined vault interpenetrate but are not essential to its maintenance. In fact, it can be shown how the cross-rib was preceded and prepared by the architect's inclination to see and conduct the ridges of a groined vault not as the interpenetration of curved surfaces but as the intersection of straight lines.[1]

→ p. 281

Shell Tales

Of the great buildings and projects designed by Louis Kahn, those on which the engineer August Komendant collaborated are the Richards Medical Research Laboratory (1957–1961), the First Unitarian Church (1959–1967), the Salk Institute (1959–1965), the Olivetti-Underwood Plant (1966–1970), the Kimbell Art Museum (1967–1972), and the projects for the Kansas City Office Tower (1966–1973) and Venice Congress Hall (1969). In their 1975 book Louis I. Kahn, Giurgola, and Mehta[2] credit Komendant as structural engineer on all these projects except for the First Unitarian Church, the Olivetti-Underwood Plant, and the Kimbell Art Museum. It is unclear why Komendant's name is omitted in the first two instances. It is remarkable that it is so in the case of the Kimbell. Perhaps it reflects in part Komendant's wish. As he writes in his memoir *18 Years with Architect Louis I. Kahn*: "There was an article before the opening ceremony in a local newspaper which ... pointed out ... that it [the structural design] was made possible by Kahn's genius only. All names in connection with the construction and supervision were given, even subcontractors were listed; I was the only exception; my name was not even mentioned. Nobody protested, so I declined the invitation for the lavish opening ceremonies [of October 1972] and numerous receptions." Since Komendant believed he had taken a design that was "structurally unsound" and transformed

Published in *Lotus International* 98, 1998, pages 28–48

it into a remarkable synthesis of structure, service, and space, the lack of acknowledgment was a bitter outcome.

The question of credit is often a vexing one among the collaborators engaged in works of architecture. While it is clear in some cases how different participants in the design have marked the outcome, it is often the most difficult to tell in the best buildings. The UNESCO building in Paris is a good example where, by the design of the collaborators, one can tell where Breuer, Nervi, and Zehrfuss each had control, while at the same time marveling at the particular quality in each one's work that came from the association. For different reasons it is clear where Nervi contributes to the design of Harry Seidler in Australia. More recently it is a more complex matter to establish the provenance of ideas and details in the work of Peter Rice with Renzo Piano and Richard Rogers, and even more so with Jack Zunz and Norman Foster, or Leslie Roberston and I. M. Pei. Most likely the best analytical approach would be to adopt the ideographic method of Ernest Fenellosa and Ezra Pound and systematically set beside one another the works of Piano and Rogers with and without Rice. It is clear, for example, that it is on the Bercy 2 Shopping Center (1987–1990) with Piano that Rice first conceived of the idea of using the geometry of the torus to rationalize the structure and cladding, a concept later applied both with and without Piano. Did that come from Piano, Rice, or the project architect Jean-François Blassel? And is Rice's stayed arch concept–borrowed, it would seem, from V. Schukov, and applied on the Rogers offices, Kansai airport, Lille TGV station and Louvre roofs with determined persistence–his or the architects', or neither?

In the case of Komendant the problem is that, unlike Rice, it is not clear that he developed a set of characteristic ideas or preoccupations that carried over from one collaboration to the next.[4] His work with Moshe Safdie on Habitat '67 is entirely unlike the work with Kahn. Even within the body of work with Kahn there are great differences from the Richards Laboratory to the Salk and Kimbell structures, besides, of course, the fact that they are all concrete. The carpentry of the Richards pre-cast system does not reappear in the later projects. The use of the Vierendeel truss frame and, most consistently, the use of prestressing and post-tensioning, the latter of which is invisible in the form, do recur but neither in a unique manner. In his textbook *Contemporary Concrete Structures*,[5] the structural system examples shown all feature some kind of pre-tensioning or post-tensioning of the concrete, including the remarkable applications to Habitat '67 and the Venice Congress Hall. However, there is no obvious formal pursuit in Komendant's work similar to Rice's stayed arch concept.

Diagram of the cycloid vault

The accounts of the development of the design of the Kimbell roof structure differ markedly. Referring to the section drawn and dated September 22, 1967, Komendant relates that: "As conceived, the preliminary layout of the shells was structurally unsound. First, Kahn misunderstood the carrying action of the shell. The arch shape confused him and so he considered a shell primarily an arch and not a beam, which it actually is. Due to this, the shell roof design was structurally completely wrong. The arrangement of ducts below the marginal beams was improper. The end support of the shells was clumsy. From a structural as well as from an architectural point of view, the roof design was dishonest and the elegance of a shell system was entirely missing. I changed the shape and layout so it would work structurally. Kahn accepted the changes after my explanations."[6]

According to Marshall Meyers, the project architect, the choice of the cycloid was initiated by his reading of Fred Angerer's book *Surface Structures in Architecture*,[7] which showed sectional curves for barrel shells: semicircle, ellipse, cycloid, and sector of circle.

"Though the cycloid was unfamiliar, I was struck by the grace of this curve and saw that it perhaps could fulfill our needs. When I showed it to Kahn he accepted it without hesitation and we began to prepare section drawings. I called our local structural engineer, Nicholas Gianopoulos, to discuss the feasibility of the cycloid structure, but when he learned that we intended to cut out a slot at the top of the curve for a skylight, he told me that we had effectively destroyed the integrity of the shell and that analysis of this was beyond his expertise. 'Call Gus,' he said. When Meyers went to see 'Gus' Komendant in Upper Montclair, New Jersey, the engineer 'looked at our drawings. Then ... opened a large German book, pointed to a drawing of a cycloid and, in his abrupt manner of speaking, just said 'yup.''"

In her fine essay on the Kimbell in *The Art Museums of Louis Kahn*, Patricia Cummings Loud describes the "vaulted shape, now more spreading and Mediterranean" of this and other drawings prepared by Kahn on that September day. She quotes Kahn from his talk in Boston in November of that year: "Here I felt that the light in the rooms structured in concrete will have the luminosity of silver. I know that rooms for the paintings and objects that fade should only most modestly be given natural light. The scheme of enclosure of the museum is a succession of cycloid vaults, each of a single span 150 feet (46 m) long and 20 feet (6 m) wide, each forming the rooms with a narrow slit to the sky, with a mirrored glass shaped to spread natural light on the sides of the vault. This light will give a touch of silver

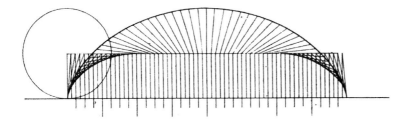

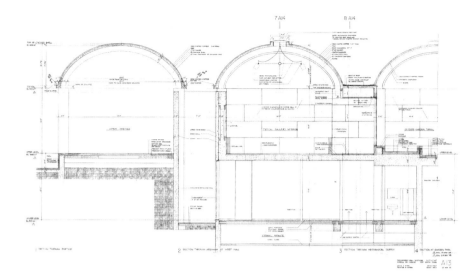

to the room without touching the objects directly, yet give the comforting feeling of knowing the time of day. Added to the skylight from the slit over the exhibit rooms, I cut across the vaults, at a right angle, a counterpoint of courts, open to the sky, of calculated dimensions and character, marking them Green Court, Yellow Court, Blue Court, named for the kind of light that I anticipate their proportions, their foliation, or their sky reflections on surfaces, or on water, will give."

To Loud, the cycloid "curve [was the one] Kahn instinctively chose for the vault." In Marshall Meyers' account he suggests that it was the museum director "[Richard] Brown [who] liked the initial schemes but felt that the shape of the roofs made the space too lofty…. So, as Kahn's project architect, the task fell to me to find a way to make a lower roof shape."[10]

Kahn himself, it seems, does not appear to have said or written directly on the question of the origin of the Kimbell vaults or shell form. He does write in 1959: "Suppose you got the right engineer, let's say Candela or Nervi to do the building for you—and then you said, 'Now, how shall we light it?'—then you're wrong. Or if you then said, 'How shall we breathe in this place?' you are also wrong. In the very fabric of making it must already be the servants that serve the very thing I've talked about—its timbre, its light, and its temperature control; the fabric of the construction must already be the container of these servants." And in the earlier poem *Order Is* (1955): "A form emerges from the structural elements inherent in the form/A dome

Preliminary building section (November 1968)
Sketch of the section (September 22, 1967)

is not conceived when questions arise how to build it/Nervi grows an arch/Fuller grows a dome?" [12]

Kahn, it seems, believed, as Fenollosa (and later Pound) would say, that "the forces which produce the branch-angles of an oak lay potent in the acorn," [13] that the structure emerges inexorably from the form. The engineering is in the realm of what Kahn would call the design, the "how," not of the "what" that is form. The accounts of the project collaborators in the design simply reinforce the case that theirs is the narrative of "how," after the fact of form. The narratives make camouflage, revealing as much of psychology as of truth.

Form and Structure

The fact remains that the shells of the Kimbell are a remarkable synthesis of form and structure. Loud has suggested that the use of a "barrel vault" form came from one or another French precedent, Boullée or the paintings by Hubert Robert of proposed designs for the Grande Galerie of the Louvre, as well as, of course, from the use of the vault by Le Corbusier on several houses. The application to the Kimbell, however, is not of the "barrel vault" structural type since the span is not across but along the axis of the "barrel." Kahn was clearly aware of this, as a student of Candela or Torroja would be by the late 1960s. His early sketches from March 1967 onward explore a variety of gull wing or folded plate shell profiles reminiscent of the Spanish engineers' work. All exploit the fact that a thin shell section of any form with sufficient symmetry and span to depth ratio will act in part like a beam. The first or "square plan" scheme of early 1967 had such a folded rather than curved roof section.

Yet while it seems clear that Kahn understood from the outset that he was working with, to quote Brown, "a direct, simple sparse shell of structural validity and integrity" [14] and not a vault, the shell concept is not so cleanly implemented either, since many of the shells, including the final schemes, are quite short in span and therefore not much more than folded slabs.

Along with the September 1967 section noted by Komendant, the mechanical drawing of the cycloid vault geometry has become a summary statement of the shell's formal concept. The mechanical drawing shows the construction of the cycloid curve by means of a hypothetical rolling circle. The figure, like Marey and Muybridge's motion studies, abstracts and marks the motion and its formal potential energy. It also insinuates the reading of the structure's strong cross-grain, as William Jordy aptly noted in 1974: [15] "... between the galleries separating

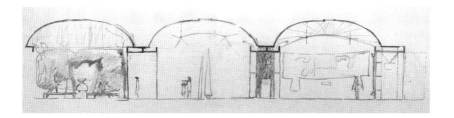

each vault are low, flat-ceiling areas, six feet (1.8 m) wide, spanned by channel beams concealing ducts for heating and cooling systems, their sides also serving as edge-stabilizers for the shells. Inside the building these stabilizers may appear to be beams supporting the shells–a possible fault in the clear expression of structure–but it is they that are supported from the edges of the vaults, which are, in fact, the structural beams. These low areas run beside the galleries as the servant spaces."

Hence the significance of this space in which Kahn reconciles opposites: maintaining loft-like regularity, continuity and flexibility, while establishing within his modular organization major rooms and subordinate areas. This compartmented and hierarchical continuity occurs, moreover, in a grid possessing what I would call "grain." Moving through the space is, alternately, to move *with* or *across* the grain, and always, in any movement one way or the other, to be conscious of the alternative as its spatial complement. However much the Corbusian image [Maisons Jaoul and Sarabhai] may have forced itself on Kahn, it must be clear that Kahn used this element in his own way. Le Corbusier was primarily interested in the long vault as a series of tunnel compartments.

In turn, that cross-grain reading registers the actual behavior of the shell structure. For the curvilinear shell, whether of circular or other profile, is both beam and arch. Like other thin shells the behavior is a variation of so-called "membrane action," meaning that the internal stresses are direct in-plane stresses without any bending of the shell plate.[16] The stresses acting along the longitudinal axis of the shell vary from compression at the crown of the shell to tension at the lower edges, providing the so-called beam action, while the "arch" stresses transverse to the axis of the shell vary from a maximum compression at the crown to zero at free edges or compression stress at restrained edges. A third action is shearing in the plane of the shell.

While the "beam action" is the primary load-carrying action, gathering load and delivering it to the support, the "arch action" will have the effect of distorting the cross section if it is not adequately resisted. This is easy to simulate by making a model of a cylindrical shell from a cardboard roll or sheet and noting the tendency of the mid-section to spread and flatten. The purpose of edge beams and end, or internal "diaphragms" is to stiffen and hold the shape. In the Kimbell, the flat edge beams serve this role as well as that of construction platform and housing for the mechanical ductwork. They are flat, as Komendant clearly explains, because their role is to hold not carry. In fact, as Jordy noted, it is the shell that carries the edge beam.

Diagram of the steel reinforcement

The beam action will also generate substantial longitudinal tension stresses along the bottom edges, and into the edge beams, which are often countered by the use of post-tensioning, or even mild steel reinforcement. Komendant uses post-tensioning. An early scheme applies straight longitudinal stressing strands and straight transverse strands near the crown. In the final design the strands are laid along parabolic lines on each flank of the shell, resolving brilliantly both the need for vertical load balancing ("suspension action" in Komendant's words) and restraint of arch action, possibly a first of its kind.

The roof structure as such is clean and clear, as is well displayed by the two portico shells. The introduction of the longitudinal light slot on the interior shells has disturbed most readers, starting with the engineer Nicholas Gianopoulos. In reality, the effect of the slot on the behavior of the shell is small since in Texas there is little likelihood of large unbalanced live loads to distort the cross section and tax the small beams that cross the light slot. Indeed, one can reread the structure as a series of gull wings from the edge beams and see that it is no different from many successful Candela, Torroja, or other designs of north-light industrial roofs. What the slot diminishes is the effectiveness and reading of the vault or arch action, but this reflects the fact that it is mostly eliminated by the parabolic post-tensioning. The upturned curb beams introduced by Komendant at the edges of the slot further strengthen the beam action and reading.

A last and memorable touch is the introduction of the tapered end "diaphragm" arch that by both Meyers' and Komendant's accounts came to be at the latter's insistence ("Komendant wouldn't budge" [17]–"Finally, I convinced him that the constant depth of the two hinged arches was statically wrong and ... would result in a very dull appearance" [18]) and led to the tapered glass "lunette window" thanks to Kahn's "artistry." [19]

The clearest exposition of the logic and intent of the structural design are Komendant's calculations, held at the Kahn archive at the University of Pennsylvania. These are only fifty pages, handwritten, complete, and succinct, covering, in order: Geometric Data; Loading; Symmetric Cycloids; Asymmetric Cycloids; Cycloids–Short Shells; Stability of Shells; Diaphragms; Beams Between Column Lines E–F, 4, 5, and E–F 10, 11; Columns; Mezzanine Floor.

The calculations are summarized as well in his *Contemporary Concrete Structures*. They make remarkable reading, on the one hand, for the simplicity and mastery of the mathematical treatment of the complex cycloid geometry and, on the other,

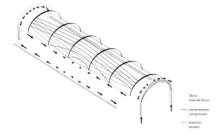

Sforzi
Internal forces

—— compressione
compression

—— trazione
tension

for their selective address of only those conditions thought critical. The localized "sky-light" curb and cross-beam stresses, for example, are ignored and (*pace* Gianopoulos) the shells are treated as solid (though in a later account Komendant writes that "the beams along the skylight are subjected to normal forces N_x and to high torsional moments caused by the bending moments in the shell and the resistance of the struts spaced 10 feet (3 m) center to center. The struts thus have to balance the bending moments of the shell and to resist the normal force N_α").[20] Komendant solves the problem with masterful virtuosity.

Form and Flow

All the analyses and discussions so far of the structure of the Kimbell Art Museum have for obvious reasons focused on the cycloid shells. This is encouraged by the sketches Kahn produced as he investigated the building form, most of which show the shells resting on the ground, as they appear to do on the "front" west elevation. That "ground" is actually the second suspended floor above the ground. The first floor above the actual ground is the level of the parking to the east and north of the building and the sculpture garden to the south. Below this level the building has a full basement that is currently used for storage of other than art objects. The structure of the first floor was designed by the associate architect and engineer Preston M. Geren and is a simple concrete slab and beam system. The "second" or gallery level, essentially the *piano nobile* of the museum, is Komendant's design. It consists of a hollowed *monocoque* (as Komendant calls it "two skinned") slab of two 3-inch-thick (7.6-cm) slabs separated by an 8-inch (20-cm) gap with 6-inch-wide (15-cm) ribs in both directions spaced three feet (0.9 m) on center and the rest void. This slab is also post-tensioned in both directions. It spans over columns spaced up to 38 feet by 30 feet (11.6 × 9 m) apart, which is considerable for a 14-inch (35.6-cm) slab, let alone a slab with an equivalent solid thickness of just over 7 inches (17.8 cm).

This was Komendant's idea and greatly impressed the contractor,[21] Thos. S. Byrne Inc. What is rarely if ever mentioned is the way the slab is supported at the two lightwells on the west side and the entrance area on the parking level at the east side. In both cases a "wall beam" extends from the flush underside of the slab up to the continuous 6-inch (15-cm) glass under the cycloid shell edge beam. This wall beam is 10.5 feet (3.2 m) deep and spans just over 100 feet (30.5 m). It is post-tensioned with steel strand draped in parabolic profiles.

Considering that there are columns on the interior of the space behind the west side lightwells, and that the south side is actually divided into offices that have not been altered in twenty-six years, it is quite a structural feat for little immediately

Section of the cycloid vault
Working drawing for typical cycloid vault with plan elevation and section by August E. Komendant
Cross section of building from East to West

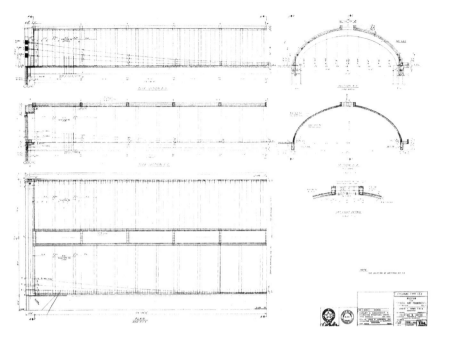

evident purpose. On the east side the result is more striking. There, the alternation of concrete and travertine stone on the upper level and concrete and void on the lower level clearly announces the constant dialogue inside the structure between void and infill, concrete, glass, and stone.

This quiet bit of structural heroism carries a greater purpose. As William Jordy and some other writers have noted, the building has a strong "cross grain" flow. It has been noted that it has good "feng shui," that it allows the flow of space to pass unhindered from west to east.

It faces west to the setting sun and the winds of oncoming fronts. This flow can cascade into the lightwells or through the entrance grove, down the stair shaft, and out the center in back. The differences in light quality from the west and from the three light courts are also marked: the former more diffuse and spreading, the latter harder and static.

Besides this broad flow of space through the building there is the continuous cavity lining the exterior north and south walls through which fresh, conditioned

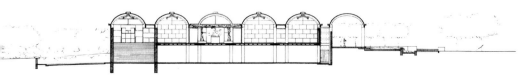

air is supplied and withdrawn. These also exceed by a wide margin what would be necessary. The final plans and especially the wall sections are striking for the pervasive porosity they show.[22] The building is truly constructed in flowing space.

Tautologies of Structure

The evident disappointment expressed by Komendant in his writings is troubling, given the obvious importance of his talent and contributions to the architecture of the Kimbell, among others. It is a feeling often expressed by engineers. The Kimbell offers an example of great architecture emerging not just from the greatness of the architect, which is clear, but of the "vortex" of the project. Pound defined vortex as "a radiant node or cluster ... from which, and through which, and into which ideas are constantly rushing."[23] A patterned energy. In his contribution to Gyorgy

Kepes' *Structure in Art and in Science* Buckminster Fuller defines structure as "patterns of inherently regenerative constellar association of energy events."[24] In the same volume Eduard F. Sekler offers that "tectonic expression [is] one result of that universal artistic activity which Paul Klee called 'making visible' ... which ... is but one manifestation of a more general mental activity which [can be descibed] as 'taking possession spiritually.' Through tectonics the architect may make visible, in a strong statement, that intensified kind of experience of reality which is the artist's domain."

The work Kahn achieved with Komendant does stand out from the rest of his work. Like the contemporary efforts of Fazlur Khan, Myron Goldsmith and Bruce Graham, and Paul Weidlinger and Gordon Bunshaft, these are "radiant nodes" in both the individual's practices and the architecture culture. This should not be surprising, of course, no more than the presence of moments in the careers of musicians like Miles Davis or Paul McCartney that are higher peaks than others thanks to the quartets or other groups they form. Perhaps what has made the understanding of this fact difficult, and often caused anguish to those involved, is the fiction of the master architect (the "servant/served"?) and the confusion of tectonic and technicality. Progress and improved practice will come once it is recognized that, as Kahn understood, "order is" to be discovered, and is not the object of will. The discipline of observation and patient learning which he applied to his practice (and which drove clients and contractors to distraction) is correct for sure, and is still applied in some practices today. Alongside the Kimbell is a garden of rock sculptures donated by Isamu Noguchi in honor of his friend Louis Kahn. They are a reminder that great architecture is the fact, about which air, light, and narrative ebb, surge, and eddy.

View of the building site with the wood formwork carpentry
Detail of the east front, with the travertine facing and the concrete structure
Detail of the cycloid vault in the entrance portico
View of the building site

Truth is the simple reality of 4-inch (10-cm) concrete shells, wall beams, and void slabs aloft in the Texas light and waterfalls, and the stains and cracks of twenty-five years of life. Truth is the vortex of genius and virtuosity, the unique aggregation of wills. "Komendant wouldn't budge," says the narrative, and the sunlight and stories come and go.

1 Simson, O. von. 1956. *The Gothic Cathedral: Origins of Gothic Architecture and the Medieval Concept of Order*. New York: Pantheon Books.

2 Giurgola R., and Mehta, J., ed. 1951. *Louis I. Kahn*. Bologna: Zanichelli [Colorado: Westview Press Boulder, 1975].

3 Komendant, A. E. 1975. *18 Years with Architect Louis Kahn*. Englewood: Aloray Publisher.

4 I owe this observation to Charles Vallhonrat.

5 Komendant, A. E. 1972. *Contemporary Concrete Structures*. New York: McGraw-Hill.

6 Komendant, A. E. *18 Years with Architect Louis Kahn*, op cit.

7 Angerer, F. 1961. *Surface Structures in Architeture*. New York: Reinhold.

8 Meyers, M. D. 1997. Making the Kimbell: A Brief Memoir. In: Louis I. Kahn, *The Construction of the Kimbell Art Museum*, ed. Luca Bellinelli, Milan: Skira.

9 Cummings Loud, P. 1989. *The Art Museums of Louis Kahn*. Durham: Duke University Press.

10 Meyers, M. D. Making the Kimbell, op cit.

11 Kahn, L. 1991. New Frontiers in Architecture: CIAM in Otterlo 1959. In: *Louis I. Kahn Writings, Lectures, Interviews*, ed. Alessandra Latour, New York: Rizzoli.

12 Latour, A. *Louis I. Kahn Writings, Lectures, Interviews*, op cit.

13 Fenollosa, E. *The Chinese Written Character as a Medium for Poetry*. New York: New Directions.

14 Cummings Loud, P. *The Art Museums of Louis Kahn*, op. cit.

15 Jordy, W. 1974. Kimbell Art Museum. *Architectural Review* (June): 330–35.

16 The best text on thin shells is Billington, D. 1965. *Thin Shell Concrete Structures*. New York: McGraw-Hill.

17 Meyers, M. D. *Making the Kimbell*, op cit.

18 Komendant, A. E. *18 Years with Architect Louis Kahn*, op cit.

19 Meyers, M. D. *Making the Kimbell*, op cit.

20 Komendant, A. E. *Contemporary Concrete Structures*, op cit.

21 See Seymour III, A. T. 1984. The Immeasurable Made Measurable: Building the Kimbell Art Museum. *VIA 7, The Building of Architecture*. University of Pennsylvania and Cambridge: MIT Press. The system allowed for "a half million pound (227,000 kg) weight reduction of the total structural floor system."

22 See the reproductions in *The Construction of the Kimbell Art Museum*, ed. Luca Bellinelli, op cit.

23 Pound, E. 1970. *Gaudier-Brezska*. New York: New Directions.

24 Kepes, G. 1965. *Structure in Art and in Science*. New York: George Braziller.

Seismic Design Requirements for Regions of Moderate Seismicity

Guy J. P. Nordenson, M.EERI, and Glenn R. Bell, M.EERI

The need for earthquake-resistant construction in areas of low to moderate seismicity has been recognized through the adoption of code requirements in the United States and other countries only in the past quarter century. This is largely a result of improved assessment of seismic hazard and examples of recent moderate earthquakes in regions of both moderate and high seismicity, including the San Fernando (1971), Mexico City (1985), Loma Prieta (1989), and Northridge (1994) earthquakes. In addition, improved understanding and estimates of older earthquakes in the eastern United States, such as Cape Ann (1755), La Malbaie, Quebec (1925), and Ossippe, New Hampshire (1940), as well as monitoring of microactivity in source areas such as La Malbaie, have increased awareness of the earthquake potential in areas of low to moderate seismicity. Both the hazard and the risk in moderate seismic zones (MSZs) differ in scale and kind from those of the zones of high seismicity. Earthquake hazard mitigation measures for new and existing construction need to be adapted from those prevailing in regions of high seismicity in recognition of these differences. Site effects are likely to dominate the damage patterns from earthquakes, with some sites suffering no damage not far from others, on soft soil, suffering near collapse. A number of new seismic codes have been developed in the past quarter century in response to these differences, including the New York City (1995) and the Massachusetts State (1975) seismic codes. Over the same period, the national model building codes that apply to most areas of low to moderate seismicity in the United States, the *Basic Building Code* of the Building Officials and Code Administrators (BOCA) and the *Southern Standard Building Code (SSBC)*, have incorporated up-to-date seismic provisions. The seismic provisions of these codes have been largely inspired by the *National Earthquake Hazard Reduction Program (NEHRP)* recommendations. Through adoption of these national codes, many state and local authorities in areas of low to moderate seismicity now have reasonably comprehensive seismic design provisions. This paper will review the background and history

Published in *Earthquake Spectra*, vol. 16, no. 1, February 2000, pages 205–25 leading up to the MSZ codes, discuss their content, and propose directions for future development.

Introduction

Design for earthquake resistance has only recently been required by law in regions of low to moderate seismicity relative to areas of high seismicity. So far, in the United States the major areas of focus have been the areas of Charleston, South Carolina; Memphis, Tennessee; New York City; and Boston, Massachusetts. This has been a direct result of the record of historic earthquakes in each of these areas, the attention drawn by recent earthquakes in areas of high seismicity, and the improving understanding of the likelihood and severity of earthquakes in moderate seismic zones. Similar development has occurred in parts of Europe, especially the northern countries, eastern Australia, New Zealand, and Japan, among others.

The principal characteristics of moderate seismic regions can be summarized as follows:

– Either very infrequent, major earthquakes or infrequent, moderate earthquakes are known to have occurred. In either case, the more recent seismic activity is minor. An example might be a region with a single recorded occurrence of a magnitude 7 or larger earthquake, and no damaging earthquake since (e.g., Memphis, Charleston, or Boston) or a string of earthquakes of magnitude 5 to 5.5 and sufficient geologic evidence to imply the possibility of a rare larger event (e.g., New York City).

– The localities are not expecting, nor are generally prepared for an earthquake, and the buildings are, for the most part, not earthquake-resistant.

– Typically, these regions are located away from tectonic plate boundaries, and major faults, and so the source of earthquakes is less well understood and hazards assessments are more difficult.

– The ground shaking caused by earthquakes diminishes, or "attenuates," much less with increasing distance from the earthquake. This means that for a given magnitude the "felt area" and extent of damage is much greater in most moderate seismic regions than in high seismic regions.

This situation is changing for a number of reasons, some of which are discussed in this paper. Generally, awareness of the disastrous consequences of earthquakes is increasing in the United States and worldwide. As earthquakes of even moderate magnitude are seen to be quite damaging, it has become clear that the risks are significant even, or perhaps especially, in regions of moderate seismicity, since the construction and communities there are unprepared, and the extent to which even a moderate earthquake is felt will be greater. In other words, a moderate earthquake will cause more damage, over a larger area, in these regions than a similar magnitude earthquake will in the high seismic regions. Nevertheless, seismic risk mitigation is a more difficult sell to developers, building owners, and other stakeholders in areas of low to moderate seismicity than it is in areas of high seismicity because of the relative infrequency of large events in such areas. (Note the experience in Memphis cited later in this paper.)

Seismic Hazard and Seismic Risk in Moderate Seismic Zones

Speaking before the National Board of Fire Underwriters in New York on May 24, 1926, Professor Bailey Willis, a geologist at Stanford University, proposed that "in California the underwriters of earthquake insurance should allow for a severe quake coming somewhere within the state, causing more or less loss, once every twenty-five years, and that in New England the underwriters should expect a disastrous quake somewhere about once in each 100 years."[1] John Freeman, from whose *Earthquake Damage and Earthquake Insurance* this quote is taken, argued further that "Manhattan Island seems one of the safest spots from earthquake hazard among all of the Atlantic seacoast cities because of its rigid bedrock foundation."

→ p. 308

The current state of knowledge embodies similar views in the approach to seismic hazard assessment and the consideration of site effects. The return periods estimated for various regions' maximum credible earthquake show that there are regional differences corresponding to a factor of four or five on the return period anticipated by current code requirements (FIG.1). A further lesson for earthquake engineering in moderate seismic zones (MSZs), reaffirmed in the 1989 Loma Prieta earthquake, is the broad variation in site factors. It is apparent now, as it was in 1926, that site effects are a key determinant of damage, second only after construction quality. This seems particularly true in the case of moderate earthquakes, with peak accelerations on the order of 10 percent of gravity and short duration. Brittle buildings may survive such earthquakes if founded on rock, but even some modern structures can be severely damaged if located on soft soils.

The devastation of San Francisco by fire following the 1906 earthquake, as well as several close calls following the 1989 Loma Prieta earthquake, confirm the critical importance of emergency response planning. In the

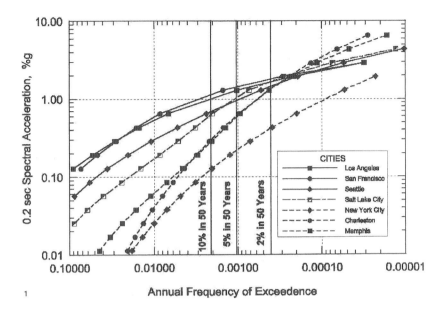

Annual Frequency of Exceedence

assessment of seismic hazard from severe ground motions and the conse-
quent risk to lives and built works, it is especially critical in moderate seismic zones to pay close attention to soil conditions and emergency response
planning.

The Northeastern United States

The recognition that earthquakes are a hazard in the northeastern United
States has evolved and gained greater acceptance only in the past quarter
century. Concern over the possibility of damaging earthquakes in the
eastern United States developed through the 1970s as a result of improved knowledge of both the history of eastern U.S. earthquake occurrences and effects, and of the underlying ground-shaking mechanisms. Of
interest here is the fact that this improved knowledge led to changes in
both national and local building codes through the seventies. The 1973
Uniform Building Code [2] included northern New York State; Boston, Massachusetts; and Charleston, South Carolina, in the next-to-highest seismic zone (Zone 2 of 3). The subsequent ATC 3-06 maps, [3] developed for
equal probabilities of occurrence and intensity nationwide, refined the
zoning further. At the same time, the Nuclear Regulatory Commission
was carefully evaluating the seismic hazards and risks at potential plant

1 Hazard curves for selected cities (BSSC 1999)

sites. In an advisory note, the Nuclear Regulatory Commission[4] commented as follows:

"Because the geologic and tectonic features of the Charleston region are similar to those in other regions of the eastern seaboard, we conclude that although there is no recent or historical evidence that other regions have experienced strong earthquakes, the historical record is not of itself sufficient ground for ruling out the occurrence in these other regions of strong seismic ground motions similar to those experienced near Charleston in 1886 (M = 7). Although the probability of strong ground motion due to an earthquake in any given year at a particular location on the eastern seaboard may be very low, deterministic and probabilistic evaluations of the seismic hazard should be made for individual sites on the eastern seaboard to establish the seismic engineering parameters for critical facilities."

The particular seismicity of New York City, which is "moderate," was characterized as follows in a study conducted in the mid-1980s:[5]

– Earthquakes with intensity of about Modified Mercalli Intensity (MMI) VII have occurred every 100 years in the New York City area.

– Regional seismicity indicates that earthquakes of MMI VII are likely to occur on average every 100 to 200 years (i.e., 20 to 40 percent probability of occurrence in 50 years).

– Larger earthquakes, with MMI VIII to IX, or magnitude 5.75 to 6.75 (probable upperbound range), may occur.

– Even larger magnitude and/or higher intensities, at very low levels of probability, cannot be excluded.

– New York City seismicity is very similar to that of the Boston area, where local seismic design provisions have been developed and are in effect.

These were the conclusions of a committee of the New York Association of Consulting Engineers formed to assess the need for seismic design in New York City.

Central and Southeastern United States

Beginning in December 1811 and for the next year, a succession of earthquakes occurred in the central Mississippi Valley "New Madrid" region, which includes southeastern Missouri, northeastern Arkansas, and western Kentucky and Tennessee. According to Myron L. Fuller, author of *The New Madrid Earthquake, a Scientific Field Account*,[6] "These shocks have not been surpassed or even equaled for number, continuance of disturbance, area affected, and severity by the more recent and better known shocks at Charleston and San Francisco." The 1811–12 events caused ground motions equivalent to MMI VI as far away as northern Illinois, mid-Georgia, and central Ohio. Because the New Madrid region was relatively unsettled at the time, damage was low and events received little attention in the common history of the region. However, hazards and seismological studies in the past two decades have confirmed the great magnitude of these events and the potential for a repeat event, albeit of low probability. As if the ground motion of the 1811–12 New Madrid events alone are not sufficient reason for comprehensive seismic design requirements in the central United States, the extent of soil lique-faction was staggering. Work by Fuller in the early 1900s shows that in the 1811–12 New Madrid events, liquefaction was pervasive in a zone extending from Memphis 93 miles (150 km) to the north, and over a width of 31 to 37 miles (50 to 60 km). Extensive ground fissuring (up to 5 miles [8 km] in length), ejection of sand and water, settlement, and landslides were common in this zone.[7]

Early recognition by building authorities of the seismic hazard in the New Madrid region came from the Memphis Building Code Advisory Board in 1965.[8] However, the board had little to draw upon but the high-hazard practices of the West Coast. With the development of the ATC 3-06 *Tentative Provisions* in 1978,[3] a national view of seismic hazard and de-sign advanced that was useful for application in the central United States, but West Coast versus central and eastern U.S. practice remained. For example, in the late 1970s it was well known that in many regions of California the design seismic hazard maps were "truncated" at 0.4 *g*. En-hanced ductility provisions were relied upon to cover any shortfall created by truncation. In the balance of the country, including the central United States, however, the design maps were not truncated, and, hence, code developers assumed that some indeterminately lower level of ductility would suffice. Such West Coast versus Elsewhere issues served to confuse and delay the adoption of seismic provisions in Memphis and other parts of the central and eastern United States.[8]

Charleston was shaken by a devastating event in 1886 resulting in sixty deaths and estimated damage (in 1886 terms) exceeding $5 million.[9] As in Memphis, the 1886 event caused widespread liquefaction. In fact, research by Obermeier et al. indicates that at least three liquefaction-inducing earthquakes have taken place within the past 7,200 years near Charleston.[10]

TABLE 1 Ratio of spectral acceleration at 0.2 seconds for 2%/50-year hazard to 10%/50-year hazard

Los Angeles	1.7
San Francisco	1.7
New York City	3.3
Charleston	5.0
Memphis	5.1

TABLE 1

Proponents of seismic design in the Charleston area recognized the political sensitivity of such provisions and recommended two important strategies for dealing with the problem:

1. Educate building officials and other stakeholders about seismic hazard and risk mitigation.
2. Focus first on the highest priorities: schools and essential facilities.[9]

Again, the absence of large events since has produced some complacency about the urgency of seismic hazard in the Charleston area, which has led to resistance to recognition of the true hazards in local building codes.

General Considerations

A number of probabilistic seismic hazard assessments developed for sites in the northeastern United States and other moderate seismic zones led to additional observations. The estimated ground motion parameters, either spectral accelerations or velocities, for increasing average return periods, maintained a steeper slope in the moderate than in the higher seismic zones. This difference in "marginal hazard" or "exceedence ratio" [11, 12] implies that buildings designed in each region in terms of the same return period or percent probability of exceedence over a given time period would not provide the same level of safety (SEE TABLE 1 AND FIG. 1).

An important implication of this idea of marginal hazard is that the prevailing notion embodied in the materials design provisions of building codes prior to the 1990s—that less ductility is required in regions of lower seismicity—is mistaken. In fact, the marginal hazard characteristic of moderate seismic zones dictates that greater ductility and energy-dissipating capacity should be required of structures designed for forces corresponding to 10%/50-year hazards.

In Boston in the 1970s and in New York City in the late 1980s, the principal concerns confronting those considering the development of a seismic code were as follows:

– What are the maximum probable (say, with a 10 to 20% probability of occurrence in 50 years) and maximum credible (say, with a 2% probability of occurrence in 50 years) earthquakes for the region, and what would be the nature of the resulting ground motion at various types of sites?
– How difficult and costly is it to provide seismic resistance to buildings?
– What would the human and economic effects of an occurrence of the maximum probable or maximum credible earthquakes be, both locally and nationally?
– To what extent would improved building codes mitigate these consequences? What other measures are needed? Should these take precedence over improved building codes? (e.g., post-disaster planning, upgrading medical or other emergency facilities and lifelines, abatement of hazardous buildings, etc.)?
– What corollary benefits are there to adopting seismic design requirements in improved design and construction practices?
– Given the cost/benefit relationships in MSZs and uncertainty in hazard predictions, what level(s) of seismic ground motion or hazard level(s) would society consider prudent for new construction?

Clearly it is necessary to assess the need for seismic code provisions alongside other human needs. With limited resources, is it right to allocate a sizable portion to seismic resistance, given the infrequency of earthquakes, as against needed housing, or education? Especially as it will affect such a small percentage of the building stock. Can one ignore an event, with extremely low probability, of such severe consequences?

Wind Versus Seismic Resistance
When considering the introduction of a seismic code in moderate seismic zones, the question arises whether the requirements for wind resistance, especially for tall buildings, can provide adequate earthquake resistance. As part of a study of the impact of the ATC 3-06 guidelines, and in a study sponsored by BSSC,[13] an approach was proposed for comparing wind and seismic resistance, based on the building density. A building of height H and depth parallel to the wind D will have a total wind base shear W equal to

$$W = {}_pHD \quad (1)$$

in units of force per unit building width, where p is the average wind pressure. The seismic base shear E would be equal to

$$E = C\varrho HD \quad (2)$$

per unit building width, where D is the building depth, or dimension parallel to the wind direction, and C is the seismic coefficient including zone, soil, structural system "ductility," and dynamic response factors. ϱ is the average building density. C relates to the building period that can be calculated approximately as

$$T = C_t H^{3/4}$$

C_t is an empirical coefficient between 0.02 and 0.03. In general, building density ranges from 10–15 pounds (4.6–6.8 kg) per cubic floor (pcf) for steel structures to 20–25 pcf for masonry and concrete structures. Combining Equations 1 and 2, one may express the earthquake demand, E, as a function of wind resistance, W:

$$E/W = C\varrho D/p \quad (3)$$

For many structures in the central and eastern United States, $E/W \le 1.0$. For others, $E/W \gg 1.0$. It is clear from Equation 3 that heavier, deeper structures designed for relatively low wind pressures will be more at risk to earthquake damage than other structures. When considering older buildings, especially pre-World War II, it is also important to remember that many were built without a complete lateral load-resisting system in the "longitudinal" direction, but instead relied on the infill masonry to stiffen the semi-rigid frames against the small wind loads acting on the narrow face of the building. This asymmetry is, of course, detrimental to seismic resistance.

Current Assessment of Seismic Hazard

The most recent developments in seismic hazard assessment for MSZs are discussed elsewhere in this volume. The 1997 *NEHRP Recommended Provisions for the Development of Seismic Regulations for New Buildings and Other Structures* [14] have incorporated a radical revision to the hazard assessments that are based on the Building Seismic Safety Council Project '97 mapping project. As part of Project '97, the United States Geological

Survey (USGS) prepared new seismic hazard maps that are a radical departure in objective and method from previous natural hazard assessments. Two notable features of this new hazard assessment are (1) the mapping of spectral values at 0.2 and 1.0 second, and (2) the use of 2%/50-year hazard levels, rather than the previous 10%/50-year values. In the 1997 *NEHRP Provisions* (and in the upcoming 2000 *International Building Code*), 2%/50-year values will be multiplied by two-thirds to recognize the margin against collapse inherent in current design procedures. The base shears resulting from $2/3 \times$ (2%/50-year values) are about equivalent to the 10%/50-year values in areas of high seismicity, but as much as 100 to 200% greater in areas of low to moderate seismicity. Thus the seismic risk posed by large, rare events in areas of low to moderate seismicity is beginning to be recognized. The effect of this on seismic risk is discussed in the next section.

Seismic Risk

General Considerations of Risk

As opposed to the western United States, the seismicity of the central and eastern United States (CEUS) is characterized by rare, damaging earthquakes. Frequently occurring events (around $M = 4.5$) damage only the most fragile structures. Studies of the cost of building seismic resistance into structures in the Northeast and the benefits to be derived therefrom generally show that the increased cost of seismic resistance is not justified on the basis of economic considerations, but that life safety is the key objective. When one considers risk as the product of hazard and vulnerability, it is vulnerability of structures to the rare, damaging events that drives seismic design in the CEUS. Over the last several years there has been considerable debate as to whether design ground motions with a 10% probability of exceedence in 50 years provides adequate protection of life safety when much larger events are reasonably foreseeable at lower risk levels (say 2% in 50 years). This has resulted, as mentioned above, in the adoption in the 1997 *NEHRP Provisions* of a basic design ground motion that is $2/3$ of the 2% in 50 years ground motion. The impact of this on seismic performance in the CEUS is discussed in the section below.

Consideration of Total Hazard

Drawing on the Commentary of ATC 3-06, the total seismic risk can be assessed by integrating the product of hazard and vulnerability to obtain an annual probability of failure as follows:

$$f = \int P[F \mid a] \frac{d\gamma}{da} da$$

where:

f = average number of failures per year

$P[F \mid a]$ = conditional probability of failure, given acceleration, a

$\frac{d\gamma}{da}$ = annual rate at which intensities of shaking are exceeded, i.e., the slope of the hazard curve

With this method, the contribution of total seismic hazard to risk of failure is obtained.

Using hazard curves developed by USGS for Project '97 and published on the Web and using generic fragility curves from a number of sources,[15, 16, 17] we (the authors) performed such integrations for ten geographic locations in the United States for two scenarios: (1) design spectral acceleration based on a 10% in 50 years probability and (2) design spectral acceleration based on two-thirds of the 2% in 50 years probability. The former represents the basis of most of the national codes up to the present. The latter represents the approach taken by the 1997 *NEHRP Provisions* as described above. The results, shown in Figures 2 and 3 for the 10%/50 years and $\frac{2}{3} \times 2\%$/ 50 years bases respectively, indicate that anchoring the design seismic hazard at 10% in 50 years results in significant disparity: areas of low to moderate seismicity are at considerably more risk than areas of high seismicity, while the newer approach provides a better balance of risk across geographic areas.

Existing Buildings

For structures in the CEUS, seismic resistance can be provided in new construction often for very little increase in construction cost, particularly for structures of light construction and relatively high inherent wind resistance. In many cases, seismic resistance is obtained only by adding detailing that ensures ductility and redundancy with no increase in design lateral forces. The principal challenge to seismic risk in the CEUS is with a large existing building stock built before earthquake design considerations were codified. Somewhat different from the western United

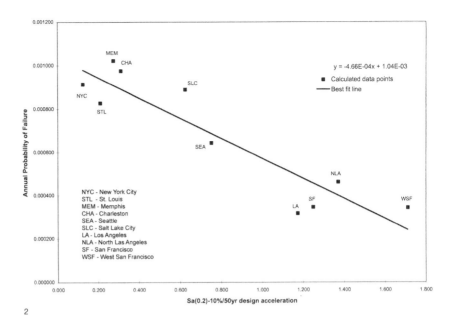

2

States, the great majority of existing buildings in the CEUS are of older, nonductile systems, were designed for little or no lateral forces, and are heavily concentrated in urban masses. Except for the so-called Presidential Order requiring evaluation of federally owned and leased facilities,[18] there are no socially mandated programs for addressing this risk. Developing and implementing such a program for existing facilities should be the top priority for seismic risk mitigation in the areas of the CEUS of moderate risk.

Massachusetts State Building Code and the BOCA Code

Massachusetts was the first eastern state to adopt specially developed seismic design provisions. The provisions, first published in 1975, were slightly modified over the next five years, but essentially remained unchanged for seventeen years. They were based, in part, on the provisions of the 1973 *Uniform Building Code (UBC)*, with modifications to reflect local knowledge and concerns.

These provisions represented the recommendations of an ad hoc committee jointly appointed by the Boston Society of Civil Engineers and the Massachusetts Section of the American Society of Civil Engineers

2 Plot of annual probability of failure in different cities versus the design acceleration for 10 % in 50-year return period
3 Plot of annual probability of failure in different cities versus the design acceleration for 2 % in 50-year return period

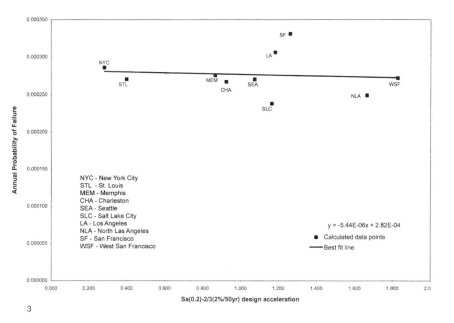

3

in July 1973. The committee considered the results of seismic risk and cost-benefit analyses previously conducted as part of the Seismic Design Decision Analysis project at the Massachusetts Institute of Technology. The primary finding of these studies was that the probable maximum earthquake intensities for Massachusetts were as large as those for *UBC* Zone 3 in California, but had much longer return periods (lower hazard levels). The cost-benefit analyses suggested that the protection of life safety could best be achieved for new construction at minimal incremental cost by comprehensive ductility requirements rather than by requirements for large lateral resistance.

In fact, the stated purpose of the original seismic design provisions of the *Massachusetts State Building Code (MSBC)* was "to protect life safety by limiting structural failure." [19] This contrasted with the intent of the *UBC* provisions embodied in the SEAoC *Recommended Lateral Force Requirements and Commentary* at that time, which was to "resist minor earthquakes without damage; to resist moderate earthquakes without structural damage, but with some nonstructural damage; and to resist major earthquakes without collapse, but with some structural as well as nonstructural damage." [20] The seismic provisions developed for

Massachusetts were intended solely to protect life safety and not to reduce expected damage. This recognized the low probability of occurrence of damaging earthquakes in Massachusetts and the economic impracticality of providing improved asset protection in new construction.

The seismic studies defined a nominal design earthquake with a peak ground acceleration on firm soil of 0.12 g (acceleration of gravity), corresponding to an epicentral intensity of between MMI VII and MMI VIII. In 1975 the return period for this nominal earthquake was estimated to be approximately 5,000 years, with bounds of 2,000 years and 10,000 years reflecting the uncertainty in seismic risk. The adoption of a zone factor of one-third in the 1973 *UBC* base shear formulation, along with special design requirements to ensure ductility and specific foundation design requirements, formed the basis of the 1975 *MSBC* seismic provisions.

For comparison, the 1973 *UBC* identified the majority of the Commonwealth of Massachusetts as Zone 2 (MMI VII and Z = ½) and a small section of northeastern Massachusetts as Zone 3 (MMI VII and Z = 1), similar to the highest zone in California. In the 1976 *UBC*, the same zonation applied in Massachusetts except that a new zone, Zone 4, was added in California; subsequently, the zone factors for Zones 2 and 3 were changed to ⅜ and ¾ respectively. In the 1987 *Basic Building Code* of the Building Officials and Codes Administrators (BOCA), a variation of the 1976 *UBC* map included the entire Commonwealth of Massachusetts in Zone 2 with Z = ⅜.

The 1988 *UBC* included a revised seismic zone map that still remains in the current 1997 *UBC*. It is similar to the 1987 BOCA *Code* map except that Zone 2 is subdivided into Zone 2A for the central and eastern United States and Zone 2B in the western United States. The zone factors were modified to represent effective peak acceleration (EPA) as a fraction of g. Massachusetts was entirely located within Zone 2A with Z = 0.15, or an EPA of 0.15 g.

The 1996 BOCA *Code* maps are based on the 1991 *NEHRP Provisions* and provide contours of the effective peak acceleration coefficient, A_a, and the effective velocity-related acceleration coefficient, A_v. The map coefficients reflect ground motions with a 10 percent probability of exceedence in 50 years, or a mean return period of 475 years. Massachusetts lies entirely within contours of 0.10 for both A_a and A_v, except for a point location with A_a and A_v equal to 0.15.

TABLE 2 Historical summary of design EPA for Boston, Massachusetts

Effective Peak Acceleration (g)	Mean Return Period (yr)	Source
0.16 [1]	not estimated	1970 *Boston Building Code* (Zone 2 of 1967 *UBC*); 1970/1973 *UBC*, Zone 2
0.12 [2]	not estimated	1976 through 1985 *UBC*
0.12	~5,000	1975 *MSBC* [3] ($Z = 1/3$)
0.09	475	USGS (Algermissen and Perkins), 1976
0.10	475	ATC 3-06, 1978; 1985/1991/1994 *NEHRP Provisions*; and 1987/1990/1993 BOCA *Codes*
0.15	475	1988 through 1997 *UBC*, Zone 2A
0.12	>500	1997 *MSBC*
0.14 [4]	Based on 2,475-year return period, but scaling base shear by $2/3$ results in an equivalent return period of about 1,300 years.	1997 *NEHRP Provisions* (proposed)

1. Correlation based on zone factor $Z = 1/2$ (MMI VII)
2. Correlation based on zone factor $Z = 3/8$ (MMI VII)
3. *Massachusetts State Building Code*
4. Design EPA shown reflects $2/3$ of EPA for mean return period shown adjusted to reflect stiff soil site

TABLE 2

The above-mentioned BOCA seismic hazard maps are based on sites with stiff soils. In contrast, the 1997 *NEHRP Provisions* incorporate the results of the USGS National Seismic Hazard Mapping Project, which maps contours of spectral acceleration at 0.2 sec (short) period, S_s, and at 1.0 sec period, S_1, for sites on rock. The design values are two-thirds of the spectral accelerations with a 2 percent probability of exceedence in 50 years, or a mean return period of 2,475 years. For example, in Boston the "equivalent" A_a and A_v are about 0.09 and 0.06 respectively, for a soil profile of rock. Adjusted by the 1997 *NEHRP Provisions* site soil coefficients to reflect stiff soils, the equivalent A_a and A_v are both about 0.14. Table 2 illustrates the change in the design EPA for Boston since 1970.

Differences Between the Sixth Edition of the MSBC and the 1993 BOCA Code

In February 1997, the Commonwealth of Massachusetts issued the sixth edition of the *Massachusetts State Building Code*. In adopting the seismic provision of the 1993 BOCA *National Building Code* with modifications, the *MSBC* reflected the first major change in some seventeen years. Specific deviations from 1993 BOCA *Code*, which is based on the 1991 *NEHRP Provisions*, are detailed below.

Design Ground Motion

During the development of the sixth edition of the *MSBC*, the USGS mapping from Project '97 was still underway. As mentioned earlier, the 1993 BOCA *Code* maps have Massachusetts entirely within contours of 0.10 for both A_a and A_v, except for a point location with A_a and A_v equal to 0.15. Given the uncertainty of seismic hazard determination in New England and with the knowledge of potentially fundamental changes in seismic hazard maps and seismic provisions arriving in the 1997 *NEHRP Provisions*, the *MSBC* adopted a single value of A_a and A_v equal to 0.12 for the entire state. This is consistent with the effective peak acceleration on 0.12 g embodied in earlier editions of the *MSBC*.

Seismic Performance Category

In the 1993 BOCA *Code*, all buildings at sites with A_v equal to 0.12 are assigned a Seismic Performance Category of C, regardless of Seismic Hazard Exposure Group. In contrast, the *MSBC* assigned buildings in Seismic Hazard Exposure Group III the Seismic Performance Category of D. Seismic Hazard Exposure Group III represents those buildings having essential facilities that are required for post-earthquake recovery. The intention of the *MSBC* is that the more stringent detailing requirements and drift limits associated with Seismic Performance Category D are justified for buildings associated with post-earthquake recovery, such as hospitals, fire and police stations, emergency preparedness centers, etc., in order to reduce the expected level of damage to these critical buildings.

Detailing Requirements

Seismic detailing provisions in the *MSBC* are in some cases more stringent or at least different from the corresponding provisions in the 1993 BOCA *Code*. The primary reason is not to weaken the detailing requirements of previous editions of the *MSBC* for similar structural systems and to recognize the damaging potential of large, rare events.

Specifically, earlier editions of the *MSBC* had detailing provisions for a single type of concrete moment frame, which were similar but not identical to the provisions for intermediate moment frames of reinforced concrete in the 1993 BOCA *Code*. Therefore, the detailing requirements for intermediate moment frames of reinforced concrete in the latest *MSBC* are slightly more stringent than those in the 1993 BOCA *Code* in order to be consistent with earlier editions of the *MSBC*. Detailing requirements for special moment frames of reinforced concrete in the latest *MSBC* follow those in the 1993 BOCA *Code*.

The *MSBC* requirements for minimum reinforcement for masonry bearing walls, interior partitions, exterior walls, parapets, chimneys, and nonstructural partitions enclosing stairwells, exits, and elevator shafts for both Seismic Performance Categories C and D differ from those in the 1993 BOCA *Code*. Generally, the requirements are greater or equal to those in the 1993 BOCA *Code* and are consistent with earlier editions of the *MSBC*.

The seismic design provisions in the *MSBC* for steel moment-resisting frames reflect the experience gained from the performance of special moment-resisting steel frames in the 1994 Northridge earthquake. During the development of the latest *MSBC, Interim Guidelines: Evaluation, Repair, Modification and Design of Steel Moment Frame Structures*,[21] also known as *FEMA 267/267A*, represented the current state of knowledge. Accordingly, the latest *MSBC* allows the use of ordinary steel moment-resisting frames provided they are configured in accordance with Section 8 of the Commentary of AISC's *Seismic Provisions for Structural Steel Buildings*.[22] Additionally, special provisions require notch toughness of weld metal, removal of bottom flange backer bars, and fillet weld reinforcement of all full penetration welds.

The latest *MSBC* requires that the design of special moment-resisting frames, eccentrically braced frames, and dual systems follow the procedures in *FEMA 267* with the following exceptions and clarifications: 1) all buildings with welded beam-to-column moment connections are to be assumed to be susceptible to connection failure; 2) the connections shown in Section 8 of the Commentary of the *AISC Seismic Provisions* are prohibited; 3) welded steel beam-to-column moment connection details used in the design of buildings with special moment-resisting frames shall be sufficiently verified by test of connections with similar geometry and member size; and 4) example designs shown in Section 7.9 of *FEMA* 267 shall not be permitted unless adequate data showing acceptable performance has been submitted and approved by the local building official.

Existing Construction

The sixth edition of the *MSBC* includes a chapter, unique to Massachusetts, outlining the scope of required structural upgrades, including seismic, to existing buildings subject to repair, alteration, addition, or change of use. As the stated scope implies, the "provisions ... are intended to maintain or *increase* [emphasis added] public safety, health, and general welfare in existing buildings by permitting repair, alteration, addition, and/or change of use without requiring full compliance with the code for new construction except where otherwise specified ...."

For the purpose of evaluating the scope of structural upgrades, building use groups are assigned a Hazard Index. A Seismic Hazard Category (1, 2, or 3) is assigned based on the change in use (or Hazard Index) and on the change in occupancy or cost of alterations. Seismic Hazard Category 3 requires full compliance with seismic design provisions with new construction, with some exceptions. For example, specific guidance is given for lateral load-resisting systems that do not meet the detailing requirements for new construction.

Where full compliance with seismic provisions for new construction is not required, the design seismic lateral force may be less than that required for new construction. For existing buildings that are not being extended in area or height, the design seismic lateral force need not exceed 75% of that required for new construction. Similarly, for existing buildings that are being increased in weight or area, the design seismic lateral force is based on the percentage increase in weight or area. For example, 10% and 70% increases in building weight or area correspond to design seismic lateral forces of 40% and 100% of that for new construction respectively.

Seismic Hazard Category 2, with some exceptions, requires evaluation and mitigation of earthquake hazards such as unreinforced parapets, inadequate diaphragm-to-masonry wall connections, and connections of precast concrete elements. Seismic Hazard Categories 1 and 2 require that alterations not reduce the existing lateral load-resisting capacity of the building.

The New York City Seismic Code

Background

The 1982 edition of ANSI (American National Standards Institute) A58.1, *Minimum Design Loads in Buildings and Other Structures*,[23] included a new seismic design section, modeled after the *UBC* and ATC 3-06, which placed New York City in Seismic Zone 2 (versus Seismic Zone 4 for California). This would, in turn, have triggered the application of the ductile design provisions of the ACI (American Concrete Institute) 318 code for concrete design.[24] The New York City Building Commissioner asked the New York Association of Consulting Engineers (NYACE) to review the matter. The initial response, in the summer of 1984, was to recommend that such requirements be omitted. However, after some discussion, NYACE decided that a group of seismologists and engineers should review the issues and advise NYACE. The committee's conclusions have been reported earlier in this paper.[5] Following this, the NYACE Board unanimously recommended to the commissioner, in June 1987, that seismic design be mandated in New York City, and that these should follow the 1988 *UBC*.[25]

At the same time (1986), the National Center for Earthquake Engineering Research (NCEER) was established in Buffalo, New York. As a result, several conferences were organized[26] that addressed the particular issues of seismic hazard and design in the eastern United States. Following these, the commissioner appointed, in April 1989, a Seismic Code Committee to draft seismic code provisions for New York City. This committee included engineers, seismologists, and representatives of the building industries and real estate community. The Seismic Code Committee voted unanimously to submit its final report to the commissioner in early 1991, and the report was submitted on April 18, 1991.

Principles and Approach

The development of the *New York City Code* was guided by several agreed principles:

– To focus on provisions for the prevention of life-threatening collapse of buildings and components, and not the protection of property *per se*.

– To seek improvements, not radical changes, in construction practices.

– To modify the characterization of the loading to reflect local seismicity.

The committee divided its efforts into five subcommittees dealing with consideration: (1) Geotechnical (2) Loads and Systems (3) Detailing (4)

Economic Implications, and (5) Nonstructural. After several months of deliberation, the committee decided to adapt the 1988 *UBC*, following the above-stated principles, for inclusion in the New York City Building Laws.

The committee's work, therefore, consisted of preparing amendments to the provisions of the 1988 *UBC*, except that the steel provisions of the 1990 Supplement to the *UBC* were referenced. The following summarizes these changes as agreed by the subcommittees. It should be noted that one- and two-family dwellings not more than three stories in height are exempt from the provisions.

Geotechnical Subcommittee

1. Seismic Zone: NYC is deemed to be in Seismic Zone 2A with a factor, or effective zero-period acceleration, of 0.15 in S_1 type rock.
2. Site geology and characteristics: Soils are classified with reference to the New York City classification system. A new soil type, S_0, is introduced for hard rock, with a factor of 0.67. The Massachusetts code provisions for evaluating soil liquefaction potential are introduced.
3. Foundations: Pile caps and caissons are to be connected, unless the soil can provide equivalent restraint. Wood stud wall plates and sills are to be bolted to foundations.
4. Site specific response spectra: These may be used for design, and are recommended for S_4 soil-type sites. However, the calculated base shear must be scaled to the equivalent static value (see below).

Loads and Systems Subcommittee

1. Analysis method: The equivalent static lateral force procedure is accepted for all buildings except irregular buildings over 400 feet (122 m) in height in Occupancy Categories I through III. These include emergency and hazardous facilities, and special occupancy structures, including those with more than 5,000 occupants. All regular buildings, of any height, can be designed by the equivalent static procedure.
2. Dual system: These are systems with shear walls or braced frames and moment frames working in parallel. The moment frames are required to carry at least 25% of the lateral load considered on their own. The system is intended to possess sufficient ductility by virtue of the moment frames. The *New York City Seismic Code* adds the provision that the walls or braced frame have sufficient shear capacity to carry 75% of the cumulative story shear (not overturning). This is in recognition of the

interaction effects of tall frame/wall structures, and the desire to ensure possible shear redistribution.

3. Period determination: The coefficients (C_t) for estimating periods have been revised for concrete moment frames, dual systems, and eccentrically braced frames.

4. Vertical component: The coefficient has been reduced in line with the local seismicity.

5. Scaling of dynamic analysis results: The *UBC* provisions have been adjusted to allow scaling to a reduced equivalent static coefficient for periods above 3 seconds. This reflects the lesser ordinates, at long periods, of response spectra developed for eastern U.S. sites. The coefficient C is calculated as 1.80 S/T for T > 3 seconds.

6. Building separation: Building separation is limited to 1 inch (2.5 cm) for every 50 feet (15 m) of total building height. Thus, a building 400 feet tall (122 m) would, at the typical 120-foot (36.6 m) zoning setback elevation, be separated by 8 inches (20 cm) from the adjacent building. The provision notes that "smaller separation may be permitted when the effects of pounding can be accommodated without collapse of the building." This provision is intentionally empirical to reflect the uncertain knowledge of the effects of pounding on building collapse.

7. Structural systems: Several new systems are recognized as follows:

— Ordinary concrete moment-resisting frames limited to sites with soils S_0 to S_2 and under 160 feet (49 m) in height.

— Dual systems combining concrete and reinforced masonry shear walls and braced frames with "Special," "Intermediate," and "Ordinary" moment-resisting frames.

Detailing Subcommittee

1. Masonry: The ACI 530-88 *Building Code Requirements for Masonry Structures* is used as a reference standard with modifications:

— All masonry bearing and shear walls shall be reinforced, regardless of whether they are designed as reinforced or unreinforced walls. Maximum spacing of vertical bars is 10 feet (3 m).

— All nonbearing backup or infill walls and nonbearing partitions shall have minimum one-way-only reinforcement to supports.

2. Concrete: ACI 318-89 is referenced without modifications.

3. Steel: The 1988 *UBC* requirements of Section 2723 are referenced without major modifications. The use of LFRD is prohibited for the design of seismic resisting elements.

4. Timber: The AITC (American Institute of Timber Construction) and APA (American Plywood Association) provisions for seismic design of plywood or other diaphragms and shear walls are referenced.

Nonstructural Subcommittee

1. Part or portion of structures: *UBC* Table 23-P is revised for nonbearing walls, so that only those around means of egress are to be designed for the specified lateral forces.
2. Exterior nonstructural components: Provisions for interior components (e.g., access floors, ceilings, etc.) have been eliminated. Exterior appendages, chimneys, stacks, trussed towers, tanks on legs, and exterior tanks and vessels are to be designed for seismic effects.

Adoption

Mayor Rudolph Giuliani signed the *New York City Seismic Code*, known as Local Law 17, on February 21, 1995, to take effect a year from that day.

New Madrid Region

The New Madrid region includes the major metropolitan areas of Memphis, Tennessee, and St. Louis, Missouri. The coincidental confluence of three states in this region (Tennessee, Missouri, and Illinois), as well the region's central location in the United States, has led to a variety of practices and approaches to code requirements, in general, and to seismic design, in particular. Code enforcement for new construction is established at the local or county level, depending on jurisdiction, and, presently, all three national model codes (BOCA, *SSBC*, and *UBC*) have been adopted in some area of the New Madrid region.

In contrast to Massachusetts and New York City, none of the jurisdictions in the New Madrid region have developed their own seismic codes, but rather have adopted one of the national model codes, in total or with some modification. After years of urging and organized effort by local engineers, the city of Memphis and Shelby County enacted their first seismic design requirements for new construction in 1992 by adopting the *Southern Standard Building Code (SSBC)*.[27] But resistance from developers, building owners, and structural engineers, along with arguments that seismic design provisions *would double the cost of construction*, resulted in compromise: the basic ground acceleration was reduced to two-thirds of the *SSBC* value. Today, the city of Memphis and Shelby County use the current version of the *SSBC* without modification. As stated elsewhere in this paper, however, these requirements greatly underestimate the damage potential of large, rare events.

Following common practice in much of Missouri, the city of St. Louis uses the 1997 *UBC* for seismic design.

Charleston, South Carolina, and Vicinity

Engineers and seismologists in the Charleston area have long recognized that potential for large, rare events in their region, but recognition of this potential in code requirements has been a slow process. Charleston is generally governed by the *SSBC*, which for many years had optional seismic requirements in its appendix. These optional requirements were adopted only by special designation in local areas, and in Charleston such a special designation was made on June 23, 1981 through *Bulletin No. 81-01*. In 1991 engineers in the Southeast were successful in convincing *SSBC* to move these optional seismic provisions in the *SSBC* to the main body of the code, thus making them mandatory unless specifically exempted by local authorities. Thus, the city of Charleston adopted its first seismic design requirements.

Not satisfied that *SSBC* or any of the other national model codes properly recognized the damage potential of large, rare events in Charleston, local engineers pushed state and local agencies to modify the provisions of the *SSBC* to include updated hazard maps and/or two-level design. These efforts met with resistance as state and local authorities were unwilling to depart from national standards. Today, Charleston uses the current version of the *SSBC*.

In the metropolitan St. Louis area, seismic design for new construction became mandatory through the earthquake provisions of the 1987 BOCA *Code*. Smaller counties in the surrounding regions did not adopt seismic provisions until much later. While adopted by code, actual implementation was variable from design office to office through the late 1980s and early 1990s. Today, seismic provisions in the region are dictated through the 1996 BOCA *Code*, and while execution has much improved since 1987, local engineers still report less than full compliance.

Conclusions

Design considerations for seismic resistance of buildings in areas of moderate seismicity are in many ways different from those in areas of high seismicity. As most codes and earthquake design procedures have advanced through consideration of areas of high seismicity and by the strong leadership of professionals with high-seismicity experience, such codes have not readily been adaptable to areas of low to moderate seismicity, leading to some resistance to adoption of seismic design procedures. As a consequence, jurisdictions like the city of New York and the Commonwealth of Massachusetts have prepared and adopted their own seismic design requirements. Other regions of the CEUS adopted one of the national model codes with or without modification but more slowly than areas that prepared region-specific codes. Some of the special considerations for areas of moderate seismicity compared with areas of high seismicity are as follows:

— The large magnitudes of rare events (2% probabilities in 50 years) as compared with the typical design basis ground motions used in most present national model codes of 10% in 50 years. Specialized seismic codes, such as those developed for New York City and Massachusetts, have addressed this by maintaining relatively conservative design ground accelerations. The 1997 *NEHRP Provisions* and the 2000 *International Building Code (IBC)* address this through the adoption of design spectra corresponding to hazards of 2% in 50 years.

— Attenuation of earth shaking is generally different in the CEUS and in the western United States. In fact, in the CEUS, the "felt areas" of moderate events have been quite large, up to one million square miles (2.59 million square kilometers). This difference in attenuation was recognized in the recent USGS national hazards mapping project.

— There is no defensible rationale for allowing new structures in moderate seismicity to have less ductility than structures in regions of high seismicity when using design accelerations based on 10%/50-year hazards. On the contrary, the large magnitudes of the rare earthquakes in regions of moderate seismicity require even greater ductility.

— In many instances, good seismic resistance for new construction in areas of low to moderate seismicity can be obtained for small incremental costs in construction. In fact, the wind load requirements for many structures in these regions will frequently exceed the seismic base shear, requiring only the addition of details yielding ductility and toughness.

— Seismic sources and hazard are less readily defined in the low to moderate seismicity regions of the CEUS. This fact, coupled with the relatively low incremental construction cost to provide seismic resistance in areas of low to moderate seismicity, argues for more conservatism in these regions.

— The existing building stock in areas of low to moderate seismicity, most of which have not had the benefit of seismic design in their original construction, present tremendous seismic risk.

Recent efforts, such as the 1997 USGS hazard mapping project, the 1997 *NEHRP Provisions*, and the preparation of the 2000 *IBC,* will advance greatly the cause of a uniform and integrated national approach to seismic design across areas of low, moderate, and high seismicity. The authors' recommendations for further advancement are given below.

Future Developments

The authors hope that future efforts by local groups will continue to advance some of the special issues in areas of low to moderate seismicity and that ongoing national efforts will integrate these efforts with a uniform and consistent national practice. Future directions should include:

– The ability to achieve seismic resistance more readily in areas of low to moderate seismicity by limited trade-off between force and ductility, allowing the designer to optimize the cost-benefit relationship.

– Improved provisions for assessment of existing buildings and the ability to maintain and improve existing buildings without undue economic hardship that would make saving or improving existing buildings cost-prohibitive.

– The advancement and codification of progressive design and analysis techniques, such as nonlinear static procedures.

– The great improvements in seismic design philosophy and procedures in the 1997 *NEHRP Provisions* and the 2000 *IBC* should be adopted across the country.

– Increasing public awareness of the earthquake hazards and risks in areas of low to moderate seismicity is particularly challenging because of the long return periods of moderate to large events. Ongoing efforts to ensure timely codification of good seismic design procedures as well as emergency preparedness are essential. We can use the silver linings of such tragedies as have occurred in Turkey, Greece, and Taiwan in 1999 to heighten such awareness.

Acknowledgments

The authors thank the following individuals, who provided information on the development of code requirements in the central and southeastern United States: Warner Howe (Consulting Structural Engineer, Germantown, Tennessee), Charles C. Theiss (EQE/Theiss, St. Louis, Missouri), and Charles Lindbergh (Charles Lindbergh & Associates, Charleston, South Carolina).

1 Freeman, J. F. 1932. *Earthquake Damage and Earthquake Insurance*. New York: McGraw-Hill.

2 International Conference of Building Officials (ICBO). 1973. *Uniform Building Code*. Whittier, CA.

3 Applied Technology Council (ATC). 1978. *Tentative Provisions for the Development of Seismic Regulations for Buildings,* ATC 3-06. Redwood City, CA.

4 Nuclear Regulatory Commission. 1983. *Division of Engineering Geosciences Plan to Address USGS Clarification Relating to Seismic Design Earthquakes in the Eastern Seaboard of the United States.* Memorandum from Richard H. Vollmer to Harold R. Denton.

5 Nordenson, G. J. P. 1987. Seismic Hazard Evaluation for New York City. *Report of the NY Association of Consulting Engineers Ad Hoc Seismology Committee*. New York, NY.

6 Fuller, M. L. 1912. *The New Madrid Earthquake*. U.S. Government Printing Office, Washington, DC.

7 Wesnousky, S. G., E. S. Schweig, and S. K. Pezzopane. 1989. Extent and Character of Soil Liquefaction during the 1811–12 New Madrid Earthquakes. *Annals of the New York Academy of Sciences* 558 (*Earthquake Hazards and the Design of Constructed Facilities in the Eastern United States*). New York, NY, 208–16.

8 Howe, W. 1989. Seismic Building Code Efforts in the Central United States. *Annals of the New York Academy of Sciences* 558 (*Earthquake Hazards and the Design of Constructed Facilities in the Eastern United States*). New York, NY, 421–34.

9 Lindbergh, C., ed. 1986. *Earthquake Hazards, Risk, and Mitigation in South Carolina and the Southeastern United States*. The South Carolina Seismic Safety Consortium, Charleston, SC.

10 Obermeier, S. F., R. E. Weems, R. B. Jacobson, and G. S. Gohn. 1989. Liquefaction Evidence for Repeated Holocene Earthquakes in the Coastal Region of South Carolina. *Annals of the New York Academy of Sciences* 558 (*Earthquake Hazards and the Design of Constructed Facilities in the Eastern United States*). New York, NY, 183–95.

11 Nordenson, G. J. P., and C. T. Statton. 1986. Seismicity and Seismic Hazard in the New York City Area. *Proceedings 3rd U.S. National Conference on Earthquake Engineering*. Charleston, SC.

12 Nordenson, G. J. P., and L. D. Reaveley. 1990. Acceptable damage in low and moderate seismic zones. *Proceedings of 4th U.S.-Japan Workshop on the Improvement of Building Structural Design Practices*, Applied Technology Council ATC 15-3, August, Kailua-Kona, HI.

13 Nordenson, G. J. P. 1984. BSSC Trial Design Program–Buildings NY-5, NY-20A and NY-32, *Weidlinger Associates Report to the National Institute of Building Science and Building Seismic Safety Council No 182-016*, ATC-3-06 Trial Design Program, New York, NY.

14 Building Seismic Safety Council (BSSC). 1998, 1997 *Edition NEHRP Recommended Provisions for the Development of Seismic Regulations for New Buildings and Other Structures*. Federal Emergency Management Agency. Washington, DC.

15 Anagnos, T., C. Rojahn, and A. S. Kiremidjian. 1995. NCEER-ATC Joint Study on Fragility of Buildings. *NCEER-95-0003.* Buffalo, NY.

16 Earthquake Engineering Research Institute (EERI) Ad Hoc Committee on Seismic Performance. 1993. *Expected Seismic Performance of Buildings*. Unpublished draft report.

17 Applied Technology Council (ATC). 1985. *Earthquake Damage Evaluation Data for California,* ATC 13. Redwood City, CA.

18 Executive Order 12941. 1994. Seismic Safety of Existing Federally Owned or Leased Buildings.

19 *Massachusetts State Building Code*. 1975. Commonwealth of Massachusetts, 2nd edition.

20 Seismology Committee Structural Engineers Association of California (SEAoC). 1973. *Recommended Lateral Force Requirements and Commentary*. California.

21 SAC Joint Venture. 1997. *Interim Guidelines: Evaluation, Repair, Modification, and Design of Welded Steel Moment Frame Structures, FEMA 267/267A*. Prepared for the Federal Emergency Management Agency, Washington, DC.

22 American Institute of Steel Construction, Inc. (AISC). 1992. *Seismic Provisions for Structural Steel Buildings*. Chicago, IL.

23 American National Standards Institute (ANSI). 1982. *Minimum Design Loads for Buildings and Other Structures, A58.1*. New York, NY.

24 American Concrete Institute (ACI). 1983. *Building Code Requirements for Structural Concrete,* ACI 318. Detroit, MI.

25 International Conference of Building Officials (ICBO). 1988. *Uniform Building Code.* Whittier, CA.

26 Jacob, K. H., and C. J. Turkstra, ed. 1989. *Annals of the New York Academy of Sciences* 558 (*Earthquake Hazards and the Design of Constructed Facilities in the Eastern United States*). New York, NY.

27 Southern Building Code Congress International, Inc. (SBCCI). 1991. *Standard Building Code.* Birmingham, AL.

References

Building Officials and Codes Administrators International, Inc. (BOCA). 1987. BOCA *National Building Code.* Country Club Hills, IL.

BOCA. 1990. BOCA *National Building Code.* Country Club Hills, IL.

BOCA. 1993. BOCA *National Building Code.* Country Club Hills, IL.

BOCA. 1996. BOCA *National Building Code.* Country Club Hills, IL.

BOCA. 1999. BOCA *National Building Code.* Country Club Hills, IL.

International Conference of Building Officials (ICBO). 1997. *Uniform Building Code.* Whittier, CA.

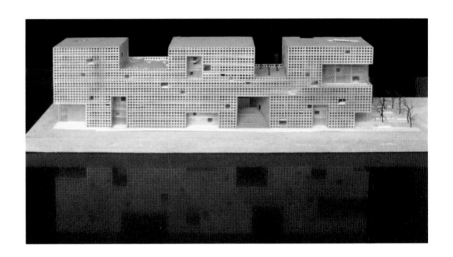

MIT Simmons Hall design model

Collaboration

Guy Nordenson spoke with the editors on several occasions about the changing role of structural engineering in architectural design. What follows is a synthesis of his responses to several questions about how engineers work and think.

NORDENSON: It is sometimes useful to think of a structural engineer's practice as being that of either a technician, an artist, or a collaborator. Obviously, these usually blend into a hybrid, but differences do exist.

The technicians solve the problem given by the architect. Sometimes that means the structure has a particular tectonic "look" about it as conceived by the architect. At other times it will mean that the structure disappears behind the scenes. I remember one engineer friend telling me he saw his task as making an exposed structural detail work as the architect imagined it did, executing a specific mechanical script. Often, the result is a great project. But, in all these cases, if uncovered, the facts will show that the script was driven by an architectural idea, not necessity or engineering.

The artists, like Maillart, Nervi, Candela, and Calatrava, develop a distinct style out of the materials and methods of structure. Usually, the form incorporates certain inventions: the deck-stiffened arch, ferro-cement, the hyperbolic parabo-loid shell. You might even say that the work is in some cases classical, or romantic, or even mannerist or baroque. The practice is clearly that of an artist working in the medium of structure.

The collaborators work as part of design, and sometimes construction teams, usually ongoing. One thinks of groupings: August Komendant and Louis Kahn, Paul Weidlinger and Marcel Breuer or Gordon Bunshaft, Fred Severud and Eero Saarinen, Peter Rice and Renzo Piano (and Tom Barker, the services engi-neer), Leslie Robertson and I. M. Pei. The collaborations evolve and deepen over a series of projects. The contributions are not always distinct or identifiable.

Published in *Perspecta 31: Reading Structures* [interview], *Yale Architecture Journal,*
New Haven, 2000, pages 36–44

Usually, the only way to discern the engineer's contribution is to look at the architect's work with or without them.

The hand of the collaborator engineer is elusive, but recognizable when projects are studied over time. It is manifested in a sensibility instead of a style. If two of Bunshaft's projects using Vierendeel trusses are compared, one with Weidlinger's involvement and one without, it is much easier to see the engineer's influence. In the Weidlinger projects, such as the Beinecke Rare Book and Manuscript Library, the delicate connections between moment-resisting intersections are articulated with a precision that reflects the participation of someone who knows what is possible; they are pushed beyond the conventional.

Where there is no such evidence, the conclusion would be that you are looking at more of a technician's practice. In fact, maybe the best way to think of these categories—technician, artist, collaborator—is as being all interconnected in a circle, so that Rice is more artist/collaborator while Fazlur Khan is maybe more collaborator/technician, and so on.

→ p. 317

EDITORS: In describing how he and his colleagues[1] worked with Steven Holl on recent projects, Nordenson elaborates on the working method of the collaborators, emphasizing how fluid the structural design process is and how it can be woven into the architect's earliest conceptions. He lays out the process of embedding structure in architecture. His thinking reflects this conceptual experience and, in turn, embeds structural thought in an intellectual culture.

NORDENSON: In Steven Holl's work the structure comes and goes in the space like an actor on the stage.

Helsinki Museum of Contemporary Art: Kiasma

The large-scale forms in the Helsinki Museum express Holl's idea of intertwining. A linear block intertwines with a curved shape. The torus geometry of the curve lent itself to a structural system comprised of trusses formed to the C-shaped section and spread along the curve every 10 feet (3 m) or so to delineate the shape of the building. The trusses rise from the ground and arch over to tall columns set inside the glass wall. The cavity in between trusses harbors the mechanical and electrical systems that feed the building.

Helsinki marked a new development in our collaboration with Holl's office. The formal moves—thick wall and glass wall—were tangled up with the technological

Kiasma curved wall—view from the north
Kiasma building section
Top floor Kiasma gallery construction

requirements of the building from the very start of the design competition. The structure and mechanical and electrical systems are all closely integrated and become occupants of the form—there is an added meaning to this form, the curved wall, when you begin to understand that it has a significant, dramatic thickness, and that the thickness is occupied by supporting systems because the wall is designated as a chase. The thickness becomes part of the character of the space.

When Mies was given his architectural licensing exam in Chicago, he was asked what he thought about technology. He drew two lines on the blackboard. He pointed to the top line and said, "This is the slab," then pointed to the bottom line and said, "This is the ceiling." Pointing to the space in between he said, "This is technology." This zone, whether it is beneath the slab or above it in a raised floor, is the stuff of technology.

At Helsinki we turned that stuff in the middle, the poché, into an actor in the design. The thickness of the curved wall implies technology on some level, but it's not technological exhibitionism. Observers do not immediately become aware or may never become aware of the technological contents of the wall, except by inference. The cuts for skylights reveal the wall's thickness, and it is up to the viewer to sense that the building is supported by the wall—both structurally and mechanically.

Cranbrook Institute of Science Addition

Again, were interested in housing mechanical and electrical systems in structural elements. The thick wall adjacent to the stairs contains these systems. The precast planks, which support the floor of this gallery space, are fabricated with hollows, to reduce dead load. We took advantage of these hollows and used them as ducts.

Within the thick central wall, flexiduct carries air from main runs to open ends of the precast planks, where it is then forced into the voids and fed out into the space through openings in the underside of the planks. This had never been done before. We took this piece of structure—this ready-made, precast, hollow core plank—and ventilated it. It is in the tradition of hollowing out structure so it can act as a plenum, except the structure itself was not designed to perform that function, but was adapted to do so.

The building structure at Cranbrook is organized around a notion of base and superstructure. There is concrete structure up to a certain datum, and above that is steel—in the form of trusses, two of which bridge between the two concrete

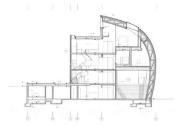

ground forms. The exterior does not reflect this structural system (the masonry runs uninterrupted between the two levels) but instead reflects the circulation system–changes in material and texture show where interior ramps are. And inside the building the idea of a steel frame popping out above masonry is expressed only locally in glimpses of the structure, a series of vignettes.

The glimpse of structure is part of the collaborator's repertoire–it is a rhetorical device, a synecdoche. At Beaubourg, you can walk right up to Peter Rice's enormous gerberette and inspect a piece of it. At Cranbrook, we have a portion of a truss sitting quietly in the corner of a gallery. The idea is that in getting quite close to a piece of structure and trying to figure out why it's shaped the way it is, one enters into a local relationship with the piece instead of reading a diagram of the whole system. In a diagram building with, say, a giant truss like on the Hancock Building, one can see and understand the structure immediately from a distance. At Cranbrook, there really is no evidence of technology at a distance. But at a smaller scale you get glimpses that add up to a knowledge of the systems figured out over time.

Since this is a place for science, the structure takes on something of an archae-ological character–you're shown a few bones of the dinosaur, and it's up to you to figure out the rest of the skeleton. The use of structure does not have to be blatant; it is not necessary to broadcast all of the components of the building at once. Much of the structure is hidden from view, or discovered by spending time in the building. Its organization–the concrete base and steel superstructure above, a full-height truss that becomes the bridge–is very straightforward. Independently, the structural vignettes have an order and clarity of organization, so that when observers want to understand what is going on through the evidence given, the exposed pieces, it is possible to assemble the system in their minds. Sometimes it's buried, sometimes it pops out, and where those things happen is chosen entirely by Holl's architectural aims in relation to one's movement through the building.

There is a tension between the episodic (slightly fetishistic) presentation of structure and the fact that it's not just a display of structure, it is the structure. This ambiv-alence is inherent in the use of the language of exhibits with structure, particularly when the glimpses occur in gallery space.

EDITORS: So you did not necessarily design a pure engineering structure to resist force, which would be selectively revealed by Steven Holl. You pay attention to where and how it is revealed and detail accordingly.

Cranbrook placement of precast hollow core plan
Cranbrook steel superstructure bridge
Cranbrook exterior expression of interior stair

NORDENSON: There is no such thing as pure. There is only organized or disorganized. You either have an overall strategy for the structure, or you have to solve problems locally and independently. Most engineers have a strategy.

What you do is weave a collection of ideas together that work off each other, starting with form, then the organization of the structure, and then the resulting implications for structural expression. One of the examples of structure participating in circulation ideas at Cranbrook is the shearing column that occurs at the pivot point of the plan. It is not just a column, but an element of a larger truss running above. The column drops down to participate in circulation. This was Holl's expression of the circulation in the structure.

College of Architecture and Landscape Architecture, University of Minnesota

The idea of structure harboring technology that was developed in Cranbrook found its way into Minnesota. Again, there was an architectural idea of removing the clutter of systems from underneath the slab and placing it in a thickened wall. A good deal of effort was required here to design the concrete frame in a way that cleared a path for these mechanical, electrical, and plumbing systems. A series of independent frames marches along the two axes, braced by precast concrete planks spanning between them. During construction, before the planks are in place, the frames will look like soldiers. In the finished building, no beams will connect the frames. The voids where perimeter beams would normally be allow for a clear reading of the zone of wall in between frames. Again, the airflow happens in the walls instead of in the floors.

Massachusetts Institute of Technology

EDITORS: When do you begin to draw structural models that work with architectural ideas? When do the back-and-forth conversations become real structural schemes?

NORDENSON: The schemes as well as the ideas can happen very early on. At MIT, Holl is developing concepts for a dormitory, and we have been drawing the structure that goes with them. In one of them, the "Folded Street," the architectural idea of having public and private spaces ramp up around the core of the building clearly depends on a clean structural solution. Rooms are in blocks on both sides of the building. Each room faces the exterior and, on the other side, opens up to the double-height public space between the core elements. Both dorm rooms and public space wrap around cores and ascend. Our structure is a series of

trusses cantilevered off the core, which allows for column-free space in the circulation areas.

In the second dorm project, the "Sponge," my colleague Christopher Diamond invented a new precast concrete "perfcon," of which the exterior walls were made.

EDITORS: You have described structure as being narrative, didactic, and rhetorical. What are the differences between these three treatments of structure?

NORDENSON: If you allow that there is a language of structure, architecture, and technology, and assume it's a language that people are somewhat familiar with, then it is possible to "write" in that language in ways that are clear, elusive, or allusive. You could develop a rhetoric of structure.

The language that is employed in narrative structure—the conventions of trusses, arches, bridges, high tech—are used to tell a clear story. At Cranbrook, the trusses were detailed in such a way that a part was able to speak for the whole. Didactic structures give as direct as possible an account of what's going on, like those of Fazlur Khan, or of Maillart. The goal is to be clear, straightforward, and complete—to show the whole of what's going on structurally.

Holl's work is more rhetorical. There is a hide-and-seek in which a revealed part represents the concealed whole. It is similar with Mies. The exterior of Crown Hall tells a structural story that is incomplete, but clear—the series of frames is visible, but how they are stabilized across the grain remains hidden. Once inside, that story is taken away—there is no way to tell what is column or mullion.

EDITORS: Can structure be subverted?

NORDENSON: Structure can be manipulated to express "weightlessness"—not just by suspending it and making the supports invisible like a magic trick, but by manipulating structure so that the scale of the things still visible gives the appearance of weightlessness. Because observers can move around in buildings, it is possible to orchestrate these kinds of experiences. Looking at Crown Hall from a distance, one can perceive that roof trusses are being supported by columns. On the interior everything is dematerialized—you see only the ceiling plane. At Peter Rice's and RFR's La Villette project in Paris, the main stability for the structure is hidden from sight: a large concrete pillar sheathed in mirror-finished metal. Some things are given, others hidden.

MIT folded street truss erection sequence
CALA framing plan and section
MIT folded street model
CALA study model

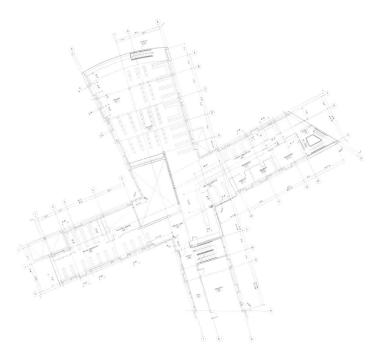

The critical analysis of structures, and their rhetoric, is impossible without
a study of construction drawings and photographs, especially in collaborative work,
such as Kahn's with Komendant. There are always drawings; ultimately, things
get worked out, or they wouldn't stand up. Defiance of gravity is purely rhetorical. The
challenge is in how to relate the reality, the deep structure of the construction
documents, to the surface structure that is visible in the architecture, and how to
work that language.

1 Ove Arup & Partners were engineers for both Kiasma and Cranbrook, with Guy Nordenson as principal in
charge and Mahadev Raman in charge of building services engineering. Guy Nordenson and Associates are the
structural engineers for CALA and MIT, collaborating with Ellerbe Beckett and Simpson, Gumpertz & Heger
respectively.

The Daily Practice of Collaboration[1]

→ p. 321

Architecture Research Office (ARO) has, like many of its contemporaries, chosen to call itself something other than its partners' names. So far, the media has not denied them this, as it has with Rem Koolhaas' OMA and Renzo Piano's Building Workshop. ARO shares with these, and with Steven Holl's practice, where Stephen Cassell and Adam Yarinsky worked and met (and where I met and worked with them in the mid-1980s), a commitment to the concept of "design research."

The term "research" is polemical and problematic. It is based on collaboration and empiricism. In positive terms, it appeals to the scientific method, finding ways to test concepts and hypotheses visually, quantitatively, and conceptually. As the English artist Michael Baldwin wrote of the work of Ian Burn and Mel Ramsden:

"Collaboration ... was not a kind of working-togetherism. It was a matter of destroying the silence of beholding with talk and puzzles, and a forcing any and every piece of artistic 'work' out of its need for incorrigibility and into the form of an essay."[2]

In negative terms, it is opposed to the creationist concept of the "Author-God." Which is not to say that the use of a formal language is entirely lost, but rather that aspects other than the surface appearance are considered in the conceptual development and end result.

Memory plays an important part in this work, having the effect of "downplaying the role of the imagination as it is usually conceived: as the expression of individual subjectivity."[3] There is a narrative structure to ARO's work, both in conception and in execution, and it has an important democratic character to it. As in any craft-based practice (in the tradition of Mies and Wright, not Le Corbusier), what Peter Rice called the "*trace de la main*" and Marc Mimram the "*faire à repenser*"[4] enters the picture, as the energetic participation of collaborators is encouraged. This can, but does not necessarily, work against abstraction.

Published in *Architecture Research Office* (Introduction), Princeton Architectural Press, New York, 2002, pages 93–95

Of the projects included by ARO in their book, the one I had most to do with was the SoHo Loft glass stair. The premise ARO and I developed in our earliest discussion was to find a way to cantilever the stair treads from a vertical plane of glass. After a few failed design tests using thick or double glass-layer walls, I suggested using a version of what the British call "cantilever" stairs,[5] a concept originally developed in Renaissance Italy[6] and best exemplified by Palladio's stair at the Accademia in Venice. The concept is to actually overcome the low resistance of stone to tension stresses caused through bending by eliminating the cantilever bending of each projecting tread. This is achieved by interlocking it with the treads above and below, which allows each tread to rest on the lower one and for the load to cascade to the bottom. The resulting torsion on each tread can be resisted by the stone and its anchorage to the wall. In fact, the cantilever stair thus becomes anti-cantilever. The glass stair in the SoHo Loft adapted this concept, using steel risers that are connected to a glass wall and interlocking them with aluminum-plate treads to achieve the cascading. The glass wall carries the remaining load that does not cascade down, and the riser torsion.

The project is conceptual, starting with the cantilever paradox and playing on interdependence. There are a number of clues in the stair (for example, the pin connecting the top tread in a slot and the free riser at the bottom) that are legible (barely) to an engineer as puzzles. And there are the machine-crafted elements, especially at the glass-to-riser connection, that are clearly far from mass-produced. What makes the result strong is, I think, that it is anything but retinal. This may also make it less appealing to the contemporary eye.

Robert Smithson said: "Look at any *word* long enough and you will see it open up into a series of faults, into a terrain of particles each containing its own void."[7] We need to understand that the same is true for buildings. In some cases, critical analysis can reveal underlying social and economic structures, and their interplay with appearance (as in the work commissioned over the years by Disney, or in the neo-Gothic skin jobs of postmodernism). In other cases, it reveals the poetic interplay of all the parts, particulars, and collaborators, as it does in good movies, and in some works of Gordon Bunshaft (Beinecke Library) and Louis Kahn (Kimbell Art Museum).[8] ARO does not have a style, nor has it engaged much with the contemporary polemics of architecture. It is focusing on the processes and facts of making and will, I think, with things if not words, change our experiences for the better.

COLLABORATIONS

1 After Gerhard Richter's "the daily practice of painting." Gerhard Richter, quoted in Richter, Gerhard. 2002. *Forty Years of Painting* (exh. cat.) New York: Museum of Modern Art.

2 Green, Charles. 2001. *The Third Hand–Collaboration in Art from Conceptualism to Postmodernism.* Minneapolis: University of Minnesota Press, 55.

3 Ibid., 97.

4 See Fromonot, Françoise. 2001. *Marc Mimram: Solferino Bridge Paris.* Basel: Birkhäuser Verlag.

5 Price, Sam. 1996. Cantilever Staircases. *Arq* 1 (spring): 76–87.

6 Probably the first instance of this is the stair in the towers of the Palazzo Ducale in Urbino, built around the 1460s to the design of Luciano Laurana.

7 Ed. Jack Flam. 1996. *Robert Smithson: The Collected Writings.* Berkeley: University of California Press, 107.

8 Nordenson, Guy. 1998. The Lineage of Structure and The Kimbell Art Museum. *Lotus International.* 28–47.

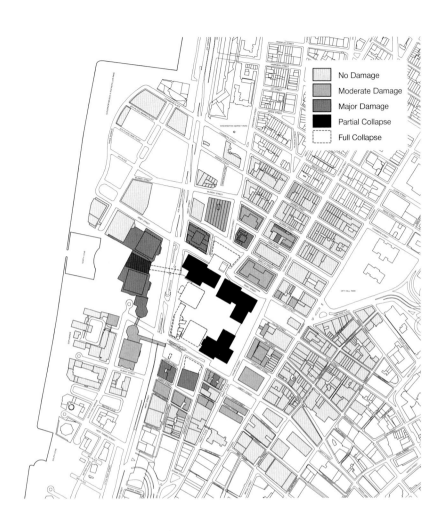

No Damage
Moderate Damage
Major Damage
Partial Collapse
Full Collapse

City Square: Structural Engineering, Democracy, and Architecture

I watched the attacks on the World Trade Center Towers at home in New York, on television. My office is on Broadway a block away from the site, but I was leaving home late that morning. Like most others I did not realize till the second plane hit at 9.03 a.m. that this was an attack. And it took me another half hour watching the fire in the North Tower to understand that it would collapse. I know these structures well, from study, the work of a design studio conducted at Princeton in 1999, and discussions with their structural engineer, Leslie Robertson. I knew, as I think the terrorists did, that they were especially robust.

I began calling my colleagues—engineers, emergency response specialists, and others in the earthquake engineering community. It was very hard to reach anyone. The city's emergency response headquarters, which I had visited in June, was destroyed with the WTC7 Tower. I was able to reach my colleagues Ramon Gilsanz and Aine Brazil, and we discussed how we might mobilize volunteer engineers through the Structural Engineers Association of New York (SEAoNY), a group we had founded together in the early 1990s. Aine's firm, LZA/Thornton Tomasetti (LZA/TT), had already been hired by the city to help on the site, to advise the contractors on safety as they assisted with the search and recovery efforts. George Tamaro and his firm, Mueser Rutledge, were hired to consult on the below-grade structures.

The Mayor's Office of Emergency Management (OEM) had assigned to the Department of Design and Construction (DDC) the supervision of construction-related work on site. The agreed to give SEAoNY a role, with LZA/TT, in providing teams of engineers, organized by the individual firms, to be on site with the four contractors (Amec, Bovis, Tully, and Turner/Plaza), around the clock on twelve-hour shifts. Each shift would begin with a briefing by the departing group and a detailed discussion of all the engineering issues of concern. These included the safety of existing structures, the design of crane platforms and access ways, and the demolition strategies.

Published in *Grey Room* 07, New York, 2002, pages 102–05

A second task was to inspect the surrounding buildings and determine which were safe for reoccupancy. On September 13 and 14, I proposed to my colleagues at SEAoNY and the DDC a methodology for inspections based on the approach taken after the last major earthquakes in California and using a database of NYC building information assembled at Princeton for a research project for FEMA. Details of this can be found at *nycem.org/default.asp* and *www.princeton.edu/pr/pwb/ 01/1008/1b.shtml*. Through SEAoNY we organized a number of inspection rounds: (1) of 400 or so buildings in the surrounding area (see map) during September 17–18; (2) of the thirty-one most damaged buildings ("dark gray" and "gray" on the map), in joint teams with the NYC Department of Buildings, on September 21; (3) again, of the 400 buildings during October 4–10; and (4) close inspections of several of the "dark gray" buildings. (1) and (3) were "rapid" visual inspections from the side-walk and with aerial photographs, (2) were more detailed walk-throughs, and (4) involved mapping and categorizing the specific damages. (1), (2), and (3) used a standard procedure with individual building checklists preprinted for each team.

On September 11, a colleague of mine at Princeton, Josiah Ober, presented a paper, "The Politics of Knowledge in Democratic Athens," at the University of Wisconsin. He referred to Heroditus' use of the concept of *isegoria,* and translated it as an "equal opportunity to speak in public: the equal right to rhetoric." He points to Pericles' Funeral Oration, regarding "democratic Athens, [where] open delib-erations and bold collective action are mutually entailing rather than mutually exclusive." Ober writes: "… the Athenians attend quite promiscuously to anyone, whether he be a smith, a shoemaker, a merchant, a sea-captain, a rich man, a poor man, of good family, or of none." Against Plato (in *Protagoras*) he is critical of the idea of "political expertise" (*politike techné*). Instead, with Aristotle he suggests that "because they are many, each can have a part (*orion*) of virtue and practical reason, and on their joining, together, the mass of people, with their many feet and hands and having many senses, become like a single human being, and [do] so also with respect to character and mind."

In retrospect, the great benefit of the SEAoNY activities at the WTC site was this "promiscuous," deliberative aspect. Engineers, construction workers, firemen, and rescue workers argued, suggested strategies and designs, acknowledged good ideas, and criticized dumb ones. Within an overall "command" structure managed by OEM and the DDC thrived a powerful, at times very emotional, and extraordinarily effective democracy. Thanks to this, the work proceeded safely, effectively, and in fact quickly. This went beyond the "public" and "private" sectors. It was in every respect a renaissance of democracy.

World Trade Center, aerial photograph, September 13, 2001
Alberto Giacometti, *La Place,* 1948

Of course, capitalism abhorred this momentary "New York Commune" and swiftly sought to impose its structure on the site. The developer barons met with the state and city officials, and their architects, and mobilized. Still, in the void there had been created an experience of real democracy. What is built must remember this.

Like so many others, I was compelled to go work on the site and was fortunate that there was something I could do. My experience with earthquake enginee-ring, my own and my colleagues' research work for FEMA, and the existence of SEAoNY proved useful to the inspection program we were asked to organize. With my colleagues I spent hours, day and night, observing the damage, the chaos, the courage, and democracy. In mid-November, I left for a long-planned trek in the Himalayas and took along *War and Peace*. Reading Tolstoy's descriptions and meditations on the great battles of Napoleon's wars, I understood that I had witnessed a battle, the awful and amazing reality of which history would never capture.

Tall Building Structures
Since the World Trade Center:
Art, Craft, and Industry

The World Trade Center Towers of New York were unique works of structural design. They were also the last, besides the Sears Tower in Chicago, of the tall building structures characteristic of the late modern period of, say, 1950 to 1975. After the hiatus of the mid-70s recession, the structural design of tall buildings, particularly in the U.S., shifted to a more industrialized approach. Before that, and especially with the WTC Towers, it was possible to find at many levels— of form, materials, and building systems—the mark of specific creative energy and invention.

The ideology of this period (1950–1975) in architecture included a strong argument for structural rationalism. This meant that certain buildings, especially tall ones, were expected to represent their tectonics and materials as clearly as possible. This was not always easy, especially since the structures had to be fire-protected and clad. Still, there was an expectation of structural legibility and "honesty," at times with even a moral overtone. This expectation had to be satisfied visually—how else is it legible? And this led, one could argue, even in the midst of this period, to a gradual disjunction between sign and meaning. Some of the best works of apparent structural rationalism—Mies van der Rohe's Crown Hall and Seagram Building, Gordon Bunshaft's Bienecke Library and Lever House, Eero Saarinen's CBS Building, and Louis Kahn's Salk Institute and Kimbell Art Museum—are, in fact, the consequence of argument and synthesis between the claims of form, light, circulation, air, structure, material, and construction. In the most successful, each of these "strata" can be interpreted as such (for example, innovations in the practice and art of "X") and as they reinforce or contradict each other (for example, organic form vs. Cartesian structure, plastic structure vs. classical order). But in the syntheses, purity is lost. Take, for instance, the Seagram Building, whose vertical bronze mullions both represent the supporting structure safely buried in concrete and create the sharp shadow lines and virtual outer plane that so stunningly make the façade. There is no simple relationship between sign and signified, but rather so much more.

Published in *Next* (*8th International Architecture Exhibition* catalogue), Venice, 2002, pages 202–03

The Hancock Tower, Chicago (1,127 feet [343.5 m], 1969), the World Trade Center Towers, New York (1,361 feet [415 m] and 1,368 feet [417 m], 1971–1973), the Sears Tower, Chicago (1,453 feet [443 m], 1974), and Standard Oil of Indiana, Chicago (1,136 feet [346 m], 1972): these are the notable very tall building structures of the postwar period 1950–1975. They divide neatly into two basic types–the perimeter tube frame and the perimeter braced frame or megastructure. Both rely on the full perimeter of the building to act as the structure resisting horizontal wind forces. In the case of the tube this means that the columns around the perimeter are closely spaced together (10 feet [3 m] or less) and tied with deep beams all rigidly welded together. The effect is to create a tight rigid grid that acts almost like a solid-walled, hollow tube. When the wind (or earthquake) acts to push the building laterally, this tube resists the bending like a cantilever stuck in the ground, with compression forces on the leeward side (away from the wind), tension a force on the windward side and shearing on the other two sides parallel to the wind direction. The difference with earlier tall structures–for example, the Empire State Building– is that they only mobilized the frames parallel to the wind to resist shearing forces. They did not gain the compression/tension force couple developed in the lee and windward faces of the tube.

The Hancock Tower acts in a similar fashion, except that very large diagonals resist the shearing forces and all the compression/tension forces caused by the wind-induced overturning are carried by huge corner members. The smaller intermediate columns do not participate in the wind resistance. The structure is, in effect, a large bridge (or offshore oil platform), truss upended. It is more efficient in its use of steel because all the diagonals and corner members act in direct tension or compression. In the tube, the columns and beams are mostly bending, which means a somewhat less efficient use of material. The WTC and Standard Oil of Indiana were single-tube structures–one tube on the perimeter. The Sears Tower is composed of nine square tubes bundled together and rising to different heights. As urban sculpture, the Sears Tower is, I think, one of the great works of 20th-century architecture, with all the majesty and energy of Rodin's *Balzac*.

The structure of the WTC Towers was designed by Leslie Robertson and John Skilling. It incorporates a number of innovations that Robertson applied elsewhere, most notably a uniquely promiscuous use of steel alloys. The superstructure consisted of three main parts: the core, the floor structure, and the perimeter tube. The core was built up of box columns made of thick steel plates welded together and standard wide-flange (I) beams. These box columns were not rigidly connected and the core did not, therefore, provide any lateral stiffness. The floor structure

consisted of 3-foot-deep (90-cm) trusses and a metal deck topped with a concrete
slab. The benefit of using trusses (a design also adopted in the Sears Tower)
was that the ventilation ducts could lace through them. This meant that the floor-
to-floor-height could be 12 feet (3.7 m) with nearly 9-foot (2.7-m) ceilings, rather
than the typical 12 feet 6 inches to 13 feet (3.8 to 4 m) of most office buildings with
standard beams and slabs: a saving of more than 50 feet (15 m) on the height,
or more rentable floors. The floor was panelized in pieces—including two trusses
and the intervening deck—which could be shipped and placed quite quickly. The
perimeter structure was made of box columns about 15 inches (38.1 cm) square,
spaced 3.5 feet (1 m) apart and linked with steel plate beams. These were assembled
off-site into "trees" three stories tall and 12 feet (3.7 m) wide that could be lifted
into place and easily assembled. While these columns and plate beams were the
same size whatever the floor level, they were often made of different steel alloys,
depending on the required strength calculated from structural analyses and
the results of detailed wind tunnel studies. What seems the same may not actually
be so, though this is illegible without recourse to the construction documents.
There is an obsessive intelligence quite apparent on close study of the engineering
design of the WTC. In my opinion, this led to their remarkable performance on
September 11, standing up to the impact and fire as long as they did. It is apparent
in retrospect that the floor trusses—light members which are difficult to fire-
protect—were, in the end, the weak link that precipitated the collapse. Nonetheless
the buildings stood long enough to allow thousands to escape. I would argue
that no other existing very tall structure except the Sears Tower could have
performed as well.

After the WTC, the design of tall building structures effectively split into three
directions: the American industrial products of speculative development,
the American megastructures, and the British craft products of so-called high
tech. The first not entirely uninteresting direction emerged with the recovery
of the U.S. real estate market in the late 1970s. It was led by developers such as
the Reichmans of Canada, Gerald Hines of Texas, and the many real estate
barons of New York, Chicago, and elsewhere. The formula is simple—a refined,
repeatable, set-assembly of internal structure and systems, enveloped in
a form and cladding of the "design" architect's making. The professional arrangement mirrors the buildings: the design architect is assigned to an established
team of producers—architects, engineers, construction managers—that follows
the direction of the developer. From an engineering design point of view this
means evolution, not invention and direction, lies in the hands of the developer's
technical managers rather than in the hands of the professionals. It can be

a very profitable and effective methodology. Apartment buildings built in New York since the 1970s are highly standardized products of this type that, as a result, go up at extraordinary speed—up to two floors a week. Of course, the resulting quality is as good as any other product designed for quick return and planned obsolescence—another case of the American disposable vernacular.

The second category, the American megastructure, is the work of a small number of creative structural engineers, including Leslie Robertson, William LeMessurier, Paul Weidlinger, and Prabodh Banavalkar. The Hancock Tower in Chicago inspired this line and it has led to the structures of the Citicorp in New York, Fountain Place in Dallas, and the Bank of China in Hong Kong. The lessons learned from the Hancock Tower were that diagonal truss systems are not only efficient for resisting wind loads but can also be used to channel the building gravity loads to discreet megacolumns placed where they best contribute to the wind resistance and least obstruct the use of space (e.g., not at the corners). LeMessurier was master of this type, going so far in the Citicorp as to omit columns at the corners to ensure that forces go where designed. Banavalkar's structural design for Henry Cobb's Fountain Place in Dallas is another case of well-matched architecture and engineering and a rare case of good design for a developer. And finally, Robertson's and I. M. Pei's Bank of China achieves a sophistication of rhetorical hide-and-seek in its selective expression of structure comparable to the virtuosity of the Seagram Building.

The British line—mostly the work of Norman Foster in collaboration with Jack Zunz and others at Ove Arup & Partners—is closer to the interrupted tradition of the WTC, a work of obsessive craft despite its constant references to industrialization. It is, as they say, always a "one-off." Like Mies and Pei, Foster is manipulating the forms and expression of engineering and materials to a specific rhetorical end. As one of his engineers once told me, it is a matter of making things appear to work the way Foster imagines they do. As such it is related, though the two men never worked together, to Peter Rice's own rhetorical investigations, including his almost mannerist dissimulation of structural order to create suspense and stimulate inquiry: How does it stand? A case in point with Foster is the repression of the top horizontal chord of the trusses on the main façade of the Hong Kong and Shanghai Bank—an essential element in its typhoon wind-resistance. Foster's work, whether the Hong Kong and Shanghai Bank, Commerzbank in Frankfurt, or the current Swiss Re building in London, all carries strong ideological messages toward which all aspects—form, material, ventilation, structure—are called to contribute. Unlike the earlier American work of Fazlur Khan and Robertson, however, they do not, as far as the structure goes, represent radical advances in technology. Instead, they demonstrate rich and exquisite craftsmanship in the science of corporate and civic image formation.

There have, of course, been a host of tall structures designed and built in recent years in the Far East, notably the Petronas Towers in Kuala Lumpur and many in Shanghai. Most of these fall in line with American industrialized developer work: a skillful package design on standardized structures. Even Leslie Robertson's recent redesign of the structure of Kohn Pedersen Fox's projected world's tallest tower in Shanghai did nothing to alter the form of the building (although, like Robertson's intervention in Philip Johnson's AT&T Building, it does carry on his habit of hiding brilliant structures inside postmodern architecture). On the whole, the inventive work in tall buildings is coming from architects new to the field, including Renzo Piano, Jean Nouvel, Rem Koolhaas, Steven Holl, and Frank Gehry. It is not clear whether any of them is engaging engineering as skillfully as did their 1960s forbears like Bunshaft or Saarinen. If we can recover some of the subtlety of collaboration obvious in buildings like the Beinecke Library and the CBS Building, and learn from the mannerist work of the likes of Peter Rice and Santiago Calatrava, there may even be a renewal of the engineering as well as of the architecture of tall buildings.

It is encouraging that some contemporary architects have established strong collaborative relationships with engineers—Gehry with Jörg Schlaich, Koolhaas with Cecil Balmond—and that these relationships are having an impact on their work. Perhaps we are at a stage where formal exploration is moving quickly and may draw in better engineering, not unlike what happened in the postwar modernist period in the U.S. What will make a great difference is the gradual recognition that the civic, monumental function of tall structures means that they should not simply be vehicles of capitalism, but also signs of aspiration. This means adopting a polemical voice, arguing for ecological responsibility—as Foster and Piano have done—or poetic enchantment—as Gehry, Holl, and even Koolhaas do—or even technological progress—as does, I think, the proposed 7 South Dearborn tower by SOM (Adrian Smith and William Baker), with its wind "confusing" gaps. In the wake of 9/11, there is no benefit to a neoconservative retreat to false urbanist contextualism. This is just another disguise of counter-democratic profiteering. Instead, as was the case with the original World Trade Center Towers, it is time to reassert the humanist and even democratic character of collaborative, inventive, and inspiring design.

1

1 Construction of the armature for the Statue of Liberty, Paris, 1881

Tall Building as Metaphor

"The 'tall buildings,' which have ... usurped a glory that affects you as rather surprised, ... the multitudinous sky-scrapers standing up to the view, from the water, like extravagant pins in a cushion already overplanted, and stuck in as in the dark, anywhere and anyhow, have at least the felicity ... of taking the sun and the shade in the manner of towers of marble. They are not all of marble, I believe, by any means, even if some may be, but they are impudently new and still more impudently 'novel'–this in common with so many other terrible things in America–and they are triumphant payers of dividends; all of which, with flash of innumerable windows and flicker of subordinate gilt attributions, is like the flare, ... of the lamps of some general permanent 'celebration.'"

Henry James, 1906 [1]

→ p. 361

After the terrorist attacks on New York and Washington on September 11, 2001, it was natural to wonder why the World Trade Center Towers and not the Statue of Liberty had been the target in New York, why Al Qaeda had chosen a symbol of commerce over a symbol of freedom.[2] Whatever the answer, there is little doubt that if it had been attacked, the statue would have been rebuilt (as was the Pentagon) and not replaced (as the World Trade Center will be). What is not as clear is how it would have been rebuilt, and what that would have meant.

Tall buildings, if only by being tall, look to stand out in a crowd. In time they may become the crowd, but it is always their intention to speak up, to declare, indeed, even to persuade us of their novelty, their sumptuousness, their responsibility to social needs and ideals, their outright beauty, and their abstraction. The World Trade Center Towers were built to revitalize downtown Manhattan and promote globalization. Like Rockefeller Center, they expressed a unique moment of civic will. And they became exponents of global commerce in the marketplace of New York City. After their destruction, the same expression of civic will did not reemerge; what did emerge was more of our own time.

Published in *Tall Buildings*, exhibition catalogue, The Museum of Modern Art, New York, 2003, pages 11–31

2

The Statue of Liberty has always remained, in its solitude, the clearest voice in that marketplace of ideas, in the agora not just of the city but at large: it stands for liberty. And it stands, in fact, because of a particular set of circumstances, ideals, talents, and resources that brought it into being. But its meaning is such that, long after all these particularities have been forgotten, it could never have been a target on September 11. This may tell us how we might begin to understand the meaning of the tall building or structure. Each is an expression, a "speech act" in the agora. And each is constituted, of necessity, not by a single artist's hand but by the condensation of events and individual talents. Thus, each becomes a metaphor.

3

Originally intended as a gift of the French nation to the United States on the centennial of the Declaration of Independence, the Statue of Liberty was the idea of a group of republican gentlemen and businessmen led by the journalist and politician Édouard-René Lefebvre de Laboulaye, who also hoped to promote the principles of *liberté, égalité, fraternité* at home in France.[3] The enterprise was conceived near Versailles in 1865, the year of Abraham Lincoln's assassination, and came of age in 1871, the year of the Paris Commune. The French sculptor Frédéric-Auguste Bartholdi was commissioned to create the statue, which he derived from an amalgam of allegorical and other sources, notably the traditional figures of Faith and Truth,[4] the great *colossi* of Thebes in Egypt, and even Eugène Delacroix's heroic canvas, *Liberty Guiding the People*, of 1830. The French architect, engineer, and critic Eugène-Emmanuel Viollet-le-Duc was asked to undertake its structural design, but died in 1879 before it could be completed. He was succeeded by the French engineer Alexandre-Gustave Eiffel, whose landmark tower in Paris—at 984 feet (299.9 m) the tallest man-made structure of the time—was erected ten years later in 1889. Surprisingly, Eiffel does not appear to have shown much interest in his work on the Statue of Liberty, and described it as designed according to "the conditions of strict economy which circumstances imposed," designing "an iron framework which would serve as a support for the whole of the copper envelope," and would form "a sort of large pylon secured at four points to the masonry base supporting the statue."[5] Eiffel's contribution, however invisible at first, subtly deepens the statue's meaning. Much of its presence and power can be attributed to its colossal scale, its almost still stance, its vast interior and paper-thin copper "skin," its sophisticated structural order of trussed spine, light outriggers, and the delicate springs and bars holding the skin, the radical pretensioned cable system anchoring the statue to the pedestal, and finally the beautifully composed pedestal evoking the great stone past, from Egypt to France, which frames the light and lightness above. Eiffel was undoubtedly the greatest engineer of his day. His contribution, perhaps

2 Sections of the Statue of Liberty, 1986; drawing by Swanke Hayden Connell Architects
3 Eero Saarinen, Paul Weidlinger, and Mario Salvadori. Aerial view of the CBS Building, New York, under construction, 1961–65
4 Frank O. Gehry. Longitudinal section of the Solomon R. Guggenheim Museum in Bilbao, Spain, 1991–97

more than those of his colleagues, does a great deal in raising the work to its iconic status.

The Statue of Liberty was the project of three men who worked independently: the sculpture by Bartholdi, the structure by Eiffel, and the pedestal by the American architect Richard Morris Hunt. Each man's work was attentive and sensitive to that of the others, and the work emerged with a sublime resonance of its own (FIG. 1). Even after more than a hundred years, the Statue of Liberty can still serve as an interpretive example of the well-made tall building, one that might be thought of as an ideogram of form, structure, program, symbol, and fabrication, as the product of a strong collaborative process, and as a "speech act" in the urban marketplace.

If the statue were ever reconstructed, it might be rebuilt in a number of ways. One possible model might be the Solomon R. Guggenheim Museum in Bilbao, Spain (1991–97), by the American architect Frank O. Gehry–like the statue, a large-scale sculptural object, powerful urban intervention, complex interior space, and individualized structure. Yet, a comparison of sections (cross sections) of the statue and the Bilbao museum (FIGS. 2, 4) makes it apparent how they differ structurally: the latter is dialectical, the former monolithic. Gehry's building is in the tradition of early expressionistic architecture (by Erich Mendelsohn and Hans Poelzig, for example) and also of the later, more technological, expressionistic works by Jørn Utzon and Eero Saarinen.[6] In Utzon's Sydney Opera House (1956–74), the architect and the structural engineers Ove Arup and Jack Zunz created, in close collaboration, parallel achievements of form and structure, each distinct and legible.[7] Similarly, Saarinen's collaboration with the engineer Fred Severud on the St. Louis Arch (1965) and with engineers Paul Weidlinger and Mario Salvadori on the CBS Building (1961–65) are instances of highly inventive structural engineering contained by and directed toward a formal objective (FIG. 3).

In contrast, such tall buildings as the Sears Tower in Chicago (1970–74) by Bruce Graham and Fazlur Khan of Skidmore, Owings & Merrill and the World Trade Center Towers in New York (1966–73) by Minoru Yamasaki and the engineers Leslie Robertson and John Skilling more fully integrate structure and form. This is largely because of the extreme demands of their scale, but also because they were conceived at the outset as expressing the means and wonder of their structural art and achievement.

These are differences of kind, not of quality or effectiveness. One kind of work (the dialectical) holds the technological and architectural meaning apart, allowing

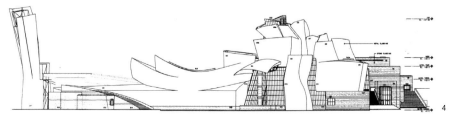

4

the meaning to emerge gradually, while the other approach (the monolithic) aims to fully integrate them in an organic whole. An example of the former, in another discipline, might be that of the Russian filmmaker Sergei Eisenstein, who developed a theory of sound and moving pictures that proposed the conjuncture of sound and image (and, for that matter, image and image–montage) as a means to "give birth to the image in which the thematic matter is most clearly embodied." [8] He even suggested a kind of narrative space with pictures in the horizontal and sound in the vertical, in effect, a kind of space structure. [9] He referred to the American orientalist and educator Ernest Fenollosa's *The Chinese Written Character as a Medium for Poetry*.[10] Fenollosa and his translator, Ezra Pound, argued that such juxtapositions made meaning and could make it new. Taking their inspiration from the visual construction of Chinese written characters or ideograms–and the way they apparently construct meaning through metaphoric relations–Fenollosa and Pound stated: "Relations are more real and more important than the things they relate. The forces which produce the branch-angles of an oak lay potent in the acorn. Similar lines of resistance, half-curbing the out-pressing vitalities, govern the branching of rivers and of nations. Thus a nerve, a wire, a roadway, and a clearing house are only varying channels which communication forces for itself. This is more than analogy, it is identity of structure." [11]

5

In 1914 Pound introduced his idea of the *vortex* as "a radiant node or cluster ... from which, and through which, and into which, ideas are constantly rushing." [12] In architecture, he pointed to the Tempio Malatestiano in Rimini (1446–68) to illustrate the vortex (FIG. 6). There, works by the architect Leon Battista Alberti, the painter Piero della Francesca, the sculptor Agostino di Duccio, and the Lombardi brothers, an architect and a sculptor, are conjoined with a preexisting church, San Francesco of Rimini, and together celebrate the achievement of its patron, the ruthless *condottiere* Sigismondo Malatesta. It is a confluence of disparate energy that weaves a cohesive and lasting pattern.

Frame Craft

Eiffel took over the structural engineering of the Statue of Liberty in 1879, the design was completed around 1880, and the statue was first erected in Paris in 1881–84. In Chicago, at the outset of tall-building architecture, the first complete steel-frame structure, the Home Insurance Building (1884–85), was constructed by the architect William Le Baron Jenney and the engineer George B. Whitney. Vertical trusses were first used, as wind bracing, on the twenty-two-story Masonic Temple (1891–92) in Chicago by Daniel Burnham and John Wellborn Root, as well as on the Unity Building of the same year by Clinton Warren (FIG. 5).

5 Clinton Warren. Unity Building, Chicago, 1891–92
6 Tempio Malatestiano, Rimini, Italy, 1446–68
7 William Holabird and Martin Roche. Gage Group, 30 and 24 South Michigan Avenue, 1898;
Louis H. Sullivan. 18 South Michigan Avenue, Chicago, 1898–99

In some cases, Chicago architects, particularly in the mid-1890s, were able to reduce the visible presence of the steel frame almost completely. For instance, in the Reliance Building (1890–95) by Charles Atwood of Burnham and Company, the terra-cotta and glass façade weaves back and forth, hiding evidence of columns in the folds of the bay windows and corners, and becoming a true curtain wall. But these cases were uncommon. More often, as in the Gage Group (1898) by William Holabird and Martin Roche and the adjacent 18 South Michigan Avenue (1898–99) by Louis Sullivan, the frame was clearly expressed as slender masonry piers and spandrels around the classic Chicago tripartite window (FIG. 7). Starting with the First Leiter Building (1879) by Jenney (which still had load-bearing masonry piers), continuing to Louis Sullivan's Carson Pirie Scott Store (1899, 1903–04, 1906) and well into the 1900s, this gave a clear and direct reading of the structural frame, from top to bottom.

The key exceptions to this are Dankmar Adler's and Louis Sullivan's Wainwright Building in St. Louis (1890–91) and their Guaranty Building in Buffalo (1894–95). Both are classical compositions in the vertical and horizontal, with the distinct base, shaft, and top advocated by Sullivan, with massive piers anchoring the corners, and uniform vertical masonry piers across the façade. The actual difference between the structural and nonstructural façade piers is obscured by their equivalent appearance.[13]

Here, at the birth of the skyscraper, we can see the distinction between direct and veiled structural expression. The Reliance, Wainwright, and Guaranty buildings allow a reading of the structure but not without some ambiguity between the primary load-bearing and secondary façade-framing structures. Atwood as well as Adler and Sullivan also sought to veil or blend these in order to express an organic and bounded whole,[14] whereas the more conventional Chicago School façades are grids of potentially infinite extension.

In his essay "Chicago Frame," the late British architectural historian Colin Rowe argued that when the European architects adopted the frame, it was as a polemical device and counterpoint to space making.[15] The Chicago architects were not, on the other hand, that interested in shaping space. And their successor Frank Lloyd Wright chose not to use the frame for his few tall building proposals, but, rather, adopted something like Eiffel's spine and outrigger (or tree-and-branch) structure for his St. Mark's Tower (1929), which was later built as the Price Tower in 1956. In doing so, he transformed the organic idea of his mentor Louis Sullivan from the outside into the plan, using the core as the center of his whirling spaces.

6   7

While Eiffel's graphical calculations for the Statue of Liberty show a clear understanding of the effect of wind load on the structure, at that time nothing was required by the New York City building code for structures up to one hundred feet (30.5 m) with respect to wind load.[16] The code simply specified an increase in the thickness of masonry walls as height increased. Many early New York skyscrapers were built as so-called cage constructions, with self-supporting exterior walls tied back to complete steel or iron frames. Other early towers were erected with load-bearing masonry. This method resembles that used in the construction of Venetian palazzi, a cage wrapped in a veneer, but at a much larger scale and with frames of steel, not wood. This may be said to reflect the similar emphasis in both mercantile cultures on the confectionary–on a stage set and not a curtain.

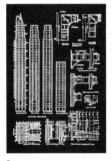

8

In 1906 the architect Cass Gilbert started his 90 West Street Building (1906–07) in New York, which was a precursor to his later design for the great Woolworth Building (1910–13) (FIG. 8). Also in 1906, Stanford White was shot in his Madison Square Garden Building of 1889–90, and Philip Johnson was born. In New York, skyscrapers have typically been more like towers than tall buildings, and they are often quite slender and stylistically derivative. The Madison Square Garden tower, for instance, was an enlarged copy of the Giralda of the Cathedral of Seville. Other buildings are inflations of the Italian campanile, and still others, like the Woolworth Building, are derived from French Gothic cathedral bell towers. Johnson's later buildings in New York, the former AT&T Headquarters (1984) and the so-called Lipstick Building (1986), perpetuated that tradition.

Generally, New York skyscrapers, in both concept and construction, divided the exterior expression and interior makeup. The cage and, later, curtain-wall constructions were taken up by New York architects as occasions to develop formal languages that were usually independent of the interior spatial, structural, or servicing realities of their buildings. This differs from both Venetian and Chicago practice. In Venice, the elaborate gothic façades of the Ca D'Oro (1421–40) and the Ducal Palace (1465–79) are at the same time patterned surfaces and an articulate expression of interior spatial arrangements and meanings.[17] They are examples of what the British critic and painter Adrian Stokes has described as: "Such artificiality in astonishing unity with such realism … where nature in exotic form conspires with good sense."[18] It was the disjunction of content and surface in New York skyscrapers that caused Henry James to write: "Crowned not only with no history, but with no credible possibility of time for history, and consecrated by no uses save the commercial at any cost, they are simply the most piercing

8 Cass Gilbert. Woolworth Building, New York, 1910–13. Elevations, plans and structural details

notes in that concert of the expensively provisional into which your supreme sense of New York resolves itself."[19]

Comparing New York structures such as the Woolworth Building to Chicago's Reliance Building, it is obvious that most New York architects and engineers went about their work separately, with little concern for harmony or metaphoric resonance. Another way to understand this is to examine the work of the partners Charles McKim and Stanford White. McKim was responsible for bringing the Guastavino masons to the United States to work on his Boston Library, and designed the Low Library dome at Columbia University (1893–1903) as a load-bearing masonry shell. White built the Gould Library at New York University's Bronx campus of steel trusses clad in stone and plaster. McKim took care to include careful craft in the execution of his work, while White, the man about town, cared mainly for the appearance. McKim had studied closely the architecture and construction methods of the Romans and understood that style was tied to craft, even when transmuted through abstraction.

Louis Sullivan wrote in *Kindergarten Chats* that his function as an architect was: "to vitalize building materials, to animate them collectively with a thought, a state of feeling, to charge them with a subjective significance and value, to make them visible parts of the genuine social fabric, to infuse into them the true life of the people, to impart to them the best that is in the people, as the eye of the poet, looking below the surface of life, sees the best that is in the people."[20] William Le Baron Jenney wrote in 1891: "There must be sufficient material and no more, for it is essential, not only for economy but also to reduce the weights on the foundations, that the construction should be as light as possible consistent with stability."[21] In Chicago, designers of tall buildings were constrained by the unstable soil conditions to take particular care in the design of their foundations and to keep the buildings light. In New York, the hard bedrock both downtown and in midtown made greater whimsy possible. Only instances such as the Statue of Liberty, which had to be built light for transport from Paris to New York, or the now-demolished, slender forty-seven-story Singer Tower (1906–08) by Ernest Flagg, required well-conceived structures that then could contribute something to the meaning of the buildings.

Citizen Skyscraper

After the Woolworth Building and the changes in the New York City building and zoning code of 1916 (which resulted from the construction of the massive Equitable Building in 1912–16), things were calm for a time. In Chicago, the creative energy of the 1890s had shifted to the residential work of the Prairie School, and the remarkable plastic and planimetric inventions of Frank Lloyd Wright. As the Italian historian Manfredo Tafuri has demonstrated in his essay "The Disenchanted Mountain," it was the Chicago Tribune Competition and exhibition of 1922 that brought together all the strange and remarkable strands that had evolved from the Chicago and New York skyscrapers. On the one hand, there was the "anarchic individual," and on the other, there were those making buildings that "had first and foremost to convey a composite significance." [22] In a discussion of the Chicago Tribune entry by Eliel Saarinen, Tafuri wrote: "His interpretation of the skyscraper is, in fact, exactly the opposite of the whole American experience in the matter of the skyscraper: not a structure materializing the concept of laissez-faire, and thus not an image of the competition among the great commercial concentrations but an element capable of exercising a formal control over the urban complex as a whole." [23] In a subsequent project for the Grand Hotel and the Chicago lakefront (1923), Eliel Saarinen extended this idea and contributed a remarkable plan that foreshadowed the nine-square plan of the Sears Tower.

As eclectic, or anarchic, as the separate designs for the Chicago Tribune Competition were, none demonstrated the weaving of "patterned energies" of structure, symbol, space, and form that exists at the Statue of Liberty or even the Reliance Building. The entry that came the closest to this was the Adolf Meyer and Walter Gropius design, a careful composite of structural expression, expressive façade articulation, skilled asymmetric massing, and memorable rendering from a three-quarter perspective. Tafuri clearly described the transformation of the type, from skyscraper to a kind of "literary image." On the work of Hugh Ferriss, including the Metropolis of Tomorrow (1929), Tafuri offered the following judgment: "The historical significance of the designs of this able conjurer of images lies in their poetic celebration of the skyscraper. The skyscraper is 'sung' by Ferriss in an attempt to restore an 'enchantment' to what could by this time be only a 'disenchanted mountain.' In this sense Ferriss was Saarinen's only follower in the 1920s, and with reason; only as a purely literary image could the skyscraper any longer assume an 'aura.' The results of the Chicago Tribune competition had made this quite clear." [24]

Tafuri's mention of Ferriss having "sung" the skyscraper was an obvious reference to Walt Whitman's "I Sing the Body Electric" from *Leaves of Grass* (1855), where the American poet wrote:

But the expression of a well-made man
   appears not only in his face,

It is in his limbs and joints also, it is curiously
    in the joints of his hips and wrists,
It is in his walk, the carriage of his neck,
    the flex of his waist and knees,
    dress does not hide him,
The strong sweet quality he has strikes
    through the cotton and broadcloth;
To see him pass conveys as much as the best
    poem, perhaps more,
You linger to see his back, and the back of
    his neck and shoulder-side. [25]

Here is the idea of a complete and self-generated whole, something new, synthetic: a vortex, in Pound's sense of the word.

The very diversity of kind and quality manifest in the Chicago Tribune Competition dissipated any notion of the city as a whole. The great tall buildings constructed between the wars in New York—Raymond Hood's Daily News and McGraw-Hill buildings (1930–31), William Van Alen's Chrysler Building (1930), and Shreve, Lamb and Harmon's Empire State Building (1931)—were strong individual objects, both self-publicizing and acquiescent to market needs. The structure of the city, the structure of the real-estate business, the structure of the construction industry, the structure of the buildings—all were unaffected by the conceptual work of design. The design styles did vary—the Daily News and McGraw-Hill buildings, built only a year apart on opposite ends of Forty-Second Street, had opposite formal emphases but equally ad hoc means of construction. The massing and façades are quite different, but all else is the same.

Even the Empire State Building, although constructed at breakneck speed (eighty-five stories in six months) and with great inventiveness by the Starrett Brothers and Eken,[26] had little to contribute to advance the arts of architecture or engineering. It does not convey the thrill of Whitman's "well-made man." The structure for the Empire State Building was designed by Homer G. Balcom for speed of erection, not lightness. With 57,480 tons of steel for 2.1 million square feet (195,096.3 sq m), it required about fifty pounds per square foot (244.1 kg per sq m) of structural steel to reach its 1,252-foot (381.6-meter) height.[27] Balcom was also the engineer of the buildings at Rockefeller Center (1931–40). His design for the former RCA Building (1931–33), in particular, is noteworthy for the fact that in the narrow direction it uses diagonal braces to resist the wind forces, but on the broad north and south façades, in the

9

10

11

other direction, it relies, as does the Empire State Building, on the interaction of the riveted-steel frame with the brick masonry and stone cladding filling in that frame to resist the wind (FIG. 9). This represents a rather typical hybrid usage of "non-structural" cladding masonry to resist wind load, characteristic of the continued ad hoc approach of New York architects and structural engineers when it comes to the means and materials of building.[28]

While Rockefeller Center may have neither the structural elegance of the Statue of Liberty nor the closely choreographed construction speed of the Empire State Building, it is of fundamental significance as a sterling instance of ensemble design and urban power. For Le Corbusier: "Rockefeller Center affirms to the world the dignity of the new times [and] the proclamation of a proper name, that of a financial success, a fortune, a monetary power. Thus in the Middle Ages, at San Gimignano in Tuscany, the struggles for control among the families of the little city brought about the construction of fantastically high towers ... San Gimignano has the appearance of a pin cushion, and the spectacle delights tourists while troubling common sense; hirsute beauty–yes beauty, why not? The cataclysms of nature–jagged rocks, Niagara, Alps, or canyons, do they not impel our admiration by the effect of power, the feeling of catastrophe?"[29] For Tafuri: "Rockefeller Center ... represented the final result of the general debate on the structure of the American city.... It demonstrated that the only type of undertaking with any real possibility of influencing urban dynamics was one limited in scale and wholly in keeping with the existing, traditional laws of urban growth.... Indeed, if Rockefeller Center contained any ideological residue, it was in this attempt to celebrate the reconciliation of the trusts and the collectivity on an urban scale.... Rockefeller Center marked the definite eclipse of the 'skyscraper as an individual.' Presenting itself as 'a city within a city,' it had no need to create shock effects, as did the McGraw-Hill, Daily News, and Chrysler buildings."[30]

Both Le Corbusier and Tafuri recognized the necessarily composite meaning of tall buildings, understanding them as urban in scale but suggestive, as well, of a way for design practice to create individual buildings. The best works, from the unintentional composite brilliance of the Statue of Liberty, the Reliance Building, and even the Monadnock Block (1889–91) (FIG. 10),[31] all the way to Le Corbusier's astonishing Cartesian Skyscraper (1935) and Obus E Project for Algiers (1939), are at least careful compositions of space, fabric, structure, and form. It is possible to find an equilibrium of forms among the rhetorical and real aspects of formal language and technological content, where neither one is diminished nor dominant. A classical language need not dress up a banal interior, nor must a technological

9 Shreve, Lamb and Harmon, Empire State Building. New York, under construction, 1931
10 Burnham and Root, Holabird and Roche. Monadnock Block, Chicago, 1889–91
11 Gordon Bunshaft, Skidmore, Owings & Merrill, and Weiskopf & Pickworth. Lever House, New York, 1950–52

imperative determine the total integration of the whole. Instead, a conjunction of forces can flow in a "patterned energy," or vortex.

Rhetoric, Poetry, and Art

John Wellborn Root, the architect of the Monadnock Block and, incidentally, the brother-in-law of the founder of *Poetry* magazine, Harriet Monroe, wrote in 1890: "Like all forms of civilization, architectural development has for centuries moved from homogeneity to heterogeneity … to be true, architecture must normally express the conditions of life about and within it, not in a fragmentary and spasmodic way, but in the mass and structure; the life of the building, in large and comprehensive type." [32]

This means incorporating the facts of the "age of steam, of electricity, of gas, of plumbing and sanitation" into a "new art, a rational and steady growth from practical conditions outward and upward toward a more or less spiritual expression." [33] According to the architect and critic Alan Colquhoun, in "Pax Americana," a chapter in his *Modern Architecture* (2002): "Perhaps the greatest single achievement of American architecture after the Second World War was the establishment of the modern corporate office building as a type, imitated all over the world." [34]

In the United States, Lever House (1950–52) and the Inland Steel Building (1956–57) by Skidmore, Owings & Merrill, and the Seagram Building (1954–58) by Ludwig Mies van der Rohe; in Brazil, the Ministry of Education and Health Building in Rio de Janeiro (1936–43) by Lucio Costa, Oscar Niemeyer, and others (with Le Corbusier consulting)–all were retranslations from Europe of earlier American frame buildings, through abstraction and free planning. The originals ranged from Mies van der Rohe's Glass Skyscraper (1921), the Chicago Tribune Building proposals (1922) of Meyer and Gropius and Ludwig Hilberseimer, and Le Corbusier's Cartesian Skyscraper and Algiers project to the various speculations of the Vesnin brothers and Ivan Leonidov in 1920s Russia. As Colin Rowe wrote: "A formula was evolved permitting the simultaneous appearance of both structural grid and considerable spatial complexity.… In the International Style an autonomous structure perforates a freely abstracted space, acting as its punctuation rather than its defining form. There is thus … no fusion of space and structure, but each in the end remains an identifiable component, and architecture is conceived, not as their confluence, but rather as their dialectical opposition, as a species of debate between them." [35] For example, with the Lever House the opposing bodies of vertical and horizontal prisms float beside and bracket a cubic negative space (FIG. 11). The columns are sharply detailed stainless-steel cladding and are clearly separate from the tightly wrapped fabric of glass and stainless-steel vertical mullions. Prior to the recent restoration, the façade was even more remarkable for its variation in spandrel-panel glass color, from light marine blue to indigo, a subtle counterpoint to the building's machined and prismatic appearance.[36] And, like the Inland Steel Building, the building also clearly segregates office space and a core or service zone.

It is instructive to compare the plan of the former RCA Building at Rockefeller Center (1930–33) and that of the Chase Manhattan Bank Headquarters (1957–61) by Gordon Bunshaft, the architect of Lever House. Both are commissions of the Rockefeller family, although a generation apart. The most significant difference seems to be that the RCA Building has been composed as a volume from the outside in–a contingent object clearly fitted to its protagonist role at the urban scale–while the Chase building is also composed in plan, with emphasis on the column-free spans. The idea of the open space without columns is an important generator of the Chase design. The columns are expressed in the exterior as stainlesssteel clad pilasters all the way up and down. Their presence on the façade suggests an open light-filled space within. The buildings of the 1920s and 1930s on the other hand, from Rockefeller Center to the Empire State Building, did not suggest that the interior spaces were likely to be all that open or pleasant.

The use of glass plays a crucial role in this context. The glass curtain wall, despite the occasional successes of the 1890s, did not gain a firm hold until the post-World War II period. Glass offers lightness, transparency, and reflection, and an allusion to crystals.[37] An interesting precursor to some of the late modern crystal-like building forms is Wenzel Hablik's 1920 Exhibition Building. It is unusual in that it prescribes both a sculpturally strong form (almost like an Easter Island figure) and a completely regular and rationalized structure of load-bearing vertices, anticipating the later investigations of Myron Goldsmith and of I. M. Pei.

The ambition has changed since Root argued that: "Looking at the problems presented by these buildings ... we may certainly guess that all preexisting architectural forms are inadequate for their solution."[38] But to Root and the American architects that followed: "Styles are found truly at the appointed time, but solely by those who, with intelligence and soberness, are working their ends by the best means at hand, and with scarce a thought of the coming new or natural style ... if the new art is to come, I believe it will be a rational and steady growth from practical conditions outward and upward toward a more or less spiritual expression."[39] This argues, as Montgomery Schuyler wrote, that expression is an organic manifestation of the "true nature" of the thing, the building–"as it must be."[40] But this of course implies ambiguity, in that it is not just as it must be but as the society would have it be: "normal." In a 1964 text, *La Tour Eiffel*, Roland Barthes counters what he regards as pseudoarguments for utility–the tower as meteorological or other scientific platform, or as a site for high-altitude medical research: "Here the utilitarian reasons, as ennobled as they might be by the myth of Science, are nothing in comparison to the imagination which, alone, serves men to be properly human. Nevertheless, as ever, the gratuitous meaning of the work is not always admitted directly; it is rationalized by usage."[41] To Barthes: "Architecture is always dream and function, the expression of a utopia and the instrument of comfort."[42]

The Anglo-Welsh Roman Catholic poet and critic David Jones, who died in 1974, wrote in a 1947 essay, "Art and Democracy," of the "gratuitous which is the *sine qua non* of art…. If we could catch the beaver placing never so small a twig *gratuitously* we could make his dam into a font, he would be patient of baptism– the whole 'sign-world' would be open to him, he would know 'sacrament' and would have a true culture, for a culture is nothing but a sign, and the *anathemata* of a culture, 'the things set up,' can be set up only to the gods."[43] To be human is to be engaged in the making of art, to be both *homo faber* and *homo sapiens*, in practice. Thus, Barthes' understanding that "functional beauty does not reside in the perception of the good 'results' of a function, but in the spectacle of the func- tion itself, seized in the moment before it is produced; to seize the functional beauty of a machine or an architecture, is in effect to suspend time, retard usage to contemplate a *fabrication*."[44]

The tall buildings of the 1950s and onward became an art medium encompassing all the sophistication of the 1920s and 1930s European avant-gardes. Le Corbusier's inventions, the *pilotis* and the *brise soleil*, and Mies van der Rohe's steel structure and glass skyscraper, among others, opened significant avenues of creative experimentation. Space, fabric, and structure can be interrelated in complex and suggestive ways. Their interaction can at times have metaphoric effects.[45] The figure of the metaphor–whether Charles Baudelaire's *correspondances*, Pound's and Feno-llosa's ideogram, Eisenstein's montage, I. A. Richard's "interaction" or Barthes' "structure"–is a key critical tool.[46] Between the elements of a metaphor as well as its context a "resonance" can occur. This was the case with a few early tall buildings, notably the Reliance, Guaranty, and Wainwright, and of course with the Statue of Liberty, but it is not until the postwar period that it is clearly implemented in new tall buildings.

The rhetoric of modern tall buildings is generative, and more so than their program- matic or urbanistic aspects. Tafuri and others have identified this clearly. Tall

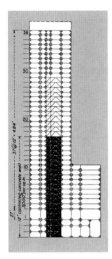

12

buildings are forms of persuasion constructed out of figures of a kind of speech, as well as material objects and building systems. In fact, those systems and materials serve as means to those figures, whether the figures are viewed as anarchic individuals or as ensembles. Robin Evans, for example, has shown how the mirror-finished cruciform columns of Mies van der Rohe's 1929 Barcelona Pavilion appear to "hold the roof down onto the walls, as if it were in danger of flying away. They hold it down more surely than they hold it up."[47] Just because a building structure looks rational does not mean it is. Critics often delight in exposing this contradiction, or labor to deny it. What is more useful is to see how the ambiguity itself constructs the meaning as metaphor.[48]

Mies van der Rohe's Crown Hall at the Illinois Institute of Technology in Chicago (1952–56) is a case in point. There is a skillful ambiguity between structural columns supporting the roof trusses and "nonstructural" mullions. In fact, the "mullions" on the side walls parallel to the trusses do support the roof. But more astonishing is the fact that, from the inside, it appears that the columns and mullions merge and all look alike, and the ceiling appears to float, independent of all of them. Eero Saarinen's General Motors Technical Center (1947–56) accomplishes a similar ambiguity by using the curtain-wall mullions as roof-supporting columns.[49] Gordon Bunshaft's and Paul Weidlinger's brilliant Beinecke Rare Book and Manuscript Library at Yale (1963) takes this even further, foreshadowing Herzog & de Meuron's manipulation of flat texture as material simulation. The Seagram Building, while technically not as advanced as these buildings, has even greater rhetorical power. Its siting, the deployment of dark and reflective surfaces and materials, and the careful proportioning of the mass are all admirable. But it is Mies van der Rohe's transformation of the I-beam, gradually detaching it from its structural function as he progressed from the Lake Shore Drive Apartments to the Seagram Building to a sharp-edged synecdoche, that most clearly demonstrated the rhetorical effectiveness of abstracted structural geometries and elements. It is truly the re-invention of classicism put at the service of the projection of a corporate and urbane identity.

For Le Corbusier, "the 'orders' are replaced by *brise-soleils* which give scale and meaning to the façade through the representation of the hierarchy of spaces within the building."[50] But whereas sections of Le Corbusier's projects, for instance the Unité d'Habitation, Marseille (1946–52), show his plastic handling of structure, a section of the Seagram Building (FIG. 12) clearly shows the pragmatic and dissociated quality of the actual structure.[51]

12 Ludwig Mies van der Rohe and Philip Johnson, and Severud Associates. Seagram Building, New York, 1954–58. Elevation of steel frame and concrete walls

Admitting the rhetorical to the architecture of tall buildings does not diminish its poetic capacities.[52] Indeed, it may be that the relationship of rhetoric and poetics is the dialectic most useful to any effort of interpretation. Rhetoric is the art of persuasion, and poetics the theory of making and judging poetry. They are inextricable. Northrop Frye sees rhetoric either as persuasion ("applied literature") or ornament ("the *lexis* or verbal texture of poetry").[53] Both are useful critical concepts. This dialectic goes back to the ancient Greeks and the most productive debates in Athens among the advocates and critics of democracy, most notably Socrates and Plato.[54] That rhetoric and poetry were illusory distractions from the true dialectics of philosophy was Plato's powerful antidemocratic argument. The interesting question of rhetoric and poetics, as it is applied to the interpretation of tall-building architecture, is then arguably a question about democracy. These "anarchic individuals" are, in a sense, diverse "speech acts" in the large agoras of our modern cities. They are not monuments, except perhaps on rare occasions when they come together as ensembles, such as Rockefeller Center. Like Auguste Rodin's *Burghers of Calais* (1884–86) and Alberto Giacometti's aptly named *City Square* (1948), they represent the demos.

The Postmodern Skyscraper

The architect-engineers Pier Luigi Nervi and R. Buckminster Fuller were invited to give the Charles Eliot Norton Lectures on Poetry at Harvard in 1961 and 1962 respectively. Both instances indicated a recognition of the poetic force of their work and its relevance to the culture. The architectural practices of both men integrated art and science. For a generation of architects and engineers, it seemed admirable that men like Nervi "combine two opposite frames of mind in one person: the synthetic, intuitive, artistic approach together with the analytic, mathematical, scientific approach."[55] The work of Nervi, and others like him, such as Felix Candela and Eduardo Torroja, was inspiring because it seemed to prove that beauty and truth could be one. This platonic fantasy seemed possible because the mathematics of thin concrete-shell design, the medium of choice, was both simple in formulation and endlessly rich in formal potential. It was like the idea of a generative grammar, which the linguist Noam Chomsky inaugurated in the mid-1950s.[56] Using a set of simple rules, he showed how the infinite richness and diversity of human creativity could emerge.

The idea of structural rationalism, at least in its postwar version, is closely related to this idea of grammar and simplicity. It is really no less than the aesthetics of structuralism itself. In structuralism, "what we generally call the signified—the meaning or conceptual content of an utterance—is now to be seen as a meaning-effect, as the objective mirage of signification generated and projected by the relationship of signifiers among themselves." [57] From the works of Nervi to the writings of Barthes, and from the "tensegrity structures" of Fuller to the fractal geometry of Benoît Mandelbrot, there is a common love of beauty as manifest in homologies of patterns, of structures, of natural forms and mathematical formulas, across scale and medium. The metallurgist and critic Cyril Stanley Smith argued that there is a "converse relationship between aesthetics and metallurgy," [58] that it is the aesthetic drive that motivates the craftsman to invent new materials and techniques, which, in turn, lead to new technology and finally scientific discovery.[59]

One of the most influential architect-engineers of the postwar period, Myron Gold-smith of Skidmore, Owings & Merrill, apprenticed with both Nervi and Mies van der Rohe and was also very much influenced by the writings of D'Arcy Thompson [60] on the similarity of natural forms at different scales, and the limits imposed on these similarities by gravity. Goldsmith taught a design studio with the structural engineer Fazlur Khan, also of Skidmore, Owings & Merrill, at the Illinois Institute of Technology for a number of years.[61] Together they experimented with structural forms for tall buildings, including varieties of braced cores, braced exteriors, rigid combinations of frames and braced cores, and ultimately the braced or rigid tube frames that became the structures of the very tall buildings built in the late 1960s and early 1970s. Their work was systematic, and relied on the use of numerical calculation on digital computers from early on. They were able to consider three-dimensional frames and hybrid structures, such as diagonally braced (or trussed) frames or shear walls linked to orthogonal, rigidly connected (or moment) frames, and were also rigorous in their experimentation with both steel and reinforced concrete, alternating the application of their structural ideas between the two.[62] They were able to test their ideas on numerous commissions at Skidmore, Owings & Merrill and to learn from the work of other engineers and architects who had been inspired by their propositions.

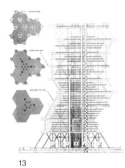

13

The idea of the perimeter tube frame is a case in point. The first appearance of this was in the Chestnut-DeWitt Apartments (1961–65) by Myron Goldsmith, Bruce Graham, and Fazlur Khan of Skidmore, Owings & Merrill, followed shortly thereafter by their Brunswick Building (1962–66). This form was adapted skillfully for the CBS Building in New York (1961–65) by Eero Saarinen. But where Skidmore, Owings & Merrill had made the tube out of a gridded frame, Saarinen and the engineers Paul Weidlinger and Mario Salvadori pushed the closely spaced columns beyond the floor beams, an approach adopted shortly thereafter by Minoru Yamasaki for the World Trade Center Towers. Ironically, their emphasis on the columns of the

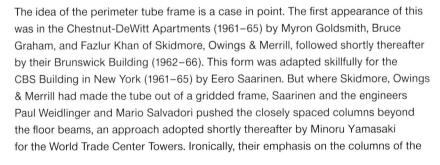

13 Louis I. Kahn and Anne Tyng. Office Tower, Philadelphia, Project, 1952–57. Section
14 R. Buckminster Fuller. Tetra City, San Francisco, Project, 1965. Photomontage

tube frame was a return to the example of Adler's and Sullivan's Guaranty and Wainwright buildings, now reinterpreted to have all the verticals as primary structure. An aesthetic reinterpretation of the frame passed through a period of abstract and rhetorical development to reemerge as the formal source of a new structural principle.

What Fredric Jameson characterized as the "relief of the postmodern"[63] has had both a productive and an alienating effect. Fuller declared in 1969 that all ideological dogmas would be "resolved" by the computer.[64] Certainly the computer, like the telescope, has opened a new universe of form and patterns, and served as a model for other forms of inquiry. It has also reinforced the kinship of science and art,[65] as the interest of science has moved to "systems of greater complexity, for methods of dealing with complicated nature as it exists."[66] The contemporary Pop and Fluxus productions illustrated wonderfully in Wolf Vostell's and Dick Higgins' *Fantastic Architecture*,[67] including Fuller's 1965 Tetra City (FIG. 14), constitute only one of many manifestations of the energetic joining of multiple scales and practices of those movements.[68] At the same time, there is "the 'effacement of the traces of production' from the object itself, from the commodity thereby produced" that is characteristic of postmodern reification.[69] This tension between production and alienation is present in the development of tall buildings from the 1960s onward.

Pop Art and the related Archigram group, as well as the Situationist and Mega-structuralist movements in architecture, worked through "play" to achieve an influential body of work that is utopian, delirious, and even at times colossal.[70] The design and construction of the Centre Pompidou (1971–75) in Paris by the team of Renzo Piano and Richard Rogers was the first clear emergence of this line into the public realm.[71] While Louis I. Kahn's and Anne Tyng's 616-foot-tall (187.8-meter) Office Tower proposal for Philadelphia (FIG. 13) could be considered a precursor, given Piano's apprenticeship in that office, the Centre Pompidou clearly initiated the production-oriented practices that followed in Europe, both in its architects' work and in that of Norman Foster.

Foster's Hong Kong and Shanghai Bank in Hong Kong (1979–86) shares with the Centre Pompidou and Kahn's 1952–57 project a lineage going back to Fuller's explorations in triangulated geometries and their techno-utopian association. But while Piano and Rogers, and the structural engineers Peter Rice and Edmund Happold, were looking for ways to show what Rice called the "trace of the hand,"[72] Foster and the engineer Jack Zunz (a colleague of Rice at Ove Arup & Partners) were re-forming their work to a machined anonymity.

14

15

Even so, both were able to achieve a result with strong popular appeal. The plaza in front of the Centre Pompidou and the public space in the Hong Kong and Shanghai Bank are both modern piazzas.[73] And both their interiors have a level of detail and craftsmanship that, not unlike earlier Victorian works in Great Britain, afford a humanistic intimacy to which its occupants seem to respond well.

Around the time the Centre Pompidou was being built, Happoid and Arup collaborated on the Multihall at Mannheim (1970–75) with the architect Frei Otto. This biomorphic freeform timber dome required a convergence of computer-based calculations of complex geometries and structural behavior, and the use of physical models and testing that set the pattern of collaborative, empirical, and visibly "made to order" (even if highly computerized and machined) as opposed to mass-produced work.[74] Indeed, Frei Otto's one-time collaborator Jörg Schlaich's recent work in designing very tall solar chimneys in the 1980s,[75] and the projects by the Arup engineers Peter Rice and Tom Barker, with Piano and then with Rogers, making early use of computational fluid dynamics to simulate large-scale air movements inside and around large buildings, are extensions of this focus on experimentation and production and the architectural use of their traces.

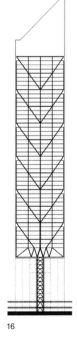

16

In the United States at that time, the completion of the Hancock and Sears towers in Chicago and the World Trade Center in New York represented, for the most part, the end of any integrated attention to production and experimentation. The World Trade Center Towers were the work of structural engineers Leslie Robertson and John Skilling, whose intensity of thought on their structure has not been rivaled in the United States. Robertson standardized the geometry of the perimeter tube and the panelized floor structure in order to achieve large-scale prefabrication and rapid assembly. Recognizing the directional variation of wind loads, the so-called "wind rose,"[76] and the wind shadowing between the towers, he also used, for each floor, beams and columns made of plates all the same thickness but of varying strength properties as a way to accommodate the asymmetrical load-and-stress patterns—an ephemeral rather than formal expression. This was mass customization on a giant scale, and a level of complex project management comparable to the contemporaneous Apollo 11 lunar expedition. The concentration of invention and integration across disciplines as well as the unexpected minimalist sculptural presence of the towers had been rivaled in New York only by the Statue of Liberty.

In Chicago the Sears Tower by Bruce Graham and Fazlur Khan of Skidmore, Owings & Merrill has a comparable sculptural power (reminiscent in stance of Rodin's

15 Bruce Graham and Fazlur Khan, Skidmore, Owings & Merrill. John Hancock Building, Chicago, 1970, under construction

16 Hugh Stubbins and William LeMessurier. Citicorp Center, New York, 1974–77. Elevation of structural frame

Balzac) and specific relationship to the wind environment.[77] Its asymmetrical form as well, like that of the World Trade Center Towers, gives it a strong role as a means of orientation in the city and a dynamic quality. While New York's twin towers were each independent single-framed tubes, the Sears Tower is itself a bundle of nine such tubes tied together. Both are constructed forms whose innovative structures are legible to the knowledgeable but still somewhat ambiguous behind either the shear black façade of the Sears Tower or the reflective ribs of the Trade Center.

The Hancock Tower in Chicago, on the other hand, appears emphatically structural; the large-scale, three-dimensional trussed tube is even a mega-structure (FIG. 15). The detailed computer analysis by Fazlur Khan and his team revealed that the large diagonal members, ostensibly there as wind bracing, drew a large portion of the building's gravity load, owing to the relative rigidity of the large diagonals and smaller columns, and the unavoidable triangulation of gravity columns, beams, and diagonal wind braces. What appears to be a clear diagram is in fact a hybrid. This discovery actually led to the most inventive tall-building structures of the late 1970s and 1980s, notably Citicorp Center (1974–77) by Hugh Stubbins and William J. LeMessurier, the Bank of the Southwest project in Houston (1982) by Helmut Jahn and LeMessurier (FIGS. 16, 17), and the Bank of China (1982–89) by I. M. Pei and Leslie Robertson (FIG. 18). The structural strategy for these buildings was to combine a small number (four to eight) of columns with cross bracing connecting them through the building; this combined the functions of carrying gravity load and effecting wind resistance into one integrated system.[78] In the case of LeMessurier's structures, the system consists of interlocking planar trusses. In the Bank of China, Robertson and Pei extended the idea into a three-dimensional triangulated space frame (FIG. 19).

In all three cases, however, the innovative structure is only partially expressed. Unlike the Hancock Tower with its exoskeleton, these buildings have manifestly thin curtain walls tightly wrapped around their forms. This is especially true of Citicorp and the Bank of China where the triangulated structure is entirely, or selectively, suppressed and displaced [79] – a practice fully in the tradition of Mies van der Rohe's Seagram Building. The Bank of China further succeeds in appearing to be a rare crystal object on a refined pedestal, appealing both to Chinese connoisseurship and early modern expressionist precedents.

This surface flatness characterizes some of the best tall-building designs of that period in the United States. The Hancock Tower in Boston (1977) and Fountain Place in Dallas (1986) by Henry Cobb of Pei Cobb Freed & Partners have a minimalist

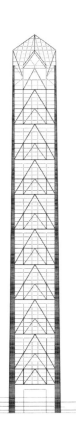

sculptural purity and minimalist structure (the latter by the skilled protégé of Fazlur Khan, the structural engineer Prabodh Banavalkar) that achieve a kind of "almost nothing" and flatness, skillfully expressing the developers' quest for a maximum "net-to-gross" floor area ratio.

The Contemporary Tall Building as Metaphor

"When John [Cage] and I first thought of separating the dance and the music, it was very difficult, because people had this idea about the music supporting the dance rhythmically. I can remember so clearly–in one piece I made some kind of very big movement, and there was no sound at all, but right after it came this incredible sound on the prepared piano, and I understood that these two separate things could make something that couldn't have happened any other way."

Merce Cunningham, 2002 [80]

In the early twentieth century, the creative step in American tall-building design, from the Chicago School to Frank Lloyd Wright, was to turn to the plan as the generator of form. A similar key turn in contemporary tall-building design has been toward the whole building section. This was signaled by Rem Koolhaas' book *Delirious New York* (1978), which drew attention to the surrealist section of the Downtown Athletic Club, New York (1926) by Starrett & Van Vleck. At the same time, both Skidmore, Owings & Merrill and Norman Foster were experimenting with the organization of office floors in clusters grouped around common spaces, usually atria, and accessible by express elevators stopping only once per cluster, with escalators in between. Skidmore, Owings & Merrill's experiment was short-lived, but for Foster this became a key concept that he developed through to the present with increasing sophistication. The earliest example was the low-rise Willis Faber Building (1971–75) in Ipswich, itself an extraordinary concentration of inventive form, materials (the earliest use of planar-bolted glass walls), and social organization. The later Hong Kong and Shanghai Bank extended both the use of modular office "villages" for organization and the intensity of technical and material invention. In Foster's Commerzbank in Frankfurt, Swiss Reinsurance Headquarters for London, and his office's World Trade Center proposal, as well as Rem Koolhaas' Togok (XL Towers) for Seoul, Korea, and Central Chinese Television (CCTV) Tower for Beijing, the range of experimentation, and accomplishment, is impressive. With the exception of Foster's World Trade Center proposal, which was developed with the New York structural engineers Ysrael Seinuk and Ahmad Rahimian, these projects were all designed in collaboration with the structural engineers at Ove Arup & Partners, notably Rem Koolhaas' collaborator Cecil Balmond. These tall buildings are, or would be, landmarks. In the case of Koolhaas' Togok (XL Towers), this

17 Helmut Jahn and William LeMessurier. Bank of the Southwest, Houston, Project 1982. Elevation of structural frame

is projected by grouping buildings into integrated ensembles, in the tradition of
Rockefeller Center. The Togok project, while alluding to the vertical patterns of
Rockefeller Center and more so even to its successors (Time-Life, McGraw-Hill, etc.)
by Harrison and Abramowitz along Sixth Avenue, literally adds a new dimension
by leaning two of its six slender towers into and alongside three of the others to form
large-scale A-frames. An equally large-scale "collar" truss ties these frames to the
other towers, and forms a high-altitude datum. The resulting structural assembly
is then interconnected with resilient dampers to control wind-induced vibrations.
The CCTV project is formally less complex than the Togok project. Sculpturally,
it is close to some of Isamu Noguchi's work and that of Tony Smith.[81] The structure
is developed on the façade as a triangulated grid of varying density reflecting the
stress distribution. The internal program is segregated into zones that differentiate
the space in the sections.

Norman Foster's tall-building projects are equally ambitious, although less Dionysian than Koolhaas'. The Frankfurt Commerzbank was a breakthrough as the
first demonstrably "ecological" skyscraper, with natural light and views, and organized
in modules or "villages" of interior space. The building also marked a calmer
formal stratagem, closer in spirit to Mies van der Rohe's minimalism than the earlier
Hong Kong and Shanghai Bank project, while still demonstrating an unusually
progressive social agenda in the organization of spaces. With this and the later Swiss
Reinsurance Headquarters and World Trade Center projects, Foster also developed
a more legible and less rhetorical structure than that of the Hong Kong building.[82]
The "diagrid" of expressed diagonals and suppressed horizontals in both projects
still maintains some of the ambivalence of expression of the Miesian tradition.
After all, the diamond pattern is only part of the triangulated structure. In both the
Swiss Reinsurance Headquarters and World Trade Center projects, these white lines
serve effectively as highlights, sharpening the optical clarity of the distinct forms.
The horizontal floor beam elements, while part of the truss structure, are visually
suppressed.

At the same time, formal exuberance has clearly emerged in force in the design
of contemporary tall buildings. Philip Johnson, with his AT&T Headquarters (1984),[83]
and Gordon Bunshaft, with his last and most minimalist skyscraper (1983) in Jedda,
had already introduced the effect of what Barthes called the "miniaturization of
the tower," a kind of mingling of model and souvenir *(maquette et bibelot)* – something not only to hold and, in a sense, domesticate but also to receive the projection
of one's own potential power as maker. It may be that the remarkable popular
support that met Foster's scheme for the World Trade Center site had not only to

18

19

do with his re-creation of the twin towers and the project's sculptural, structural, and ecological qualities, but also with this scalability.

The Swiss Reinsurance Headquarters at 30 St. Mary Axe has a different, if equally ambitious, urban charge. Despite its size – at 590 feet (179.8 m), only sixty percent of the height of the Eiffel Tower – it will become a distinct focus, or landmark, for London. The building form, in effect that of a bullet, is circular in plan and tapers both at the top and, slightly, at its base. The shape reduces the apparent size of the building seen close-up, and seems to have also reduced the degree to which the wind is deflected by the building down to the street level. There are spiraling atria that divide the floor plates into distinct work areas and that link these visually across floors. The atria can also draw natural ventilation as they bridge areas of positive and negative wind pressure. The exterior structure is a rigid and redundant system that can efficiently resist the wind load and effectively redistribute the gravity load in case an accidental blast damages any element (the building was constructed on the site of a damaging IRA attack). One striking, if invisible, detail is the adjustment (or truing) of the building frame and the way it was accomplished during construction. A number of pockets left open in the slab allowed radial adjustment of the exterior frame to the floor, like the spokes on a bicycle wheel.

The tall building as a landmark, such as Swiss Reinsurance, can reorient an older city center, mark new areas of development, or create the image of new cities. Teodoro González de León's Arcos Bosques Corporativo buildings in Mexico City have had this effect for its new area of high-technology development. It also belongs to a group of new buildings, starting with Peter Eisenman's proposed Max Reinhardt Haus for Berlin and Koolhaas' CCTV Tower, that form a closed, looped shape. This has important advantages for circulation, for safety (offering many more routes of escape in a fire), and for structure. It also offers a much larger area of accessible space at the highest level. Since September 11, this has become a consistent element of many proposals for tall buildings.

There is clearly an increased complexity in the development of tall buildings, which is visible in their sections. They no longer comprise the simple extensions of repeated commercially viable floor areas. For one thing, there are the social and environmental agendas of architects like Norman Foster. But also there is the imperative of mass-transportation access, the notion of the tall building as transit hub, pioneered with the World Trade Center.[84] This strengthens the ecological justification of tall buildings as energy and open-space savers (and advances the late-capitalist objective of routing workers through shopping malls). Thus we

18 I. M. Pei, Pei Cobb Freed & Partners, and Leslie Robertson. Bank of China, Hong Kong, 1982–89, under construction
19 I. M. Pei, Pei Cobb Freed & Partners, and Leslie Robertson. Bank of China, Hong Kong, 1982–89. Construction photograph showing a corner of the three-dimensional triangulated space frame before the corner concrete columns were poured

have generated multiple hybrid programs consisting of transit, shopping (often all the way to the upper floors), entertainment, and observation. Hans Hollein's Monte Laa PORR Towers is a clear manifestation of this, as are of course the United Architects and Norman Foster proposals for the World Trade Center site. It also recalls Hollein's iconic Aircraft Carrier City of 1964 (FIG. 20)—an ironic but also telling precursor to this use of program to make unexpected form.

This also links to the increasing sculptural ambition of many recent projects. In one sense, this is a return to the traditions of *colossi*, of the Statue of Liberty and its precursors. One project of this type is the proposal for the New York Times Head-quarters on Manhattan's West Side by Frank O. Gehry with David Childs of Skidmore, Owings & Merrill, a highly accomplished abstract colossal sculpture. The façade is made of "wrappers" [85] of curved sheets of vertically ribbed glass curtain wall and extends far above the roof level as a huge parapet. These wrappers are held away and distinct from the building structure. The floor plates vary according to the billowing profile of the exterior. The structure itself, a simple frame, is of the usually deadpan straight-man kind favored by Gehry.

Kohn Pedersen Fox's Kowloon Station Tower shares with Gehry's project the effect of a glass façade peeling from its mass. The tower is one of two very tall develop-ments over new mass-transit stations in Hong Kong. The other tower, by César Pelli, is across the water on Hong Kong Island. Each is over 1,542 feet (470.0 m) high, taller than the Sears Tower. The Kowloon tower is located on an unusually deep and narrow deposit of very soft soil, so that its orientation bridging this underground valley at an angle to the local city grid, in fact, literally marks the contours of the land it is founded on. As with most of the new very tall buildings (over 1,300 feet [396.2 m]), the structure is made up of a continuous concrete-wall-enclosed core and a series of outrigger steel trusses at regular vertical intervals that are tied to eight very large columns on the perimeter aligned with the faces of the core shaft. In Asia, these outrigger trusses, occupying full-story height, can easily occur at the "refuge" floors that are required for fire safety at about 200-foot (61 m) intervals. This "mast" concept is the same as Eiffel's pylon and outrigger truss structure for the Statue of Liberty. The great benefit is to free the façade from the structural role it had in the perimeter-tube frames of the Sears and World Trade Center Towers, opening the view, and opening the possibility of sculptural play.

The idea of a "mast" tied with outriggers to perimeter columns (or "stays") was explored by Fazlur Khan in the 1960s but did not emerge in the design of tall structures until the 1980s proposal for the Miglin-Beitler tower in Chicago by César

Pelli and the engineer Charles Thornton, and the same team's Petronas Towers in Kuala Lumpur (1991–97). The reemergence of this structural type is due in part to the increasing attention to wind-induced vibrations that cause discomfort for workers in very tall buildings. Since mass and damping are generally more effective at reducing vibrations than stiffness, the trend, starting in the 1980s, was to increase building density and add mechanical damping to tall slender structures.[86]

The Jin Mao Tower in Shanghai and the 7 South Dearborn mixed-use tower project for Chicago, both by the Skidmore, Owings & Merrill office in Chicago, have adopted this core-mast idea. On the Jin Mao structure this allows the building façade considerable freedom, while providing a strong underlying formal structure to the plan; a kind of Greek-cross configuration is maintained owing to the geometry of the core, outriggers, and exterior stay-columns. What is most interesting about Jin Mao, however, is the sectional inversion that takes place at the top floors where the program shifts to a hotel. Here, in the tradition of John Portman's atrium hotels, the shaft of the core is made void as the elevators and services are shifted to one side. The core concrete walls remain, turning into the separation between the room and the continuous balcony facing into the huge atrium. This topological inversion is both simple and quite awe inspiring, and has become a tourist attraction in its own right.

The 7 South Dearborn project was to be 2,000 feet (609.6 m) tall and include three digital transmission antennae. Indeed, the tower is not easily categorized, since its raison d'être was to have been the revenue from the antennae. The program starts with offices at the base, apartments in the middle, and broadcast studios at the top. The separation into these modules is articulated with gaps made possible by the fact that the floors of the top three modules are cantilevered from the central concrete core. There is only one set of outriggers on this mast, located at the top of the base portion. The fact that the area of the core near the top is greater than the residential area around it creates an ambiguity of type. It also tends to a very direct expression of functional equilibrium and formal simplicity.

The idea of having gaps belongs to a rather unusual long-term experiment on the part of Skidmore, Owings & Merrill in collaboration with Nicholas Isyumov of the Boundary Layer Wind Tunnel in Canada. Isyumov and Baker, as well as Baker's predecessors at the firm, have investigated ways to reduce the effective wind load on tall structures by "confusing" it, as Baker describes it. It turns out that one of the principal sources of problematic vibrations in tall slender structures is the aerodynamic phenomenon of vortex shedding. This effect occurs when a steady

20 Hans Hollein. Aircraft Carrier City in Landscape. Project, 1964. Perspective, cut-and-pasted printed paper on gelatin silver photographs, mounted on board

wind, at a particular velocity (not necessarily that great) interacts with a building's size and shape such that regular vortices form alternately at opposite corners of the leeward side. These vortices form and detach steadily at regular intervals. When that temporal rhythm coincides with one of the building's natural periods of vibration, the sway that results (actually perpendicular to the wind's direction) can be felt. To counteract this, Isyumov and the Skidmore, Owings & Merrill engineers have experimented with large holes in buildings and, in this case, gaps to disrupt the vortex formations. On 7 South Dearborn it worked well enough in the wind tunnel to reduce the wind effects by twenty-five percent.

Another way to counter wind vibration is to use dampers. These can be large masses located high in the building (such as the Citicorp Center) on sliding surfaces and between carefully calibrated springs. These are designed to move opposite to the building motion and dampen its effect. Or, they can be mechanical dampers, like shock absorbers (such as the viscoelastic dampers on the World Trade Center), that directly absorb energy.

The Highcliff and Summit apartment buildings in Hong Kong by Dennis Lau Wing-kwong and the engineer Ad Gouwerok of Magnusson Klemencic Associates make use of a very effective damping device, the tuned "sloshing" damper. This is made up of two sets of paired water tanks that allow water to slosh back and forth between the tanks, both countering the building sway and dissipating energy through the water's turbulence. The apartments themselves, especially in Highcliff, have a nautical quality, narrowing as they do from the center core and ending in the master bedroom and bathtub at the "prow." These apartments have extraordinary views since the building is not only 827 feet (252.1 m) tall, but is perched high on the hillside overlooking the harbor. Some apartments are at least 1,300 feet (396.2 m) above sea level. The pairing of the two towers, one convex the other concave, and their extreme slenderness, shapes the space around them as well. The towers are, in fact, quite prominent in the skyline of Hong Kong Island, as they extend above the top line of the mountains, so their identity is as a pair, not twins, and their spatial interplay is as interesting as their individual qualities.

The use of damping devices to reduce wind vibration and the design of tall-building ensembles are both literally the means of making a design out of interactions. The Togok (XL Towers) by Rem Koolhaas is an excellent example of both. The design uses the differential movements of the towers to drive dampers and dissipate wind energy: the prevention of physical resonance, as it were, juxtaposed with the metaphoric resonance between things. The JR Ueno Railway Station Redevelopment

tower project by Arata Isozaki, with the engineer Toshihiko Kimura and his associates, uses extremely large trussed struts to help stiffen the narrow direction of the building against earthquakes. The tower is part of a projected complex of retail and office spaces on top of a train station, a program that was applied with very interesting results in Japan in the 1980s (at Kyoto and Nagoya). The struts are attached to the distinct structural "belt trusses" at the fifth points of the tower height.[87] The projected cladding geometry is also quite distinct, creating both lenticular cuts at the corners and a pillowing effect between the "belts."

Renzo Piano's projected London Bridge Tower, at 1,016 feet (309.7 m) and seventy-seven stories tall, is a slender pyramid clad in what Piano describes as "shards" of glass. The building site is directly above London Bridge Station and includes offices, live/work, public, residential, and broadcast facilities, in that order, from bottom to top. The structure is also a stayed mast consisting of a concrete core (to be cast using a self-supporting "jump" form—one where the form is in parts that move by each one "jumping" over the one just above, rather than "slipping" as a whole, as is sometimes the method) and steel floor framing, outriggers, and composite steel and concrete stays, or "outrigger" columns. The central heating system uses the waste heat from the office areas to heat the residential areas. The mechanical engineer John Berry of Ove Arup & Partners predicts that, overall, the carbon dioxide emission will be about 9,000 tons a year or about two-thirds that of a typical office building. There is interaction in the actual heat exchange, just as there is interaction of structural movement and dampers to dissipate the dynamic energy of the wind. Increasingly, buildings are active participants, even to actual motion, fluid flows, and exchanges of energy with the environment. It is no wonder that the mapping of these exchanges and physical patterns has become a source of structural ornamentation as rich and organic as Louis Sullivan's and Dankmar Adler's earlier dialogues on ornament and pragmatism.

The structural engineer Cecil Balmond of Ove Arup & Partners has explored this pattern-making, drawing on number theory[88] and Mandelbrot's theories of fractal geometry to create some remarkable structural patterns, notably in the Victoria and Albert Museum with Daniel Libeskind, and currently on the CCTV exterior bracing structure with Rem Koolhaas. Starting from a uniform grid, Balmond and his team evolved a pattern reflecting the varied stresses in the diagonal members of the CCTV façade by reducing their number where stresses are low.

A similar strategy was used on the Edificio Manantiales, Santiago, Chile, by Luis Izquierdo W., Antonia Lehman S. B., Raimundo Lira V., José Domingo Peñafiel E., and the engineer Luis Soler P. Here, responding to the need to resist earthquake effects, the designers devised a combined system of a concrete core and partial perimeter bracing. The perimeter bracing is made of eleven-and-one-half-inch (29.2-cm) diameter round concrete struts, both vertical and inclined, that counter-intuitively increase in extent with the height. The reason is that they serve to counteract the building's tendency to twist (torsion) caused by the placement of the concrete core off center (necessary to preserve good leasable space). As the building plan grows out at the lower floor, that eccentricity diminishes and the necessity for the exterior bracing is lessened.

For both the CCTV and Edificio Manantiales structures, the configuration required repeated iteration of the analysis to arrive at a balanced result. Each step in that interaction was then the evaluation of the interaction of structural parts, an adjustment (or tuning), and a replay. The final design is the trace of that development and, in effect, the evidence of a physical process. Louis Sullivan would have appreciated this fine balance of rhetoric and poetry.

The Standard Model

The so-called Standard Model of subatomic particle physics, first formulated in the 1970s [89] and largely confirmed by experiments since, accounts for the basic effects of three of the four fundamental forces: electromagnetism, the strong and weak forces, and gravity. The model diagrams the interactions of matter particles (the fermions: electrons, quarks, muons, and taus) and force carriers (photons, gluons, and other bosons). The model allows for their particular interactions, which have so far given a good prediction of the complex interactions observed in high-energy particle physics experiments. This is no orbital model of stars and planets. Its geometry is far more complex, akin to the universes of Paul Klee and John Cage, and it exceeds physical intuition. So, perhaps the present postmodern culture might at last elude the hold of idealism in Western thought and come to accept poetry and rhetoric as closer to the real, not, as Plato argued, the faint shadow of a reality available only to an elite few.

The best recent evidence of this may have been the recovery efforts at the World Trade Center site following the disaster and horror of September 11. It was the best evidence, since the 1960s, of democracy's effectiveness at the ground level. People worked and argued to solve problems and keep everyone safe. Things got taken care of through individual initiative tempered with deliberation, a flexible re-ordering of priorities, and a supple executive structure.

Democracy is itself a "standard model," and the best tall buildings are, at times, its best advocates on the skyline. They can inspire society by the dignity of their language, the example of their social and environmental thoughtfulness, and the evident quality of the social processes by which they are made. The trace of the hand, as Peter Rice would say, is the "speech act" of the worker, there to please and inspire his fellow citizens.

Since the completion of the World Trade Center Towers in 1973, there has been a redirection of energy within the United States practice of tall-building design toward an industrial method, much like its automobile industry: the body is styled but the chassis is standard. This worked quite well for American developers but led, in general, to silent buildings.

It is encouraging that some architects, such as Norman Foster and Frank Gehry, have drawn their technologies and some inspiration from aerospace. Prototyping and computer-aided customized manufacturing processes have helped them make not only complex buildings but rich and complex practices within their own offices—constructive in both the social and artistic realms.

Once again, more balanced teams are coming together to collaborate on projects, recapturing some of the quality of engineering design that existed in the 1950s and 1960s, which was mostly lost with the advent of post-1969 formalism.[90] Here, the evolving model, drawing from the example of filmmaking, seems to help provide a framework: an audience that has learned to appreciate the difference in art between the actor's work and the director's work, and the pleasure that is found in discovering and distinguishing those differences, can begin to see the gain achieved in strong collaborations. The work of Frank Gehry and Rem Koolhaas has grown stronger in collaboration with more thoughtful and creative engineers, such as Jörg Schlaich and Cecil Balmond.

Ove Arup once described his theory of the architectural "star system" as the right choice of a metaphor or idea toward which to navigate a project, regardless of the occasional detours. This can be a metaphor that unites the energies of a team, much like the historic convergences that form the vortices of Ezra Pound's *Cantos*. After all, the history and practice of tall-building design shows that, like the history of jazz, it is utterly urban, street smart, and at its best in those rare moments when everyone is playing well together.

1   James, Henry. 1906. New York Revisited. *Harper's Monthly Magazine* 112 (Feb.): 402; quoted in Sarah B. Landau and Carl Condit. 1996. *Rise of the New York Skyscraper, 1865–1913*. New Haven: Yale University Press, 285.

2   For a list of Osama bin Laden's prospective targets, see Lichtblau, Eric. 2003. Bin Laden Chose 9/11 Targets, Al Qaeda Leader Says. *The New York Times*, March 20, A22.

3   Trachtenberg, Marvin. 1976. *The Statue of Liberty*. (New York: Viking Press; London: Penguin Books, 1976): 35.

4   Ibid, 79.

5   Talansier, Charles. 1883. La Statue de la Liberté éclairant le monde. In *Le Génie Civil*, 15. Paris; quoted in Loyrette Henri. 1985. *Gustave Eiffel*. New York: Rizzoli, 100.

6   For an excellent discussion of expressionist architecture and its universalist politics, see Colquhoun, Alan. 2002. *Modern Architecture*. Oxford and New York: Oxford University Press, 89.

7   Fromonot, Françoise. 1998. *Jørn Utzon: The Sydney Opera House*. Corte Madera, CA: Ginko; Milan: Electa, 91, 107.

8   Eisenstein, Sergei M. 1942. Synchronization of Senses. In *The Film Sense*, ed. Jay Leyda, 69. New York: Harcourt, Brace.

9   Ibid, 74–75.

10   Fenollosa, Ernest. 1968. *The Chinese Written Character as a Medium for Poetry*. Ed. Ezra Pound. San Francisco: City Lights Books. See also Eisenstein, Sergei M. 1949. The Cinematographic Principle and the Ideogram. Idem, *Film Form*. New York: Harcourt, Brace, 28–44.

11   Fenollosa. Op cit, 26. See also Kenner, Hugh. 1971. *The Pound Era*. Berkeley and Los Angeles: University of California Press.

12   Pound, Ezra. 1970. *Gaudier-Brzeska: A Memoir*. New York: New Directions, 92.

13   Colquhoun, Alan. 1981. The Displacement of Concepts in Le Corbusier. Idem, *Essays in Architectural Criticism*. Cambridge, MA: MIT Press, 52.

14   The Reliance Building is always photographed from the southeast at three-quarter view because it has only two sides of white terra cotta. The other two are plain brick party walls. See Merwood, Joanna. 2001. The Mechanization of Cladding: The Reliance Building and Narratives of Modern Architecture. Grey Room 04 (Summer): 53–69. With its 1999 restoration, the Reliance Building has gone from the drab gray of early engravings and black-and-white photographs to a brilliant white. This radiance is a reminder of the key role of color and glaze in lightening the appearance of curtain walls and giving even the truly massive masonry Monadnock Block dazzling highlights.

15   Rowe Colin. 1976. Chicago Frame. Idem, *The Mathematics of the Ideal Villa and Other Essays*. Cambridge, MA: MIT Press, 89–117. In full: "An autonomous structure perforates a freely abstracted space."

16   Prior to the December 6, 1968, edition of the New York City Building Laws, the code did not require any wind-force calculations for buildings under 100 feet (30.5 m), nor under 150 feet (47.7 m) before 1935 (James Colgate and Mark Topping, Department of Buildings, and Irwin Cantor, personal communications to the author, 2003).

17   Stokes, Adrian. 1978. Venice. In *The Critical Writings of Adrian Stokes: Volume II, 1937–1938*, ed. Lawrence Gowing. London: Thames & Hudson, 91.

18   Ibid, 93.

19   James, Henry. Op cit, 402.

20   See Sullivan, Louis H. 1947. *Kindergarten Chats (Revised 1918) and Other Writings.* Documents of Modern Art. New York: Wittenborn, Schultz.

21   Jenney, William Le Baron. 1891. The Chicago Construction, or Tall Buildings on a Compressible Soil. *Inland Architect and News Record* 18 (Nov.): 41; quoted in Merwood, op cit, 56.

22   Tafuri, Manfredo. 1980. The Disenchanted Mountain: The Skyscraper and the City. In *The American City: From the Civil War to the New Deal*, Giorgio Ciucci, Francesco Dal Co, Mario Manieri-Elia, and Manfredo Tafuri. London: Granada, 390–391.

23   Ibid, 419.

24   Ibid, 448. The 1982 film *Blade Runner* offered a contemporary analogue to Tafuri's interpretation in its intensely architectural and urban character. The movie set, part collage, image, and representation, conveyed the potential emotive impact of a city–the very impact that both Eliel Saarinen and Hugh Ferriss hoped to create with architecture.

25 Whitman, Walt. 1926. "I Sing the Body Electric." Idem, *Leaves of Grass*, Inclusive Edition, ed. Emory Holloway. Garden City, New York: Doubleday, 79–80.

26 See Willis, Carol, ed. 1998. *Building the Empire State*. New York: W. W. Norton. It is striking how similar the Empire State Building is to Eliel Saarinen's Grand Hotel scheme (1923), especially in early renderings that do not include the antennae.

27 Ibid, 11. The Chrysler Building required 21,000 tons for 850,000 square feet (78,967.6 sq m), or about fifty pounds per square foot (244.1 kg per sq m) as well.

28 The structural engineers Weiskopf & Pickworth did the same on the Daily News Building by Raymond Hood, using braced frames in one direction (the narrow one) and relying on the interaction of frame and masonry infill in the other for wind resistance. In the case of the Daily News, the architect also allowed the outer wythe of ceramic glazed white brick to run continuously and be self-supporting rather than run as a "curtain" relieved on each floor. Again, the pragmatism of New York designers tended to mix methods without much conceptual consistency.

29 Le Corbusier. 1947. *When the Cathedrals Were White*. Cornwall, NY: Reynal & Hitchcock, 54–56.

30 Tafuri. Op cit, 483–484.

31 The Monadnock Block by John Wellborn Root is a sixteen-story-tall office building of load-bearing exterior brick walls that are up to six feet (1.8 m) thick at the base. It represented the limit of bearing-wall construction at the birth of steel-skeleton framing. Despite this, the simplicity of its lines, the deep glow of purple indigo and slightly glazed brick, and the clear expression of mass is a forerunner of later rationalist structural expression.

32 Root, John Wellborn. 1890. A Great American Problem. *Inland Architect and New Record* 15, no. 5 (June): 69. I wish to thank Henry Cobb for giving me a copy of this essay.

33 Ibid, 70.

34 Colquhoun. *Modern Architecture,* 237.

35 Rowe. Op cit, 99.

36 The 2001 restoration of the Lever House replaced the two-piece spandrel glass panel with a single piece covered by an applied horizontal metal girt. The original two-piece spandrel glass panels had on occasion been replaced since 1952 by glass of a darker blue than the original, weaving a random pattern of subtle color differences. See color illustration in Colquhoun, *Modern Architecture:* 238 (FIG. 163).

37 The orthogonal crystal forms of Bruno Taut's glass architecture, of Kazimir Malevich's *Arkitektens* (c. 1924), and of Eliel Saarinen's 1920s skyscraper designs had a strong influence on Hugh Ferriss' and Raymond Hood's skyscraper massing experiments.

38 Root. Op cit, 69.

39 Ibid, 70.

40 Schuyler, Montgomery. 1907. Some Recent Skyscrapers. *Architectural Record 22*, no. 3 (September): 164.

41 Barthes, Roland, and André Martin. 1964. *La Tour Eiffel*. Paris: Delpire, 33. Trans. Guy Nordenson. "C'est qu'ici les raisons utilitaires, si ennoblies qu'elles soient par le mythe de la Science, ne sont rient en comparaison de la grande fonction imaginaire qui, elle, sert aux hommes à être proprement humains. Cependant, comme toujours, le sens gratuit de l'oeuvre n'est jamais avoué directement il est rationalisé sous l'usage."

42 Ibid, 64. Trans. Guy Nordenson. "L'architecture est toujours rêve et fonction, expression d'une utopie et instrument d'un confort."

43 Jones, David. 1959. Art and Democracy. In *Epoch and Artist*. New York: Chilmark Press, 87–89.

44 Barthes and Martin. Op cit, 64. Trans. Guy Nordenson. "La beauté fonctionnelle ne réside pas dans la perception des bons 'résultats' d'une fonction, mais dans le spectacle de la fonction elle même, saisie dans un moment antérieur à ce qu'elle produit; saisir la beauté fonctionnelle d'une machine ou d'une architecture, c'est en somme suspendre le temps, retarder l'usage pour contempler une fabrication."

45 For an excellent discussion of metaphor, rhetoric, and poetics, see Preminger, Alex, ed. 1965. *Princeton Encyclopedia of Poetry and Poetics*. Princeton, NJ: Princeton University Press, 490, 702.

46 For the application of ideograms and for I. A. Richard's ideas on architecture and planning, see Smithson, Alison, ed. 1968. *Team 10 Primer*. Cambridge, MA: MIT Press.

47 Evans, Robin. 1997. Mies van der Rohe's Paradoxical Symmetries. Idem, *Translations from Drawing to Building and Other Essays*. Cambridge, MA: MIT Press, 242.

48 See Empson, William. 1966. *Seven Types of Ambiguity*. New York: New Directions, 2. "Metaphor is the synthesis of several units of observation into one commanding image; it is the expression of a complex idea,

not by analysis, nor by direct statement, but by a sudden perception of an objective relation." Also note Empson's deconstruction of the idea of "atmosphere" as a psychological, and not poetic, effect.

49 Martin, Reinhold. 2003. *The Organizational Complex: Architecture, Media, and Corporate Space*. Cambridge, MA: MIT Press, 242.

50 Colquhoun. *Modern Architecture*, 211.

51 T. S. Eliot's critical concept of the "dissociation of sensibility" is applicable. Writing of the metaphysical poets, he observed that "the structure of the sentences ... is something far from simple, but this is not a vice; it is a fidelity to thought and feeling," and that "the poet must become more and more comprehensive, more allusive, more indirect, in order to force, to dislocate if necessary, language into his meaning." Idem, 1964. *Selected Essays*. New York: Harcourt, Brace, 245, 248.

52 The Girasole apartment building in Rome (1949–50) by Luigi Moretti is an astonishing example of the rhetoric and poetic deployment of space and structure with profound results.

53 Herrick, Marrin T. Rhetoric and Feeling. In *Princeton Encyclopedia*, Preminger, 704.

54 Ober, Josiah. 1998. *Political Dissent in Democratic Athens*. Princeton, NJ: Princeton University Press.

55 Nervi, Pier Luigi. 1956. *Structures*. Trans. Giuseppina and Mario Salvadori. New York: F. W. Dodge, vi.

56 See Chomsky, Noam. 1957. *Syntactic Structures*. The Hague: Mouton. Also idem, 1965. *Aspects of the Theory of Syntax*. Cambridge, MA: MIT Press, 3–10.

57 Jameson, Fredric. 1991. *Postmodernism, or, The Cultural Logic of Late Capitalism*. Durham: Duke University Press, 26.

58 Smith, Cyril Stanley. 1965. Structure, Substructure, Superstructure. In *Structure in Art and in Science*, ed. Gyorgy Kepes. New York: George Braziller, 29.

59 See Smith, Cyril Stanley. 1981. *A Search for Structure*. Cambridge, MA: MIT Press. Also idem, 1980. *From Art to Science: Seventy-Two Objects Illustrating the Nature of Discovery*. Cambridge, MA: MIT Press.

60 Thompson, D'Arcy. 1961. *On Growth and Form*. Cambridge and New York: Cambridge University Press.

61 Goldsmith, Myron. 1987. *Myron Goldsmith: Buildings and Concepts*. New York: Rizzoli.

62 Goldsmith was the Spinoza of Skidmore, Owings & Merrill structural rationalism, carefully developing the formal implications of purist structural ideas. His 50 × 50 House drawings for Mies van der Rohe's office of April 8, 1952, already show his synthetic genius; see Lambert, Phyllis, ed. 2001. *Mies in America*. New York: Abrams, 459. From the Brunswick Building to the Rochester Building, the Sears Tower, and the Haj Terminal at Jedda airport, his influence on Fazlur Khan and others at Skidmore, Owings & Merrill is pervasive.

63 Jameson. Op cit, 313.

64 Fuller, R. Buckminster. 1970. *Operating Manual for Spaceship Earth*. New York: Pocket Books, 120.

65 There was an MIT vortex in the 1960s: from Noam Chomsky's linguistics to Warren McCulloch and Jerome Y. Lettvin's physiological studies of the brain (see McCulloch, Warren S. 1965. *Embodiments of Mind*. Cambridge, MA: MIT Press); from Cyril Smith's studies of the metallurgical arts and sciences to Giorgio di Santillana's writings on the astronomical discoveries of the pre-Socratics; and from Norbert Wiener's cybernetics to the "discovery" of chaos science by Edward Lorenz. This was a powerful, if still unrecognized, renaissance in American intellectual life.

66 Smith. Structure, Substructure, Superstructure, 41.

67 "This documentature ... is architecture!" From Vostell, Wolf, and Dick Higgins. 1969. *Fantastic Architecture*. New York: Something Else Press. Trans. of the German ed.: 1969. *Pop Architektur, Concept Art*. Düsseldorf: Droste.

68 Klüver, Billy, Julie Martin, and Barbara Rose, eds. 1972. *Pavilion, by Experiments in Art and Technology*. New York: E. P. Dutton. This is the account of a collaborative experiment for a fog-enveloped polygonal structure for multimedia performances at EXPO '70 in Osaka, Japan.

69 Jameson. Op cit, 314.

70 Colquhoun. *Modern Architecture*, 226. Also see Derrida, Jacques. 1967. La structure, le signe et le jeu dans les discours des sciences humaines. In *L'écriture at la différence*. Paris: Editions du Seuil, 409–428. Noam Chomsky told the author in 1977 that Derrida had written to him before coming to the United States the first time to ask if he would be safe there.

71 See Colquhoun. Plateau Beaubourg. Idem, *Essays in Architectural Criticism.*

72 Peter Rice was referring, in particular, to the evidence of the casting and assembly of structure being easily legible. See his *An Engineer Imagines*. 1994. London: Artemis.

73 The open space under the Hong Kong and Shanghai Bank is used on weekends as a meeting place and "job fair" for mostly Filipino housekeepers. It seems that in some tropical cities such open spaces under buildings are well-used public places (another example is Lina Bo Bardi's Museo de Arte São Paulo, Brazil).

74 The Mannheim Multihall is notable both as a free form (akin to Heinz Isler's contemporaneous investigations into freeform thin concrete shells), and as the vortex that brought Frei Otto, Ove Arup, and Edmund Happold together. Since the dome was a compressive inversion of Otto's tensile investigations, he needed help from Arup and Happold to understand the limits imposed by buckling on its thinness. The project introduced Happold and, through him, Peter Rice to lightweight structures and to the problem of analyzing large displacements in geometrically nonlinear structures. While Rice and Happold (who later left Arup to start his own office) evolved the "dynamic relaxation" approach to handling these analyses, Jörg Schlaich, a past collaborator with Otto on the Munich Stadium in 1972, took a separate analytical tack using the finite-element methods. Happold, Rice, and Schlaich later developed rich and diverse bodies of work based on both these analytical and detailing practices. The Multihall is a Tempio Malatestiano of postwar structural design; see Institute for Lightweight Structures. 1978. *IL-13 Multihalle Mannheim*. Stuttgart: Heinrich Fink.

75 Holgate, Alan. 1997. *The Art of Structural Engineering: The Work of Jörg Schlaich and His Team*. Stuttgart, Edition Axel Menges, 273–275.

76 The wind rose is a diagram of the maximum velocities of the wind measured for a particular period of time and plotted over the cardinal directions. It shows the directions of prevailing winds for a particular location.

77 The wind-tunnel studies for the Sears Tower by Alan G. Davenport and his colleagues demonstrated that the orientation of the top twenty stories of the building was critical to the overall aerodynamics of the structure. The top part of the building consists of two of the nine ninety-foot-square (27.4-meter-square) plan modules. Because these were oriented with the long axis perpendicular to the prevailing westerly winds, the effects of vortex shedding were minimized and, in fact, created a damping effect on the building. (Herbert Rothman and John Zils, personal communications to the author, 2003).

78 See Rastorfer, Darl. 1985. William J. LeMessurier's Super-tall Structures: A Search for the Ideal. *Architectural Record* 173, no. 1 (Jan.), 141–151.

79 The Bank of China takes the form of a crystal on a carved wood stand, a typical collector's *objet d'art* in China. The base of the tower, a postmodern study in geometric decoration, clearly reinforces this reading, which would have appealed to the gentlemen bankers that were Pei's clients. The crystal form lent itself to the space structure design that Robertson and Pei devised for it, but the purity of the geometry ruled throughout, forcing the structural geometry back from the concentric surface lines of the curtain wall. The corner mega-columns of concrete cleanly resolve that structural "eccentricity" so that it benefits the structure and its construction. The façade lines, in turn, rewrite the traces and widths of the structural geometry for a deceptively pure reading. These poetics and rhetoric of the building's structure and appearance are worthy of the Seagram Building.

80 Merce Cunningham, quoted in Tomkins, Calvin. 2002. The Creative Life: A Troupe Turns Fifty. *The New Yorker*, July 8, 26.

81 There is also an interesting link between the work of Rem Koolhaas and Alberto Giacometti. Koolhaas' brilliant competition entry for the Bibliothèque National in Paris is quite similar to Giacometti's *Cage* sculptures in terms of the idea of a box of things (quite like a box of toys) suspended in space. This gives both works a frame and therefore an intense negative space between the positive volumes, a fact Giacometti and Koolhaas each develop elsewhere.

82 The trusses that support the floors below on the façade of the Hong Kong and Shanghai Bank are the same as the interior trusses that do the same with the omission of the top horizontal "chord" member. This omission reinforces the appearance of suspension but elides the fact that the trusses also play a key role as the beams of the "mega" moment frames that resist winds in the east-west, or longitudinal, direction of the building.

83 The structure of the AT&T Building was Robertson's last tall-building structural design in the United States. It is another brilliant example of Robertson's use of steel. The structure is part truss, part steel shear walls (an innovation at the time), and all clear and symmetrical. Its craft is a suitable match to the care with which the thick stone curtain wall is detailed, and its disappearance behind that wall is appropriately postmodern.

84 The idea of a tall building astride a train station has a sad history in Manhattan, with the demolition of Penn Station and the construction of the Pan Am Building over Grand Central Station (despite the romance of its helicopter pad). It has become, however, an important type around the world.

85 See Fredric Jameson's discussion of the "strategy of the wrapper" in idem, *Postmodernism*, 97–129; also see his analysis of Gehry's Santa Monica House.

86 The Canadian wind engineer Peter Irwin transformed the design of tall thin Manhattan towers in the 1980s (the three towers around Carnegie Hall and the Millennium Hotel across from the World Trade Center site, all by the structural engineer Jacob Grossman) by emphasizing the importance of density as a means of limiting wind vibration. Since steel buildings are less than half the density of concrete ones (twelve vs. twenty-five pounds per cubic foot [192.2 vs. 400.5 kg per cubic meter]) and since inexpensive foundations on rock are the norm in Manhattan, the very slender (up to 1:15) towers of that era were all made of concrete.

87 One of the fascinating and unwritten aspects of modern tall-building design is the frequent use of proportional relations, often related to the golden section and the Fibonacci series (1:2, 2:3, 3:5, etc.), to regulate geometries.

88 See Balmond, Cecil. 1998. *Number 9*. Munich: Prestel. Also idem, *Informal*. 2002. Munich: Prestel. The idea of expressing the geometries of nonlinear or chaos processes and patterns has appeared more frequently in the 1990s, on such buildings as the Edificio Mantiales, Steven Holl's Simmons Hall at MIT, and Balmond's and Koolhaas' CCTV Tower.

89 See Weinberg, Steven. 1983. *The Discovery of Subatomic Particles*. New York: Scientific American Library. Also Kane, Gordon. 2003. The Dawn of Physics Beyond the Standard Model. *Scientific American* 288, no. 6 (June), 68–75.

90 See discussion of 1969 Conference of Architects for the Study of the Environment (CASE) held at The Museum of Modern Art, in Drexler, Arthur. 1975. *Five Architects*. New York: Oxford University Press.

1

1 Berthold Lubetkin, Ove Arup, and Felix Samuely, Penguin Pool, London Zoo, 1935

Concrete Theater

"[Robert Maillart] respected the function of every element of the structure, through the monolithic forming of the material."

Max Bill

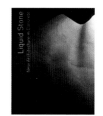

Concrete structures are either cast in place or prefabricated off site, for assembly in place. The concrete work of Robert Maillart (1872–1940) and Le Corbusier (1887–1965), two quite different designers, was always cast in place. The concrete work of Pier Luigi Nervi (1891–1979) was always precast, sometimes off and sometimes on site, and assembled. Cast-in-place concrete is a plastic art; the assemblage of prefabricated concrete is, like steel and timber work, an art of framing and joint-making.

Across this difference of plastic gesture and assemblage there is the opposition of empirical and formalist practices. Maillart closely monitored the cracks in his bridges to learn from his structures and adapt his craft. For Le Corbusier, concrete was the material of an art of sculpture and the massive ground for the play of light and color.

Louis I. Kahn (1901–1974) designed both with precast and cast-in-place concrete. The Richards Medical Research Laboratories at the University of Pennsylvania in Philadelphia (1961), and parts of the Jonas Salk Institute in La Jolla, California (1965), are precast. The Yale University Art Gallery in New Haven, Connecticut (1954), and Kimbell Art Museum in Fort Worth, Texas (1972), are cast in place. The difference is that the precast projects seem–like timber architecture–transient, and the cast-in-place structures seem monumental. This is ironic since the jointing of precast concrete structures, by separating and freeing the elements, often improves the durability of structures, whereas the monolithic nature of cast-in-place structures makes them susceptible to unforeseen crack patterns and decay.

Concrete is always, after all, a composite material. It is *reinforced* concrete. The placement of steel–size, length, location, detailing–is critical. Thanks to the

Published in *Liquid Stone: New Architecture in Concrete*, Princeton Architectural Press, New York, 2006, pages 62–63

2

great engineer and amateur philosopher Hardy Cross (1885–1959), the techniques of "moment distribution," or "relaxation," allowed engineers to calculate on which side (top or bottom of a beam; near, left, far, or right side of a column) an element saw tension and thus to place the steel where it was needed. Contemporary computer-based analysis methods speed this analysis, but the issue remains the correct placement of steel. The proof is in the cracking.

The plasticity of concrete makes for monolithic structures. They are, to use Cross' term, "continuous" structures. All the elements are joined in one whole, the likely behavior of which can only approximately be known. As Maillart is quoted as saying in Max Bill's *Robert Maillart* of 1955, "the calculation results can either undergo direct application or, on the other hand, modification, and the latter will be the case when not a calculator, but a constructor is at work."

"Freedom and indeterminacy are antecedent to and larger than order."
Donald Judd

It makes a difference whether a structure is a monolithic totality or an assemblage of parts separated at joints. It also makes a difference whether the work expresses the will of one artist or somehow the joint idea of several collaborators; there is no analog, however. The monolithic Penguin Pool ramp structure at the London Zoo (1935) was the work of the architect Berthold Lubetkin (1901–1990) and the engineers Ove Arup (1895–1988) and Felix Samuely (1902–1959), though how their ideas came together is not known (FIG. 1). Thanks to landscape historian Marc Treib's research, Le Corbusier's Philips Pavilion in Brussels, Belgium (1959), is well understood as the assembled (precast) structure conceived (mostly) by Iannis Xenakis (1922–2001) and the Dutch contractor Strabel and its engineer/director Hoyte C. Duyster (b. 1937), who created an exuberant *poeme electronique*–multi-media and multiauthored (FIG. 3). The impossibly thin and numerous hyperbolic paraboloid shells of Felix Candela (1910–1997) are, on the other hand, the sole invention (form, calculation, construction–the works) of Candela, made possible by the freedom of operation he found for a limited, golden decade (1950 to 1961) in Mexico. Similarly, the extraordinary work of the Swiss engineer Heinz Isler (b.1926), a lyrical successor to Candela, found realization (only) in Switzerland.

As proponents of the New Criticism–or rather, practical criticism–might see it, the work stripped bare of authorship may be composite or singular–assembled or monolithic. This does not follow from whether it is precast or cast in place, or singly or collectively authored. Either it is good, or not, and that's all.

2 T. Y. Lin and Myron Goldsmith, Ruck-A-Chucky Bridge Project, Auburn CA 1977
3 Le Corbusier and Iannis Xenakis, Philips Pavilion, Brussels, Belgium 1959

"Aesthetic of the Engineer, Architecture."

Le Corbusier

The "miracle" of concrete is now old. That isn't to say that its monuments—the works of Le Corbusier, Nervi, Kahn, Candela, and Isler, and of Eduardo Torroja (1899–1961) and Christian Menn (b. 1927) as well—no longer thrill. In fact, like the work of great old actors, theirs is stronger for its unexpected presence. It remains new.

Today, the best works of concrete are the bridges: the Sunniberg Bridge near Klosters, Switzerland (1999), by Menn; the Oresund Bridge connecting Sweden and Denmark (2000), by Jørgen Nissen (b. 1935); the Millau Viaduct in Millau, France (2005), by Michel Virlogeux (b. 1946) and Norman Foster (b. 1935); and the great Ruck-A-Chucky Bridge design proposal for the American River in Auburn, California (1977), by T. Y. Lin (2003) and Myron Goldsmith (1918–1996) (FIG. 2). These are, for the most part, segmentally precast concrete decks suspended on cable stays from slip-formed concrete towers—part precast, part cast-in-place.

In buildings, the most interesting work is arguably performative. The Menil Collection in Houston, Texas (1986), by Peter Rice (1935–1992) and Renzo Piano (b. 1937), inaugurated a practice of experimentation in precast concrete (or ferro-cement, in this case) that led to a remarkable series of refined precast concrete projects by John Thornton, in conjunction with Michael Hopkins (b. 1935) and Patty Hopkins (b. 1942), from their Inland Revenue buildings in Nottingham, England (1995), to their recent Parliament Portcullis House office building in London (2001). In the spirit of Rice's motto *"la trace de la main,"* these projects fashion precast slab panels, formed with industrial precision, into structure, light reflector, and thermal sink. Their refinement is a humanist retort to the contemporary scenography of neoconservative historicism.

In the works of these practitioners, and in the best work of contemporary engineers and architects, concrete is made performative. This theatricality sometimes manifests itself in baroque expressions: concrete forced into fluid expression, seldom recognizing the actual force flow. Most often, though, the limits of contemporary cast-in-place craftsmanship lead to prefabrication, which, in turn, sometimes becomes theatrical in its execution and leaves a trace of its production in joints and texture. This turn within the concrete theater opens to a more democratic space of expression, which is welcome.

3

1

1 Ezra Pound, Fuller, and Noguchi at the Spoleto Festival in Italy, 1971

With Great Joy and Expectations

In his 1968 autobiography Isamu Noguchi quoted Marcel Duchamp's advice to him: "Don't do anything that pleases you—only do that which you dislike and cannot help but do. This is the way to find yourself. But it is also true that we cannot ever be more than we are." [1] This turns against the grain of desire, but does not deny desire or passion. It stills and sublimates it.

Buckminster Fuller and Isamu Noguchi met at Romany Marie's tavern, for which we are told Bucky designed the décor.[2] Fuller would often stand on a table and declaim his Homeric account of four-dimensional science and art, of triangles and tetrahedra and the "new consciously disciplined relationship of man to his physical universe." [3] He enchanted an audience that included Noguchi, Mark Tobey, Willem de Kooning, The Museum of Modern Art's Dorothy Miller, the paleontologist Walter Granger, and even Vilhjálmur Stefánsson, the Arctic explorer, with epics that were part mathematics, part physics and chemistry, and part neo-Buddhist mysticism *avant-la-lettre*, "what the scientist-artist speaks of as intuition is the intellect-initiated and synergetically precessional event evolution into conscious objective anticipatory evolutionary conceptual formulation, realized in thought described words, mathematical relationship rotation, graphical schematics, three-dimensional static and four-dimensional kinetic modelling." [4]

→ p. 373

In 1976 I worked as an intern in Noguchi's Long Island City studio for Fuller and Shoji Sadao, making tensegrity models with Rob Grip, one of Bucky's assistants, for that fall's inaugural exhibition at the Cooper Hewitt Museum, titled *Man Transforms.* Fuller stopped by one day and took me aside for tête-à-tête in his and Sadao's drafting office. He sat perched on a table; I took a chair, he turned off his hearing aid and started off. Unfortunately, I don't remember what he spoke of, but I do remember I said nothing, figuring he could not or did not want to hear. Twenty-five years later I learned from his daughter Allegra Fuller Snyder that he would turn off his hearing aid at the start of a conversation so that he would not be distracted by ambient noises and could concentrate, reading lips. I had completely misunderstood.

Published in *Best of Friends: Buckminster Fuller and Isamu Noguchi*, exhibition catalogue Noguchi Museum, Long Island City, 2006, page 11

Fuller and Noguchi were brothers. Reading their correspondence from the 1930s, one sees they were constantly looking out for each other, promoting the other's work, seeking and developing good contacts, in the thick of the culture, making it up together. If one agrees with the contemporary philosopher Kwame Anthony Appiah's idea that "the right approach ... starts by taking individuals—not nations, tribes or 'peoples'—as the proper object of moral concern,"[5] it is encouraging to reflect on the fifty-four-year-long friendship of these two individuals, both dedicated, each in his own way, to cosmopolitanism. Fuller was very much a citizen of the world. Noguchi was one as well, though, as Fuller pointed out, "he had a deep yearning for the security of 'belonging'—if possible to a strong culture—at least to some identifiable social group."[6] Coming from an established New England family with its own island in Maine, Fuller had a secure base even if he considered himself the family's black sheep. Bear Island was always there for him in a way that the Japanese island or his native America were not for Noguchi. Not just because he was nine years younger than Fuller did Noguchi long address Bucky as "Mr. Fuller." Bucky was representative of a stable culture that might patronize Noguchi, but would not have him belong.

Of course, Fuller's career was clear proof that the scientist-artist had no place in the Yankee mercantilist world, or in any other precinct of American capitalism at the time. Then again, I remember discussions with Noguchi in the 1970s on the morality of accepting commissions from the likes of the shah of Iran or Imelda Marcos. The 1970s were hard times for art and design, and these were the clients. At the time Fuller was developing ideas for the completion of the Cathedral of St. John the Divine in New York City, which was, as I recall, to be funded by the sister of the shah. To we youngsters at the time this seemed wrong. What I learned from discussing this with Noguchi, and less directly from Fuller, was that both men, perhaps because of their experiences in the Depression and living through world war, had adopted a discreet disengagement from the categorical moralizing of our politics. Their cosmopolitanism freed them. As wandering scientist-artists they were neither attached to nor accountable for the misdeeds of capitalists and their politicians. The work mattered and it in time would change things and ideas. This disengagement worked both ways.

There is a delightful photograph (FIG. 1), taken by Robin Chandler Duke at the summer 1971 Spoleto Festival in Italy, that shows the poet Ezra Pound, Fuller, and Noguchi standing together arm in arm. Each is a decade older than the other—born in 1885, 1895, and 1904 respectively. Fuller, in the middle, looks squarely at the camera. Noguchi has a broad smile, his shirt unbuttoned and his reading glasses pulling his shirt pocket to the right side. Pound, in a light suit and sweater, with white hair and a beard, looks away to the left side. This is a year before Pound died and a few years after he apologized to Allen Ginsberg for his "stupid, suburban anti-Semitic prejudice."[7] In October 1970 Pound had attended four of Bucky's lectures at the International University of Art in Venice and enjoyed the four-hour harangues on the worthless "value of metals" and the case Fuller made for the real value that comes "from the wealth of the minds of world man."[8] Pound wrote in *Canto 113:* "No man can see his own end./The Gods have not returned. 'They have never left us.'/They have not returned."

When Pound died, his widow, Olga Rudge, asked Noguchi if he would make a copy of the French sculptor Henri Gaudier-Brzeska's (1891–1915) great *Hieratic Head of Ezra Pound* (1913) to stand on his grave in Hailey, Idaho. Noguchi was happy to oblige, but in the end Pound was buried in San Michele Cemetery on the island of San Giorgio Maggiore in Venice.

The travails and achievements of these artist-scientists are Homeric not simply because they piled glory on themselves with their works and deeds, but because they took to their chosen battles with great joy and expectations. They battled not for nation or tribe, but for honor, truth, culture, and especially friendship.

1 *Isamu Noguchi: A Sculptor's World*. 1968. New York: Harper & Row, 34.

2 See www.nysonglines.com.

3 Fuller, R. Buckminster. 2001. Isamu Noguchi. In *Isamu Noguchi: Sculptural Design*. Berlin/Weil am Rhein, Germany: Vitra Design Museum, 252.

4 Ibid, 254.

5 Appiah, Kwame Anthony. 2006. The Case for Contamination. *New York Times Magazine*, January.

6 Fuller. Op cit, 245.

7 Kenner, Hugh. 1971. *The Pound Era*. Berkeley, CA: University of California Press, 556.

8 Ibid, 560.

Freedom From Fear

There is still time to take the fear out of the Freedom Tower. Despite reports that Gov. Eliot Spitzer has now decided to back the project, the fact is that with a little time it is still possible to rethink the tower and make it both secure and welcoming without setting back the overall ground zero construction schedule.

The current design, which was unveiled in 2006, was created under pressure from former Gov. George Pataki, who tied his presidential ambitions to its swift completion. In this plan, the architects and engineers, for several reasons, took a very conservative approach. The result, a 20-story fortified wall around the base of a 1,776-foot (541-m) tower, hardly evokes freedom—rather, it embodies fear and anxiety.

I write from experience. Some four years ago I began working with David Childs, the principal architect, on the first version of the Freedom Tower. This was a 2,000-foot-tall (610-m) structure of torquing glass and steel; the bottom half contained the office building while the top half was a broadcast tower composed of an open framework of cables and trusses. (Also in 2002, *The New York Times Magazine* published a proposal of mine for a 2,000-foot-tall (610-m) broadcast tower on the site that we have been working on intermittently ever since.) The structure would have given the tower the widest TV broadcast capacity possible, at the maximum height allowed by the Federal Aviation Administration. The office floors ended at about 70 stories, matching the tallest downtown office building, with as much overall floor area as the current design and with every floor having direct access to the ground level by elevator. The open, cable-stayed upper 1,000 feet (305 m) of the structure would have had wind turbines that would have met more than 20 percent of the building's energy needs, a fitting symbol for a city whose seal includes a windmill.

While the basic design won over almost everyone involved with the project, including many of the governor's advisers, Mr. Pataki asked the architect to amend it in late 2003. Specifically, he wanted Mr. Childs to reduce the upper structure from 2,000 to 1,500 feet (610 to 457 m), and to add a slender 276-foot (84-m) antenna to make it a symbolic 1,776 feet (541 m) tall. The alterations, unfortunately, made the design impossible to build, and eventually the entire concept was abandoned.

So Mr. Childs presented the revised Freedom Tower, which meets Mr. Pataki's interests but bears no resemblance to his initial design. It is in every way inferior, and those flaws—in terms of aesthetics, economics, security, and ethics—are all rooted in the way in which it was conceived.

First, the aesthetics. The critics have not been kind to the Freedom Tower. The solid geometry is self-centered—this newspaper's critic wrote that it "evokes a gigantic glass paperweight with a toothpick stuck on top"—without any sense of orientation or any recognition of its place in the skyline. This is a shame, especially consider-ing what the same architects showed they were capable of next door, in the elegant new 7 World Trade Center building.

But it is understandable: not only were the architects rushed by Mr. Pataki, but after the ordeal of the first design's development and rejection, it seems natural that Mr. Childs would reach for a simple geometry the second time around. The result, unfortunately, would be second-rate in Chicago, Dubai, or Shanghai, and should not be the symbol of New York City, let alone freedom.

Second, the finances of the new building are a disaster. The Freedom Tower will most likely cost around $3 billion to build, for 2.6 million square feet (0.24 million sq m) of office space. The cost of $1,150 a square foot (0.093 sq m) is nearly twice what it cost to build the new Museum of Modern Art, for which I was also the engineer. Of the cost, about $1 billion will be paid with insurance money collected by the ground zero leaseholder, Larry Silverstein.

Assuming that the owners of the Freedom Tower, the Port Authority, are able to sign government or other tenants on at market rate rents of $50 to $60 per square foot, the income on the entire property, after expenses and taxes and including the rent on the TV antennas, will be at most $100 million dollars a year, which is less than 4 percent return on the investment. The Port Authority would do better buying back its bonds, which now offer a return of more than 5 percent. What is more, the property is probably uninsurable, so the Port Authority will be spending billions for a below-market return and a substantial risk.

Third, the security concerns that have blocked so many facets of the plan remain unresolved. Last January, I sat in a meeting in the New York City police commissioner's conference room and listened to a debate on various security plans and blast-resistant designs for the different projects at ground zero. In the end, James Kallstrom, Governor Pataki's senior counterterrorism adviser and the security coordinator for ground zero, closed the discussion by saying, "Structural engineers will have to certify that the design meets the threat basis."

I understood this to mean that as long as the engineers signed off on the design, everything would be considered fine. This is worrisome, especially given that the computer software that is being used to simulate the blast effects is proprietary and classified by the federal government, and that the structural engineers being asked to certify the building do not have clearance or direct access to the program, only the data given them by the software.

In contrast, the approach taken by most private building owners in the city—which generally includes physical tests, repeated independent computer simulations, and help from the Defense Department's technical support working group—provides real assurances of security. The Freedom Tower deserves the same sound engineering approach as any commercial project.

The final problem with the tower is less obvious: the politically charged situation under which it was conceived has led to ethical problems in terms of tenancy. Mr. Silverstein never wanted to build the Freedom Tower, and few could blame him. The site is awkward, too far from public transportation and Wall Street, and the tower is too big for the downtown real estate market to absorb in time to realize a good profit. Last year, he exchanged this problem for the three towers he is now developing on the site, leaving the Port Authority saddled with the Freedom Tower.

The authority itself, however, will not occupy the Freedom Tower but will rent space from Mr. Silverstein in Tower Four, at the opposite corner of the site. So far, state agencies, under pressure from Mr. Pataki, have signed on for about 400,000 square feet (37,161 sq m) (roughly one-sixth of the tower's floor space). Federal agencies, including the Customs Service and the Secret Service, will most likely sign on for 600,000 square feet (55,742 sq m).

In other words, government employees are being conscripted to occupy a tower that no private company or authority—including the building's owner—will take.

At a time when there is considerable anguish over the 20,000 additional troops that President Bush wants to send to Baghdad, it seems that the ethics of forcing thousands of state and federal employees to work in fear in the Freedom Tower is fundamentally flawed.

The good news is that it is not too late to change things. The current construction of the foundation and subterranean levels does not lock us into a final design above ground. The work should continue up to the ground level and stop (this should take about a year), so that the architects and engineers are given another chance to design a Freedom Tower that, like other buildings rising downtown, is financially viable and a secure and welcoming work environment worthy of its place in the skyline.

Apocryphal

"Let us go and see."
Bruno Munari

The blackout as a chance to reflect on nightfall

Somewhere in James Gleick's biography of the physicist Richard Feynman, he tells the story of Feynman taking a date out for a walk late one evening. If I remember correctly, it was on the high plateau of Los Alamos. This was the day he realized that the energy of stars was released by fusion reactions. He stood there looking up at the stars, knowing that at that moment he alone on Earth knew this. Should he tell her?

Of course, I was unable to find the passage again in the book, *Genius. The Life and Science of Richard Feynman.* Did I dream it? No, in fact it wasn't even about Feynman. The website metafilter.com traces the story to the physicists Fritz Houtermans and his future (first and fourth) wife Charlotte Riefenstahl, and wonders whether it might actually be apocryphal.

Knowing a universal truth that is hidden from all others is a lonely state. It is not the same as knowing a worldly secret. It is the difference between night and shadows.

What happens in a disaster, a catastrophe, an accident, a blackout? For an instant everything is concentrated on survival, on cognition, on information. What is going on? Where is my family? How can I reach anyone? In the first moments of an earthquake you don't even know if it is your mind or the planet playing a trick on you. In the first moment of a blackout you check the light bulb, the fuse, and then recognize what is happening.

The Northeast America blackout of August 14, 2003, came to New York less than two years after the 9/11 disaster. Communications were poor and we did not know if this was another crime or just a malfunction. Everyone was out in the

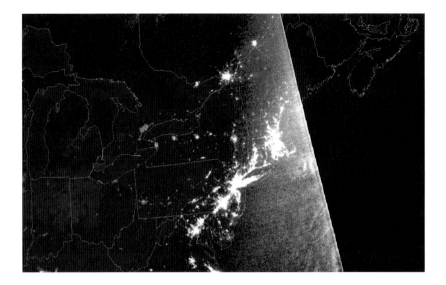

streets walking home and spreading rumors. It was calm, though. All you could do was ask, wonder, and walk home.

These are moments when starlight is all that glimmers on gold.

"In the gloom the gold gathers the light against it."
Ezra Pound, Canto XI

We are each on our own, and on our own together.

Technology, culture, and cities are our constructs. They crumble fast when the forces unleashed by the fusion of stars—earthquakes, hurricanes and floods—jerk out of balance. These disruptions cause havoc and misery in the mechanisms of commerce and communications. They call it the fog of war, and as in war the intricately linked gears of the global market are impossible to comprehend from within the fight. Only when it is stopped by disaster can you see how this light, this enlightened world, casts a deeper shadow than the night. But in that night we also find and help each other (viz. Bruno Munari's *Nella Notte Buia/In the Darkness of the Night).*

Satellite imagery from one day before and the day of the August 14, 2003 blackout

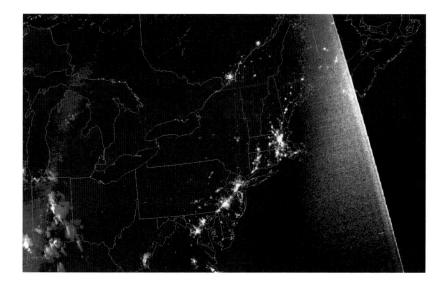

When I was working at Ground Zero in the months after 9/11, I was struck by
how obsessive the drive to clean up was. Later I marvelled at how intensely it was
argued that the nearby Bankers Trust/Deutsche Bank building was polluted
and had to be torn down when in fact it was not, and this was simply a cover story
to hide the greed of those who wanted to collect the insurance money and gain
the chance for greater profits from the site. The entire "rebuilding" effort has been
a rush to profit, whether politically, professionally, or financially, as money flowed
into the vacuum of that "point zero." It is no more about rebuilding than the war in
Iraq has been about building democracy.

It is a cacophony filling the frightening void of a catastrophe's revealing silence.
Yet in that first 9/11 silence, as in the suffering of the Iraqi people, there is solidarity.

As the rising catastrophe of climate change promises more blackouts, storms,
floods and eventually wars and misery, it is a good time to reflect on the nightfall.

Henry N. Cobb, Pei Cobb Freed & Partners, Fountain Place, Dallas, 1986

Truth in Tall Buildings

For HNC

"Ce double trait d'une taille qui limite et illimite à la fois, la ligne divisée sur laquelle un colosse viens à se tailler, s'entaillant sans taille, voilà le sublime."

Jacques Derrida, "Parergon, Le colossal" [1]

"The artist must scorn all judgment that is not based on an intelligent observation of character."

Paul Cézanne [2]

→ p. 392

"Here again the road leads over capitalism's dead body, but here again this road is a good one."

Bertolt Brecht [3]

Rhetoric and Fact

The skyscraper is a form of secular idealism, of one kind or another. Some, like the 1913 Woolworth Building, preen in elaborate dress to celebrate civilizing commerce, and others, like the 1986 Hong Kong and Shanghai Bank, blast manifestos of ideal labor organization, technological optimism, and nationalism. Skyscrapers reach, idealize, and dependably distort the truth of their making.

This is why the name "skyscraper" has lately been scrapped in favor of the dull "tall buildings," a measure of both skepticism and cynicism. Rem Koolhaas, in promoting his China Central Television (CCTV) Tower, describes its triumphal arch as an anti-skyscraper. He claims in an interview in *Icon* magazine that he is on "a campaign to 'kill the skyscraper.'" [4] Of course this kind of iconoclastic rhetoric, like Mies van der Rohe's Zen-like claim of just "building art," works well to restore the architect's power to grant authenticity to his client's authoritarianism.

There is no escaping the rhetorical discourse of tall buildings – and no reason to. Together, the collection of tall buildings that stands up in the world's central

Published in *Harvard Design Magazine*, Spring/Summer 2007, pages 30–37

business districts is the clear voice of each society's economic oligopoly or democracy, just as the slow persistent spread of the ideology and practice of "green" tall buildings is principally a self-representation of cities and societies as environmentally responsible.

Modern building is not an experimental science. Cities may be laboratories, but the problem is that few scientists are watching the experiments. Consider for example the "green" design of tall buildings. There is a worthy idealism driving the designs of Norman Foster and Ove Arup & Partners for the Commerzbank in Frankfurt, Germany, and the St. Mary Axe (Swiss Re) tower in London. Both are carefully conceived and executed; each is an unmistakable icon in its city. Both have captured centers of attention in their skylines and city spaces and so resoundingly serve as advocates for environmentally responsible design. They are aspirational in the best sense.

But who knows how well their green building systems work? To my knowledge and that of colleagues involved in the designs, there have been no post-occupancy studies to test the original design's energy consumption projections and natural ventilation simulations. Foster claims that 30 St. Mary Axe consumes forty percent less energy than a "typical" office building. If this is true, then the benefit of the inventions that make this possible should be measured, modeled, and disseminated in the scientific literature so that every office building could follow its "leed." The general lack of empiricism is not the fault of the designers, whether architects or engineers. I know that the engineers would like nothing better than to study their works in operation and calibrate their design tools to find out whether their green theories work. Those to blame are the clients, academies, and governments who commission, theorize, and legislate without much investment in empirical research.

The question of truth in tall buildings is both impossible and essential. There is not more (or less) truth in architecture than in painting. But sealed, air-conditioned office buildings are profligate users of nonrenewable energy sources in both their construction and their operation, and the impact that each million square feet of office space in, say, New York has on the remaining Greenland ice sheet is real. The correlation may be positive (i.e., greater urban density could help reduce global warming), or more likely it is negative and even nonlinear. In that case, which million square feet is going to be the one that sets off the cascade of ice that raises the world's sea level by seven meters?[5]

OMA, Kill the Skyscraper, 2003, from AMO/OMA and Rem Koolhaas, *Content* (book)
Pei, Cobb and Freed, Oversea-Chinese Banking Corporation Center, Singapore, 1976

To even try to answer these questions, the first step would be to undertake a massive applied research program that would calculate the energy embodied in selected buildings, compile the simulations that went into their design, calibrate these to the actual conditions in use, and maintain real-time monitoring. The study of selected groups of tall buildings could follow the protocols of long-range medical studies: establish benchmark data sets and then monitor key factors to understand trends. Research could include control experiments or, more likely, use comparative studies between different city climates and tall building practices to isolate idiosyncrasies.

Another model research program is the U.S. Geological Survey National Strong-Motion Mega-Project,[6] which has instrumented hundreds of sites and buildings to be able to acquire data during earthquakes that can be used to develop codes of earthquake engineering practice and to calibrate analysis tools. The technology of active structural control is yet another model of active monitoring.[7] This technology enables structures to adjust to load actions using their own built-in monitoring, feedback, and actuators–similar to airplanes' active controls. For this to work, active control systems link detailed virtual computer models of the building structure to distributed accelerometers that monitor motion and hydraulic or other actuators that drive bracing that counters the effects of those motions. A by-product is a complete data set of building response that can be used to study the system's functioning.

49 Squares

I made a list of my favorite forty-nine tall structures–forty-two built, and seven unbuilt–and arranged them on a 7 × 7 square grid. The two-dimensional range is from Experiment (empiricism) to Art (idea) and from Rhetoric (discourse) to Real (invention). These are fuzzy categories, and the arrangement is entirely subjective, but it shows the constellation of tall building types and is a kind of ideogram of this essay's argument. The reader can try his or her own version with these and other buildings.

The list of tall structures follows. Some of them–marked with an *–were included in the MoMA exhibition on tall buildings that; curated with Terence Riley in 2004. The names in parentheses are the architect followed, after the I, by the structural engineer. Unbuilt projects are assigned letters.

RHETORIC (discourse)

EXPERIMENT (empiricism)

ART (idea)

REAL (invention)

Formal
Structural
Ecological
Ideological

1 Statue of Liberty, New York, NY (1886, Frédéric-Auguste Bartholdi | Gustave Eiffel)
2 Wainwright Building, St. Louis, MO (1891, Louis Sullivan | Dankmar Adler)
3 Woolworth Building, New York, NY (1913, Cass Gilbert | Gunvald Aus)
A Friedrichstrasse Skyscraper, Berlin, Germany (1921, Mies van der Rohe)
4 Chrysler Building, New York, NY (1930, William van Alen | Ralph Squire and Sons)
5 Empire State Building, New York, NY (1931, Shreve, Lamb and Harmon | Homer G. Balcom)
6 Lever House, New York, NY (1952, SOM/Gordon Bunschaft | Weiskopf and Pickworth)
7 Latin American Tower, Mexico City, Mexico (1956, Manuel de la Colina and Augusto Alvarez | Adolfo and Leonardo Zeevaert)
B City Tower, Philadelphia, PA (1957, Louis Kahn and Anne Tyng)

TALL BUILDINGS

8 Seagram Building, New York, NY (1958, Mies van der Rohe | Fred Severud)

9 Pirelli Building, Milan, Italy (1959, Gio Ponti | Pier Luigi Nervi)

10 CBS Building, New York, NY (1964, Eero Saarinen | Paul Weidlinger and Mario Salvadori)

11 Standard Bank Centre, Johannesburg, South Africa (1968, Hentrich-Petschnigg & Partner | Ove Arup & Partners)

12 Hancock Tower, Chicago, IL (1970, SOM/Bruce Graham | SOM/Fazlur Khan)

13 U.S. Steel Tower, Pittsburgh, PA (1970, Harrison Abramowitz & Abbe Architects | Leslie Robertson)

14 One Liberty Plaza (formerly U.S. Steel Tower), New York, NY (1972, SOM/Roy Allen | Paul Weidlinger)

15 88 Pine Street (Wall Street Plaza), New York, NY (1973, James Freed | Office of James Ruderman)

16 Solow Building, New York, NY (1974 SOM/Gordon Bunschaft | Paul Weidlinger)

17 Sears Tower, Chicago, IL (1976, SOM/Bruce Graham | SOM/Fazlur Khan)

18 Hancock Tower, Boston, MA (1976, Henry N. Cobb | Office of James Ruderman)

19 Oversea-Chinese Banking Corporation Centre, Singapore (1976, I. M. Pei | Ove Arup & Partners)

20 World Trade Center, New York, NY (1977, Minoru Yamasaki | Leslie Robertson)

21 Citicorp Tower, New York, NY (1978, Hugh Stubbins Associates | William LeMessurier)

C Bank of the Southwest Tower, Houston, TX (1982, Helmut Jahn | William LeMessurier)

22 Bank of America Plaza, Dallas, TX (1985, Brockette Davis Drake | William LeMessurier)

23 Hong Kong and Shanghai Bank, Hong Kong, China (1986, Norman Foster | Ove Arup & Partners/
Jack Zunz and Tony Fitzpatrick)

24 Fountain Place (originally Allied Bank Tower), Dallas, TX (1986, Henry N. Cobb | CBM Engineers/
PV Banavalkar)

25 Grosvenor Place, Sydney, Australia (1988, Harry Seidler & Associates | Ove Arup & Partners/Ian Ainsworth)

26 Temasek Tower (formerly Treasury Building), Singapore (1988, Hugh Stubbins Associates | William
LeMessurier and Ove Arup & Partners)

27 U.S. Bank Tower (formerly Library Tower, originally First Interstate World Center), Los Angeles, CA
(1989, Henry N. Cobb | CBM Engineers/PV Banavalkar)

D Tour sans fin, Paris, France (1989, Jean Nouvel and Tony Fitzpatrick | Ove Arup & Partners/Tony Fitzpatrick)

28 Bank of China, Hong Kong, China (1990, I. M. Pei | Leslie Robertson)

E *JR Ueno Railway Station redevelopment, Ueno, Tokyo, Japan (1995, Arata Isozaki | Toshihiko Kimura
and Mutsuro Sasaki)

29 Commerzbank Tower, Frankfurt, Germany (1997, Norman Foster | Ove Arup & Partners/Tony Fitzpatrick)

30 Petronas Towers, Kuala Lumpur, Malaysia (1998, Cesar Pelli | Thornton-Tomasetti and Ranhill Bersekutu)

31 *Jin Mao Tower, Shanghai, China (1998, SOM/Adrian Smith | SOM/William Baker)

32 *Edificio Manantiales, Santiago, Chile (1999, Luis Izquierdo, Antonia Lehmann, Raimundo Lira,
Jose Domingo Penafiel | Luis Soler)

33 Aurora Place, 88 Phillip Street (Amro Tower), Sydney, Australia (2000, Renzo Piano Building Workshop |
Ove Arup & Partners)

F *Togok (XL Towers), Seoul, Korea (2002, OMA/Rem Koolhaas | Ove Arup & Partners/Cecil Balmond
and Philip Dilley)

G WTC Tower 1, New York, NY (2003, Guy Nordenson and SOM/David Childs)

34 Deutsche Post AG, Bonn, Germany (2003, Helmut Jahn | Werner Sobek)

35 *30 St. Mary Axe, London, England (2004, Norman Foster | Ove Arup & Partners/John Brazier)

36 *Turning Torso, Malmo, Sweden (2005, Santiago Calatrava)

37 *New York Times Building, New York, NY (2006, Renzo Piano Building Workshop | Thornton-Tomasetti/
Thomas Scarangello)

38 Hearst Tower, New York, NY (2006, Norman Foster | Cantor Seinuk Group/Ahmed Rahimian)

H 7 Stems, New York, NY (2006, Guy Nordenson and Henry Cobb)

39 Shanghai World Financial Center, Shanghai, China (2008, Kohn Pedersen Fox | Leslie Robertson)

40 *CCTV Tower, Beijing, China (2008, OMA/Rem Koolhaas and Ole Scheeren | Ove Arup & Partners/
Cecil Balmond and Rory McGowan)

41 Burj Dubai Tower, Dubai, UAE (2009, SOM/Adrian Smith | SOM/William Baker)

42 Union Square Phase 7 (Kowloon Station Tower), West Kowloon, Hong Kong, China (2010, Kohn Pedersen
Fox | Maunsell Group and Ove Arup & Partners)

Invention and Evolution

An empirical and rhetorical theory of tall buildings would have to accommodate all of the examples in the list above. For example, the ambiguous relationships of structure and architecture in the Seagram Building, the Bank of China, and the Dallas Fountain Place create formal or conceptual tensions that, once known, strengthen their rhetorical impact. Because these ambiguities are apparent only from construction photographs or on the working drawings, they do not generally get any attention in conventional criticism, which attends mostly to final appearance, personality, and discourse. Henry Cobb once remarked (in jest) that he and his commercial clients would be delighted if the structure of their commercial tall buildings were reduced to nothing. In fact this "real virtuality" (to quote Vito Acconci) of structure is nearly achieved in the Seagram façade, the absolute structural minimalism of Cobb's Boston Hancock and Dallas Fountain Place towers, and the surface (as opposed to structural) geometry of I. M. Pei and Leslie Robertson's Bank of China. This contrasts to the industrial muscularity of SOM's Chicago John Hancock Center, the Victorian machine aesthetic of Foster and Arup's Hong Kong and Shanghai Bank, and the brooding exoskeletal frameworks of Harrison and Robertson's U.S. Steel Tower in Pittsburgh and Bunschaft and Weidlinger's U.S. Steel Building (now Liberty Plaza) in New York. Their stances, refined or heroic, James Bond or Rambo, cannot be fully understood until a close look at the final appearance of the buildings is supplemented by an understanding of the construction and mechanism behind those appearances. This requires *both* rhetorical and empirical studies.

It would be instructive to parse, as an example, the history of the Seagram and Lever House buildings from their inception and reception to their recent purchase and "renovation" by the New York developer RFR Realty. How have the real and mediated images of these buildings evolved, and what contribution have the engineering and architecture made to those images? At the outset, you have the aspirations of both the clients (Canadian liquor merchants across the street from soap salesmen) and the architects (Mies and Bunschaft) realized with cold precision: ad hoc structures and services in compliant instrumental support of Modernist abstraction and rhetorical finesse. For fifty years, the buildings stand in reserve and potential—easily the best pairing in tall building architecture in the U.S. Then, once real estate fashions swing around to favor the suave lightness of mid-century Modernism, they are purchased and "renewed." Whereas before the façade of the Lever House was a delicate pattern of jade and aquamarine spandrel panels, the new owners, with their architect *collaborateurs*, have changed the curtain wall design by substituting false metal spandrel girt horizontals and using one-piece green

Guy Nordenson and Henry Cobb, 7 Stems Broadcast Tower, Bayonne, New Jersey, 2005–2007.

spandrels rather than the original real girts and two-part colored spandrels. Putting aside the nostalgia of my analysis,[8] it would be worthwhile to analyze in more detail how the value of these properties has fluctuated with fashions and how we can try to understand what gives such great tall buildings meaning in the context of the cultural flows *and* the realities of their detailing and construction.

How do we read tall buildings? And how does that reading factor in the "truth" of the engineering or environmental claims or of the social experience?

Ove Arup wrote that "the scientist wants to explore nature…. The engineer wants to change [it]."[9] But nature is dynamic and changes through evolution *and* catastrophe. The difference between nature and built things is not the difference between evolution and invention, between incremental and sudden, even catastrophic, change.[10] There are in fact clear lineages in tall building design and clear instances of radical inventions. There is also evolution and invention in the rhetorical or representational spaces of tall building design. The Miesian conceit of "building art" uses the naturalization of architecture as a rhetorical device better to convince through inevitability and astonish by the result. Rem Koolhaas as well positions himself in the flow of culture and history as an artist who acts as what Ezra Pound called the antennae of the race: "Once you are interested in how things evolve, you have a kind of never-ending perspective, because it means you are interested in articulating the evolution, and therefore the potential change, the potential redefinition."[11] The challenge for the critic is to calibrate this space of invention and evolution, reality and rhetoric, and not to create false oppositions.

The more interesting tall buildings work these ambiguities, sometimes in a deadpan manner, and articulate their authenticity through the use of structure and technique as ornament. One current crop of tall buildings, including OMA's CCTV building in Beijing and Renzo Piano's NY Times Headquarters, has renewed the use of structure as ornament that Mies and Saarinen and before them Louis Sullivan had perfected. Both the pattern of diagonals of CCTV and the strange uniformity of the exposed diagonal rods on the NY Times building façade (immune apparently to the 800-fold increase in wind shear from top to bottom) are rhetorical representations of structural rationality, not the actual backbones themselves. In a less immediate but similar manner, the use of a Future Systems aesthetic by Norman Foster to signal ecological concern is an obviously rhetorical device that in this case reveals that there is more truth than meets the eye! The paradox is often that where the claims to invention are loudest, the truth is evolutionary, and where there is true invention, you will find a Wittgensteinian silence.

And so? For one, there is no need to fear empiricism. If the curtain wall is drawn back, there is still some truth, even if it is not what one expects. As William Empson wrote in *The Structure of Complex Words*, "language is essentially a social product, and much concerned with social relations, but we tend to hide this in our forms of speech so as to appear to utter impersonal truths."[12] A William Empson of architecture and engineering criticism would study the "canonical" works of architecture and help us understand how to interpret invention and evolution, truth and meaning. A radical interpretation (to use a term of philosopher Donald Davidson)[13] of architecture and engineering would integrate the forms of rhetoric and the functional operations of buildings and, where they exist, the truths or inventions that are "compositionally" related. So a radical interpretation of, say, OMA's CCTV project would note the extreme weight of the structural system and its debt to the structural inventions of Leslie Robertson in the 1960s and '70s (including the World Trade Center), the formal debt to the sculpture of Isamu Noguchi and Tony Smith, and the meaning of its representation of the state control of media (and of meaning and truth), all the while acknowledging that, like the Sydney Opera House (also a "complex work," if there ever were one), it is already an icon.

Returning to Empson:

"Cases where a word seems to leave its usual range successfully often occur when the conscious mind has its eye on a few important elements in the situation and the classifying subconscious is called on for a suggestive word. This is how people invent metaphors, but you can get the same effect of surprise from an unexpected word which seems to fit very well, even when there is no need to call it a metaphor. The process may be like a 'construction' in Euclidean geometry; you draw a couple of lines joining points which are already in the diagram, and then the proof seems obvious, though till then the right 'aspect' of the thing was nowhere in sight. It seems clear that when a man is hitting on the *mot juste* he does not have to notice whether it is a metaphor or not."[14]

Theory is a kind of "looking" so that the "right 'aspect' of the thing" might be seen. With scientific experiment, there is validation or falsification. However, as the tall building chart proposes, in the range from the diagonal opposition of the "real/experiment" corner (i.e., theory looking for proof) and the "rhetoric/art" corner (of idealist autonomy), the "space" of interpretation expands to a broader plane of more complex relationships, between the realism of science and anti-realism of abstraction.

SOM, John Hancock Center, Chicago 1970

1 Bennington, Geoff, and Ian McLeod, trans. 1987. *The Truth in Painting*. Chicago: University of Chicago Press, 144. "This double line of a size that both limits and unlimits a divided line against which a colossus comes to size itself, incised without size, is the sublime." Originally published in *La Vérité en Peinture*. 1978. Paris: Flammarion, 165.

2 Cézanne, Paul. Letter to Emile Bernard, May 12, 1904. In *Paul Cézanne Letters*, Rewald, John, ed. 1976. Oxford, U.K.: Bruno Cassirer, 302.

3 *Threepenny Trial*, 1931.

4 www.icon-magazine.co.uk/issues/013/rem_text.htm "Usually people in my position are polite about what other architects do," he says, "but in this case; find it interesting to really go on the warpath against offices like SOM, KPF, or anyone else who is doing huge, thoughtless towers and see what happens."

5 Dowdeswell, Julian A. 2006. The Greenland Ice Sheet and Global Sea-Level Rise. *Science*, February 17, 963–964.

6 http://nsmp.wr.usgs.gov/about_nsmp.html

7 Chu, S. Y., T. T. Soong, and A. M. Reinhorn. 2005. *Active, Hybrid, and Semi-active Structural Control: A Design and Implementation Handbook*. New York: John Wiley & Sons.

8 When; was quite young and impressionable, Isamu Noguchi told me he thought Lever House was the best tall building in New York, so; have watched it closely since and was saddened to see it so dulled by this "renovation."

9 In Jones, Peter. 2006. *Ove Arup: Masterbuilder of the Twentieth Century*. New Haven, CT: Yale University Press.

10 Eldredge, N. and S. J. Gould. 1972. Punctuated equilibria: an alternative to phyletic gradualism. In *Models in Paleobiology*, ed. Thomas J. M. Schopf. San Francisco: Freeman, Cooper & Co, 82–115.

11 www.icon-magazine.co.uk/issues/013/rem_text.htm

12 Empson, William. 1951. *The Structure of Complex Words*. Norfolk, CT: New Direction Books, 18.

13 See http://plato.stanford.edu/entries/davidson/ and books including *Inquiries into Truth and Interpretation*.

14 Empson. Op cit, 335.

Earthquake Loss Estimation for the New York City Metropolitan Region

Michael W. Tantala, Guy J. P. Nordenson, George Deodatis, Klaus Jacob

Abstract

This study is a thorough risk and loss assessment of potential earthquakes in the New York–New Jersey–Connecticut metropolitan region. This study documents the scale and extent of damage and disruption that may result if earthquakes of various magnitudes occurred in this area.

Combined with a detailed geotechnical soil characterization of the region, scenario earthquakes were modeled in HAZUS (Hazards US), a standardized earthquake loss estimation methodology and modeling program. Deterministic and probabilistic earthquake scenarios were modeled and simulated, which provided intensities of ground shaking, dollar losses associated with capital (the building inventory), and subsequent income losses. This study has also implemented a detailed critical (essential) facilities analysis, assessing damage probabilities and facility functionality after an earthquake. When viewed in context with additional information about regional demographics and seismic hazards, the model and results serve as a tool to identify the areas, structures, and systems with the highest risk and to quantify and ultimately reduce those risks.

1. Introduction

While natural disasters cannot be avoided, there are ways to improve safety, minimize loss and injury, and increase public awareness of the risks involved. One of the most effective ways to lessen the impact of natural disasters on people and property is through risk assessment and mitigation—the topic of this study. An important objective of this study is to convey that a low-probability event is a potential reality, carrying with it consequences for which the metropolitan area may be ill-prepared. As part of this outreach, a consortium was formed—the New York City Area Consortium for Earthquake Loss Mitigation (NYCEM). The consortium is an umbrella group of interested organizations and major public and private stakeholders from such areas as emergency management, public service, engineering, architecture, financial services, insurance, and academia.

Published in *Soil Dynamics and Earthquake Engineering* 28 (2008), pages 812–35

→ p. 426

The likelihood of an earthquake in the New York metropolitan area has been assessed as "moderate" by the U.S. Geological Survey (USGS). As recent as 2001 and 2002, two earthquakes of magnitude 2.4 and 2.6 respectively, had epicenters around Central Park. Earthquakes of magnitude 5.2 have a 20–40% probability of occurrence in 50 years in the study area.[1, 4] Based on seismic records, thousands of earthquakes with magnitudes larger than 2.0 have occurred in New York State over the past few centuries. Catastrophic events with magnitudes 6 and larger are possibilities.[8] In order to be prepared for such natural disasters, we must be able to estimate and predict the risk associated with these potential losses. The economic impact of a damaging earthquake in New York City alone would be in the billions of dollars due to direct structural damage, not to mention the additional impacts on the infrastructure, building contents, business continuity, fire suppression, and human safety.[1] Thus, we believe this study is important to emergency management officials, facilities managers, building architects, engineers, utility companies, insurance companies, business owners, and policymakers at all levels—local, state, and federal.

To predict what might happen in several "what-if" scenarios, this study used Geographic Information Systems (GIS) and a model of the Tri-State area, including detailed data on the buildings and soils of the region. This information, supplemented with additional data about regional geology and the history of earthquakes in the region (location, frequency, and magnitude), enabled us to identify the areas, structures, and systems at the highest risk. After identifying possible scenarios, this study used Hazards US (HAZUS)[28] to estimate probable consequences and potential losses. Developed by the Federal Emergency Management Agency (FEMA) in partnership with the National Institute of Building Sciences (NIBS), HAZUS is a standardized, nationally applicable tool for performing loss estimations. Using HAZUS formats, we were able to establish the building inventory information for New York at the level of individual buildings, a unique accomplishment for HAZUS applications. This paper is an abridged version of the technical report titled "NYCEM: Earthquake Risks and Mitigation in the New York/New Jersey/Connecticut Region."[1]

2. Earthquakes in the region

Although earthquake losses in the United States are known to occur predominantly in California and Alaska, many significant earthquakes in the Northeast have occurred and more are projected, largely in the areas that

1 This map catalogs the epicenters of thousands of earthquakes with magnitudes larger than 3 that have occurred over the past few centuries. More significant and related events are labeled

1

have been active in the last few centuries. More than 400 earthquakes with magnitude greater than 2.0 are on record in New York State between 1730 and 1986, but many more have occurred unrecorded. East of the Rocky Mountains, only South Carolina, Tennessee, and Missouri were more seismically active during this period and, as such, New York State ranks the third highest in earthquake activity level east of the Mississippi River.[2] Figure 1 identifies the most significant seismic events in New York State in the past few centuries, and shows the epicenters of thousands of other earthquakes of M3.0 intensity or higher that have occurred in and near the northeastern United States over the past few centuries; thousands more occur with magnitudes below 3.0.[4] Among the largest historic earthquakes that have occurred in eastern North America (east of the Rocky Mountains) are the 1663 M7, Charlevoix, Quebec earthquake; three events in 1811/1812 with M7 or larger along the Mississippi River (in the New Madrid Seismic Zone near the Tennessee–Missouri boundary); and in 1886 about M7 near Charleston, SC. Together, these events prove that such large earthquakes are possible, albeit rare, in eastern North America. Locally, within the New York City region, chimneys reportedly fell when a magnitude 5–5.5 earthquake rocked New York City on December 18, 1737. Another moderate M5.2 quake occurred in the New York City area on August 10, 1884. This 1884 event remains the best-documented earthquake for this region. It was a strong shock, centered off Rockaway Beach, about 17 miles (27 km) southeast of New York City Hall, and was felt across 70,000 square miles (181,300 sq km)—from Vermont to Maryland.[4]

New York City's seismic risk is a growing concern.[3] A study conducted in the mid-1980s,[8, 9] which characterized the seismicity of New York City as "moderate," had the following findings:
– In past centuries, earthquakes with magnitude 5.0 have occurred about every 100 years in the New York City area. Modern New York City is ill-prepared even for such moderate events.
– Regional seismicity indicates that future earthquakes of magnitude 5.2 are likely to occur on average every 100 to 200 years, with a 20–40% probability of occurrence in any 50-year period.
– Larger earthquakes with magnitudes up to 6.8, the probable upper bound, may occur less frequently.
– Even larger magnitudes at very low levels of probability cannot be excluded.

Although New York City is a region with low seismic hazard (infrequent damaging earthquakes), it actually has high seismic risk because of its tremendous assets, concentration of buildings, and the fragility of its structures, most of which have not been seismically designed.[1, 2] The seismicity of New York City is similar to that of the Boston area, where local seismic design provisions have been in effect for a few decades. The first seismic building code for New York City was passed only in 1995.[8] The consensus opinion is that retrofitting thousands of New York buildings to meet seismic standards is impractical and economically unrealistic. Therefore, it is even more important to identify the areas of highest potential vulnerability to earthquake ground shaking so that mitigation, emergency response, and recovery approaches can be strengthened.

3. Methodology
This study used FEMA's HAZUS standardized methodology for assessing potential earthquake consequences (including physical damage and economic loss) to estimate the scale and extent of damage and disruption that

2 A conceptual view of the HAZUS methodology, used to compute estimates of damage and loss

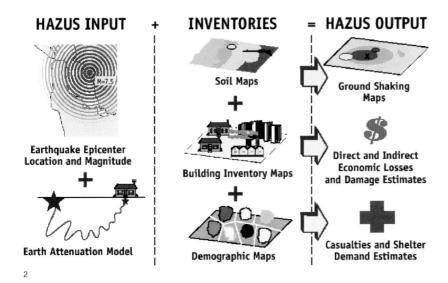

HAZUS INPUT + INVENTORIES = HAZUS OUTPUT

Earthquake Epicenter Location and Magnitude

+

Earth Attenuation Model

Soil Maps

+

Building Inventory Maps

+

Demographic Maps

Ground Shaking Maps

Direct and Indirect Economic Losses and Damage Estimates

Casualties and Shelter Demand Estimates

2

may result from potential earthquakes in the NY–NJ–CT region. Although this research chose the HAZUS methodology, several other methodologies have also been developed and implemented, including SELENA,[21] which is based on the HAZUS methodology but more easily enables applications outside the United States, DBELA,[22] which can also be implemented outside the United States and has its strengths in accounting for uncertainties, or EQSIM.[23]

A conceptual view of how the HAZUS methodology works is shown in Figure 2. The HAZUS methodology uses six "module" analyses to estimate consequences: Potential Earth Science Hazard (PESH), Inventory, Direct Physical Damage, Induced Physical Damage, Direct Economic/Social Loss, and Indirect Economic Loss.

3.1. Potential earth science hazards (PESH)

Initially, an earthquake scenario is specified within a study region. Ground motion estimates are characterized by: (1) spectral response, based on a standard spectrum shape, (2) peak ground acceleration (PGA), and (3) peak ground velocity. The spatial distribution of ground motion can be determined using either deterministic ground motion analysis or probabilistic ground motion maps (that is, by USGS or arbitrarily).

For a deterministic event magnitude, attenuation relationships are used to calculate ground-shaking demand for rock sites (NEHRP Site Class B),

DETERMINISTIC EVENTS SPECIFIED AT THE
1884 EPICENTER FOR M5, M6, M7

Ground Shaking (PGA) is attenuated from the
epicenter (star) for the three magnitudes, and
then related to soil and building information to
estimate losses.

PROBABILISTIC SCENARIO 500-YR RETURN PERIOD
[10% CHANCE IN 50 YEARS]

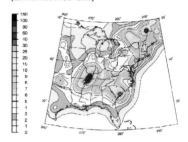

PROBABILISTIC SCENARIO 100-YR RETURN PERIOD
[40% CHANCE IN 50 YEARS]

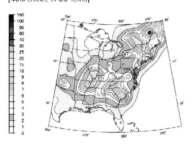

Ground Shaking (PGA) is determined based on
all historic earthquakes and regional ground
motion attenuation, and then related to soil
and building information to estimate losses.

PROBABILISTIC SCENARIO 2500-YR RETURN PERIOD
[2% CHANCE IN 50 YEARS]

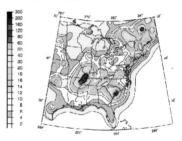

The probabilistic, 2500-yr-return-period ground
motions are the basis for the design of new
buildings. This is the so-called "Maximum
Considered Earthquake." Code-designed new
buildings may be damaged by this level of
hazard, but they should not collapse or cause
major loss of life. Results for this case will
correlate with current design practice expectations for new buildings.

3

which is then amplified by factors based on local soil conditions when a soil map is supplied by the user. Amplification of ground shaking to account for local site conditions is based on the site classes and soil amplification factors proposed for the 1997 *NEHRP Provisions*.[29] In HAZUS, the analysis has been simplified so that ground motion demand is computed at the centroid of a census tract. Ground shaking is attenuated with distance from the source using relationships provided with the methodology. The attenuation relationship used in this region is the Project 97 relationship, which is a combination of the attenuation relationships defined by 50% contribution by Toro et al.[20] and 50% contribution by Frankel et al.[19]

For a probabilistic analysis, the ground-shaking demand is characterized by spectral contour maps developed by the USGS as part of the 2002 update of the National Seismic Hazard Maps.[19] The methodology includes maps for eight probabilistic hazard levels: ranging from ground shaking with a 39% probability of being exceeded in 50 years (100-year return period) to the ground shaking with a 2% probability of being exceeded in 50 years (2,500-year return period). The USGS maps describe ground-shaking demand for rock (Site Class B) sites, which the methodology amplifies based on local soil conditions (FIG. 3).

3.2. Building inventory and damage

Damage estimates are expressed in terms of probabilities of reaching or exceeding discrete states of damage for a given level of ground motion or failure. These estimates are provided for representative building categories and types. Damage estimates also include time to restore function of essential facilities and lifelines and anticipated service outages for potable water and electric power systems.

The HAZUS earthquake building damage functions have two basic components: capacity curves and fragility curves. The capacity curves are based on engineering parameters (such as yield and ultimate levels) of structural strength that characterize the nonlinear pushover structural behavior of the 36 different types of model buildings.[24, 25] For each of these building types, capacity parameters distinguish between different levels of seismic design and anticipated seismic performance. The fragility curves describe the probability of damage to a model building's structural system. For a given level of building response, fragility curves distribute damage between four physical damage states: slight, moderate, extensive, and complete. The methodology predicts a structural and nonstructural damage state in terms of one of four ranges of damage or "damage states": slight, moderate, extensive, and complete. Damage predictions resulting from this physical damage estimation method are then expressed in terms of the probability of a building being in any of these four damage states. The HAZUS *Technical Manual* [26, 27] may be referred to for a more thorough description of building damage functions.

The results of damage estimation methods are used in other modules of the methodology to estimate: (1) casualties due to structural damage, including fatalities; (2) monetary losses due to building damage (that is, cost of repairing or replacing damaged buildings and their contents); (3) monetary losses resulting from building damage and closure (such as losses due to business interruption); (4) social impacts (for example, loss of shelter); and, (5) other economic and social impacts.

3.3. Direct economic and social loss

The HAZUS methodology provides estimates of the structural and non-structural repair costs caused by building damage and the associated loss of building contents and business inventory using structural repair and replacement ratios that are weighted by the probability of a given occupancy being in a given structural damage state. Similar calculations are performed for nonstructural damage and building contents. For social losses (casualties, injuries, and people displaced), HAZUS is based on the assumption that there is a strong correlation between building damage (both structural and nonstructural) and the number and severity of casualties. The model estimates casualties directly caused by structural or nonstructural damage although nonstructural casualties are not directly derived from nonstructural damage but instead are derived from structural damage output. The output from the module consists of a casualty breakdown by injury severity level, defined by a four-level injury severity scale. Casualties are calculated at the census tract level. The population for each census tract is distributed into basic groups (residential, commercial, educational, industrial, and hotel). The default population distribution is calculated for the three times of day for each census tract. The population distribution is inferred from Census Bureau data and Dun & Bradstreet data and has an inherent error associated with the distribution. Casualties caused by a postulated earthquake can be modeled by developing a tree of events leading to their occurrence. The earthquake-related casualty event tree begins with an initiating event (earthquake scenario) and follows the possible course of events leading to loss of life or injuries.

4 Metropolitan study region with select county populations and building replacement values. Shaded counties used more detailed, building-by-building data for analysis

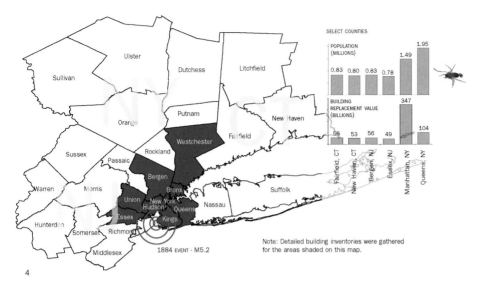

SELECT COUNTIES

POPULATION
(MILLIONS)

BUILDING
REPLACEMENT VALUE
(BILLIONS)

Note: Detailed building inventories were gathered
for the areas shaded on this map.

4

3.4. Functionality of essential facilities

Facilities that provide services to the community and those that should be functional following an earthquake are considered to be essential facilities. The damage state descriptions provide a basis for establishing loss of function and repair time. Restoration curves of essential facilities are approximated as normal curves characterized by a mean and a standard deviation. The parameters of these restoration curves include information on facility functionality for hospitals (with small to large capacities by number of beds) and police stations.

4. Inventories

To generate more accurate estimates, this study collected and incorporated region-specific inventories, including soil maps, building inventory maps, and demographic maps.

4.1. Building inventory

A building-by-building database was assembled for New York City's five boroughs and Westchester County and select counties in New Jersey (Bergen, Union, and Essex). Figure 4 shows the NY, NJ, CT study region. This building database at the individual building level was assembled using tax assessor databases and local building base maps. The developed building inventory maps (for example, how buildings were constructed,

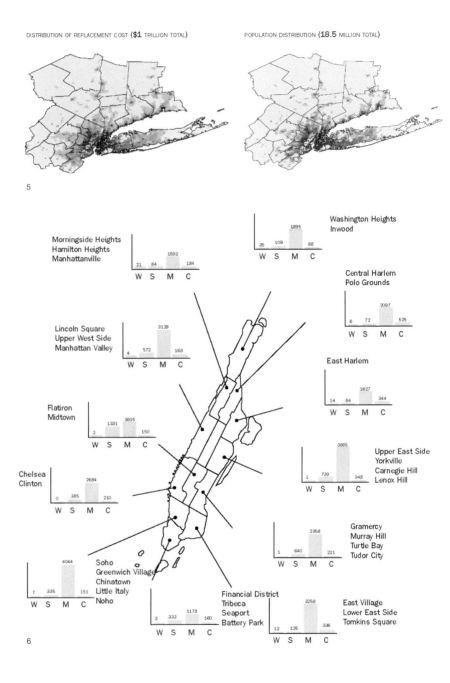

DISTRIBUTION OF REPLACEMENT COST ($1 TRILLION TOTAL)

POPULATION DISTRIBUTION (18.5 MILLION TOTAL)

5

Morningside Heights
Hamilton Heights
Manhattanville

Washington Heights
Inwood

Central Harlem
Polo Grounds

Lincoln Square
Upper West Side
Manhattan Valley

East Harlem

Flatiron
Midtown

Upper East Side
Yorkville
Carnegie Hill
Lenox Hill

Chelsea
Clinton

Gramercy
Murray Hill
Turtle Bay
Tudor City

Soho
Greenwich Village
Chinatown
Little Italy
Noho

Financial District
Tribeca
Seaport
Battery Park

East Village
Lower East Side
Tomkins Square

6

5 The distribution of population (A) and the $1 trillion replacement values (B) vary within
the region as shown in this figure

6 Building type in Manhattan neighborhoods

how old, how tall, their value, etc.) were essential for calculating economic losses and estimating damages. The Manhattan inventories were verified by field survey of the building in select census tracts. For the other counties in NY, NJ, and CT, default HAZUS building inventories were used; these are derived from building cluster model assumptions and census data.[6, 7] In the event of a damaging earthquake in the NY–NJ–CT region, about 18.5 million people in 7 million households would be at risk.[7] The number of human fatalities is the ultimate measure of severity in any disaster. The large population lives and works in about 3.5 million buildings with a combined 13 billion square feet (1.2 billion sq m) and a total replacement value of $1 trillion, excluding contents.[1] About 95% of the buildings are residential. Figure 5 shows the relative spatial distribution of population and building replacement values. The region occupies nearly 12,000 square miles (31,080 sq km), has 28 counties, and contains about 5,000 census tracts.[6] The region has a very valuable infrastructure that would be severely at risk in the event of a damaging earthquake. Replacing transportation and utility systems alone is estimated to cost $200 billion. Add to this the damage to essential facilities, and the value at risk increases significantly:

— 246 hospitals
— 123 emergency operation facilities
— 878 fire stations
— 1,348 dams (402 considered "high hazard")
— 744 police stations
— 53,095 hazardous material sites, and
— 2 nuclear power plants.

The building inventory includes residential, commercial, industrial, agricultural, religious, government, and educational buildings. The damage state probability of the general building stock is computed at the centroid of the census tract. The entire composition of the general building stock within a given census tract is lumped at the centroid of the census tract. The inventory information required for the analysis to evaluate the probability of damage to occupancy classes is the relationship between the specific occupancy class and the model building types. This can be computed directly from the specific occupancy class square-footage inventory. Figure 6 shows the relative distribution of the number of buildings in each of these four categories (wood, steel, masonry, concrete) within 12 different neighborhoods in Manhattan.[15, 16] The predominant building types by count are these: unreinforced masonry (M on the bars in Figure 6; totaling

29,352 buildings), steel (S), reinforced concrete (C), and wood (W). The results indicate that most buildings (in 9 of 12 Manhattan neighborhoods) are constructed of unreinforced masonry, whereas there are few wood buildings.[15] Unfortunately, buildings made of unreinforced masonry (URM) represent the largest concentration and are also the most vulnerable to damage during an earthquake because unreinforced masonry is brittle and does not absorb motion as well as more ductile wood and steel buildings.

4.2. Rock and soil types in the region

Knowing the local soil conditions in a region is critical for assessing earthquake losses. This study used different data sources and procedures to map the modification of ground shaking by these local geological factors, employing a prescribed HAZUS format. Soils were defined using the *NEHRP* Site Classification Scheme. The 1997 *National Earthquake Hazard Reduction Program (NEHRP)* provides rules for classifying sites according to the stiffness of geological materials.[19] The site classes range from A to E, where A represents the hardest rocks and E the softest soils. These classifications are used in Figures 7 and 8. The bulk of soil data was collected from state geological maps for NY, NJ, and CT.[11, 14, 15] Higher-resolution soil data was collected in Manhattan and derived directly from soil borings. To classify sites according to the *NEHRP* site classes A through E, this study obtained geotechnical data from a variety of different sources with varying quality and spatial resolution.[5, 11, 14] In the regions outside Manhattan and in the surrounding Tri-State region of NY–NJ–CT (SEE FIG. 7), site classification is based on lower-resolution surface geology maps provided by the different state geological surveys. The three states mapped similar rock and soil units differently. This study established assigned geological units on the site maps to the *NEHRP* site classes A through E using a Theissen polygon (equal-area method) analysis of specific boring data and their locations. For loss computations in HAZUS, the maps of site classes in the NY–NJ–CT region outside Manhattan (SEE FIG. 8) were overlaid with the outlines of census tracts. Census tracts are small areas within a county or city used for population and related statistics. This study assigned a single site class to each census tract based on the site class that was found at the center of each tract.[16]

With a high density of buildings in Manhattan, this study used higher-resolution methods to determine rock and soil properties in greater detail. Most data came from geotechnical borings of pre-existing construction

7 Types of *NEHRP* soils in the metropolitan region

8 Higher resolution of *NEHRP* soil data in Manhattan

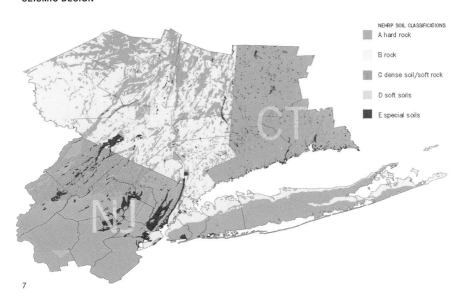

NEHRP SOIL CLASSIFICATIONS

A hard rock

B rock

C dense soil/soft rock

D soft soils

E special soils

7

Boring data map for Manhattan which was used to create the next "Thiessen Polygon" map.

"Thiessen Polygon" map of site classes in Manhattan derived from depth-to-bedrock data only.

Census-tract-based map of site classes in lower Manhattan using all boring data and additional geological information.

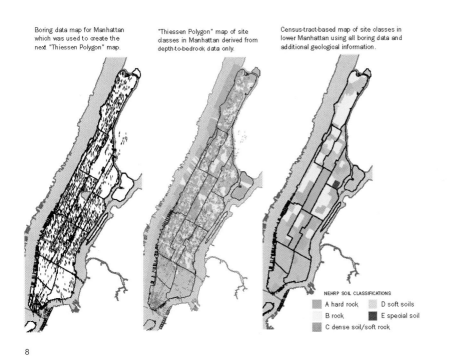

NEHRP SOIL CLASSIFICATIONS

A hard rock   D soft soils

B rock   E special soil

C dense soil/soft rock

8

projects. Several different data sources and analytical procedures were used. Soil types were defined using boring information collected by NYC's Department of Design and Construction. These borings included newer Standard Penetration Test (SPT) "blow counts" information and older Depth-to-Bedrock (DBR) borings recordings. Depending on the distribution of blow counts with depth in the boreholes, a single *NEHRP* site class (from A to E) is assigned to each borehole site.[1, 4] Older data represent only DBR borings, in which the stiffness of the overlying soil layers was not determined for each boring. The DBR borings constitute almost 90% of all data in Manhattan.[4] This study derived a standard profile of soil stiffness as a function of soil depth. Then the depth-to-bedrock boring directly translates into a site class from A (rock at very shallow depth or outcropping) to D (with very large depth to bedrock). This method does not allow assigning the softest soil class E. The black dots (SEE FIG. 8) represent more than 3,000 boring sites gathered from the past 100 years of construction.[1] The middle graphic in Figure 8 is derived from DBR point data and the Thiessen polygon analysis, which defines representative individual and areas of influence around sets of points. Using this equal-area method, this study was able to contour the site class point data, optimized to the spatial distribution of the borings. The right graphic in Figure 8 uses DBR and SPT point data, plus census tracts employed by HAZUS, assigning a predominant site class to each census tract, based on the borings it contains. Census-tract-based maps assign a single site class to a sizeable census tract, which often may contain rapidly varying site geology.[4] Nevertheless, such maps are useful in improving the loss computations generated by HAZUS. The results from both types of maps indicate that lower Manhattan and the Upper East Side are predominately soft soil (Class D). Most of the remainder of Manhattan has relatively stiffer soils (Class B and C).[4] A more detailed discussion of the development of the soil inventory is presented by Jacob.[4, 30]

5. Results

5.1. Key findings

Table 1 summarizes the discussion in sections 5.2–5.11 of the damage and disruption that could happen in each of the scenarios studied:

– M5, M6, and M7 (fixed location scenarios) are the different magnitude earthquakes located at a historic epicenter, namely, the M5.2 quake in NYC in 1884 (latitude: 40.561N and longitude: 741W about 12.5 miles (19 km) south of the Empire State Building in lower Manhattan)

TABLE 1 Key results of this study for the metropolitan region and for scenarios listed

Scenario earthquake	Economic losses			People requiring		No. of fires	Buildings destroyed	Debris (m tons)
	Building	Income (US$bn)	Total	Hospital	Shelter			
Deterministic								
Events centered on a 1884 historic epicenter with different magnitudes								
M5	4.4	0.4	4.8	24	2,800	500	45	1.6
M6	28.5	10.8	39.3	2,296	197,705	900	2,600	31.9
M7	139.8	57.1	196.8	13,171	766,746	1,200	12,800	132.1
Probabilistic								
Events defined by a given return period								
100-year	0.1	0.1	0.2	None	None	None	None	0.2
500-year	6.1	2.0	8.1	28	575	50	100	3.1
2,500-year	64.3	20.4	84.8	1,430	84,626	900	2,200	34.0
Annualized losses	0.1	0.1	0.2	–	–	–	–	–
9/11/2001 for comparison	13.0	52–64	98.0	6,000	300	10	20	1.6

TABLE 1

— 100-year, 500-year, 2,500-year "return periods" (probabilistic scenarios), based on what has historically happened in this area. The 2,500-year event is the so-called "maximum considered earthquake" and is of particular interest because it is the basis for the design of new buildings, and
— a 9/11 scenario supplied for comparison, listing actual losses from the attacks.

For the deterministic scenarios, the hypocenter depth assumed is 6.2 miles (10 km). The return periods of these deterministic events were estimated at 2,475; 19,500; and 160,000 years for M5, M6, and M7 respectively, and based on a common seismogenic area. The soil attenuation model used is the Project 97 relationship, which is a combination of the attenuation relationships defined by 50% contribution by Toro et al.[20] and 50% contribution by Frankel et al.[19] Estimates in table 1 do not include lifeline losses, which could easily increase these amounts by 30%.[2]

5.2. Expected ground shaking
PGA is one measure used to quantify ground motion. For deterministic scenario events shown in Figure 9 (M5, M6, and M7), the PGA pattern is

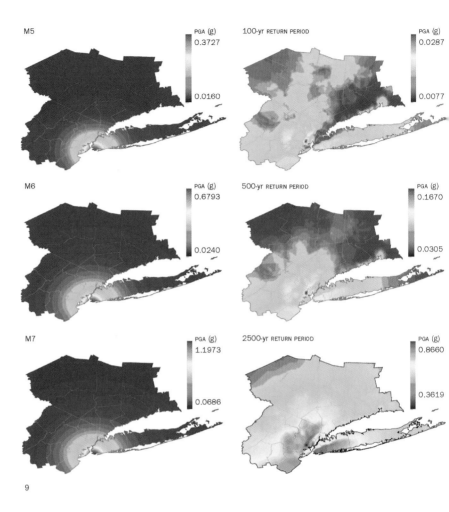

M5   PGA (g)
      0.3727
      0.0160

100-yr RETURN PERIOD   PGA (g)
                        0.0287
                        0.0077

M6   PGA (g)
      0.6793
      0.0240

500-yr RETURN PERIOD   PGA (g)
                        0.1670
                        0.0305

M7   PGA (g)
      1.1973
      0.0686

2500-yr RETURN PERIOD   PGA (g)
                         0.8660
                         0.3619

9

9 PGA estimates for scenarios

based on the location and magnitudes of the scenario earthquakes, as well as the local geology. For probabilistic scenarios (100-, 500-, 2,500-year), the PGA levels increase with the return period. PGA is a good index of hazard to buildings because there is a strong correlation between it and the damage a building might experience. In this study, attenuation relationships were used to calculate ground shaking for rock sites. These values were then amplified by different factors to account for local soil conditions. Since for the three deterministic scenarios (M5, M6, and M7) lower Manhattan is closer to the earthquake epicenter, the highest ground motions (PGA) are expected in its vicinity, as shown in Figure 9. Figure 9 also provides PGA values for the three probabilistic scenarios: the largest PGA values (areas in yellow and red) occur generally near the historically largest magnitude earthquakes and in the regions of the softest soils. Note also the increase of PGA shaking levels with increasing recurrence periods (FIGS. 10 AND 6).

5.3. Building damage and losses

HAZUS subdivides building damage into five categories: no damage (N), slight damage (S), moderate damage (M), extensive damage (E), and complete damage (C).

Figure 11 shows the likely distribution of damage in twelve Manhattan neighborhoods for an earthquake with magnitude 7.0, centered at the 1884 historic site. The results indicate that an earthquake of this magnitude and location would result in the collapse, or in the imminent danger of collapse, of 1,667 buildings in Manhattan (the sum of all bars marked C, in FIG. 11).[6] Figure 12 summarizes the total building-related losses per census tract for the region of study, based on the magnitude of the deterministic scenario earthquakes (M5, M6, and M7) or the average return period (100, 500, and 2,500 years) for the probabilistic case. The total value listed next to each figure includes both direct building losses and building-related business interruption losses:

— Direct building losses (also known as "capital stock loss") are the estimated costs to repair or replace the damage caused to the building.

— Business interruption losses (also known as "income-related loss") are financial losses related to the length of time a facility is nonoperational, including relocation expenses, loss of services or sales, wage loss, and rental income loss to building owners.

Figure 12 indicates that in a 2,500-year event, New York County (Manhattan) would experience the greatest building-related loss in the region,

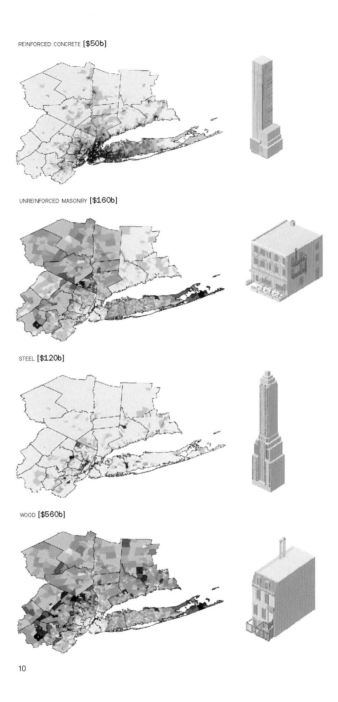

REINFORCED CONCRETE [$50b]

UNREINFORCED MASONRY [$160b]

STEEL [$120b]

WOOD [$560b]

10

10 Regional building types
11 Building damage in Manhattan (magnitude 7 event). The version of HAZUS used in this study (HAZUS-SR2)
derives the number of buildings in each of the five damage states from the damage state distributions of the
total square footage in a census tract. The number of buildings assigned to each category is based on average
building square-footage size. Consequently, the actual number of buildings assigned to each damage state
may be overestimated

SEISMIC DESIGN

N **NO DAMAGE**

S **SLIGHT DAMAGE**
Minor cracks

M **MODERATE DAMAGE**
Larger cracks and some connection failures.

E **EXTENSIVE DAMAGE**
Although people may escape safely, the building will eventually have to be demolished. Significant cracks and connection failures.

C **COMPLETE DAMAGE**
Structure is collapsed or in imminent danger of collapse. Extensive member and connection failures and major foundation cracking.

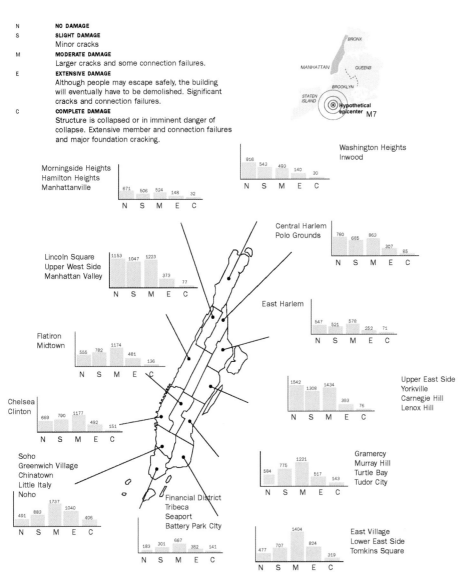

Washington Heights Inwood

916 543 493 140 30
N S M E C

Morningside Heights Hamilton Heights Manhattanville

671 506 524 148 32
N S M E C

Central Harlem Polo Grounds

760 685 863 307 85
N S M E C

Lincoln Square Upper West Side Manhattan Valley

1153 1047 1223 373 77
N S M E C

East Harlem

547 521 578 252 71
N S M E C

Flatiron Midtown

555 782 1174 481 136
N S M E C

Upper East Side Yorkville Carnegie Hill Lenox Hill

1542 1308 1434 393 76
N S M E C

Chelsea Clinton

669 790 1177 492 151
N S M E C

Gramercy Murray Hill Turtle Bay Tudor City

584 775 1221 517 143
N S M E C

Soho Greenwich Village Chinatown Little Italy Noho

491 883 1737 1040 406
N S M E C

Financial District Tribeca Seaport Battery Park City

183 301 667 382 141
N S M E C

East Village Lower East Side Tomkins Square

477 707 1404 824 319
N S M E C

[1] The version of *HAZUS* used in this study (*HAZUS*-SR2) derives the number of buildings in each of the five damage states from the damage state distributions of the total square footage in a census tract. The number of buildings assigned to each category is based on average building square footage size. Consequently, the actual number of buildings assigned to each damage state may be over estimated.

11

411

estimated at $11.45 billion. The majority of total losses would be produced by residential structures (roughly 50–60% of the total loss estimates, depending on the scenario), which are predominately unreinforced masonry. For the probabilistic 2,500-year recurrence period, the combined building losses ($64.3 billion) and income losses ($20.4 billion) for the entire 31 county, Tri-State region could amount to $84.8 billion, and for the M7 deterministic scenario event, the expected loss could amount to $196.8 billion, as stated in table 1 of this paper.[1]

5.4. Injuries

Damage to buildings and their contents causes most injuries. For example, in the 1989 Loma Prieta earthquake in California (M6.9), 95% of the injuries did not involve structural collapse. They were caused by people falling or being struck by falling objects. In fact, the most earthquake-related injuries often result from nonstructural damage, such as light fixtures falling.[3] The methodology for determining injuries and casualties is based on the strong correlation between building damage (both structural and nonstructural) and the number and severity of casualties. In smaller earthquakes, nonstructural damage will most likely control the casualty estimates. In severe earthquakes, where there will be a large number of collapses and partial collapses, there will be a proportionately larger number of fatalities. Figure 13 provides injury estimates for the different earthquake scenarios in the entire NY–NJ–CT region, occurring at 2 p.m. As expected, a proportionately larger number of injuries (compared with deaths) occur (for example, 13,171 for a M7 quake, which is about the size of the Loma Prieta event). The color code indicates that the highest number of injuries would be concentrated in the New York City metropolitan area because of high population concentration.

5.5. Casualties

Building damage has short- and long-term implications. In the short term, people may be injured or killed by falling objects. However, most deaths occur in earthquakes when structures collapse. In fact, all of the 63 deaths in the 1989 Loma Prieta, CA, earthquake resulted from structural collapse. The second major cause of death in earthquakes is fire. To estimate the number of casualties for the earthquake scenarios in our study, this study used HAZUS software to predict the number of casualties at different times of the day; namely, 2 a.m. (when people are asleep and at home), 2 p.m. (when people are at work), and 5 p.m. (when most people are commuting).

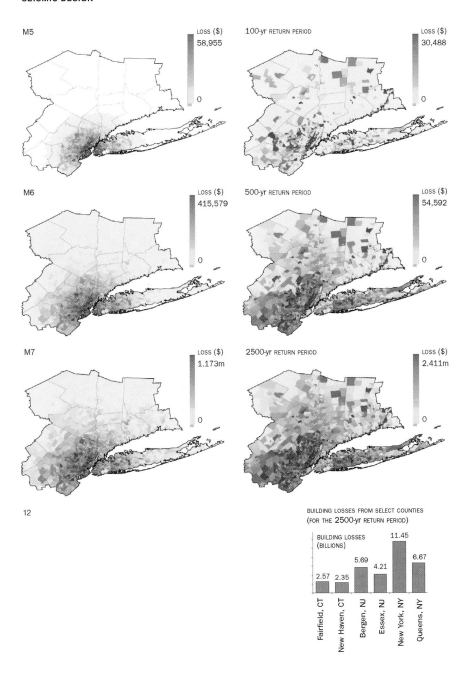

M5 | LOSS ($) 58,955 — 0

100-yr RETURN PERIOD | LOSS ($) 30,488 — 0

M6 | LOSS ($) 415,579 — 0

500-yr RETURN PERIOD | LOSS ($) 54,592 — 0

M7 | LOSS ($) 1.173m — 0

2500-yr RETURN PERIOD | LOSS ($) 2.411m — 0

12

BUILDING LOSSES FROM SELECT COUNTIES
(FOR THE 2500-yr RETURN PERIOD)

BUILDING LOSSES
(BILLIONS)

- Fairfield, CT: 2.57
- New Haven, CT: 2.35
- Bergen, NJ: 5.69
- Essex, NJ: 4.21
- New York, NY: 11.45
- Queens, NY: 6.67

M5 [24 people]

100-yr RETURN PERIOD [0 people]

M6 [2,296 people]

500-yr RETURN PERIOD [28 people]

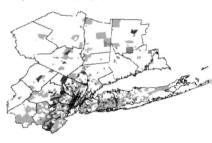

M7 [13,171 people]

2500-yr RETURN PERIOD [1,430 people]

The number of injuries listed at each figure is the total for the entire region.

13

These figures show the concentrations of people that are injured or require hospitalization directly after an earthquake occurring at 2 pm. The blue dots indicate major medical facilities (hospitals).

Because of commuting and variations in regional population during the day, people are exposed to different structures of varying vulnerability. Consequently, fatality and injury estimates will vary, depending on the time of day.[15] Our results indicate that a 2 p.m. earthquake would result in more injuries and deaths, with 5 p.m. slightly fewer, and 2 a.m. the fewest. In a M7 event (about the size of the Loma Prieta, CA, earthquake in 1989), there would be an estimated 6,705 deaths in the region, due primarily to structural collapse. Most deaths would be concentrated in the densely populated New York City metropolitan area.[2]

5.6. Shelter
Ground shaking can cause massive and immediate financial losses, casualties, disruptions in critical facilities and services, and severe long-term economic and social losses. Estimates of the number of people requiring shelter following an earthquake are classified as "social losses" within the HAZUS model. Whether long-term or short-term, these "social losses" are often missing from other attempts to measure earthquake losses; however, HAZUS provides the capability to include shelter requirements for displaced people in our loss estimations. Low-income populations may be the most severely affected, since they have fewer means for relocating to new housing if their residences are damaged. Therefore, homelessness and dislocation may increase, creating long-term shelter needs. The concentrations of short-term shelter needs for various earthquake scenarios were assessed. Even in a moderate M6 earthquake, nearly 200,000 people in the region would be displaced and require shelter. The greatest need for short-term shelter would be in the densely populated areas around Manhattan.[7] Ability to shelter people would be extremely taxed, requiring the use of unconventional facilities, shelter outside the region, and maximum use of available spaces. Schools often serve as temporary public shelters in emergencies. However, to be suitable as public shelters, they must be able to accommodate the displaced population. Our projections for a magnitude 5 event show that about 2,800 people in the region would need shelter, and the available temporary public shelters could accommodate them.[1, 15] However, for M6 and M7 events and for scenario return periods greater than 500 years, which have larger shelter needs and very low school functionality, the region would not be able to accommodate the demand for shelter. More specifically, in a 2,500-year event (the so-called "maximum considered earthquake"), an estimated 84,626 people would require short-term shelter in the existing 6,466 schools, identified

in Figure 12. In these scenario earthquakes, therefore, the region could not accommodate the displaced population.[1]

5.7. Critical facilities

After an earthquake, people are at their most vulnerable state. Collapsed and burning buildings, spreading fires, homelessness, and social chaos are just a few examples of secondary crises that follow in the wake of an earthquake and magnify its effects. In these critical moments, earthquake response is crucial. The fire department must be able to fight the flames that erupt. Hospitals must be prepared to treat the potential influx of injured. The police must ensure social order and facilitate urban search and rescue activities to save as many lives as possible. Schools must be open to provide temporary shelter. These facilities are critical to the efficient and effective management of scarce resources in a disaster situation and must remain functional. Critical facilities are those facilities that must remain in operation after an earthquake for response operations (such as hospitals, police/rescue stations, and fire stations). These facilities provide required services to victims of an earthquake and are primarily responsible for the rate of recovery in the affected area. Thus, to be effective, the structures containing these facilities must remain fully functional and structurally sound. The structure's ability to function is directly related to its particular damage state (in other words, slightly damaged facilities will still be able to aid in recovery operations while those that are extensively damaged will not). Losses to critical facilities in an earthquake (or any other disaster) will have a magnifying effect on loss estimations in both economic terms and in human lives. The estimate must include not only the cost of the facility itself, but also losses for all the victims in its service area. While support services from outside the affected region can be moved to aid in the response efforts, the total loss resulting from an earthquake will be controlled by the reliability of the critical facilities within that region. In assessing the vulnerability of critical facilities in the region, this study considered the number of hospital beds (86,272), and their location.[17] Our results indicate that hospital functionality (the percentage of the number of beds available to its total capacity) would be adequate for most scenarios, except for a M7 event, in which the estimated 13,171 injured would require 26% more than the available number of beds.[17] Patients would need to be transported to hospitals outside the affected region.

5.8. Hospitals

Typically, the first 24 hours after an earthquake are the most critical for rescue operations to save lives and mitigate serious injuries. To complicate matters, if the structural and nonstructural components of the hospital are heavily damaged, then the hospital population must find alternative facilities in other accessible regions, or forego treatment. Because of transportation difficulties and overwhelmed medical facilities, the affected population would face an increased risk of casualties. Figure 14 shows the functionalities of several of the 20 major medical facilities in Manhattan (about 10,000 beds) with contours that represent the distance to the nearest hospital for those located in each contour range.[17] Figure 14 also indicates the number of people (dots on the map) who would most likely need medical care at a hospital, based on distance to the nearest major medical facility. Most of the areas of Manhattan are within 300 yards of major medical facilities, with the exception of the Upper West Side. Consequently, in a magnitude 5 earthquake, hospital functionality would likely be adequate. The scenarios considered in these cases are for a 2 p.m. earthquake, the worst-case time of occurrence. As the scenario event becomes larger, hospital functionality decreases dramatically. For example, in a magnitude 7 scenario (shown in Figure 14), our results indicate that there would be an insufficient number of beds for that scenario. Even though 2,000 beds would be available, 900 more would be needed.[1, 17]

5.9. Police stations

In regions with heavy damage to police stations, impaired police activity could potentially result in looting and other crimes. Police inability to respond would also yield increased social losses in the form of social and economic disruption. Figure 15 shows the functionalities of several of the 36 major emergency rescue facilities in Manhattan (which include police stations) with contours representing the distance to the nearest police station for those located in each contour range. These functionalities are related to the likelihood of exceeding extensive damage of the facility, which is also a measure of the facilities' ability to respond. Figure 15 also shows the number of people (dots on the map) that would most likely need rescue. The scenarios considered in these cases are for a 2 p.m. earthquake, the worst-case time of occurrence. According to our estimates, rescue functionality would most likely be adequate in a M5 or M6 earthquake.[1] However, as the scenario event becomes larger, rescue functionality decreases dramatically, particularly for the M7 event (SHOWN IN FIG. 15) and the 2,500-year

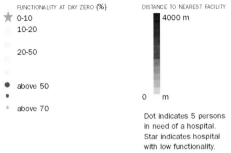

FUNCTIONALITY AT DAY ZERO (%)

⭐ 0-10

10-20

20-50

● above 50

▪ above 70

DISTANCE TO NEAREST FACILITY

▮ 4000 m

0   m

Dot indicates 5 persons
in need of a hospital.
Star indicates hospital
with low functionality.

BEDS
available: 2,000
needed: 2,900

In a Magnitude 7 earthquake,
there would be insufficient
hospital beds.

14

14 Hospital supply and injury demand for magnitude 7
15 Police station supply and rescue demand for magnitude 7

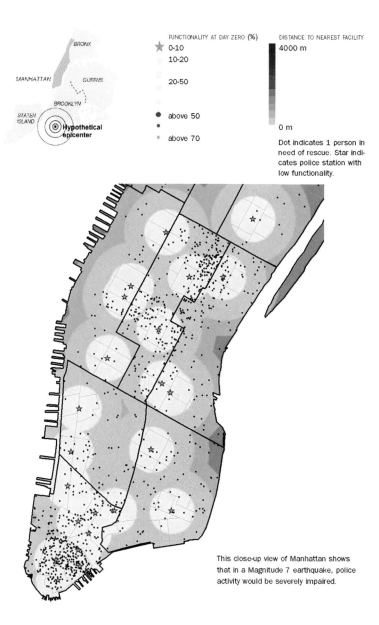

FUNCTIONALITY AT DAY ZERO (%)
0-10
10-20
20-50
above 50
above 70

DISTANCE TO NEAREST FACILITY
4000 m
0 m

Dot indicates 1 person in need of rescue. Star indicates police station with low functionality.

Hypothetical epicenter

BRONX
MANHATTAN
QUEENS
BROOKLYN
STATEN ISLAND

This close-up view of Manhattan shows that in a Magnitude 7 earthquake, police activity would be severely impaired.

15

return period (not shown), both of which would reduce police station functionality significantly.[17] Fire departments and urban search and rescue teams would be critical for rescue operations.

5.10. Fire stations

Historically, large-magnitude earthquakes have resulted in significant damage and loss of life due to structural failure. However, in many instances, even greater property damage was caused by fire damage, related indirectly to the seismic event. For instance, the fires resulting from the 1906 San Francisco earthquake destroyed more of the city than the actual earthquake did. Seismic damage rendered the water systems and firefighting units inoperable. While the primary cause of death is structural collapse, the second most significant cause of fatalities is fire. The severity of fires following an earthquake can be affected by many factors: ignition sources, types and density of fuel, weather conditions, functionality of water systems, and the building's susceptibility to fire. A complete model of a fire after an earthquake requires extensive input with respect to the level of readiness of local fire departments, as well as the types and availability (functionality) of water systems. Figure 16 shows the functionalities of 54 major fire stations with contours that represent the probable gallons-per-minute (GPM) demand of the fires for scenarios M5, M6, and M7.[1] Figure 16 also shows relative locations of probable ignitions and the number of people who would most likely be exposed to those fires. As a general rule, larger scenarios indicate more likely fires and a greater chance that the fire stations would have limited functionality and would not be able to supply the gallons-per-minute needed to suppress the fires. For example, in the M7 scenario, demand is more than 14 times the available water supply. That scenario also has the largest amount of property ($15.2 billion) and people exposed (69,000 people who are injured, killed, or displaced by the fire).[17] According to our estimates, although the number and relative placement of fire stations in Manhattan seem reasonable, the vulnerability and capacity of these structures may not be adequate for larger events (M6 or 2,500-year), where as many as 900 fires could break out simultaneously in the Tri-State region, requiring more than the available gallons-per-minute to fight them.[1]

5.11. Debris

Like fire, debris is considered an induced hazard or secondary effect of an earthquake. Using HAZUS, this study was able to estimate the total

16 Fires, fire stations, and water demand for M5, M6, and M7 scenarios

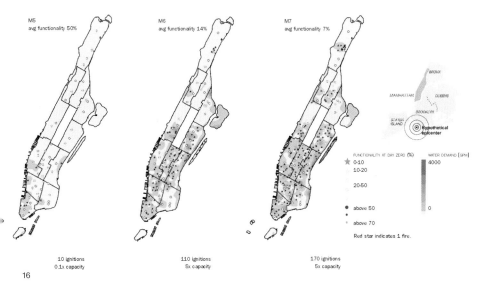

amount (in thousands of tons) of debris generated by the scenario earthquakes. The greatest amounts of debris correspond to damage estimates where the PGA is highest and unreinforced masonry structures are the most concentrated.[13] Although this is a unique application of the software, its empirical approach has proven quite useful in estimating debris totals. HAZUS classifies debris into two types:

— Debris that falls in large pieces, such as steel members or reinforced concrete elements. These require special treatment to break into smaller pieces before they are hauled away.

— Debris that is smaller and more easily moved with bulldozers and other machinery and tools, including brick, wood, glass, building contents, and other materials.

The debris estimates for the scenario events in the Tri-State region (shown in FIG. 17) include both types of debris that would be generated. The results suggest that in a moderate M5 earthquake, an estimated 1.6 million tons of debris would be generated in the region, equal to the 1.6 million tons of debris generated by the terrorist attacks on 9/11.[1, 12] This quantity would be about 21 times greater (34 million tons) in the 2,500-year return-period scenario, the so-called "maximum considered earthquake." Even in a moderate M5 earthquake there would be an estimated 88,000 tons of debris (10,000 truckloads), which is 136 times the garbage cleared in Manhattan on an average day. For the M5, M6, and M7 scenarios, the

M5 [1.6 million tons]

100-yr RETURN PERIOD [0.2 million tons]

M6 [31.9 million tons]

500-yr RETURN PERIOD [3.1 million tons]

M7 [132.1 million tons]

2500-yr RETURN PERIOD [34.0 million tons]

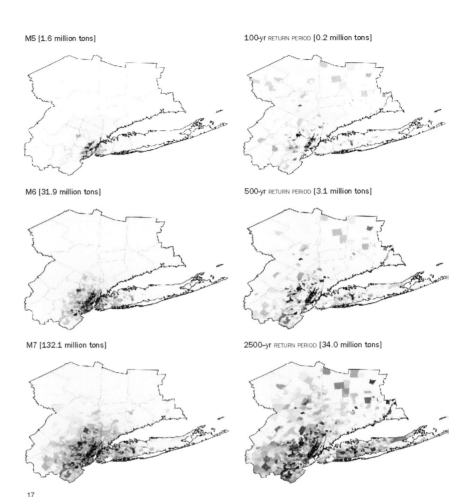

17

17 Debris generated for scenario events

debris would be concentrated in Midtown and Grammercy.[1] For 100-, 500-, and 2,500-year return periods (not shown), the debris would be concentrated in northern Manhattan, specifically Washington Heights.

6. Verification, implementation, and applications

It is important to ask, "How well does HAZUS predict loss?" The M5 earthquake at Au Sable Forks in Upstate New York on April 20, 2002 provided an opportunity to compare actual losses in the region with HAZUS predictions.[1] A preliminary validation of the HAZUS model was conducted by the New York State Emergency Management Office (SEMO) using the Au Sable Forks earthquake as a test case. First, we input earthquake scenario data in HAZUS, mirroring the Au Sable Forks event (5.0MW; depth 6.8 miles (11 km); Project 97 East Coast attenuation function; soil type B used over the entire six-county study region of Essex, Clinton, Warren, Franklin, Hamilton, and Washington).[2] Then a comparison was made of the "direct economic losses to buildings" sustained from this event with HAZUS-estimated losses. The results suggest that HAZUS did well in its estimates and that there is good agreement between actual losses and predicted losses.[1]

Actual losses from the Au Sable Forks earthquake, including damage to lifelines, were in excess of $8 million. Of this figure, approximately $5.85 million were attributed to structural and nonstructural building elements. This estimate includes $3.85 million to residential structures and $2 million to nonresidential structures.[1] This is derived from FEMA's "Individual Assistance" (IA) disaster assistance program, which paid out $2.85 million in grant monies, as of July 2002, to repair residences. In addition to accounting for individuals not applying for assistance and nondiscovery of damages, an additional $1 million was factored to the IA grant monies to arrive at the figure of $3.85 million in damages to residential structures.[1,2] As the "Public Assistance" category of disaster aid was not included in the Presidential Disaster Declaration for the Au Sable Forks earthquake (FEMA-1415-DR-NY), comprehensive damage figures on publicly owned buildings were not documented through a disaster assistance process. A rough damage estimate of $2 million for publicly owned and other nonresidential structures was collected during the damage assessment.[1] Most of the damage was to building foundations and chimneys. Very little damage to building "contents" was reported. Simulating the same earthquake, HAZUS predicted that the structural and nonstructural losses for this event would be $4.53 million, just $1.32 million less than the $5.85 million estimated actual damage.[1] This is a generally acceptable level of error; in fact, it may have been even less if more detailed soil maps had been used. Additionally, HAZUS estimated that there would be $3.8 million in "contents" losses and $32,000 in inventory loss. In actuality, very little "contents" damage was reported; however, if a comparable earthquake had occurred down-state in the New York City metro area, then the predicted "contents" losses might apply.

Credible estimates of future loss can be effective tools in encouraging area stakeholders to mitigate against the possible future damaging conse-quences of earthquakes. Therefore, we are continuing to develop the neces-sary databases of geologic and building information to verify and improve the default database in HAZUS. These efforts include:

– simulating real earthquakes (April 20, 2002, in Au Sable Forks, NY) to verify the accuracy of loss estimates generated with HAZUS software;[1]
– improving the analysis capability of HAZUS' assessment of tall build-ings, a "uniquely metropolitan" infrastructure that concentrates value and people,[13] and continuing to develop soil data and building inventories to refine the default data contained within HAZUS;
– extending our comprehensive building inventories (1 million individual records) for use with assessing and mapping building damage at Ground Zero, as well as estimating roof damage and debris, and predicting losses from the 9/11 terrorist attacks several weeks after they happened, with a modified form of the HAZUS loss estimation methodology.[10, 12, 18]

In the application of this work, some key implementation strategies for mitigating risk and minimizing losses have already been initiated. This includes establishing a seismic building code for NYC (signed by Mayor Giuliani in 1995), initiated by the Seismic Code Committee (formed in 1989), and implemented by the Structural Engineers Association of New York (formed in 1996).[8]

7. Conclusions

The overall conclusion of this research suggests that by considering the ar-ea's historic seismicity, population density, and vulnerability of the region's built environment, it is clear that even a moderate earthquake would have significant impact on the lives and economy of the Tri-State region. Specifi-cally, this research, its methods, and application indicate the following:

– HAZUS is a useful loss estimation methodology for this NY–NJ–CT metropolitan region.
– The building inventory of the Tri-State region represents a total replace-ment value of $1 trillion, excluding contents and lifeline infrastructure

systems. In a 2,500-year event, which is used as a criterion in designing new buildings, the combined loss of buildings and building-related income could be nearly $85 billion.

— Even in a moderate M5 quake, building and income losses would total $4.8 billion. The greatest loss is incurred from a magnitude 7.0 earthquake at the 1884 historic site with $198.6 billion, which is about 20% of the total building-replacement value for the entire Tri-State region. Because of its dense built environment, New York City represents over half of the losses of the Tri-State region for each scenario.

— Hospital functionality would most likely be adequate for most scenarios, except for a M7 event, in which the estimated 13,200 injured would require 26% more than the available number of beds.

— In all scenarios, low-income housing, which is often concentrated in older buildings, may be the most severely affected, leading to homelessness and dislocation. In a moderate M6 quake, the number could be close to 197,700. In a 2,500-year event, over 84,600 people would require short-term shelter.

— Although the number and location of fire stations in Manhattan seem adequate for all scenarios, for larger events (4M6 or 2,500-year), as many as 900 fires could break out simultaneously in the Tri-State study region, demanding more than the available gallons-per-minute to fight them.

— In a moderate M6 quake, an estimated 2,600 buildings would have complete damage. In a 2,500-year event, about 2,200 buildings would be damaged.

— Predictably, the greatest concentration of deaths would be in and around the densely populated New York City metro area. In larger events, where there would be more collapses and partial collapses, there would also be proportionately more fatalities with additional threats from fire, which is not included in these estimates.

Although the building inventories and soil data developed in this work are invaluable for future regional studies, further involvement by emergency responders, planners, builders, and health and human services officials will help improve the effectiveness of this work. The NYCEM continues to update building and soil information, refining and verifying HAZUS as a tool for assisting planners, responders, and stakeholders. Additional data collection and study of regional lifeline systems (water, gas, sewerage, waste-water treatment, highway, and public transportation systems) will significantly enhance the risk characterizations that HAZUS can provide for this region. Uncertainty (epistemic or aleatory) has not been explicitly quantified in our results; there are other studies analyzing uncertainty in HAZUS.[31] These methods should also be extended to assess a multi-hazard assessment, including hurricanes, floods, tornadoes, and earthquakes.

Acknowledgments

The study was partly funded by the Federal Emergency Management Agency (Region II), the New York State Emergency Management Office, the New Jersey State Police Office of Emergency Management, the National Science Foundation, the Multidisciplinary Center for Earthquake Engineering Research, and others. The work is a collaborative effort of the authors and Michael Augustyniak (New Jersey State Police), Bruce Swiren (Federal Emergency Management Agency, Region II), Andrea Dargush (Multidisciplinary Center for Earthquake Engineering Research), Mary-Ann Marrocolo (New York City Emergency Management Office), Daniel O'Brien (New York State Emergency Management Office), and others. Technical reports, research papers, articles, contact information, and soil and building data are available at the New York City Area Consortium for Earthquake Loss Mitigation (NYCEM) website at: http://www.nycem.org.

1 Tantala, M., G. J. P. Nordenson, et al. 2005. NYCEM: Earthquake risks and mitigation in the New York/New Jersey/Connecticut Region. Multidisciplinary Center for Earthquake Engineering (MCEER) Technical report MCEER-03-SP02.

2 Dargush, A., M. Augustyniak, G. Deodatis, K. Jacob, L. McGinty, G. Mylonakis, et al. 2001. Estimating Earthquake Losses for the Greater New York City Area (research progress and accomplishments 2000–2001). *Multidisciplinary Center for Earthquake Engineering Research (MCEER),* University at Buffalo, State University of New York, publication no. MCEER-01-SP01 (May).

3 Dunlop, D. W. 2002. Designing Buildings to Resist Earthquakes. *The New York Times* (June 30).

4 Jacob, K., N. Edelblum, and J. Arnold. 2000. NEHRP Site Classes for Census Tracts in Manhattan, New York City. *NYCEM 2nd-Year Technical Report.* Lamont-Doherty Earth Observatory of Columbia University.

5 McGinty, L., and S. Wear. 2001. Initial Earthquake Loss Estimation Analysis for Westchester County, New York. *Report to New York Emergency Management Organization,* West Chester County Department of Information Technology.

6 Nordenson, G. J. P., G. Deodatis, K. H. Jacob, and M. W. Tantala. 2000. Earthquake Loss Estimation for the New York City Area. *Proceedings of the 12th World Conference on Earthquake Engineering,* New Zealand.

7 Nordenson, G. J. P., G. Deodatis, M. W. Tantala, and A. L. Kumpf. 1999. Earthquake Loss Estimation Study for the New York City Area. Technical report prepared for MCEER, Princeton University, Princeton, NJ.

8 Nordenson, G. J. P., and G. Bell. 2000. Seismic Design Requirements for Regions of Moderate Seismicity. *Earthquake Spectra,* vol. 16, no. 1 (Feb.).

9 Nordenson, G. J. P. 1987. Seismic Hazard Evaluation for New York City. Report of the NY Association of Consulting Engineers Ad Hoc Seismology Committee, New York, NY.

10 Nordenson, G., et al. 2003. World Trade Center Emergency Damage Assessment of Buildings, Structural Engineers Association of New York Inspections of September and October 2001.

11 Stanford, S., R. Pristas, D. Hall, and J. Waldner. 1999. Geologic Component of the Earthquake Loss Estimation Study for Hudson County. New Jersey. New Jersey Geological Survey.

12 Ed. Nordenson, Guy, and Associates, LZA Technology/Thornton-Tomasetti. 2003. Structural Engineers Association of New York, World Trade Center Emergency Damage Assessment of Buildings.

13 Tantala, M., and G. Deodatis. 2002. Development of Seismic Fragility Curves for Tall Buildings. *Proceedings of ASCE 15th Engineering Mechanics Conference*. New York: Columbia University (June).

14 Tantala, M., and G. Deodatis. 2001. Earthquake Loss Estimation Study for Essex and Bergen Counties in New Jersey. Technical report, Department of Civil and Environmental Engineering, Princeton University, submitted to and funded by the New Jersey State Police, Office of Emergency Management (NJSP-OEM).

15 Tantala, M., G. J. P. Nordenson, and G. Deodatis. 2002. Earthquake Loss Estimation Study for the New York City Area. *2nd-Year Technical Report*. Department of Civil and Environmental Engineering, Princeton University, submitted to MCEER and funded by FEMA (January).

16 Tantala, M. W., A. Dargush, G. Deodatis, K. Jacob, G. J. P. Nordenson, D. O'Brien, et al. 2002. Earthquake Loss Estimation for the New York City Area. *Proceedings of 7th National Conference on Earthquake Engineering (7NCEE)*, Earthquake Engineering Research Institute (EERI), Boston, MA (July).

17 Tantala, M., and G. Deodatis. 2002. Essential Facilities Performance Study for Seismic Scenarios in Manhattan. Urban Hazards Forum, John Jay College of Criminal Justice of the City University of New York, New York (January).

18 Thompson, W.C., Jr. 2002. One Year Later: The Fiscal Impact of 9/11 on New York City. City of New York comptroller report (September 4).

19 Frankel, A. D., M. D. Peterson, C. S. Mueller, K. M. Haller, R. L. Wheleler, E. V. Leyendecker, et al. 2002. Documentation for the 2002 Update of the National Seismic Hazard Maps. *USGS* open-file report 02-420.

20 Toro, G. R., N. A. Abrahamson, and J. F. Schneider. 1997. Engineering model of strong ground motions from earthquakes in the Central and Eastern United States. *Seismological Research Letters* 68: 41–57.

21 Molina, S., and C. Lindholm. 2005. A Logic Tree Extension of the Capacity Spectrum Method Developed to Estimate Seismic Risk in Oslo, Norway. *Journal of Earthquake Engineering* 9: 877–97.

22 Crowley, H., R. Pinho, and J. J. Bommer. 2004. A Probabilistic Displacement-based Vulnerability Assessment Procedure for Earthquake Loss Estimation. Bulletin of Earthquake Engineering 2(2):173–219.

23 Markus, M., F. Fiedrich, J. Leebmann, C. Schweier, and E. Steinle. 2004. Concept for an Integrated Disaster Management Tool. *Proceedings of the 13th World Conference on Earthquake Engineering*, paper no. 3094, Vancouver, BC, Canada.

24 Kircher, C. A., A. A. Nassar, O. Kustu, and W. T. Holmes. 1997a. Development of Building Damage Functions for Earthquake Loss Estimation. *Earthquake Spectra* 13, no. 4: 663–82.

25 Kircher, C. A., R. K. Reitherman, R. V. Whitman, and C. Arnold. 1997b. Estimation of Earthquake Losses to Buildings. *Earthquake Spectra* 13, no. 4: 703–20.

26 National Institute of Building Science NIBS. 1999. HAZUS99 *Technical Manual,* developed by the Federal Emergency Management Agency, Washington, DC.

27 National Institute of Building Science NIBS. 2001. HAZUS99-SR1 *Validation Study,* developed by the Federal Emergency Management Agency, Washington, DC.

28 Whitman, R. V., T. Anagnos, C. A. Kircher, H. J. Lagorio, R. S. Lawson, and P. Schneider. 1997. Development of a National Earthquake Loss Estimation Methodology. *Earthquake Spectra* 13, no. 4: 643–61.

29 1997. *NEHRP Recommended Provisions for Seismic Regulations for New Buildings and Other Structures.* Developed by the Building Seismic Safety Council (BSSC) for the Federal Emergency Management Agency (FEMA), Washington, DC, in press.

30 Jacob, K. 1999. Site Conditions Effecting Earthquake Loss Estimates for New York City. *NYCEM 1st-Year Technical Report*. Lamont-Doherty Earth Observatory of Columbia University.

31 Grossi, P. A. 2000. Quantifying the Uncertainty in Seismic Risk and Loss Estimation. Department of Operations and Information Management, The Wharton School, Philadelphia, PA.

Action and Practice

The editors asked structural engineer Guy Nordenson if he would be interested in contributing to *Perspecta 40*. Nordenson's response was as follows:

Thank you for the request but I think I will have to pass on this one.

As much as I like Perspecta and would want to be able to contribute, I find your theme of "monster" unconvincing. It is rather narcissistic in fact. Do you really believe it is architecture that is monstrous? Perhaps there are other forces out there that better deserve the description. And the allusion to the permissiveness of engineering is rather shortsighted–isn't the Sydney Opera House or the World Trade Center for that matter a good example of engineering making outscale and willful building possible? Once again it is this fashion of making today the great crisis of architecture (now there's a theme).

That said, I am happy to talk to you about your project–but as it is, I don't think I would be a good contributor.

All the Best,
Guy

Perspecta 40 followed up with an interview on September 26, 2006.

GN: Automatically, this discussion about monsters leads me to think of the movie *Godzilla*, which I recently watched in Japanese on a flight between Tokyo and Seoul. I think the classic interpretation is that Godzilla represents the Atom Bomb and the terror it caused. Today, there seems to be a kind of slippage which has happened. A film like *Godzilla* expressed the absolute horror of Hiroshima and Nagasaki and the possibility of nuclear annihilation. There used to be widespread motivation to actually talk about eliminating nuclear weapons. I remember the great June 12, 1982, nuclear freeze demonstration in New York. I think there were one million people at the New York City demonstration on the Great Lawn in Central

   Published in *Perspecta 40: Monster*, 2008, *Yale Architecture Journal*, New Haven, pages 198–201

Park. There were so many people marching towards Central Park that half of the people had to march down Fifth and the other half had to march down Eighth Avenue.

There is quite a difference between a million people walking into the park protesting the possibility of the use of tactical nuclear weapons, and what we are used to today. At that time, it was just a matter of basing Pershing missiles in Germany. Today, if you read Seymour M. Hersh, you know that there are actually plans in the Pentagon for using weapons in Iran.[1] Nevertheless, there is not a peep from the public, and I don't see rivers of people walking into the park worrying about it.

→ p. 431

So, while watching *Godzilla*, I thought it was striking, the distance that we have traveled domesticating our terror of nuclear annihilation. Maybe climate change has frightened people more—I don't know—but I think part of my reaction was that those realities are getting so much worse than thirty or forty years ago. Consequently, I find it a little bit disconcerting that architects are preoccupied with the idea of "the monster," as in Daniel Libeskind's building in Denver. It's almost a sublimation of the other issues—such as the potential use of nuclear weapons against Iran—into the aesthetic realm for the sake of distraction.

P40: Actually, this is an issue we'd like to explore. One (possibly unfortunate) role for architecture today is to attempt to create a safe bubble, a new take on Oscar Newman's "defensible space" perhaps. Just look at the new 7 World Trade Center around the corner from here, or the revised design for the Freedom Tower with a 20-story, windowless, fortified concrete base. With the Freedom Tower especially, we are actually seeing an architectural attempt to defend against terrorist attack.

GN: I think the issues at stake here are very similar to the debates that were going on with deterrent theory in the 1970s, which at that time argued for tactical nuclear weapons in Europe. What we are seeing with the Bush administration is a return of the repressive and reactionary attitudes that were in play during the Vietnam War and then during the Nixon and Ford administrations. For a lot of the people involved, particularly Cheney and Rumsfeld, there were missed opportunities and missed understandings about what the ideological issues were and what should have been done to achieve a different outcome. So now there is a chance to replay the scenario, this time with the substitution of "Islamo-Fascism." The status today is fueled by the classic "man-needs-to-replay-the-trials-of-his-youth-and-win-this-time" situation. This is why, I think, there is such a strong fantasy component in our foreign policy today.

The deterrent theory in the '70s argued for using tactical nuclear weapons in Europe. It was necessary to put nuclear weapons in the front line because doing so would trigger a sequence of events, which the other side would realize and then be forced to act in a certain way. It is like playing a game of chess.

In the case of the World Trade Center buildings, the question is: Who decides what the threat is? Whoever decides what the threat is basically decides what the architecture is. Early on we had a design for the World Trade Center site which was this twisting parallelogram. After some time in the schematic design process the client came to a point where they realized it couldn't be built, in part because of the adjustments Pataki had made to the design. Conveniently, the police came along and said, "Well, you can't build it anyway because it is not according to what we want." Essentially getting the "right" design was about adjusting it to the level of threat. "You've designed it for X threat, but we've decided now that it is not good enough. You will have to design it for 3X or 6X. So, please come back to me and tell me what your architecture is, now that the threat has changed." If the client is really, truly sophisticated, perhaps he can get you to design it in Gothic rather than Modern simply by changing the threat and tweaking the parameters just right. This situation is all based on the construction of a monster, namely, the Terrorist.

One bureaucratic entity takes the issue to another bureaucratic entity; they arrive at some compromise where they all agree to believe in the same fiction regarding what the threat is, and that is what we design according to. Thus, when something bad happens at least we can all say, "Governor Pataki told me what to do." This is where the Monster is constructed, and I think this is the area where I find it hard to articulate what is going on in terms of architecture and engineering.

P40: Is there any way that the architect and the engineer can engage in the discussion proactively as the supposed expert, as the one who should be able to step in and say, "This isn't solving the problem"?

GN: Noam Chomsky would say that it is a question of the intelligentsia's role. We got away with what we did on the World Trade Center Tower One, because we had no contract, we weren't getting paid—we were free. We could have just as easily stood up in the middle of Central Park and made a speech, but as it was, Hyde Park Corner happened to be in the conference room at Skidmore, Owings & Merrill. However, the role wasn't any more official than if we had been in the middle of Central Park. There were already other engineers involved, there were architects

Gojira, 1954, directed by Ishirô Honda

involved, there was a political process involved. So the only thing we had was the ability to influence the process through our argument. We got involved in the World Trade Center, partly because we didn't agree with the ideological connotations of Libeskind's design. I felt that it was demagogic, so there was an opportunity to oppose a kind of romantic, neo-expressionist reaction with a rational, classical response. It was a truly ideological exercise, which we took all the way to Governor Pataki and through his intermediaries, explaining: "If you build that way, people will die, and if you build this way, they will not die. Therefore let's build this way." The problem is, once you are acting as an expert—the role that Chomsky is trying to play as a social critic—you become an outsider. You are not going to be asked to design the building.

The generation of architects who were born in the 1930s all made the same decision at the end of the 1960s, be they "whites" or "grays": no more "blue jean architecture." Arthur Drexler argued against political engagement because that muddied the waters. Architects should, by his argument, work in an autonomous practice where somebody else carves out our domain so the work can proceed. What the World Trade Center has shown is that for a lot of people who have grown up in a form of practice from the late 1960s—Libeskind is a good example—it is very hard to reconcile politics and architecture. I think it is very hard for everybody nowadays to reconcile politics and architecture. It's hard for them to deal with the monstrous side.

P40: Do you try to do that in your own work?

GN: To some extent, but only because we are given opportunities to do things where expectations are different. Again, for the World Trade Center Tower One nobody asked us to design the building; we were asked to come in there and react to ideas. Personally, I have found that in the last few years there have been more and more occasions where it has been possible to combine political action and practice. Ground Zero is a case in point. There, we have seen a number of occasions where it was possible to resist certain ideological thrusts through certain design approaches, like the different work we did on Tower One or, the work we are doing on the slurry wall right now ... we are trying to preserve good ideas within the difficult environment, as are a lot of other people.

1 "One of the military's initial option plans, as presented to the White House by the Pentagon this winter, calls for the use of a bunker-buster tactical nuclear weapon, such as the B61-11, against underground nuclear sites. One target is Iran's main centrifuge plant, at Natanz, nearly two hundred miles (322 km) south of Tehran." From Hersh, Seymour M. 2006. The Iran Plans: Would President Bush go to war to stop Tehran from getting the bomb? *The New Yorker* (April 17).

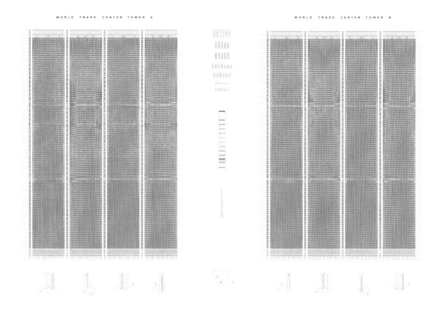

WORLD TRADE CENTER TOWER A

WORLD TRADE CENTER TOWER B

1

1 Guy Nordenson et al., World Trade Center Towers A and B structural steel grates (diagram 2004). 55'' × 7'5''
(139.7 × 226.1 cm). Guy Nordenson and Associates. This color-coded diagram shows the 14 types of steel
used in the construction of the perimeter tube structure of the World Trade Center, as shown in tables in the
working drawings of Skilling, Helle, Christiansen, and Robertson, engineers.

Constellations

"In Candela's work, we have, then, an example of how complete mastery by one mind of all the facts affecting a design can produce that balanced perfection which makes a building or structure into a work of art."[1]

Ove Arup

Ideas and things

In his book of essays *El arco y la lira (The Bow and the Lyre)*, the Mexican diplomat and poet Octavio Paz (1914–1998) writes that "justice and order are categories of being," that "both political and cosmic justice are not properly laws that are over the nature of things, but things themselves in their mutual movement, engendering themselves and devouring each other, produce justice."[2] Felix Candela, born January 27, 1910, embraced a strong sense of justice and order in his life and work. In his early years, growing up, studying and practicing architecture in Madrid, Candela led an active life of sports (he was Spain's national ski champion in 1932), mountain climbing, engineering, and design, and, from 1936, absorbed "some of the lessons portioned out by revolution and civil war."[3] At the end of the Spanish Civil War, he was lucky to be one of only a few hundred Republicans selected—from among more than 50,000 imprisoned in the French concentration camps near Perpignan—for evacuation to Mexico on a ship chartered by the Society of Friends. He arrived there in June 1939, working first in Acapulco, then in Mexico City, and within ten years was able to establish himself as a builder and designer. There followed in the ten years from the Fernández Factory (1950) to the Bacardi Rum Factory (1960) an astonishing eighty-three works (thirty-nine of which were completed in 1955 alone), all variations on the thin concrete shell form of the hyperbolic paraboloid (hypar) for which he is so admired. The range of forms—from the subtle Cosmic Rays Pavilion at the National University of Mexico in Mexico City (1951; FIG. 2) to the whimsical Lake Tequesquitengo signpost in Morelos (1957; FIG. 3)—all have a rugged presence and exuberant freedom.

→ p. 445

I met Felix Candela in 1983, when he taught my second class, at the suggestion of Mario Salvadori, after I had delivered a disastrous first lecture to my students at

Published in Guy Nordenson, *Seven Structural Engineers: The Felix Candela Lectures*, The Museum of Modern Art, New York, 2008, pages 8–27 the Parsons School of Design in New York. At that time, Candela and his wife, Dorothy, were living in the city, having emigrated from Mexico in 1971. He spoke to the class about his design and construction work, about the importance of direct observation and judgment, and about the limits of complex calculations and the natural resistance of shell forms. He described with relish how his design of the Palacio de los Deportes for the XIXth Olympics in Mexico (1968; FIG. 6) was created and calculated in only a few weeks. The commission was assigned to Candela, Enrique Castañeda, and Antonio Peiri only eight months before the opening ceremonies. The initial approximate calculations by Candela were confirmed by detailed computations just days before the structure was successfully completed.

Candela delighted in the freedom and lightness that were possible with the geometric and structural order he had adopted. The syntax of the hypar forms allowed poetic expressions from the Antonio Gaudí-like chiaroscuro of the Church of La Virgen Milagrosa in Narvarte (1954–1955; FIG. 7) to the surreal Sales Office in Guadalajara (1960; FIG. 8). Even when he took up steel, wood, and copper for the prickly Palacio de los Deportes, he applied the same simplicity and invention (FIG. 9). The tension-stayed X-framed arches prefigure by a quarter-century the engineer Peter Rice's (1935–1992) own beautiful mastlike structures (such as the TGV Station roof with the SNCF design bureau, and the MOMI tent in Lille, France [1992]), designed with Future Systems of London. And, of course, the hypar form, even in this steel design, holds pride of place (FIG. 10).

In early 1997 I contacted Candela with the idea of organizing a lecture series named in his honor to be held yearly at The Museum of Modern Art and at the Princeton University and MIT schools of architecture. The Museum lecture would be cosponsored by the Structural Engineers Association of New York, an organization I had founded with a group of New York structural engineers two years previously. The idea of the lecture series had many sources. One was David P. Billington's concept of structural engineering as an art "parallel to but independent of architecture in the same way that photography ... is parallel to but independent of painting."[4] As Billington argues in *The Art of Structural Design: A Swiss Legacy*, the key to understanding this art is to follow "the way in which mechanics and aesthetics are linked through practice."[5] Often, he claims, the art of structural engineering is misinterpreted along the lines of two competing theories.

"The first expresses the belief that all structure is merely a part of architecture and that the engineer's work is purely technical while the architect determines the

2 Felix Candela, Cosmic Rays Pavilion, National University of Mexico, Mexico City
3 Felix Candela, Signpost, Lake Tequesquitengo, Morelos, Mexico

aesthetics. The second holds that engineering is applied science and hence any aesthetic arises from the laws of nature, which dictate an optimum for each case…. Both ideologies are particularly damaging to the wider understanding of structural art in bridges because the first often implies that beauty requires great cost and thus little economic discipline, while the second suggests (erroneously) that beauty naturally occurs because efficiency automatically leads to elegance."[6]

Besides the Swiss structural engineers that Billington highlights in his book – Robert Maillart (1872–1940), Othmar H. Ammann (1879–1965), Heinz Isler (born 1926), and Christian Menn (born 1927) – the other structural engineers he acknowledges as artists of this kind include the Spaniard Eduardo Torroja (1899–1961), the Italian Pier Luigi Nervi (1891–1979), and, of course, Candela. Their arts are diverse, from the plasticity of Torroja's Coal Silo (1951; FIG. 4) and Nervi's St. Mary's Cathedral in San Francisco (1970), both late works, to the minimalism of Maillart and Amman. In the case of the work of Ammann, there is not a single line of aesthetic development – the George Washington Bridge (1931), the Bronx Whitestone Bridge (1935), and the Verrazano Narrows Bridge (1964), all in New York City, do not readily appear to be the work of the same artist. In fact the visual and intellectual strength of Amman's work comes from the distinct individuality of each project. In the work of others, like Nervi's and Candela's, the focus on and development of a particular formal aesthetic is more obvious. In Maillart's case, one can follow the interplay of two distinct lines of development: the three-hinged arch (for example, the Salginatobel Bridge, 1930) and the deck-stiffened arch (for example, the Schwandbach Bridge, 1933; FIG. 5).

Besides the aesthetic qualities highlighted by Billington, what links the work of these engineers, from the particularism of Ammann to the dual research of Maillart and the narrow focus of Candela, is a strong empirical focus, a direct concentration on things.

–Say it, no ideas but in things–
nothing but the blank faces of the houses
and cylindrical trees
bent, forked by preconception and accident–
split, furrowed, creased, mottled, strained–
secret–into the body of the light![7]

These well-known lines from the poem *Paterson* by William Carlos Williams capture the balance of aesthetic pleasure and objective attention that is present

2

3

4

5

in the best of the art of structural engineering. Form is considered a category (indeed a constellation) of things, teased out by the arts of empiricism, practice, and observation.

While this applies well to the seven engineers presented in this collection of essays, there is also apparent in their work and words a struggle with "questions [that] are not answered by either empirical observation or formal deduction,"[8] questions that are philosophical and are subject to moral, social, or political inquiry, and reason. If "rationality rests on the belief that one can think and act for reasons that one can understand, and not merely as the product of occult causal factors which breed 'ideologies' and cannot, in any case, be altered by their victims,"[9] then the consciousness that emerges from engineering practice expands beyond the aesthetic and formal to these other questions. Through the connection to things, reason is then able to ask questions of fact and reach others through the physical expression of this reasoned inquiry.

The direct engagement with things that is characteristic of the work of Candela and these artist-engineers expresses human values broadly. This is clear from Candela's stark chapel in Lomas de Cuernavaca (1958–1959) and his Sales Office (FIG. 8) in Guadalajara. The buildings address directly the question of what it is to be a man, a woman, in a particular time, going to church, going to work, or going to shop. The hyperbolic paraboloid form, the rough concrete work, the obvious evidence of handcrafting, the soaring, thin line of the shell's edge, all these touch, as Isaiah Berlin lists them: "The basic categories (with their corresponding concepts) in terms of which we define men—such notions as society, freedom, sense of time and change, suffering, happiness, productivity, good and bad, right and wrong, choice, effort, truth, illusion (to value them wholly at random)."[10]

Ove Arup's quote at the beginning of this essay is a clear allusion to romantic heroism—to the perfect act "in which freedom and self-fulfillment lie in the recognition by men of themselves as involved in the purposive process of cosmic creation."[11] Arup's admiration for Candela as the master builder echoed the Bauhaus "idea of creating a new unity of the welding together of many 'arts' and movements: a unity having its basis in Man himself and significant only as a living organism."[12] Arup shared with Walter Gropius this ideal of a "total architecture" and of the perfect work as a perfectly integrated organism. This ideal of totality requires the absolute authority of the work's author, a captain who will guide the ship of design to complete integration.

4 Eduardo Torroja, Coal Silo, Instituto de Ciencias de la Construcción, Madrid
5 Robert Maillart, Schwandbach Bridge, Hinterfultigen, Switzerland
6 Felix Candela, Sports Palace, Palacio de los Deportes for the XIXth Olympics, Mexico City
7 Felix Candela, Church of La Virgen Milagrosa, Colonia Vertiz Navarte, Mexico City

In one sense this idea of romantic heroism could apply to the man, Candela, who in 1936 joined the Republican cause "with enthusiasm,"[13] and who later, given the opportunity to build shells in Mexico, felt "as though all the previous events of my life began to make sense and to have meaning. I began to feel 'in form,' like an athlete, but mentally as well. I felt the moment had arrived to do something."[14]

But Candela's work belies this interpretation. The repetition of the hypar form stands apart from the architecture. As the critic Colin Faber wrote, "Once a structure stands, I believe it is dead to Candela. The forms are dropped and the last support is slammed away. As its forces start to play, the shell comes alive. It stands. That is all Candela needs to know and already, for him, 'it belongs in history.'"[15]

This is not total architecture. It is closer to the detached "stance" of the confident ironist, the observer and handler of "things." As Paz writes in his luminous essay on Marcel Duchamp's *Large Glass, Marcel Duchamp; or The Castle of Purity,* "Irony is the antidote that counteracts any element that is 'too serious, such as eroticism' or too sublime, like the Idea. Irony is the Handler of Gravity, the question mark of *et-qui-libre?*"[16] Candela is closer in practice to the dialectical and antiretinal practice of Duchamp ("the beauty of indifference") than to the metamorphic and fertile heroism of Pablo Picasso. Rather than represent Arup's "balanced perfection," the work of Candela presents the concrete outcomes of a quizzical attention to things that actually suspends mastery. Engineering is not, as Billington correctly states, a simple reading or re-creation of nature. This is why the work of Candela continues to delight as well as serve us so well as a provocation to fresh thoughts about structure and architecture.

Constellations

Felix Candela was to have been the first lecturer in the series named for him, but in late 1997 he fell ill and on December 7 he died in Durham, North Carolina. Following Candela's wish, David Billington gave the first Candela lecture in April 1998, speaking on Candela's work. In the talk, Billington linked the work of Candela to those of other concrete shell designers and structural artists, including Anton Tedesko (1903–1994), Pier Luigi Nervi, and Heinz Isler. The essay by Billington and Maria Garlock that is included here is a further development of this lecture and serves to situate Candela alongside these peers. In 1999 the second Candela lecture was presented by the German engineer Jörg Schlaich. After Schlaich, the lectures were presented by Christian Menn (Switzerland) in 2000; Mamoru Kawaguchi (Japan) in 2001; Heinz Isler (Switzerland) in 2002;

6

7

Leslie E. Robertson (U.S.) in 2003; Cecil Balmond (U.K. and Sri Lanka) in 2004; and Stanford Anderson on Eladio Dieste (Uruguay) in 2005.

The Candela lecturers were selected to "honor the most distinguished structural engineers active in design in the world today" by a committee that included Terence Riley (MoMA), Herbert Einstein and (until 2004) Stanford Anderson (MIT), Ralph Lerner, Stan Allen, and David Billington (Princeton) and, after 2000, Mutsuro Sasaki (Japan), Ricky Burdett (UK), and Antoine Picon (France). The Structural Engineers Association of New York was represented in the selection process each year by its president and president-elect. The lectures were intended as both an honor and an occasion for the engineers to present their work and consider the meaning of that work and its connection to, or distinctness from, the practice of architecture. Each talk was given with accompanying slides and, for the most part, in the informal narrative style that is usual in project-based architecture and engineering lectures. While the museum venue was an explicit challenge to the engineers who were speaking, and to those in the audience, to reflect on the place of the engineer's work in the context of modern art, the speakers seized this opportunity, to varying degrees, to highlight the extent to which they saw their work as art, invention, or problem-solving technique.

Dieste's work, as Stanford Anderson describes it here and in his book *Eladio Dieste, Innovation in Structural Art,*[17] is infused with the engineer's strong social convictions. As he wrote, "We, the nations of the third world, should not make the mistake of confusing the ends. Development is not an end in itself. Development will be beneficial as long as it is in accord with the ends of mankind and it will be detrimental if it forgets these ends."[18] He added, "When faced with the seduction of power, wealth, and efficiency, without content, we must react."[19] For Dieste, the purpose of design is to enclose everyday life with lightness and natural light, employing local materials to achieve this end. Like Candela, he followed in the practical and poetic tradition of the Catalans Rafael Guastavino (1842–1908) and Antonio Gaudí (1852–1926),[20] joining the means of construction and the resistance of forms and materials in designs that also embody human hopes and values.

This tradition is evident also in the work of the Swiss engineer Heinz Isler (born 1926). Like Candela, Isler has concentrated his practice on thin concrete shells, inventing forms even freer and more playful than Candela's. Isler derives his forms not from analytical geometry (as were Candela's hypars) but directly from physical and funicular models–flexible membranes that assume the least energy, or minimal surface, for a specific boundary and force patterns. In the mid-1950s,

8 Felix Candela, Sales Office, Guadalajara. Candela is standing at the left
9 and 10 Felix Candela, Palacio de los Deportes under construction, Mexico City

Isler invented two new form-making techniques, the first by using pneumatic models and the second by experimenting with hanging cloth models sprayed with water and put out to freeze in wintertime. Later, in 1965, he added a third technique that made shapes "by the flow method, by which the advancing velocity of a liquid inside a tube is varied. At the wall, velocity is zero because of friction, whereas in the center there is maximum velocity. A slowly expanding form leaves a square tube and forms a dome shape. This natural function produces lovely shapes."[21]

While the frozen cloths conform to the funicular[22] shape given by gravity, the other methods, pneumatic and flow, are hydraulic. Although constrained by physical processes, these experiments are not determined by gravity. The forms of projects like the BP Service Station in Deitingen (1968; FIG. 11) and the Sicli Company Building in Geneva (1969–70; FIG. 12) are adjusted for the site geometry, for the "loveliness" of their shape, and even the subtle interplay of light and shade that follows the necessity to curl the shell edge to prevent buckling.

Jörg Schlaich (born 1934) has been described by the architect Frank Gehry (born 1929) as the world's best living structural engineer. Schlaich, in his turn, has said that he thinks that Christian Menn is the world's greatest living bridge designer. Whatever else these opinions indicate, they point to the difference between Schlaich's team-based practice and the more solitary career of Menn. Alan Holgate's 1997 book on Schlaich, entitled *The Art of Structural Engineering: The Work of Jörg Schlaich and His Team,*[23] refers not only to his office and to his lab at the University of Stuttgart's Institute for Lightweight Structures (founded in 1964 by Frei Otto) but also to his collaborative relationships with architects. Schlaich worked first in the office of the great German engineering firm of Leonhardt und Andrä, where he helped design several telecommunication towers, and collaborated on the remarkable 1968 Munich Olympic Stadium roof. This membrane roof was designed by the architect Gunter Behnisch (born 1922) and a team that at first included Heinz Isler and then Frei Otto (born 1925), the great tensile-structures experimentalist, together with Leonhardt, Andrä, Schlaich and Bergermann. In 1980 Schlaich formed an independent practice with Rolf Bergermann.

The early work of Schlaich and his partners is classical in the sense that it is based on the evolution of existing types. Most obvious are projects like the GRC Shell for the Stuttgart Federal Garden Exhibition (1977), an explicit adaptation of Candela's Los Manantiales restaurant in Xochimilco (1958) by other material and construction means. Their cable net and glass grid structures are both developments of the Munich Olympic Stadium roof, using clamp connectors to join continuous, twinned,

8   9   10   **439**

tension cables or compression bars. The use of steel castings, facilitated by a close collaboration with German steelmakers, is another consistent element, applied recently to the twin lattice tower proposal of the THINK team for the redevelopment of the World Trade Center site in New York in 2003. Schlaich, like his contemporary and peer the Irish engineer Peter Rice (for example, the Pompidou Center in Paris, 1972–1976), uses cast steel joints in a conscious recovery of a late-nineteenth-century, particularly Victorian, technology, both for their expressive as well as functional potential. Rice, in particular, valued the *"trace de la main,"* or craftsmanship, that is indicated by the roughness of the casting surface (FIG. 14).

Like Isler's shells, the glass grid roof structures of Schlaich Bergermann und Partner are shaped to follow the funicular form delineated by the geometry of the supporting boundaries and the glass self-weight. In recent projects with Frank Gehry, such as the Berlin DG Bank Building and the proposed Museum of Tolerance in Jerusalem, the funicular form is further warped by Gehry's sculptural will. It is testimony to the open-mindedness and curiosity of Schlaich and his partner in these projects, Hans Schober, that they are happy to adapt their glass shells to these improvisations with Gehry and his partners, Craig Webb and Edwin Chan.

The early bridges of Christian Menn are also evolutionary, drawing on the work of Robert Maillart for a series of elegant concrete deck-stiffened arch bridges beginning in 1957. In 1969 Menn designed his first prestressed concrete hollow-box beam bridge, the Salvanei Bridge. In 1971 he was appointed professor at the ETH (Federal Institute of Technology), where he had received his doctorate in 1956 with Pierre Lardy (1903–1958).[24] Since the 1970s, Swiss law has limited Menn to consulting on a few select projects, all of which have been concentrated and original works of bridge design.

In their later bridge work, both Schlaich and Menn have been open to original forms, with little regard for "taste." Marcel Duchamp once proposed "the search for 'prime words' ('divisible only by themselves and by unity')"[25]–an apt description of both men's bridge designs. Schlaich's Ting Kau Bridge in Hong Kong violates any precedents of "good" cable-stayed bridge design and for that reason remains indelible in one's memory. Menn's great Felsenau (1974), Ganter (1980), and Sunniberg (1998) bridges are all of brilliant intelligence and raw simplicity. The towers of the Sunniberg Bridge, in particular, recall his fellow Swiss Alberto Giacometti's *Spoon Woman* (1926–1927)–enigmatic and curled. Even now, after years of familiarity, the Ganter Bridge remains iconoclastic.

11 Heinz Isler, BP Service Station, Deitingen
12 Heinz Isler. Sicli Company Building, Geneva

Mamoru Kawaguchi (born 1932) is, like Schlaich, a great collaborator. Kawaguchi contributed to several of the key projects at EXPO 70 in Osaka, including the space frame by Kenzo Tange (1913–2005) and the inflated Fuji Group Pavilion. Like Schlaich, Kawaguchi is also rooted in a strong lineage of engineer designers. He worked with the remarkable Yoshikatsu Tsuboi (1907–1990) and Tange on the cable-stayed roof of the Yoyogi Indoor Stadium for the 1964 Tokyo Olympics and with Arata Isozaki (born 1931) on the unfolding Palau Sant Jordi Sports Palace for the 1992 Barcelona Olympics. The 1998 Centennial Hall in Nara, also with Isozaki, even displays the deployment hinges as ornaments–an echo of the projecting construction corbels of the Roman Pont du Gard in Nîmes, France. Kawaguchi, of all the engineers in this collection, is the most whimsical and humorous. He designs air arches, springing pantadomes, and flying fish. His exuberance adds a theatricality to his designs. Not only are many of the projects–for EXPOs, Olympics, and festivals–ephemeral, but their construction is an event, a happening, like the extraordinary Osaka EXPO "Pavilion" of Billy Kluver (1927–2004;) and others.[26] As did Candela, Kawaguchi delights in the dramatic moment "when the forms are dropped and the last support is slammed away…. It stands.'"[27]

Leslie Robertson (born 1928) is the only U.S. engineer in this collection. He belongs to the two generations of U.S. structural engineers that include Fred Severud (1899–1990), August Komendant (1906–1992), Paul Weidlinger (1914–1999), Fazlur Khan (1929–1982), and William LeMessurier (born 1927), whose originality found expression in collaborations with architects. Severud was associated with Eero Saarinen and Philip Johnson, Komendant with Louis Kahn and Moshe Safdie, Weidlinger with Gordon Bunshaft and Marcel Breuer, Kahn with Myron Goldsmith and Bruce Graham, and LeMessurier with Hugh Stubbins and Helmut Jahn. Robertson has worked with Minoru Yamasaki (1912–1986), Wallace Harrison (1895–1981), Gunnar Birkerts (born 1925), and, most notably, with I. M. Pei (born 1917). Robertson paints ideas with steel. On the World Trade Center Towers (1970–2001) he used fourteen different steels (FIG. 1) for the perimeter "tube" structure. By applying high-strength steel in some parts, he was able to use smaller plate thickness and thereby reduce their stiffness, to shed stress to the thicker, lower strength steel elements. The spectrum of steels used is the invisible expression of an integration, across all the possible extreme winds, measured by wind tunnel models of the surrounding urban terrain and the climatic idiosyncrasies (the "wind rose")[28] of the New York City area. This WTC design marked the culmination of similar uses of multiple steels on the IBM and U.S. Steel Buildings in Pittsburgh.

11

12

Robertson's collaboration with Pei developed in the 1980s with the Bank of China Tower in Hong Kong (1990) and culminated in the remarkable bridge and tunnel at Miho, Japan (1996). The Bank of China Tower is particularly intriguing for the fact that the crystalline geometry of the outer surface disguises the offset geometry of the unique, three-dimensional space-frame structure of steel and concrete. This apparent flattening [29] of the structure to the minimal surface is reminiscent of both Mies and Severud's Seagram Building in New York (1958) and Bunshaft and Weidlinger's Beinecke Rare Book Library at Yale (1963), both instances where the structure is thinned to a surface of shadows and light (FIG. 13).

Cecil Balmond (born 1943) is best known for his collaborative work with Rem Koolhaas (born 1944), Daniel Libeskind (born 1946), and Alvaro Siza (born 1933). Balmond is especially preoccupied with number and pattern. His first book, *Number 9,*[30] begins with the story of a boy mathematician faced with a riddle: "What is the fixed point of the wind?"

13

"To solve the riddle, Enjil went to a secluded spot and sat in the shade of a banyon tree and blanked everything he knew out of his mind. The great blackness descended. Nothing moved. Shadows went into deeper shadows, layer into layer. A black disc grew. First as a dot, then a circle, then a rushing blind movement. Then the numbers came out, tumbling one over the other, rolling the patterns over in his head. There were the star patterns, zigzags, squares, cubes, seesaws, and the weaving patterns going in and out, all twisting over each other…. And there in the simplest patterns were points that did not move or change, no matter what the numbers were. And they were the fixed points."[31]

Though Balmond looks to manifest the patterns he discovers in his designs, he shares with Robertson the interest in the abstraction of structure. The spiral extension to the Victoria and Albert Museum (2003), designed with Libeskind, is an astonishing act of creative editing by Balmond that, like Ezra Pound's reduction of T. S. Eliot's draft of *The Waste Land* [32] to its final form, promises to be Libeskind's best work. The Bordeaux house (1998) and the Beijing CCTV Headquarters with OMA and Rem Koolhaas (under construction) both elaborate and display the structure as ornament—an ambiguous and ironic use of the structure's usual implications of authenticity, while the delicate, stressed, concrete sheet of the Portuguese Pavilion for the 1998 Lisbon EXPO, with Alvaro Siza Vieira (born 1933), and the later tensile roof of Braga Stadium (2000–2004), with Eduardo Souto de Moura (born 1952), link Balmond's example to the historical lineage of Candela's funicular abstraction.

13 Gordon Bunshaft and Paul Weidlinger. Beinecke Rare Book Library, New Haven, Connecticut
14 Peter Rice, Renzo Piano, and Richard Rogers, "Gerberettes" for the Centre Georges Pompidou, Paris, in the Krupp casting factory in Germany
15 Gustave Eiffel and Frédéric-Auguste Bartholdi. Interior of the Statue of Liberty, showing secondary iron frame and armature supporting copper skin of toga

UNE CONSTELLATION
froide d'oubli et de désuétude
pas tant
qu'elle n'énumère
sur quelque surface vacante et supérieure
le heurt successif
sidéralement
d'un compte total en formation [33]

Economy

The word "economy" has a vast etymology that extends back through the Greek words for "home" (*oikos)* and "law" (*nomos*) to the more contradictory terms of parish and village, number and nomad. Economy is central to engineering and its aesthetic. Candela's shells are reductive, not as total works of art but as simplification. For the Greek astronomers and the writers and scientists who followed them, the ideal was the cold purity of the patterns apparent in the stars and constellations and their motions. The poem of Stéphane Mallarmé (1842–1898) *Un coup de dés jamais n'abolira le hasard* has been a modern icon of this ideal ever since Mallarmé showed the original manuscript to his friend Paul Valéry (1871–1945), because it is as cold, impenetrable, and beautiful as the stars. Like all great poems its economy is also absolute. Admirers of *Un coup de dés,* from Valéry to T. S. Eliot and Marcel Duchamp, have been drawn, I think, to the absoluteness of sublimation that the work presents. There is a kind of mysticism to it as well. It is–to use other oppositions–Apollonian, classical, not Dionysian or romantic.

Type is, at its root, a kind of constellation, and engineering is necessarily typological. That is not to say there is no iconoclastic structural art. In fact, we see in the work of some of the engineers in this collection clear examples of this. But the iconoclasms are not instances of "cosmic creation" as Berlin describes those of the great romantics. They are instances of economic discovery, the uncovering of some new laws of making things that spring from a particular culture or situation–hypar shells in Mexico, frozen shells in Switzerland, masonry vaults in Uruguay, steel castings in Germany, multiple varieties of U.S. steel, and highly industrialized structural machines in China and Japan. The types that emerge are works of art in the realm of things and orders, not feeling and self-expression.

This idea of type as constellation can also be explained by reference to the difference between the Brooklyn Bridge (1888), and the Statue of Liberty (1884).

14　　　　　　　　　　15　　　　　　　**443**

The Brooklyn Bridge is much more than just a bridge, as its utilitarian neighbors, the Manhattan and Williamsburg bridges, make clear. The ephemeral deck truss hung from the parabolic main cable and radiating stay cables contrasts with the thick granite and gothic towers to embody both heaven and earth–the same opposites that animate Mallarmé's poem. The bridge is perfectly proportioned and unforgettable. The structure designed by Gustave Eiffel (1832–1923) for the Statue of Liberty is, on the other hand, revealed only on the inside, and piecemeal at that. It is effectively invisible, and yet once it is understood through drawings and photographs (FIG. 15), it is of astonishing originality and *delicatesse*. It is an idea caught lightly, invisibly, in a thing.

16

"Thus structure, the intangible concept, is realized though construction and given visual expression through tectonics,"[34] Eduard F. Sekler writes, "[and the] atectonic is used ... to describe a manner in which the expressive interaction of load and support in architecture is visually neglected or obscured."[35] Or, referring to a verse by Henry Wadsworth Longfellow that Ludwig Wittgenstein claimed as his motto:

In the elder days of art
Builders wrought with greatest care
Each minute and unseen part,
For the Gods are everywhere.[36]

This economy is a manner of conscience and practice, that is, a series of choices made on the belief "in the intelligibility of the notion of objective inquiry ... [and] the discipline required by the dedication to the ideal of *correctness*."[37] Tectonics is an expression of the economy of design that pays homage to the economy of evolution–and survival–"with greatest care."[38] The atectonic rather sublimates the structure into ornament, or just nothing. Construction itself can offer, on occasion, a time for theater and performance that may echo in the cultural memory of the built thing.

The works of the engineers that are represented in this collection divide into two general categories. Dieste, Isler, and Menn are structural artists; each had or has an autonomous practice that transforms the meaning of the art. They invent and develop forms that have a clear structure, are constructed in a direct and legible way, and "give visual expression" to these facts through their form and details. Like the Brooklyn Bridge, they are made of what you see, even if they are open to multiple readings. Their "engineering ... is a fairly anonymous art"[39] since they are in public use and do not carry a signature. But each has a distinct

16 Marcel Duchamp. *Étant donnés: 1e la chute d'eau, 2e le gaz d'eclairage*. 1946–1966. Mixed-media assemblage, approx. 7' 11½'' high, 70'' wide. Philadelphia Museum of Art. Gift of the Cassandra Foundation, 1969

way of working and has developed a new formal language that has changed
the history of the art for those who practice it.

Balmond, Kawaguchi, Robertson, and Schlaich are not visual artists in the same
way as the other three, but that only makes their work more challenging to think
about. This is where the example of Duchamp is instructive. "Structure, the intangible concept" and the "unseen part" that are "realized through construction"
could just as easily be a description of the "Ordre des 15 operations de montage
général" for his *Étant donnés: 1ᵉ la chute d'eau, 2ᵉ le gaz d'éclairage*[40] (FIG. 16),
as indeed it could be for that other prefabricated lady–the Statue of Liberty.
These four engineers always work in collaboration with architects. While Balmond
and Schlaich have developed geometric patterns and structural ideas that persist
across different collaborations,[41] these four mostly apply a hidden hand. These
degrees of anonymity or impersonality lend, for those sufficiently curious and willing
to research, a suspense and even (in the case of Kawaguchi) a sense of theater
and humor to their work. The invisible creativity of Robertson's World Trade Center
structural design is, especially after the tower's destruction, as poignant and
memorable as any great work of conceptual art.

1 Arup, Ove N. 1963. Foreword to *Candela: The Shell Builder*, by Colin Faber, 8. New York: Reinhold.

2 Paz, Octavio. The Heroic World. *The Bow and the Lyre*. trans. 1973, Ruth L. C. Simms. New York:
McGraw-Hill, 183.

3 Faber. op. cit., 12.

4 Billington, David P. 2003. *The Art of Structural Design: A Swiss Legacy*. New Haven: Yale University Press, 13.

5 Ibid., 15.

6 Ibid., 14–15.

7 Williams, William Carlos. 1992. The Delineaments of the Giants. *Paterson: Book I*, rev. ed. New York:
New Direction Publishing, 6–7

8 Berlin, Isaiah. 1998. Does Political Theory Still Exist? *The Proper Study of Mankind*. New York:
Farrar, Straus and Giroux, 84.

9 Ibid., 89.

10 Ibid., 83.

11 Ibid., 72.

12 Giedion, Sigfried. 1967. *Space, Time and Architecture*, 5th ed. Cambridge: Harvard University Press, 511.

13 Faber. op. cit., 12.

14 Ibid., 13.

15 Ibid., 77.

16 Paz, Octavio. *Marcel Duchamp; or The Castle of Purity,* trans. 1970, Donald Gardner. London: Cape
Goliard, 31.

17 Anderson, Stanford, ed. 2004. *Eladio Dieste, Innovation in Structural Art*. New York: Princeton
Architectural Press.

18 Dieste, Eladio. 1996. Tecnica y Subdesarrollo. *Eladio Dieste 1943–1996*. Ed. Antonio Jimenez T et al.
Montevideo: Dir. General de Arquitectura y Vivienda, 262.

19 Ibid., 263.

20 Allen, Edward. 2004. Guastavino, Dieste, and the Two Revolutions in Masonry Vaulting. *Eladio Dieste*. Ed. Stanford Anderson. New York: Princeton Architectural Press, 66–75.

21 Billington. *Art of Structural Design*. 139.

22 Funicular, as in *funis + -iculus,* or little rope, is used to describe the shape of a suspended string or net of strings. Also *funiculi', funicula'!*

23 Holgate, Alan. 1997. *The Art of Structural Engineering: The Work of Jörg Schlaich and His Team*. Stuttgart: Edition Axel Menges.

24 See Billington, *Art of Structural Design,* for a discussion of the key role of Pierre Lardy.

25 Marcel Duchamp, in Paz, Octavio. *Marcel Duchamp; or the Castle of Purity,* 10.

26 Kluver, Billy et al. 1972. *Pavilion/Experiments in Art and Technology*. New York: E.P. Dutton.

27 Faber. op. cit., 77.

28 The "wind rose" is the diagram of the fastest winds measured for a particular time-exposure period over the cardinal coordinates. The "petals" are the directions of prevailing wind–in New York, the Northeast, and Northwest mostly. See http://www.wcc.nrcs.usda.gov/climate/windrose.html.

29 "No terms taken from other art–whether from antecedent paintings or from Picasso's own subsequent Cubism–describe the drama of so much depth under stress. This is an interior space in compression, like the inside of pleated bellows, like the feel of an inhabited pocket, a contracting sheath heated by the massed human presence." Leo Steinberg, quoted by Rosalind Kraus, 2004, in Flattening Space. *London Review of Books* 26, no. 7, April 1.

30 Balmond, Cecil. 1998. *Number 9: The Search for the Sigma Code*. New York: Prestel.

31 Ibid., 19.

32 T. S. Eliot. 1971. *The Waste Land: A Facsimile and Transcript of the Original Drafts*. Ed. Valerie Eliot. New York: Harcourt Brace Jovanovich.

33 Mallarmé, Stéphane. 1914. *Un Coup de dés jamais n'abolira le hasard*. Paris: Gallimard.

34 Sekler, Eduard F. 1965. Structure, Construction, Tectonics. *The Structure of Art and Science*. Ed. Gyorgy Kepes. New York: George Braziller.

35 Sekler, Eduard F. 1967. The Stoclet House by Joseph Hoffmann. *Essays in the History of Architecture Presented to Rudolf Wittkower*. London: Phaidon Press 230–31, quoted in Frampton, Kenneth. 1995. *Studies in Tectonic Culture*. Cambridge: MIT Press.

36 Longfellow, as quoted in Frankfurt, Harry G. 2005. *On Bullshit*. Princeton: Princeton University Press, 20. "Wittgenstein once said that the following bit of verse by Longfellow could serve him as a motto."

37 Ibid., 65.

38 Cf. the sculptor Richard Serra: "Since I chose to build in steel it was a necessity to know who had dealt with the material in the most significant, the most inventive, the most economic way," in Foster, Hal. 2000. The Un/making of Sculpture (1998). *Richard Serra*. Ed. Hal Foster. Cambridge: MIT Press, 186.

39 "Until lately art has been one thing and everything else something else. These structures are art and so is everything made. The distinctions have to be made within this assumption. The forms of art and of non-art have always been connected: their occurrences shouldn't be separated as they have been. More or less, the separation is due to collecting and connoisseurship, from which art history developed. It is better to consider art and non-art one thing and make the distinctions ones of degree. Engineering forms are more general and less particular than the forms of the best art. They aren't highly general though, as some well designed utensils are. Simple geometric forms with little detail are usually both aesthetic and general." Judd, Donald. 1975. Review of *Twentieth Century Engineering* exhibition at The Museum of Modern Art, 1964, in *Donald Judd: Complete Writings 1959–1975*. New York: New York University Press, 138.

40 Duchamp, Marcel. 1987. *Manual of Instructions for Marcel Duchamp, Étant donnés: 1e la chute d'eau, 2e le gaz d'éclairage*. Philadelphia: Philadelphia Museum of Art.

41 The art-historical technique of using side-by-side slides as a means of interpreting artworks is useful when studying the works of engineers who act in collaborations, such as Peter Rice, August Komendant, or Paul Weidlinger, as well as the four included here. Renzo Piano, with and without Rice, Louis Kahn, with and without Komendant, or Gordon Bunschaft, with and without Weidlinger, all do very different work, as do these same engineers with other collaborators (such as Richard Rogers, Moshe Safdie, and Marcel Breuer respectively).

Duelling Partners

Book review of Andrew Saint's *Architect and Engineer: A Study in Sibling Rivalry*, Yale University Press

"If there is a moral to the story of the [Millennium] bridge," writes Andrew Saint, "it is that the strands of art and engineering run parallel, often intertwine creatively, but in the last analysis are distinct. They should remain so and be seen to be so." In his encyclopedic survey *Architect and Engineer: A Study in Sibling Rivalry,* Saint weaves these strands in a web that is always instructive and enjoyable, if in the end without a clear pattern. The "sibling" metaphor may lead one to expect a pattern, but Saint admits at the start that the reader "may feel in want of a clear thread." Why sibling? Why not married? Or parallel? Are violinists and pianists siblings? Actors and directors? Painters and sculptors? As one who has practiced for some time as a structural engineer, I don't see that architects are any more my sisters than sculptors are my brothers. Rather, I find that in professional practices like acting and directing, writing and engineering, we operate in that material and social practice for the necessary time, then step out. Saint quotes the British engineer Anthony Hunt referring to "the engineer in me," a role, not the whole. One of the pleasures of contemporary culture is the versatile vigor of some of its protean characters. Think Clint Eastwood, George Clooney, Miles Davis, or David Byrne. We may lack equivalent figures in architecture and engineering, at least since Charles and Ray Eames, but that doesn't mean versatility is not possible.

Saint divides his book into distinct topical chapters: Imperial Works and Worthy Kings; Iron; Concrete; Bridges; Reconciliation; and A Question of Upbringing. Each section is a beautifully illustrated article on the history of approaches to prac-tice, material, or type as far back as the 17th century. There are many wonderful surprises, from the works and ideas of the French bridge engineers Emiland-Marie Gauthey and Paul Séjourné to Le Corbusier's under-appreciated collaborator, Vladimir Bodiansky. In the section Reconciliation, Saint gives an excellent historical account of the postwar British and American structural engineering scene, but

Published in: *The Architect's Newspaper* 12, 07.09.2008, pages 23–24 says little about the contribution of mechanical engineers as of the mid-1960s. Tom Barker, the partner and collaborator to Peter Rice and Renzo Piano, goes unmentioned, as does the natural ventilation and other building services developments that are detailed in Reyner Banham's *The Architecture of the Well Tempered Environment* (1969), which have only become more relevant since then. The "engineer" of this book is the structural engineer of bridges and buildings, and his or her contribution is to the visual arts of architecture and engineering. But also, as Saint freely acknowledges, there is only a modest attempt at a theoretical or philosophical overview.

There are a few tantalizing suggestions. Quoting some by Saint: "What mattered was an architect's ability to open eyes and raise the game by articulating a technical challenge in the language of art."

"The architect harnesses known techniques to perfectionist ends, while the engineer forwards technology, often leaving the details of his work rough."

"The further a structure departs from logic and economy, the less reasonable, objective, and truly dialectical becomes the relationship between the architect and engineer."

Not to mention other gems, such as this one from Mies van der Rohe: "Wherever technology reaches its real fulfillment, it transcends into architecture."

And Guy de Maupassant: "When you see an engineer, take a gun and shoot him," and "the engineer instinctively goes for the ugly, as the duck makes for water."

Perhaps the reason that Saint chose the "sibling" analogy is to resist the obvious dualism of many of these suggestions: body/mind, matter/spirit, art/science, architect/engineer. The family connection runs counter to that absolute dialectic. My preference is to look elsewhere for analogies, to music or film, where there are tribal connections that are neither dualistic nor kin-based. The architect-engineer-builder-user-client tribe in which we operate has, in its best moments, mobilized all parties to come together for the best works—Crown Hall, Beinecke Library, Kimbell Art Museum, and the de Menil Collection are great examples of what Ezra Pound would call tribal "vortices." In this way, making architecture can be as richly muddled and networked as making movies and making music.

Describing the way the tapered windows under the ends of the Kimbell Art Museum's cycloid shells were shaped by the Aquavit-fueled standoff between Louis Kahn and August Komendant, Saint concludes: "It was a simple touch; but the feature has come to be revered for its grace and candor." This book is similarly refreshing and stimulating for its grace and candor. By example, it nudges us to consider lifting grace and candor over cause and effect as we expand our field and versatilities.

Index

Publications

Books

On the Water | Palisade Bay. With
C. Seavitt and A. Yarinsky. Berlin: Hatje Cantz
Verlag / The Museum of Modern Art
Publications, 2010.

*Seven Structural Engineers – The Felix
Candela Lectures in Structural Engineering.*
Ed. New York: The Museum of Modern
Art Publications, 2008.

*New York Consortium for Earthquake
Hazard Mitigations.* Summary Report with
M. Tantala et al. Buffalo, NY: MCEER
Publication, 2003.

Tall Buildings. With Terence Riley.
New York: The Museum of Modern Art
Publications, 2003.

*WTC Emergency – Damage Assessment
of Buildings Structural Engineers
Association of NY Inspection of September
and October 2001.* Volume A Summary
Report, and B-F on DVD. New York:
SEAoNY, 2003.

Research Reports

"Earthquake Loss Estimation Study
for the New York City Metropolitan Region."
With M. W. Tantala, G. Deodatis, and
K. H. Jacob. *Journal of Soil Dynamics and
Earthquake Engineering*, vol. 28,
no. 10-11, October / November 2008.

"Earthquake Loss Estimation Study for the
New York City Area." Final report, Princeton
University, School of Architecture and
Dept of Civil and Environmental Engineering,
funded by FEMA, January 2003.

"Earthquake Loss Estimation Study for the
New York City Area." Second year technical
report, Princeton University, Dept of Civil and
Environmental Engineering, submitted to
MCEER and funded by FEMA, January 2000.

"Earthquake Loss Estimation for the New York
City Area." With G. Deodatis, K. H. Jacob,

and M. W. Tantala. Technical report prepared
for MCEER, Princeton University. Princeton,
NJ, 1999.

"Seismic Hazard Evaluation for New York
City." *Report of the NYACE Ad-hoc
Seismology Committee.* New York, October
1986.

Articles

"Palisade Bay, New York." With C. Seavitt
and Architecture Research Office. *Workbook*
(catalogue for *Workshopping*, The US
Pavilion, 12th Venice Biennale International
Architecture Exhibition), Venice, Italy, 2010.

"Earthquake, Hurricane and Flood Resistant
Housing for Haiti." With Rebecca Nixon.
Pamphlet Architecture 31: New Haiti Villages,
New York, 2010.

"Magical Structuralism." *Solid States:
Concrete in Transition*, eds Michael Bell and
Craig Buckley. Princeton Architectural Press,
New York, 2010.

"On the Water: Palisade Bay." With S. Cassell,
M. Koch, C. Seavitt, J. Smith, M. W. Tantala,
and A. Yarinsky. In *306090*, no. 13, 2009.

"Infrathin." *Engineered Transparency – The
Technical, Visual, and Spatial Effects of Glass*,
eds Michael Bell and Jeannie Kim. Princeton
Architectural Press, New York, 2009.

"On the Water: The New York-New
Jersey Upper Bay." With S. Cassell, M. Koch,
C. Seavitt, J. Smith, M. W. Tantala, and
A. Yarinsky. *Places*, November 2, 2008.

"Duelling Partners." *The Architect's
Newspaper*, New York, July 9, 2008.

"Action and Practice." *Perspecta 40
"Monster": The Yale Architectural Journal*,
2008.

"Constellations." Introduction to *Seven
Structural Engineers: The Felix Candela

Lectures.* New York: The Museum of Modern
Art Publications, 2008.

"Glass Pavilion, Toledo Museum of Art." With
Brett Schneider. *Structural Engineering
International*, Zurich, Switzerland, February
2008.

"Truth in Tall Buildings." *Harvard Design
Magazine*, Cambridge, MA, Spring / Summer
2007.

"Apocryphal." *domus*, Rozzano, Italy,
December 2007.

"Freedom From Fear." *The New York Times*,
New York, February 16, 2007.

"Building Bridges." With Noah Klersfeld
and Jiro Takagi. *Civil Engineering*, Reston,
VA, February 2007.

"Concrete Theater." *Liquid Stone:
New Architecture in Concrete*, Princeton
Architectural Press, New York, 2006.

"With Great Joy and Expectations." *Best
of Friends: Buckminster Fuller and Isamu
Noguchi*, exhibition catalogue, Noguchi
Museum, Long Island City, New York, 2006.

"Tall Building as Metaphor." Introduction
to *Tall Buildings*, exhibition catalogue,
New York: The Museum of Modern Art
Publications, 2003.

"Tall Building Structures Since the World
Trade Center: Art, Craft, and Industry." *Next
(8th International Architecture Exhibition
catalogue)*, Venice, Italy 2002.

"City Square: Structural Engineering,
Democracy and Architecture." *Grey Room 7*,
New York, 2002.

"The Daily Practice of Collaboration."
Introduction to *Architecture Research Office*,
Princeton Architectural Press, New York,
2002.

"Earthquake Loss Estimation for the New York City Area." With G. Deodatis, K. H. Jacob, and M. W. Tantala. 7th National Conference on Earthquake Engineering (7NCEE), Earthquake Engineering Research Institute (EERI), Boston, MA, July 2002.

"Collaboration." *Perspecta 31 "Reading Structures": The Yale Architectural Journal*, New Haven, CT, 2000.

"Seismic Design Procedures for Regions of Moderate Seismicity." With G. R. Bell. *Earthquake Spectra,* vol. 16, no. 1, Oakland, CA, February 2000.

"Seismic Design Requirements for Regions of Moderate Seismicity." With G. R. Bell. Proceedings from the 12th World Conference in Earthquake Engineering, Auckland, New Zealand, 2000.

"Earthquake Loss Estimation for the New York City Area." With G. Deodatis, K. H. Jacob, and M. W. Tantala. Proceedings from the 12th World Conference in Earthquake Engineering, Auckland, New Zealand, 2000.

"4 Experimental Projects." *Dialogue*, Taipei, Taiwan, 1999.

"The Lineage of Structure and the Kimbell Art Museum." *Lotus International 98,* Milan, Italy, 1998.

"Light Construction Symposium." *Columbia Documents of Architecture and Theory*, New York, 1997.

"Notes on Bucky: Patterns and Structure." *ANY 17,* New York, 1997.

"Notes on Light and Structure." *Architectural Design*, London, UK, April 1997.

"Built Value and Earthquake Risk." *Economic Consequences of Earthquakes: Preparing for the Unexpected*, New York, January 1997.

"Critical Mass." *Daidalos* 61, Berlin, Germany, September 1996.

"Time and Section Study." On Santiago Calatrava in *Columbia University Newsline,* New York, 1993.

"The Spirit of Measure." Introduction to *Harry Wolf,* Editorial Gustavo Gili SA, Barcelona, Spain, 1993.

"Seismic Codes." *Monograph 2 on the Mitigation of Damage to the Built Environment,* National Earthquake Conference, Memphis, TN, 1993.

"An Inventive Nature." *Sites,* New York, 1991.

"Earthquake Hazard Reduction in Urban Areas of Moderate Seismicity." *3rd US-Japan Workshop on Urban Earthquake Hazard Reduction,* Honolulu, HI, November 1991.

"Adapting Seismic Codes for Zones of Moderate Seismicity: the New York City Experience." New Jersey Section, ASCE, October 1990.

"Acceptable Damage in Low and Moderate Seismic Zones." With L. D. Reaveley. *ATC 15-3 4th US-Japan Workshop on the Improvement of Building Structural Design Practices,* Kailua-Kona, HI, August 1990.

"Seismic Design of Suspended Boiler Structures." With P. J. Donelan and M. Garkawe, *Proceedings of the 4th US National Conference on Earthquake Engineering,* vol. 3, Palm Springs, CA, May 1990.

"Evaluation of Earthquake Resistance of Existing Building Practice in New York City." *Proceedings from the 9th World Conference on Earthquake Engineering,* Tokyo, Japan, 1988.

"Wind Versus Seismic Design." *Earthquake Hazards and the Design of Constructed Facilities in the Eastern United States,* New York Academy of Sciences, New York, February 1988.

"Some Limitations of Current Seismic Codes for Eastern US Earthquake Resistant Design." *Proceedings from the Symposium on Seismic Hazards, Ground Motions, Soil Liquefaction and Engineering Practice in Eastern North America,* Sterling Forest, NY, October 20-22, 1987.

"Seismicity and Seismic Hazard in the New York City Area." With C. T. Statton. *Proceedings from the 3rd US National Conference on Earthquake Engineering,* vol. 1, Charleston, SC, 1986.

"Review of Current and Proposed US Seismic Codes for Steel Structures." *Proceedings ECCS-IABSE Symposium on Steel in Building,* Luxemboug, 1985.

"Notes on the Seismic Design of Concentrically Braced Steel Frames." *Proceedings from 8th World Conference on Earthquake Engineering,* vol. V, San Francisco, CA, 1984.

"BSSC Trial Design Program-Buildings NY-5, NY-20A and NY-32." *Weidlinger Associates Report* to the National Institute of Building Science/Building Seismic Safety Council No 182-016, "ATC-3-06 Trial Design Program," New York, 1984.

"Aseismic Reinforcement of Existing Buildings." With N. F. Forell. *Journal of the Structural Division, ASCE,* vol. 106, no. ST9, September 1980.

Rune, the MIT Arts & Letters Magazine. Cambridge, 1976-present, founding editor.

"Tensegrity from Greece to Cambridge." *The Tech*, Cambridge, MA, April 15, 1975.

"In Search of Ezra Pound." *The Tech*, Cambridge, MA, March 7, 1975.

Biography

Guy Nordenson is a structural engineer and professor of architecture and engineering at Princeton University. He was born in Neuilly sur Seine, France, and lives in New York. Nordenson worked in San Francisco for Forell/Elsesser and in New York for Weidlinger Associates before establishing the New York office of Ove Arup & Partners in 1987. In 1997 he founded Guy Nordenson and Associates. Nordenson was the structural engineer for the Museum of Modern Art expansion in New York, the Jubilee Church in Rome, the Glass Pavilion at the Toledo Museum of Art in Ohio, the Nelson-Atkins Museum of Art in Kansas City, two pedestrian bridges for Yale University, and over 100 other projects. He was the editor of *Tall Buildings* (MoMA 2003) and *Seven Structural Engineers: The Felix Candela Lectures* (MoMA 2008), and the co-author of *On the Water | Palisade Bay* (Hatje Cantz Verlag/MoMA 2010).

Acknowledgments

The writings collected in these pages cover a range of 37 years and many forms, fields, and subjects. Some are in response to an invitation; others were at my own initiative. Each is associated with a particular venue, periodical, or publication and I am indebted to all of these and their stewards for the opportunities. There are too many to name. Fritz Drury as the editor of the Andover journal *The Mirror* was kind enough to publish my first poem; Donlyn Lyndon, Bruce Mazlish, Ron McNeil, and Muriel Cooper at MIT were godparents to our *Rune*, which included some more of my poetry. My earthquake engineering co-authors, including Nick Forell, Tom Statton, Glenn Bell, and Mike Tantala among others, often did far more than their fair share of the writing and underlying work. As I began to write as a critic of engineering and architecture I was encouraged and supported by many collaborators, including Dennis Dollens at *Sites*, Cynthia Davidson at *ANY*, and of course my friends Terry Riley and Barry Bergdoll at The Museum of Modern Art. MoMA has unexpectedly offered a supportive environment to me as a co-curator, editor, and writer, and I am very grateful for their support and encouragement over the last dozen or so years.

This book would not exist but for the encouragement, support, and creative energy of Lars Müller and his team, most notably Ellen Mey. Lars is old school— a serious and genuine champion of culture and creativity, and a deft and delightful collaborator. I am grateful also to the Graham Foundation and to the Department of Art and Archaeology's publications fund at Princeton University for their support, and in particular Sarah Herda at the Graham Foundation and Hal Foster and Stan Allen at Princeton University.

My intellectual development over the years has been spurred along by many friends, and these writings reflect their influence. Many are mentioned in the introduction but I want to add to that my thanks to Michael Castro, Mohamed Chalabi, Michael Halley, and Susan Weller, whose conversation and thoughtfulness have been direct influences.

Rebecca Veit has been my indefatigable and enthusiastic co-conspirator and editor in this and other book projects. Her intelligence, wit, and energy are everywhere evident in the quality of the book.

My mother Charlotte always set a high standard of aspiration and opened many worlds and opportunities for me. She did much to direct me into engineering. Her influence is woven into the patterns of this collection in numerous ways. Without her this book would not be.

This book is dedicated to the memory of my father Lars, whose absence has much to do with its contents, and to my wife Catherine and my sons Sébastien and Pierre, whose loving and bubbling presence, curiosity and adventurous spirit I revel in every day.

Photo Credits

p. 15: Courtesy MIT Museum; p. 38: Collection of Mrs. Pound, drawing by Henri Gaudier-Brzeska; p. 112: © Hoberman Associates; p. 149: D'Arcy Thompson; p. 152: © 2010, ProLitteris, Zurich; *Time* Magazine; Estate of R. Buckminster Fuller; © 2010, ProLitteris, Zurich; p. 153: Estate of R. Buckminster Fuller; pp. 154, 158: Paul Warchol; p. 160: Luc Boegly; p. 270: Marshall D. Meyers Collection, the Architectural Archives, University of Pennsylvania; Kimbell Art Museum, Fort Worth, Photograph © Robert Wharton; pp. 273, 274, 275, 278, 279: Louis I. Kahn Collection, University of Pennsylvania and the Pennsylvania Historical and Museum Commission; pp. 280, 281: Marshall D. Meyers Collection, the Architectural Archives, University of Pennsylvania; pp. 310, 313, 316, 317: Courtesy Steven Holl Architects; p. 312: Paul Warchol; p. 324: Photo by the National Oceanic and Atmospheric Administration (NOAA); p. 325: © Succession Giacometti/2010, ProLitteris, Zurich; p. 332: Photography Collection, Miriam and Ira D. Wallach Division of Art, Prints and Photographs, The New York Public Library, Astor, Lenox and Tilden Foundations; p. 334: Swanke Hayden Connel Architect; Courtesy Weidlinger Associates; p. 335: Gehry Partners LLP; p. 336: Author unknown; p. 337: Liberto Perugi; Courtesy The Museum of Modern Art, New York, Digital Image © 2003; p. 338: Author unknown; p. 342: Photography Collection, Miriam and Ira D. Wallach Division of Art, Prints and Photographs; Chicago Historical Society; p. 344: Ezra Stoller/Esto; p. 346: Severud Associates; p. 348: Louis I. Kahn Collection, University of Pennsylvania and the Pennsylvania Historical and Museum Commission; p. 349: Estate of R. Buckminster Fuller; p. 350: Ezra Stoller/Esto; Courtesy William LeMessurier; 352: Courtesy William LeMessurier; p. 354: © Pei Cobb Freed & Partners and Leslie E. Robertson Associates; p. 357: © The Museum of Modern Art/Licensed by SCALA/Art Resource, NY; p. 368: T. Y. Lin International; p. 369: Iannis Xenakis Archives, Bibliothèque Nationale de France, Paris; p. 370: ©The Isamu Noguchi Foundation and Garden Museum, New York; pp. 380, 381: NASA; p. 382: Courtesy Pei Cobb Freed, photo by Norman McGrath; p. 384: OMA/Rem Koolhaas; p. 385: Courtesy Pei Cobb Freed, photo by Kouo Shang-Wei, Singapore; p. 390: Ezra Stoller/Esto; p. 430: Courtesy Toho Company Ltd. © 1954; pp. 435, 437, 439: Dorothy Candela; p. 436: Jose Antonio Fernandez Ordonez and Jose Ramon Navarro Vera, Eduardo Torroja; David P. Billington; p. 441: David P. Billington/Heinz Isler; p. 442: Wolfgang Hoyt/Esto; p. 443: Arup; Historic American Engineering Record; p. 444: © 2010, ProLitteris, Zurich

Guy Nordenson

Patterns and Structure
Selected Writings 1972–2008

Editing: Ellen Mey and Rebecca Veit
Copyediting and proofreading: Rita Forbes, Danko Szabó
Design: Integral Lars Müller/Lars Müller and Nadine Unterharrer
Lithography: Lithotronic GmbH, Dreieich, Germany
Paper: Luxo Samtoffset 135 g/m²
Printing and Binding: Kösel, Altusried-Krugzell, Germany

The cover motif incorporates the pattern from the corrugated web
steel plate girders of the Hillhouse Pedestrian Bridges in New Haven, CT
by Guy Nordenson and Associates.

Lars Müller Publishers
Baden, Switzerland
www.lars-muller-publishers.com

ISBN 978-3-03778-219-4

Printed in Germany

9 8 7 6 5 4 3 2 1